Acts of Faith

*The publisher gratefully acknowledges
the generous contribution to this book
provided by the General Endowment Fund
of the Associates of the University of California Press.*

Acts of Faith

Explaining the Human Side of Religion

Rodney Stark

and

Roger Finke

UNIVERSITY OF CALIFORNIA PRESS

Berkeley   Los Angeles   London

University of California Press
Berkeley and Los Angeles, California

University of California Press, Ltd.
London, England

© 2000 by the Regents of the University of California

Library of Congress Cataloging-in-Publication Data

Stark, Rodney.
    Acts of faith : explaining the human side of religion / Rodney Stark and Roger Finke.
       p. cm.
    Includes bibliographical references and index.
    ISBN 0-520-22201-6 (alk. paper)—ISBN 0-520-22202-4 (pbk. : alk. paper)
      1. Religion and sociology.   I. Finke, Roger, 1954– II. Title.

  BL60 .S675   2000
  306.6—dc21

                                                 99-088220

Manufactured in the United States of America

09 08 07 06 05 04 03 02

10 9 8 7 6 5 4 3 2

CONTENTS

Introduction

Atheism, Faith, and the Social Scientific Study of Religion

Until quite recently there was very little science in the social scientific study of religion. As a child of the "Enlightenment," social science began with the conviction that religion was not only false but wicked and best gotten rid of as soon as possible. Of course, there was nothing new about atheism: many ancient Greek philosophers rejected the gods, as did various schools of Indian and Chinese philosophy (Collins 1998). Indeed, according to Clifford Geertz (1966), atheists exist in preliterate and "primitive" societies, making it likely that there were atheists even in Neanderthal times.

What Thomas Hobbes and his friends began more than three centuries ago was, however, something quite original. Not only were they the first to use the tools of a developing social science to attack religion, but they tried to make a religion out of their science—an intellectual tradition that reached full flower more than three centuries later in Carl Sagan's recent popularizations, in which the "Cosmos" is the proper object of awe and "Nature" is always capitalized (Barbour 1990; Ross 1985). In one paragraph of his enormously influential work *Leviathan,* Hobbes dismissed all religion as "credulity," "ignorance," and "lies," explaining that although the gods exist only in the minds of believers, and are but "creatures of their own fancy," humans "stand in awe of their own imaginations" ([1651] 1956, 1: 98). Two centuries later, there had been a considerable evolution in academic jargon, as demonstrated by the German philosopher Ludwig von Feuerbach when he made a similar claim in his book *Das Wesen des Christentums:* "Man—this is the mystery of religion—projects his being into objectivity, and then again makes himself an object to this projected image of himself thus converted into a subject.... God is the highest subjectivity of man

An earlier version of this chapter appeared as Rodney Stark, "Atheism, Faith, and the Social Scientific Study of Religion." *Journal of Contemporary Religion,* (1999) 14:41–62.

abstracted from himself" ([1841] 1957, 29–31). Religion is merely a reflection of society, which is why "the secret of theology is nothing else than anthropology" (ibid., 207). Seventy years later, Emile Durkheim reiterated (without attribution) Feuerbach's major premise, asserting that "god ... can be nothing else than [society] itself, personified and represented to the imagination" (1915, 206). This is one of the two themes that have dominated social scientific theories of religion for more than three centuries: first, that the gods are illusions generated by social processes; second, that the gods are illusions generated by psychological processes. Only recently has the scientific standing of these claims been effectively challenged by social scientists.

In this introduction, we first summarize the intellectual history of the social scientific study of religion as atheism, tracing the links through major scholars across the centuries. Then we examine the recent shift toward a more truly scientific approach, documenting the fact that this transformation was mainly the result of the increased participation of persons of faith. Against this background, we note "survivals" of the traditional atheistic biases, albeit in a somewhat muffled form, and seek to show that a scientific study of religion is entirely possible for both believers and unbelievers, if not perhaps for aggressive ideologues of either commitment. Finally, we offer an overview of the remaining chapters.

WHEN ATHEISM WENT PUBLIC

At the start of the English Civil War, with *Leviathan* written but not yet published, Hobbes fled London for Paris. This was the first of several Paris sojourns to evade punishment for his views—by Oliver Cromwell for his defense of monarchy and by the Royalists for his attacks on religion. However, Hobbes's political difficulties ended in 1660, when the Restoration placed Charles II on the English throne, for Hobbes had been the new king's boyhood tutor, and Charles was sympathetic to his views. Indeed, under Charles II, an intellectual climate favorable to irreligion flourished in England, which has continued ever since, perhaps culminating in the spectacle of Anglican bishops ridiculing belief in "the Old Man in the sky" (see Robinson 1963), while a Cambridge theologian (Cupitt 1997) is praised in the *Times Literary Supplement* by another British theologian (Nineham 1997) for dismissing "God" as pure subjectivity.

When Voltaire spent three years in England (1726–28), he was startled by the open and widespread atheism there, remarking, "In France I am looked upon as having too little religion; in England as having too much." Similarly, Montesquieu reported from England in 1731, "There is no religion in England ... if religion is spoken of everyone laughs" (both quoted in Durant and Durant 1965, 116). This climate of opinion favored a new generation of militantly atheistic social thinkers, the most famous of them today being David Hume, who wrote in his famous essay "Of Miracles":

There is not to be found in all history any miracle attested by a sufficient number of men, of such unquestioned good sense, education, and learning, as to secure us against all delusion in themselves; of such undoubted integrity as to place them beyond all suspicions of any design to deceive others.... It forms a strong presumption against all supernatural and miraculous relations, that they are observed chiefly to abound among ignorant and barbarous nations; or if a civilized people has ever given admission to any of them, that people will be found to have received them from ignorant and barbarous ancestors.... It is strange that such prodigious events never happen in our days. But it is nothing strange ... that men should lie in all ages. (Hume [1748] 1962, 121–23)

Meanwhile, across the Channel, stimulated by the English example, French *philosophes* were also devoting themselves to bringing about a world free of all illusion and superstition—a world beyond belief. "All children are atheists—they have no idea of God," Jean Meslier (1664–1729), a Catholic priest who was in secret an atheist, asserted in his posthumously published *Testament.* "Men believe in God only upon the word of those who have no more idea of him than they themselves. Our nurses are our first theologians; they talk to children about God as they talk to them of werewolves" (quoted in Durant and Durant 1965, 613–14).

For more than three centuries, social scientists tried not only to explain religion away but to replace it. Voltaire wrote endlessly of the need to attack religion in preparation for the coming triumph of philosophy. The *philosophes* were "fanatic; they preach incessantly, and their avowed doctrine is atheism," the English M.P. and littérateur Horace Walpole (1717–97) wrote home to a friend in 1765, after having become acquainted with Voltaire, Turgot, Condorcet, Diderot, and Rousseau (quoted in Durant and Durant 1965, 781). And so it went. Early in the nineteenth century, Auguste Comte coined the word "sociology" to identify a new social science that would replace religion as the basis for making moral judgments. In their turn, Marx and Engels hailed the coming victory of scientific atheism, just as Freud later promised the triumph of psychotherapy over the neurotic illusions of religion. All of these attacks on religion were presented as "social science," taking two primary forms: the *cultural* or comparative approach, and the *psychological* approach. It is therefore appropriate to trace the role of atheism in the history of social science by giving primary attention to these two fields.

ATHEISM AND THE CULTURAL APPROACH

In any era when there is a substantial amount of travel, humans notice cultural variations, and when they do, religious comparisons always come to the fore. Thus, more than two millennia ago, the Greeks took a particular interest in the similarities and differences among religions in their part of the world. In his *History,* Herodotus paid extensive attention to comparing gods and rituals and to tracing how they might have spread, based on his personal observations of about fifty different societies. For example, he wrote:

> I will never believe that the rites [of Dionysus] in Egypt and those in Greece can resemble each other by coincidence.... The names of nearly all the gods came from Egypt to Greece ... but the making of the Hermes statues with the phallus erect, *that* they did not learn from the Egyptians but from the Pelasgians, and it was the Athenians first of all the Greeks who took over this practice, and from the Athenians, all the rest. ([ca. 450 B.C.] 1987, 152–53)

The European Age of Exploration produced a new era of travelers' tales and once more prompted cultural comparisons, and when what many historians regard as the "first [serious] work of comparative religion" (Preus 1987, 8) was composed in 1593 by Jean Bodin, a former Carmelite monk, it was written on behalf of atheism. In the *Colloquium of the Seven about Secrets of the Sublime,* Bodin argued that by virtue of the competing claims to truth made by the clutter of faiths found around the world, "all are refuted by all." Although he did not dare publish it,[1] his manuscript was "circulated widely and became an underground classic widely read by seventeenth-century free-thinkers" (Preus 1987, 9).

A century later, however, opponents of religion hit upon the device of disguising their intentions by writing books and pamphlets to discredit *pagan* religions, including not only Greco-Roman paganism, but all of the non-Christian faiths found in the New World, Africa, and Asia. By appending perfunctory professions of Christian faith, they deflected accusations of heresy or atheism, knowing full well that their readers would recognize how these same critiques of paganism applied to Christianity (Manuel 1959). In 1697, Pierre Bayle published his *Dictionaire historique et critique* in Rotterdam. In it he concentrated on the myriad sexual sins committed by the Greco-Roman gods and goddesses, including incest, indiscriminate adultery, castration, and homosexual and heterosexual rape, all "spelled out and discoursed upon with mock solemnity." As Frank Manuel has noted: "The more evidence Bayle could accumulate on the lusts of the gods and goddesses, the degrading acts to which they were impelled by their passions, the greater his delight.... Bayle recreated a world of sex-mad divinities" (1959, 27).

As we have seen, Bayle's emphasis on sexuality had been anticipated by Herodotus, who also seems to have missed no opportunity to report sexual aspects of religion, especially if they were bizarre. For example, in his discussion of the worship of Pan, who was portrayed as a goat both in Egypt and Greece, Herodotus acknowledged that no one really believed that Pan was a goat, "nay, they think him like other gods; but why he is so depicted is not pleasant for me to say." He explained, however, that this practice had originated in Egypt among the Mendesians: "In this province, in my time, a monstrosity took place: a he-goat coupled with a woman, plain, for all to see. This was done in the nature of a public exhibition" ([ca. 450 B.C.] 1987, 151).

Attacks on paganism also provided a safe device for revealing priests as impious, lecherous frauds, and miracles as nothing but trickery or credulity. For example, in his *Histoire des oracles* (1687), a "best-seller" of the time, Bernard Le Bouvier de Fontenelle feigned an air of piety in "unmasking" pagan religious ceremonies, and especially the oracles at Delphi, as carefully planned and staged fakery. In witty, readable prose (quite unlike the ponderous texts of some contemporary Dutch and German scholars), Fontenelle regaled his readers with tales of priestly trickery and deceit, confident that they would know that his real target was *all* religion, and particularly Christianity. Fontenelle's *De l'origine des fables* (written before 1680, but not published until 1724) portrayed the religion of "savages" and "backward peoples" around the world. How are we to account for the astonishing myths that are accepted as factual among various human groups? "Men see marvels in proportion to their ignorance and lack of experience." The roots of religion are in "the unimaginable ignorance" of early mankind (Fontenelle quoted in Preus 1987, 42).

By the time Fontenelle wrote, educated Europeans knew a good deal about non-European faiths, because by then comparative religion had become a very active field of scholarship, drawing upon the flood of new accounts written by travelers, missionaries, and colonial administrators—in 1661, for example, the Dutch scholar Godefridus Carolinus produced a 50-volume work on the many "heathen" faiths.

In addition to describing beliefs and practices, many such writings were works of synthesis, in which the emphasis was given to similarities among religions, or what Fontenelle described as "an astonishing conformity" across cultures. Thus, the universality of serpent cults was detailed at length, and, although unmentioned, the similarity to the account of the Fall in Genesis would have been noticed by every reader. Most scholars of comparative religion agreed with Fontenelle that these similarities were owing to the fact that religious beliefs had been "drawn from barbarism by the same means, and that the imaginations of ... distant people are in agreement" (Fontenelle quoted in Preus 1987, 43).

Few, if any, early writers of works on comparative religion were motivated primarily by scholarly concerns. Rather, they were mainly engaged in demonstrating Bodin's principle that "all are refuted by all":

> There was no innocence in Fontenelle's history of oracles; nothing which touched
> the origins, mechanics, ritual, and beliefs of any religion was treated without premeditation during this revolutionary period in the spiritual consciousness of Europe.... Throughout the eighteenth century no discussion of pagan or exotic religion ever lost its heretical overtones, however fervid the philosophers' protests that they were only combatting the false gods.... When the Holbachian atheists appeared in mid-century they found no difficulty in translating the[se] works ... into virulent anti-Christian tirades. (Manuel 1959, 50)

The use of the comparative method to attack religion was not a short-lived tactic of skeptics in a more repressive time. The effort to expose the human origins of any particular religion by stressing its similarities to all religions has long been a standard feature of social science. It is inherent in the "critical attitude of the anthropologists," Thomas Whittaker pointed out, to reveal that even "the most distinctive [Christian rituals] are transformations of worldwide savage or barbaric rites" (1911, 3). The most famous work of this kind is, of course, Sir James Frazer's *The Golden Bough,* first published in 1890 and then issued in twelve volumes from 1907 through 1915. Frazer compiled an enormous set of examples in order to argue that tales of crucifixion and resurrection are standards of world mythology, dwelling at length on myths of gods or princes who died upon or next to a sacred tree—the "golden bough." The fame of the book (as with Freud's similar works) has much more to do with its literary appeal than with any contributions to social science (which are at best slight). Frazer's appeal to professional anthropologists would seem to have been his devotion to documenting that there is nothing original whatever in any Christian tradition, or in any religious tradition, for that matter. All is generic, occurring again and again (especially if one's standards of similarity are sufficiently elastic).

Although, as we have seen, this method did not originate with Frazer, his example turned it into a virtual cottage industry for several generations of anthropologists—especially those who did little or no fieldwork. Hence, in addition to "identifying" many myths as concerning crucifixion and/or resurrection, among the more frequently cited "similarities" are those equating various forms of ritual cannibalism with the Christian practice of communion, and those showing that the Christ story is but one of many in which a god impregnates a human female. This approach has been especially prominent in textbooks, where one easily detects that the authors' intentions were, not to convey that the religions of preliterate societies are more sophisticated than we might suppose, but that Christianity is far less sophisticated than we might like to believe.

From the start, comparative students of religion attempted to further discredit religions by ratifying Fontenelle's assertion that their origins are to be found in the inadequacies of the "primitive mind." Thus, in a book published anonymously in Brussels in 1704, a writer named La Créquinière depicted various rites and practices of mystics in India, Hebrew prophets, and Greco-Roman priests, and "what is perhaps most significant, compared them all to children.... A psychology of infantile primitive mentality was already in the making" (Manuel 1959, 18). That is, it was claimed that religion arose among credulous and not very bright "savages" and continues in "civilized" societies because of its appeal to the "lower orders," whose mental development remains at the primitive level. As already noted, this view was fully developed by Fontenelle in his book on the origins of myths. Indeed, Durkheim's famous contemporary Lucien Lévy-Bruhl praised Fontenelle's work as "wonderfully correct" for being the first to propose an evolutionary theory of religion, tracing it from its brutish origins to modern times (1899, 135–38). In fact, Comte's evolutionary stages of religious development were explicitly built upon Fontenelle's beginnings (Preus 1987). Comte claimed that the most primitive stage of such evolution is the "theological" or religious stage. During this stage, human culture is held in thrall by "the hallucinations produced by an intellectual activity so at the mercy of the passions" (1896, 2: 554).

But if Comte attributed religious ideas to hallucinations rooted in the passions, at least he did not propose that the primitive mind reflected inferior biology, as Charles Darwin did. In *The Voyage of the Beagle, 1831–36*, Darwin described the people of Tierra del Fuego as subhuman beasts, no more capable of enjoying life than "the lower animals" ([1839] 1906, 228–31). Similarly, Darwin's cousin Francis Galton (1890, 82) claimed that his dog had more intelligence than did the natives in South Africa. Galton's friend Herbert Spencer (1896, 1: 87–88) agreed that the "primitive mind" lacks "the idea of causation" and is without "curiosity." These views were virtually universal throughout the nineteenth century and, in slightly more moderate form, persisted well into the twentieth—as late as the 1920s, Lévy-Bruhl wrote several entire books to illustrate that the mind of primitive peoples is "prelogical," a view Durkheim (1913) emphatically endorsed.

Indeed, Durkheim based his famous theory of religion on (quite inaccurate) ethnographic accounts of Australian tribes precisely because he believed them to be the most primitive contemporary humans and thought that they would thus exhibit the "most primitive and simple form" of all religion (1915, 3). He admitted that some religions "call into play higher mental functions ... are richer in ideas and sentiments.... [and contain] more concepts." But, he argued, these variations are not sufficient to preclude application of lessons learned from study of the most primitive faiths to the most complex. Durkheim thus traced the religion of primitive and modern believers alike to the collective representation of society. "[T]his reality, which mythologies have represented under many different forms, but which is the universal and eternal objective cause of these sensations *sui generis* out of which religious experience is made, is society," he wrote (ibid., 418). That is, religion consists of members of a society in effect worshipping their own reflection—a secret that only scientists, and not believers, can penetrate. A careful reading of Durkheim suggests that he was not nearly so concerned to show that the religious rituals of primitives such as Australian aborigines were as sophisticated as those of Christians as he was to show that the rituals practiced in Christianity were not much more sophisticated than those of "savages." For the truth is that Durkheim and the other early social scientists mentioned thus far were not really all that interested in primitive religion. Their real agenda was to link all religion to primitive irrationality and thus to bring contemporary religion into intellectual disrepute. No one has put this better than E. E. Evans-Pritchard:

> [T]he persons whose writing have been most influential [on the subject of the primitive mind] have been at the time they wrote agnostics or atheists.... They

sought, and found, in primitive religions a weapon which could, they thought, be used with deadly effect against Christianity. If primitive religion could be explained away as an intellectual aberration, as a mirage induced by emotional stress, or by its social function, it was implied that the higher religions could be discredited and disposed of in the same way.... Religious belief was to these anthropologists absurd. (1965, 15)

Nevertheless, the "primitive mind" was a doomed concept once scholars actually began to do fieldwork. For the fact is that, unlike Darwin, none of the prominent social scientific proponents of the primitive mind thesis had ever actually met a member of a primitive culture. All of their information came from the library, from written reports by various travelers. It has subsequently been shown that the source material used by the pioneers in the social scientific study of religion, from Comte and Spencer to Lévy-Bruhl and Durkheim (Freud was mostly content to intuit his material) was incorrect, extremely misleading, and often simply fabricated (Evans-Pritchard 1965, 6). Once trained anthropologists came face-to-face with the objects of their study, the primitive mind notion collapsed under irresistible contrary evidence. The fatal blow was delivered by Bronislaw Malinowski, who carefully demonstrated the ability of the Trobriand Islanders to think rationally and to fully comprehend cause and effect. In a famous passage ([1925] 1992, 28–29), Malinowski explained that these "primitives" resorted to supernatural means *only* as a *last* resort. They did not employ supernatural means in an effort to rid their gardens of weeds or to repair fences. They did turn to the supernatural to try to influence the weather. Malinowski's views were soon embraced by all of the leading anthropologists of the time, and at the end of his life, even Lévy-Bruhl recanted (Evans-Pritchard 1981, 120).

Unfortunately, the collapse of the primitive mind thesis did not also result in the collapse of the notion that religion was, at its basis, essentially irrational—indeed, Malinowski was content to argue only that it was not irrational for primitive believers to believe, given the state of knowledge available to them. But he was not willing to grant equal rationality to civilized believers, for they should know better—Malinowski was as opposed to religion as any of his peers or predecessors (Evans-Pritchard 1965).

This double standard has continued to dominate comparative analyses of religion. In an essay in which he condemns the practice of dismissing religious beliefs as irrational merely because science "knows" them not to be true, the distinguished Melford E. Spiro noted:

> Implicit in my argument that the rationality of belief, regardless of its truth, must be assessed relative to the scientific development of the society in which it is found, is the thesis that irrationality is peculiarly characteristic of Western religious belief. It is in Western culture that the findings and the world-view of science are salient; it is in Western culture, therefore, that religious beliefs are often antithetical to scientific beliefs. (Spiro 1964, 109)

The comparative approach has thus converged with psychology in attributing religiousness to mental incapacities. And in proportion to their retreat from tracing religion to deficiencies of the primitive mind, social scientists have been busy imputing it to ignorance and to psychological abnormalities. Weston La Barre, a famous anthropologist, traced all religion to psychosexual problems, for example, claiming, "A god is only a shaman's dream about his father" (1972, 19).

ATHEISM AND THE PSYCHOLOGICAL APPROACH

In his famous *Treatise of Human Nature*, David Hume proposed that "the science of man is the only solid foundation for the other sciences" ([1739–40] 1969, 42–43). Moreover, he claimed that only through the study of this science can we adequately comprehend religion, for only as we are "thoroughly acquainted with the extent and force of human understanding, [can we] explain the nature of the ideas we employ." Hume's belief that psychology was the science to which religion must succumb was widely shared. As Peter Gay has put it: "Not content with making psychology into a science, the Enlightenment made it ... into the strategic science. It was strategic in offering good, 'scientific' grounds for the philosophes' attack on religion" (1969, 167).

This line of attack did not start with Hume. The science of the "psychology of religion" had already begun to develop in England by the late 1600s, encouraged by the climate of opinion favorable to religious skepticism mentioned earlier. Of course, even during the reign of Charles II, one needed at least to pretend to accept the existence of God, however distant and inactive one's conception of divinity. But within this limit, pretty much anything went—anything not very pious, that is, since devout Puritans and Catholics alike were regarded as enemies of the crown. "Englishmen did not need to expose the impostures of pagan oracles ... when their real target was ritualistic Judaism and Christianity" (Manuel 1959, 58). In any event, it was the third earl of Shaftesbury who seems to have originated the psychology of religion (or, more accurately, the *abnormal* psychology of religion) in his immensely influential, *Characteristics of Men, Manners, Opinions, Times*. Of course, he did not employ the term "psychology"—it was another century before it came into use. Instead, Shaftesbury referred to a new science concerned with "the Study of *Minds*" ([1711] 1978, 1: 290; all emphasis in original), its aim being "Comprehension of ourselves" (285–86). This new science "has Pre-eminence above all other Science ... teaching the Measure of each and assigning the just Value of every thing in Life," and "By this Science *Religion* itself is judged" (297). By application of this "superior science," Shaftesbury reduced religion to fear, anxiety, and illusion. Thus, "there are certain humours in mankind which of necessity must have vent. The human mind and body are both of them naturally subject to commotions" (14) and religious enthusiasm occurs "when we are full of Disturbances and Fears *within,* and have, by Sufferance and Anxiety, lost so much of the natural Calm and Easiness of our Temper" (33). Furthermore, religious revivals and belief in miracles are rooted in mass delusions—a sort of pious contagion:

> And in this state their very Looks are infectious. The Fury flies from Face to Face: and the Disease is no sooner seen than caught.... And thus is Religion also Pannick; when Enthusiasm of any kind gets up; as oft on melancholy occasions, it will do. For Vapors naturally rise; and in bad times especially, when the Spirits of Men are low, as either in publick Calamitys, or during the Unwholesomeness of Air or Diet, or when Convulsions happen in Nature, Storms, Earthquakes, or other Amazing Prodigys. (ibid., 15–16)

Another Englishman, a friend of Shaftesbury's named John Trenchard, was a co-founder of the discipline that might be called the abnormal psychology of religion. Trenchard's *Natural History of Superstition* (1709) also blamed religious zeal on an unbalanced mind. This 50-page pamphlet caused a considerable stir and was translated into French, becoming a favorite of continental atheists. As Manuel (1959, 72) has observed, Trenchard's *Natural History* undoubtedly influenced Hume's attacks on religion, and it was denounced by the bishop of Mann as a "most pestilent book."

Trenchard gained much greater prominence and influence, however, when, in collaboration with Thomas Gordon, he began to publish a weekly newspaper in London in 1719 called the *Independent Whig.* In it, for several years, Trenchard continued his denunciations of all but the most tepid, "rationalistic" Deism. His lasting fame came in 1720, when the *London Journal* began to run a weekly column by him and Gordon under the pseudonym "Cato." Trenchard thus gained access to a large national audience—the *Journal* being England's most influential paper at that time.

In all, 138 of *Cato's Letters* appeared, most of them on issues of political philosophy and good governance, but some continuing Trenchard's efforts to reveal the psychological inadequacies of religious believers. He characterized the "holy enthusiast" as a "mischievous madman" (essay of April 6, 1723) and observed that such piety was "doubtless a fever in the head, and, like other fevers, is spreading and infectious.... The enthusiast heats his own head by extravagant imaginations, then makes the all-wise spirit of God to be the author of his hot head ... because he takes his own frenzy for inspiration." At this point in the essay, Trenchard digressed to explain the rise of Islam:

> a barbarous, poor, and desert nation, half-naked, without arts, unskilled in war, and but half-armed, animated by a mad prophet, and a new religion, which made them all mad.... It is amazing how much they suffered, and what great things they did, without any capacity for doing them, but a religion which was strong in proportion as it wanted charity, probability, and common sense. (Trenchard and Gordon [1720–24] 1995, 849–55)

He concluded with a plea that the truth of any religion must be found through reason, not revelation. The next week came more of the same, in an attack on claims by a prominent Quaker that faith can be discovered from within, through meditation and reflection, for "Jesus Christ is operating within us." Trenchard would have none of this. He claimed to know that

> there are many thousands ... who have actually tried all experiments of watching, internal prayer, outward and inward resignation, separation from worldly thoughts and actions, acquiescence of mind, and submission to the operations of the deity, yet have found themselves, after all, just where they set out ... and there-fore, until I can feel something in my self, or discover some traces in others, *which I cannot account for from lower motives,* I shall take the liberty to call the pretenders to it, enthusiasts. (ibid., 855–64; emphasis added)

Trenchard then rehashed all of his claims about religion as madness. *Cato's Letters* were a huge success and subsequently were reissued in what eventually added up to eight volumes, all of which have since been reprinted many times.

A book entitled *Pantheisticon: or, The form of celebrating the Socratic-Society* (originally published in Latin in 1720 and in English translation in 1751) by John Toland, another English pioneer in the psychology of religion, added a new element by distinguishing between the religion of the masses and the religion of the enlightened elite. Toland devised a religious service to be conducted only behind closed doors, *Praise to the All,* and included hymns to free inquiry, to truth, and to knowledge, none of these to be sung until the servants had withdrawn from the banquet room. "We shall be in Safety," he wrote, "if we separate ourselves from the multitude; for the multitude is Proof of what is worst. . . . Persons of the strictest Moderation, behave Towards frantic, foolish, and stubborn Men, as fond Nurses do towards their babbling Minions. . . . Those who flatter not Infants in these Trifles are odious and disagreeable to them" (quoted in Manuel 1959, 67). As Manuel has explained, according to Toland, in agreement with Shaftesbury and Bayle, there were "two religions in every society, one for men of reason and one for fanatics, one for those who comprehended the marvelous order of the world and one for ... ignorant men full of terrors which they allayed with ludicrous rituals" (ibid., 66).

These are not, we should note, merely "antiquated" views. Whether religion is attributed to outright psychopathology, to groundless fears, or merely to faulty reasoning and misperceptions, the claim that it is irrational still permeates the psychology of religion. Until recently, the notion that normal, sophisticated people could be religious has been limited to a few social scientists willing to allow their own brand of very mild, "intrinsic" religiousness to pass the test of rationality.[2] Gordon W. Allport, who coined the term "intrinsic" religion, suggested that mature adults could have faith, so long as it was subject to continuing and constructive doubts, but dismissed stronger affirmations of faith as "primitive credulity," and as "childish, authoritarian, and irrational" (1960, 122). Indeed, Allport's distinction between intrinsic and extrinsic religion precisely parallels the distinction between the religion of reasonable people and of fanatics proclaimed by Shaftesbury, Trenchard, and Toland three centuries ago.

The irrationalist premise persists in many forms. The most influential of these equates religion with psychopathology and is notable for the open contempt and antagonism expressed toward its subject. Sigmund Freud thus explained on *one* page of his famous psychoanalytic exposé of faith, *The Future of an Illusion*, that religion is an "illusion," a "sweet—or bittersweet—poison," a "neurosis," an "intoxicant," and "childishness to be overcome" ([1927] 1961, 88). As to the causes of this dreadful illusion, Freud offered a story about how in primitive times a dominant father hoarded all of the females. To gain sexual access to females, the sons rebelled and killed and ate their father in a cannibalistic orgy. From their subsequent guilt and their concern to prevent reenactments of this occurrence, the sons established religious taboos against incest and cannibalism, and began to worship their martyred father as God—thus did religion come into the world.

This Freudian "explanation," which surely is as crude and implausible as any myth of even the most "primitive" people, is respectfully summarized at great length in many textbooks—Daniel L. Pals's highly praised and widely used *Seven Theories of Religion* (1996) gives it a lengthy chapter, as does J. Samuel Preus in his well-known *Explaining Religion* (1987). Given that Freud's theory of personality has been widely discredited and rejected in psychology, one can but wonder why his work on religion lives on. In *Religion and the Individual*, C. Daniel Bateson, Patricia Schoenrade, and W. Larry Ventis suggest an answer: "[E]ven a cursory look at this literature underscores the fact that one can pursue a psychological study of religion for motives other than an honest attempt to understand the nature and consequences of religion. To be blunt, some psychologists have tried to conduct smear campaigns against religion in the guise of science" (Bateson, Schoenrade, and Ventis 1993, 15). Among them is Michael P. Carroll, who recently filled many pages in the *Journal for the Scientific Study of Religion* with claims that praying the Rosary is "a disguised gratification of repressed analerotic desires"—a substitute for playing "with one's feces" (Carroll 1987, 491). In similar fashion, Mortimer Ostow asserts that Evangelical Protestantism is merely regression "to the state of mind of the child who resists differentiation from its mother. The messiah and the group itself represent the returning mother" (Ostow 1990, 113).

Contemporary non-Freudian psychologists also have been prolific in diagnosing the "religious mentality." At first glance, their views seem more credible, because they do not claim that religious people are mentally ill per se. Instead, they are content to claim that sincerely religious people just do not think very well, having very rigid intellectual processes—that faith reflects "authoritarianism." The invocation of authoritarianism to explain "fundamentalism" has been common since World War II. It began when T. W. Adorno and his colleagues (Adorno et al. 1950) conceived of an "Authoritarian Personality" for whom religious belief relieves pressures stemming from inability to tolerate any intellectual contradictions or ambiguities. Authoritarianism not only makes people religious, they claimed, but the two factors combine to make them bigots as well—all this despite the fact that no competent study ever has demonstrated any correlation between authoritarianism and religiousness (see Stark 1971b; Bergin 1983). Gordon W. Allport (1963) made similar claims about what he called extrinsic religion. As should be clear from the earlier quotation from his work, Allport's motives were polemical, not scientific, and his writing on the subject amounts to little more than claims that his own brand of liberal social values, slightly tinged with vague notions of the sacred, is *good* religion, while anything involving serious belief in the supernatural is *bad* religion. Slowly, psychologists have begun to acknowledge the fundamental biases in Allport's work, especially James Dittes (1971) and most recently Kirkpatrick and Hood (1990).

ATHEISM AND LIBERTY

As will be clear from the chapters that follow, we do not think that an "outbreak" of irreligion began in the seventeenth century because religion was losing its credibility in an age of science. For one thing, this was hardly the birth of atheism, which is probably as old as religion. As noted, irreligiousness is ubiquitous—common in "primitive" societies as well as in the most modern. Indeed, the Bible takes note of atheists in Old Testament times (e.g., Psalm 14) and the noncanonical Wisdom of Solomon deals with them at length. Nonbelievers were "a fairly frequent phenomenon in the Middle Ages," Max Gauna acknowledges (1992, 34). "There are many who believe neither in good or evil angels, nor in life after death, nor in any other spiritual and invisible thing," the prior of Holy Trinity, London, wrote late in the twelfth century (quoted in Coulton 1930, 3: 7). François Berriot (1984) provides an extensive portrait of what Gauna characterizes as "the hidden current of the Renaissance [which was] 'atheism' itself" (1992, 18). In 1542, Antoine Fumée wrote in answer to John Calvin's request for information about atheists in Paris that "unbelievers were numerous" there (quoted in Gauna, 1992, 74). Calvin's letter of inquiry was prompted by his conflicts with powerful atheists in Geneva (Collins 1968).

What was unusual during the "Enlightenment" was the extensive public expression of atheism—that it was possible to form and sustain an anti-religious social movement. Thus, in 1672, Sir Charles Wolseley wrote that "irreligion in its practice hath been the companion of every age, but its open and public defense seems to be peculiar to this" (in Durant and Durant 1963, 567). Even this was not a first. Almost 2,000 years earlier the Greek philosophical school known as the Epicurians denied the existence of any gods—arguing that even if supernatural creatures do exist, they are irrelevant, for they do not know that humans exist and take no interest in the material world (Gaskin 1989; Whittaker 1911). What was unusual about this period in Greco-Roman history was also what was unusual about the era of the "Enlightenment," not the existence of irreligiousness, but the *freedom* to express it in public. Shaftesbury was fully aware of this parallel, noting:

> Not only the Visionaries and [religious] Enthusiasts of all kinds were tolerated, your Lordship knows, by the Antients: but on the other side, Philosophy had as free a course, and was permitted as a Ballance against Superstition. And whilst some Sects, such as the *Pythagorean* and latter *Platonick*, join'd in with the Superstition and Enthusiasm of the Times; the *Epicurean*, the *Academick*, and others, were allowed to use all the Force of Wit and Raillery against it. ([1711] 1978, 1: 18)

The prominence of "village atheism" in nineteenth-century America had the same basis. And, as is demonstrated by the fate of the village atheist, atheistic expression soon loses its shock value and then its audience. Believers learn to ignore it and unbelievers aren't interested—which is why organized atheism has become so anemic. Indeed, as will be seen, that is why the professional atheist so often finds academic employment in "religious" disciplines such as religious studies, religion, or theology faculties (Allen 1996). Competent social scientists, let alone real historians, would have nothing to do with such preening silliness as the "Jesus Seminar."

FAITH AND A SCIENTIFIC APPROACH TO RELIGION

Now, more than three centuries later, any of these early social scientists, "granted a ... glimpse of the intellectual future" would be amazed "by the spectacle of numerous scholars of our own day expending their energies in the study of religion" (O'Toole 1984, 1). What early social scientists would find particularly upsetting is that there is no lack of things to study—that religion not only has failed to disappear, but is, in many ways, stronger than ever. And what the pioneers might find even more offensive is that the field no longer consists primarily of militant irreligion. Granted, even today most social scientists continue to display a substantial bias against those who take their religion very seriously ("fundamentalist" being a deadly epithet), but unabashed village atheism no longer passes for scholarship. These days one must discuss the causes of the decline in Catholic religious vocations, for example, in appropriately sober tones, not merely herald it as proof that people are becoming immune to "papist foolishness." This is not to deny that a substantial proportion of modern social scientists are atheists. But the unintended consequences of their atheism has been to assume that religion is a rapidly dying institution and not worth studying. Consequently, scholars interested in the social scientific study religion were driven to construct their own special institutional niche, combining greater respect for the subject matter with greater respect for the canons of science. It is worthwhile briefly to recount these developments.

The militant atheism of the early social scientists was motivated partly by politics. As Jeffrey Hadden reminds us, the social sciences emerged as part of a new political "order that was at war with the old order" (1987, 590). This new order aimed to overthrow the traditional European ruling elites and repressive political and economic structures, a battle in which the churches, Protestant as well as Catholic, often gave vigorous support to the old order. In response, social scientists declared against religion as well as state. And, although most probably were not prepared to follow Denis Diderot's proposal "Let us strangle the last king with the guts of the last priest," most found the pairing apt and the end result desirable.

However, in the early part of the twentieth century, as the center of gravity of the social sciences shifted from Europe to America, the image of religion as a political enemy waned and anti-religious antagonisms were muted. Lacking a compelling motive to attack religion, but also tending to be personally irreligious (Leuba 1916), American social scientists mostly ignored religion altogether (Swatos 1989).[3] Like insects embedded in amber, the views of the founders were dutifully displayed to generations of students, but the social scientific study of religion was far more of a museum than an area of research—"It was as if the founders had said it all" (Hammond 1985, 2).

Following World War II, a rapidly increasing number of American social scientists began to do research on religious phenomena. Their interest was stimulated by the vigor of American religion, which not only refused to wither away, but seemed to grow in popularity. Indeed, during the 1940s and the 1950s, a substantial religious revival appeared to be taking place in the United States. This was probably primarily a media event, sustained by the proliferation of church construction projects, which were necessitated by the rapid growth of new suburbs. Nonetheless, it stimulated a great deal of research and legitimated support for such research by major granting agencies. Research on religion also was stimulated at this time by the repeated encounter with stubborn religious "effects" by those working in other areas—for example, religion has a substantial independent impact on marriage, divorce, fertility, educational attainment, infidelity, crime, and drug and alcohol consumption, to name but a few areas (Wuthnow 1979; Stark and Bainbridge 1997; Beit-Hallahmi and Argyle 1997).

But, perhaps ironically, the most important factor in creating a truly scientific study of religion was the growing participation in it of persons of faith. This initially was stimulated by the growth of social science in church-affiliated colleges and universities and the creation of denominational research departments. This soon led to the formation of new organizations to sustain "religious" sociologists in the face of the militant disdain and discrimination they encountered in secular social science circles. Thus, the American Catholic Sociological Society (ACSS) was organized in 1938 by 220 American Catholic sociologists seeking shelter against the withering atheistic (and often Marxist) abuse they suffered within the American Sociological Society.[4] Many of these members specialized in "church sociology," in that they used social science methods to evaluate various Catholic programs and institutions. In 1940, the American Catholic Sociological Society began to publish its own journal, the *American Catholic Sociological Review.* Then, as the ecumenical spirit grew in post–World

War II America, the Catholics were prompted to rename their journal *Sociological Analysis*. By then many members of the ACSS held appointments in secular schools, and the work of non-Catholics soon began to appear in *Sociological Analysis*. With the change in name, there also came a change in editorial policy; the journal was forthwith devoted entirely to social scientific research and theorizing on religion. By 1970, leaders of the ACSS found that its designation as a Catholic organization had become unrealistic, and so the name was changed to the Association for the Sociology of Religion. Then, to be consistent, in 1993, *Sociological Analysis* was renamed *Sociology of Religion*. Thus, ended the era of American Catholic sociology. But, while it lasted, it sustained some very gifted scholars, who made major contributions to the scientific study of religion, including Joseph Fichter, Thomas F. O'Dea, and, of course, Andrew Greeley, whose career has far transcended "Catholic" sociology.

The Religious Research Association (RRA) was the Protestant counterpart of ACSS, its initial members being staff of the research divisions of various denominations. This group originated as an informal "committee" that began to meet in 1944 (Hadden 1974). These meetings were formalized in 1951. In 1959, the RRA began to publish the *Review of Religious Research*.

The first stirrings of concern for a scientific approach to religion among Americans in secular academic circles took the form of a regular faculty seminar that began at Harvard during the 1940s, involving scholars most of whom had at least mild personal religious commitments, including Walter Huston Clark, Gordon Allport, Horace Kallen, James Luther Adams, Paul Tillich, Pitirim Sorokin, J. Paul Williams, and Talcott Parsons (Newman 1974; Glock 1998). This seminar led directly in 1949 to the organization of the Committee for the Scientific Study of Religion, which in 1956 was renamed the Society for the Scientific Study of Religion (SSSR). In 1961, the SSSR first published the *Journal for the Scientific Study of Religion*. In response to the journal, membership in SSSR leaped from around 200 in 1960 to more than 800 by 1962 (Newman 1974).

Meanwhile, stimulated in part by these American developments, the social scientific study of religion was resumed in Europe with the formation of small organizations in France, Germany, and the Netherlands, each of them consisting of Catholic scholars. In 1948, the International Conference for the Sociology of Religion was organized by sixteen Catholic social scientists from France, Belgium, and the Netherlands (Dobbelaere 1989). Like their American counterpart, these European groups have ceased to be exclusively Catholic, and they now even accept members from the New World. However, they have remained quite small and, consequently, several European journals devoted to the social scientific study of religion proved to be very short-lived (Beckford 1990). Nevertheless, two of these efforts succeeded: *Archives de Sciences sociales des Religions* and *Social Compass*, both founded in the 1950s, the former in France and the latter in the Netherlands. In 1985, British social scientists founded *Religion Today*, which subsequently was renamed the *Journal of Contemporary Religion*.

These journals were founded to provide an outlet for articles reporting social scientific research on religion, which the existing journals too often rejected on the assumption that the subject was passé—that these were merely studies of a dying and objectionable phenomenon (Beckford 1985b; Thompson 1990). The existence of these new journals stimulated a considerable increase in the number of social scientists working in the area. By 1973, the SSSR had become an international organization, with 1,468 members.

It is important to recognize that while many of the founders of these groups and journals were men and women of deep religious commitment, they also had been well trained in research methods, most had attended the leading graduate schools,[5] and all were extremely concerned to obtain unbiased results. Indeed, because sociologists of faith were so accustomed to being dismissed as incapable of objectivity, they virtually sanctified the canons of scientific research. To read their work is to encounter constant reminders of the obligations to meet textbook methodological standards and for objectivity—a concern far greater than any expressed in the secular publications of the time.

During the 1960s, these new journals and their respectable contents helped to attract a new generation of talented social scientists from leading secular universities to the field. Some of these scholars were personally religious, and many of them were not, but all were genuinely interested in religious phenomena and unwilling to prejudge research results. And they had something else in common: most of them belonged to or were closely identified with the "Berkeley Circle" made up of Charles Y. Glock and the faculty and students whom he recruited, encouraged, and funded at the University of California, Berkeley during the 1960s and early 1970s.

Charles Glock left Columbia University for Berkeley in 1958, where he founded the Survey Research Center. An active Lutheran and trustee of several seminaries, Glock was always on the lookout for funds and opportunities to do research on religion. Before the 1960s ended, he had helped to add Robert N. Bellah and Guy Swanson to the list of Berkeley professors. But even more important was the extraordinary collection of Berkeley graduate students (and visitors) who became involved in the social scientific study of religion. It was they who recreated the field, and here too most of the credit goes to Glock. More than forty persons who have published work in the sociology of religion were students at Berkeley during the 1960s.[6] Had they studied elsewhere, most of them would not have done work on religion. But as a critical mass of unusually talented young students gathered around Glock (in part simply because he had research assistantships to offer), others were influenced by their example, and soon, by their sheer numbers, they made religion a "hot" topic. Many other prominent scholars (including Raymond Currie, Leo Driedger, Jeffrey K. Hadden, Phillip Hammond, Barbara Hargrove, Hans Mol, W. G. Runcimen, Ruth Underhill, and Bryan Wilson) became associated with the Berkeley Circle by frequent visits or by spending a year or two in residence. In the ensuing decades, members of the Circle have trained scores of graduate students, many of whom have gone on to train others. Thus, an extraordinary number of sociologists of religion in the world today can trace their intellectual "family tree" directly back to the Circle. Consider that when the Section on Religion was established within the American Sociological Association in 1994, three of the first four chairs of this section had been student members of the Berkeley Circle—Robert Wuthnow, Rodney Stark, and Ruth Wallace.

As a result of all this activity, "a vast, rapidly growing literature" (Warner 1993, 1044) soon began to pile up, competent new studies by now numbering in the thousands. Moreover, this was not primarily a literature of polemics or of speculation. Rather, as Bryan Wilson has remarked, "sociological interest in religion has found increasingly empirical expression" (1982, 11). That is, the new literature deals primarily in *fact* (Argyle 1959; Argyle and Beit-Hallahmi 1975; Beit-Hallahmi and Argyle 1997). Consequently, once religion became the object of real research, it began to appear in a rather more favorable light. For example, researchers tried to determine whether authoritarianism was indeed related to religiousness, rather than to simply assert this as self-evident the way Adorno et al. (1950) had done. In similar fashion, studies reporting that the higher their incomes, the more frequently people in North America and Great Britain attend church had to be taken seriously, because they were based on valid samples, the data were properly analyzed, and the findings were consistent in study after study (Demerath 1965; Stark 1964; 1971a). The same applies to the immense pile of studies that have explored the link between religiousness and psychopathology, and their consistent finding that religious people enjoy better mental (and physical) health (Ellison, 1993; 1991; Stark and Bainbridge 1997).

As these findings make clear, the "facts" often are entirely at odds with nearly three centuries of "theorizing." As a result, it now is impossible to do credible work in the social scientific study of religion based on the assumption that religiousness is a sign of stupidity, neurosis, poverty, ignorance, or false consciousness, or represents a flight from modernity. Unfortunately, social scientists not involved in the study of religion have been very slow to get the word, and most still accept the old impieties. Although that often results in arrogantly incorrect reviews of papers on religion when they are submitted to general social science journals, it has no great impact on the field itself. What do have an impact, however, are the residual biases that remain within the subgroup itself. That is, many of the traditional attacks on religion live on in modified forms that distort the field. In the remainder of this introduction, we discuss the more important of these.

PREVAILING BIASES

The first major bias concerns the emphasis on weird and obscure groups—that is, the space a religious group receives in journals is almost directly inverse to its size and conventionality. A coven of nine witches in Lund, Sweden, is far more apt to be the object of a case study than is, say, the Episcopal Church, with more than 2 million American members. Some of this merely reflects that it is rather easier to get one's work published if the details are sufficiently lurid or if the group is previously undocumented. A recitation of Episcopalian theology and excerpts from the Book of Common Prayer will not arouse nearly the interest (prurient or otherwise) that can be generated by tales of blondes upon the altar and sexual contacts with animals. However, some of this preference for religious exotica also reflects the tradition, going all the way back to Jean Bodin, of seeking to show that religion is rooted in fraud, foolishness, fakery, and perversion. Thus, it is that, even when selecting from among groups well outside of the mainstream, there is a very strong preference for the trivial and strange. For example, over the past thirty-five years, the *Journal for the Scientific Study of Religion* has published three articles each on Rajneesh and the International Society for Krishna Consciousness, but only one on the Jehovah's Witnesses. Similarly, since 1970, *Sociological Analysis* (now *Sociology of Religion*) has published five articles on the Unification Church (the Moonies), but only one on the Seventh-day Adventists.

Obviously, we are not suggesting that we not study new or obscure religious movements. Of course they ought to be studied, if for no other reason than they are our equivalent of the fruit fly, as William Sims Bainbridge (see, e.g., Bainbridge 1985) loves to put it. What we are saying is that we ought to give at least as much attention to large, socially significant religious groups and movements—even if their behavior is respectable.

The second primary bias is greater antagonism toward groups to the extent that their members are highly committed, and the more vivid the images they project of the supernatural are. It is almost as if groups are "better" the closer they come to disbelief. Indeed, the effort by activists in the North American Association for the Study of Religion (NASSR) to omit all supernatural elements from the definition of religion is intended to justify aggressive atheism as the rationale of religious studies (Allen 1996). If religion can be redefined as recognizing the "sacred" in human relationships or in the majesty of nature, then those obsessed with ridding students of belief in the supernatural can claim to be religious scholars, and hence to have the right to enlighten students by teaching that most of the Bible is false, that Jesus said few of the things attributed to him and died a failed revolutionary (or that Jesus was gay, or a Zen master, or a magician, or a marginal Jew, or did not exist) and that the history of Christianity is but an unending "history of atrocities" (Spong 1998; Mack 1996; Borg 1995; Crossan 1991). This was anticipated by Ernst Troeltsch nearly a century ago when he opposed the creation of "a Department of Religious Studies" on grounds that it would either be "staffed by dilettantes without specialization, and committed to religious research without religious commitment, which would bring joy to no one, least of all itself; or [it would] be the object of quarrels between believers and unbelievers" (Troeltsch [1906] 1991, 113).

Clearly, today, the personal religious beliefs of students are treated with far more respect in social science courses than often is the case in religion or theology departments (Allen 1996).[7] But, even authentic social scientists of religion freely express hostility toward any group showing the slightest sign of "fundamentalism." Consequently, there are hundreds of articles to warn against the Christian Right and to explore the social psychology of its adherents (it's still okay to equate fundamentalism and psychopathology), but not one exposé of the Christian Left. No doubt many readers wonder what could be said against the Christian Left. Consider a simple and revealing example.

Several years ago Stephen Johnson and Joseph Tamney (1988, 44) discovered that some Americans both oppose abortion when there is no concern for the mother's health or for severe birth defects and also support capital punishment under some circumstances. This struck them as so illogical that they devoted an entire paper to trying to reveal the twisted thinking behind it, settling for the conclusion that such people "tend to be authoritarians and dogmatic authoritarians tend to ignore or compartmentalize inconsistent beliefs." It is worth noting that the overwhelming majority of Americans in fact hold this "inconsistent" position. Moreover, it does not seem to have occurred to Johnson and Tamney (who have done many excellent studies), or to the editor of the *Review of Religious Research*, or to reviewers, to wonder about the comparable inconsistency of supporting abortion in all instances and opposing capital punishment in all cases—which is, of course, the prevailing view on the Christian Left.

Finally, even among many of the most objective practitioners, the notion persists that that the social scientific study of religion per se is necessarily corrosive of faith. The basis of this fallacy is the notion that to be true, religions must be immune to social scientific analysis, being inexplicable enigmas. For example, it is assumed that if believers, and especially leaders or founders, can be shown to behave in predictable ways, to be subject to normal human desires and motivations, then their religion must be a wholly naturalistic phenomenon, having no supernatural aspects. From this view, the fact that people mainly convert to a new religion because their relatives and friends have already done so, rather than being attracted by the new doctrines, is seen as discreditable proof that religion is no more than a human invention. Why else, skeptics ask, would converts require social support, rather than being moved by spiritual guidance? Why would movements spread through networks on the basis of interpersonal relations rather than on the basis of scriptural merit?

This typical form of attack on the credibility of religion ignores what all believers readily acknowledge—that there is always a human side to religious phenomena. For example, adherents of many religions, including Muslims, Christians, and Jews, believe that the divine could convert the whole world in an instant, that the option to sin could be removed, and that other such miracles could easily be accomplished. But followers of these faiths also assume that this is not the divine intention. Rather, they believe that the divine acts through history, employing imperfect human agents, and, indeed, many faiths depict the humanity even of their founders. Thus, for example, there is nothing inherently discreditable in discovering that following his first revelation, Muhammad feared that he was losing his sanity, that Jesus agonized in Gethsemane ("My father, if it be possible, let this cup pass from me" [Matt. 26:39]), or, at a more mundane level, that those who train and supervise missionaries are concerned with developing effective tactics, with sustaining morale, and with all the other common issues arising from organized human action. Consequently, from the point of view of believers, there is nothing blasphemous about examining the human side of religion in human terms. The social scientific study of religion does nothing more.

In the end, what distinguishes the scientific from the old atheistic approach to religion is fundamentally a matter of motives. As social scientists, our purpose should neither be to discredit religion nor to advance a religion of science. Rather, our fundamental quest is to apply social scientific tools to the relationship between human beings and what they experience as divine. Science may examine any aspect of that relationship except its authenticity.

Finally, social scientists are unlikely even to grasp the human side of phenomena for which they have no empathy. While it is not necessary that social scientists who want to understand religion be religious, it is necessary that they be able sufficiently to suspend their unbelief so as gain some sense of the phenomenology of faith and worship. Even Durkheim knew this. In remarks made to a meeting of "free thinkers" in 1914, he expressed it as well as has ever been done: "[W]hat I ask of the free thinker is that he should confront religion in the same mental state as the believer.... [H]e who does not bring to the study of religion a sort of religious sentiment cannot speak about it! He is like a blind man trying to talk about color" (quoted in Fields 1995, xvii).

THE PLAN OF THE BOOK

This book combines very explicit theorizing about religion with extensive summaries of research testing elements of the theory. We begin at the micro level of analysis, with the individual, and build up the larger structures—many of which will emerge as we aggregate more micro processes. Part 1 comes under the heading of old business. In it we attempt to fully clear the site so that new structures can be erected. Chapter 1 explains the emergence of what has come to be known as the new paradigm in the social scientific study of religion and compares the old and the new paradigms on central issues—each of which is taken up at length later in the book. Next, chapter 2 attempts to rid the social sciences of various pernicious views of the individual mentality of religious persons. In it we show why our first theoretical axiom, that, given their information and options, humans generally act in a rational way, is the preferable starting point for all theories of human action, including their religious actions. Chapter

3 then disposes of the secularization thesis (the doctrine that religion is on its way out) by showing that it is and always was inconsistent with reality.

Part 2 is focused on the religious individual. In Chapter 4 we ask the most fundamental question about religion: why are people religious, what do they seek from the gods? In proposing an answer, we assemble a micro theory of religion that serves as the foundation for all of the subsequent theorizing in the book. Chapter 5 pursues a theory of religious choices, analyzing the processes of conversion and reaffiliation.

Part 3 raises the level of analysis to that of the religious group. In Chapter 6 we explain why people do not just worship in private. We suggest that only as religion is sustained by group processes can a high level of commitment be generated. This line of theory allows us to explain a phenomenon that so puzzled proponents of the old paradigm: other things being equal, people seem to prefer more costly faiths—those that require a higher level of personal sacrifice. It is this that sustained so many claims about the irrationality of religious behavior. Thus, we show that costly churches are strong churches *because* they are costly—that rational actors will prefer more demanding churches because they offer a more favorable cost/benefit ratio. Within limits, the more your religious group asks of you, the more resources it has to reward you. Chapter 7 applies the theoretical model developed in Chapter 6 to closely examine the recent history of Roman Catholic orders.

Part 4 is devoted to analyses of the religious economy—to explaining religious activity taking place within whole societies and other large social aggregates. Chapter 8 synthesizes many previous theoretical works into a general theoretical model of religious economies. Chapter 9 greatly extends our previous work on how pluralism and competition generate higher levels of religious participation. We then apply these same theoretical principles to explain why the apparent "secularization" of Europe is the result of a lack of energetic and attractive religious "firms" rather than a lack of religious "demand." We also use these theoretical insights to show how new religious movements prosper to the degree that conventional churches are weak or lazy. Chapter 10 summarizes a host of empirical tests of one of the most controversial deductions from our theoretical model: that liberal religious groups can turn conservative.

We have been helped and encouraged by many colleagues. Laurence R. Iannaccone, collaborated on some of the essays drawn upon in this volume, and we thank him for his contributions and friendship. We also must acknowledge the contributions of Lawrence A. Young. In addition to many helpful suggestions, several of which are acknowledged in the text, he and his colleagues at Brigham Young University sponsored a conference on rational choice and religion at the Sundance Resort in April 1994 and thus enabled us to discuss our work with other scholars.

Besides the two Larrys, an amazing number of scholars have given us valuable suggestions. If we attempted to name them all, the list would be so long as to be meaningless and still some colleagues deserving mention would surely be overlooked. Consequently, we shall only note those who played a continuing part in the undertaking: William Sims Bainbridge, Eileen Barker, Randall Collins, Christopher Ellison, William Garrett, Anthony Gill, Andrew Greeley, Jeffrey Hadden, Eva Hamberg, Phillip Hammond, Roger O'Toole, Benton Johnson, Jennifer McKinney, Alan Miller, Kent Miller, Lyle E. Schaller, Darren Sherkat, William Silverman, John Simpson, Christian Smith, William Swatos, Stephen Warner, Michael Williams, and Patricia Wittberg.

PART ONE

Paradigms in Conflict

CHAPTER 1

A New Look at Old Issues

An immense intellectual shift is taking place in the social scientific study of religion. During the past few years, many of its most venerated theoretical positions—faithfully passed down from the famous founders of the field—have been overturned. The changes have become so dramatic and far-reaching that R. Stephen Warner identified them "as a paradigm shift in progress" (1993, 1044), an assessment that since then "has been spectacularly fulfilled," according to Andrew Greeley (1996, 1).

As is typical in science, the emergence of a new paradigm rests on both an empirical and a theoretical basis (Greeley 1996; Warner 1993). As described in the introduction, there has been a resurgence in research on religious topics and a substantial number of well-established facts have been accumulated. Most of these have turned out to be inconsistent with the old paradigm, and in response to the growing incompatibility between fact and traditional theory, new theories have been constructed to interpret the empirical literature. These incorporate new insights, some of them imported from other branches of social science.

Given that we have played an active part in empirical studies of religious phenomena and have led the way in developing new theories, it seemed appropriate to gather our many scattered works into an integrated and synthetic presentation. What follows is not, however, a collection of our recent essays. Rather, most of the chapters integrate a variety of studies, by us and by others, into what we hope are coherent syntheses reflecting our current positions. Indeed, we caution those most familiar with our publications not to assume that they already know what we have to say here.

This chapter contrasts elements of the new and old paradigms and, in doing so, serves as an overview of the remainder of the book.

ELEMENTS OF THE OLD PARADIGM

In the beginning, religion was a central concern of social scientists. Adam Smith, David Hume, Auguste Comte, Karl Marx, Friedrich Engels, Herbert Spencer, Edward Tyler, Max Weber, Ernst Troeltsch, Emile Durkheim, William James, Lucien Lévy-Bruhl, Carl Jung, and Sigmund Freud each wrote extensively about religious phenomena—a corpus of "theorizing" that was for generations the received wisdom on the subject. Indeed, although these founders of social science disagreed about many things, with the exception of Adam Smith, and to a lesser extent Max Weber and Ernst Troeltsch, there was remarkable consensus among them on key issues concerning religion.

First, it has been asserted that religion is false and harmful. It is claimed that religion harms the individual because it impedes rational thought and harms society because it sanctifies tyrants.

The introduction reviewed three centuries of claims that the causes of religion reside in abnormal psychology. Chapter 2 conclusively dismisses the thesis that religion is irrational. But of at least equal importance to the old paradigm is the claim that religion must always serve the ruling elite and facilitate exploitation of the masses. According to Marx and Engels, religion "is a great retarding force, is the *vis inertiae* of history" (1964, 313); as they put it in the *Communist Manifesto*, "the parson has ever gone hand in hand with the landlord" (1964, 89). Given the general acceptance of such views, it has been a virtual article of social scientific faith that religious movements typically are reactionary responses against enlightenment and progress. Thus, the recent growth of evangelical Protestant groups is dismissed as a "flight from modernity" by the contemporary heirs of the received wisdom (Bruce 1986; Hunter 1983; 1987)—that people who feel threatened by the erosion of traditional morality are flocking to religious havens. American evangelical Protestant churches "are like besieged fortresses, and their mood tends toward a militancy that only superficially covers an underlying sense of panic," according to Peter Berger (1969, 11).

A corollary of this line of analysis is that, in addition to being harmful, religion serves as a painkiller for frustration, deprivation, and suffering. The influential German sociologist Georg Simmel pronounced religion "a sedative for the turbulence of the soul" ([ca. 1905] 1959, 32). As Kingsley Davis explained:

> [T]he ego can stand only a certain amount of frustration.... The culture that drives him to seek goals that he cannot reach also, for the sake of sanity, provides him with goals that anybody can reach. These are goals that transcend the world of actual experience, with the consequence that no evidence to attain them can be conclusive. If the individual believes he has gained them, that is sufficient. All he needs is sufficient faith, and faith feeds on subjective need. The greater his disappointment in this life, the greater his faith in the next. (Davis 1949, 532)

Marx put it rather more succinctly, identifying religion as opium, a view that prompted his collaborator Friedrich Engels to claim that early Christianity "first appeared as a religion of slaves and emancipated slaves, of poor people deprived of all rights, of peoples subjugated and dispersed by Rome" (Marx and Engels 1964, 316). Hence, the received wisdom: religion appeals most strongly to the lower classes.

The second key element of the old paradigm is that religion is doomed.

As the social sciences emerged in the wake of the "Enlightenment," the leading figures eagerly proclaimed the demise of religion. "The philosophers of the eighteenth century explained in a very simple manner the gradual decay of religious faith. Religious zeal, said they, must necessarily fail the more generally liberty is established and knowledge diffused," Alexis de Tocqueville observed in *Democracy in America* ([1840] 1954, 2: 319).

This came to be known as the "secularization thesis": that in response to modernization, "religious institutions, actions, and consciousness, [will] lose their social significance" (Wilson 1982, 149). Tocqueville, as we shall see, was virtually alone in his rejection of the secularization thesis—perhaps no other social scientific prediction enjoyed such nearly universal acceptance for so long. "The evolutionary future of religion is extinction," Anthony F.C. Wallace, a prominent anthropologist, asserted in an undergraduate textbook. "Belief in supernatural beings and supernatural forces that affect nature without obeying nature's laws will erode and become only an interesting historical memory.... Belief in supernatural powers is doomed to die out, all over the world, as the result of the increasing adequacy and diffusion of scientific knowledge" (1966, 265).

A third basis of consensus among the founders of the social sciences was that religion is an epiphenomenon.

Despite imputing so many harmful effects to religion, the founders clung to the claim that religion was not "real"—that it was but a reflection of more fundamental social phenomena. "All religion ... is nothing but the fantastic reflection in men's minds of those external forces which control their daily lives," Marx and Engels explained ([1878] 1964, 16). In Marxist analysis, these external forces are variously the mode of production, nature, and "the forces of history." In similar fashion, in his famous study of suicide, although the topic of religion takes up a substantial portion of the book, Emile Durkheim ([1987] 1951) did not treat religion as something in itself, but only as an elaborate reflection of the more basic reality: degree of social integration (Stark and Bainbridge 1997). Seeking to explain why religious movements arise, Bryan Wilson invoked a litany of secular crises and disturbances:

> Change in the economic position of a particular group ... disturbance of normal social relations ... industrialization and urbanization; the failure of the social system to accommodate particular age, sex and status groups.... Particular groups are rendered marginal by some process of social change.... Insecurity, differential status anxiety, cultural neglect, prompt a need for readjustment. (Wilson 1967, 31)

Over the decades, this tendency of social scientists always to seek more "fundamental"—that is, material and secular—causes of all things religious has become such a basic assumption that it is routinely invoked by the news media. Among the more common suggestions as to why evangelical churches grow are repressed sexuality, divorce, urbanization, racism, sexism, status anxieties, and rapid social change. Never do proponents of the old paradigm even explore possible religious explanations: for example, that people are drawn to the evangelical churches by a superior religious product. From their viewpoint, since all religions are false and all gods are imaginary, there can be no point in examining whether some religions are more plausible and satisfying than others. One surely need not be a believer to see the absurdity of this position—imagine applying it to science fiction novels or to horror movies.

Fourth, proponents of the old paradigm rarely examine religion as a social phenomenon, as a property of groups or collectivities; instead, they treat it as fundamentally psychological.

They often talk about religion in collective terms, but in the end they reduce it to mental states and do not use aggregate or group units of analysis. Discussions of sects, for example, typically devolve into studies of sectarian attitudes rather than comparisons of religious groups. Even when the object of study is a group (a specific sect, for example), the usual result is a case study utterly lacking in systematic comparisons with other groups. The founders of the social sciences rarely examined such things as the interplay among religious groups or variations in religious social structures across societies, and their heirs seldom do so either. Even the "obvious" exceptions to this claim turn out not to be very exceptional. Thus, when Durkheim devoted a book to the thesis that religion is, in effect, society worshipping itself, his research focused on the inner life of Australian aborigines, and his conclusions about such things as totemism would not have survived even rudimentary cross-cultural comparisons (Goldenweiser 1915; Runciman 1969; Evans-Pritchard 1981). Even when Max Weber attempted to trace the rise of capitalism to the "Protestant Ethic," he for the most part conceived of that ethic as a psychological property of individuals (Hamilton 1996)—although, quite unlike most of his peers, he did attempt to contrast several societies in terms of the presence of absence of this property. The writings of Marx and Engels on religion are also overwhelmingly psychological, despite their mandatory mentions of modes of production and social evolution. The complete version of Marx's most famous observation on this subject is typical: "Religion is the sigh of the oppressed creature, the heart of a heartless world, just as it is the spirit of a spiritless situation. It is the *opium* of the people" ([1844] 1964, 11).

This tendency continues in the overwhelming preponderance in contemporary studies of research based on individuals rather than on groups. But no amount of surveys of individual opinions will reveal answers to questions such as why some new religions succeed, while most fail, or why rates of religious participation are so much higher in some societies than in others. These are not questions primarily about individuals and can only be answered adequately by reference to attributes of groups—in these instances, to attributes of new religions or of societies.

Finally, to the extent that the founders of the social sciences did take any interest in religion as part of a social system (rather than of the individual consciousness), their primary concern was to condemn the harmful effects of religious pluralism and to stress the superiority of monopoly faiths.

Only monopolies, it was asserted, can sustain the unchallenged authority on which all religions depend. This was, of course, merely a variant of the old atheistic principle that "all refute all." For, as Durkheim explained, where multiple religious groups compete, religion becomes open to question, dispute and doubt, and thereby "the less it dominates lives" ([1897] 1951, 159). Even with the contrary American example staring them in the face, those committed to the old paradigm continue to express their faith in this doctrine. "[P]luralism threatens the plausibility of religious belief systems by exposing their human origins," writes Steve Bruce. "By forcing people to do religion as a matter of personal choice rather than as fate, pluralism universalizes 'heresy.' A chosen religion is weaker than a religion of fate because we are aware that we chose the gods rather than the gods choosing us" (1992, 170). Like Durkheim, Bruce conforms to the practice of reducing a social phenomenon—competing religious groups—to its presumed psychological effects.

THE EMERGENCE OF THE NEW PARADIGM

The introduction described the formation of a subfield devoted to the social scientific study of religion. The rapid growth of this subfield during the 1950s and 1960s produced a huge new body of research findings, many entirely inconsistent with the received wisdom. Thus, as early as 1973, Charles Y. Glock and Phillip E. Hammond recognized that the strain between the received theoretical wisdom and the expanding corpus of research findings necessitated a new paradigm, albeit they were rather pessimistic that one soon would be forthcoming. However, slightly more than a decade later, introducing a volume of essays that attempted to explain the failure of the secularization thesis, Hammond recognized that the first fragments of "a new paradigm" were already in view. "Findings may seem scattered ... and theories fragmented, though this is only because the master schemes—the eventual replacements of the secularization model—have not yet come into focus. Obviously, the successor volume to this one is waiting to be born," he concluded (1985, 3).

The new paradigm arrived as predicted, and we offer this book as the awaited "successor volume." The new paradigm not only rejects each of the elements of the old paradigm outlined above, it proposes the precise opposite of each.

Religion and Abnormal Psychology

As to the claim that religion is harmful at the individual level, the new paradigm cites a huge, and growing literature that finds religion to be a reliable source of better mental and even physical health (Ellison 1991; 1993; Pargament and Park 1995; Levin 1996; Idler and Kasl 1997a; 1997b). Two literature reviews, published nearly simultaneously in 1987, each pointed to the positive health effects of religious involvement, regardless of the age, sex, race, ethnicity, nationality, or time period of the population being studied (Jarvis and Northcutt 1987; Levin and Schiller 1987). In a more recent review, Jeffrey S. Levin finds that the relationship still holds and suggests that the results generally point to a "protective epidemiologic effect of religiosity" (1996, 850).

In the field of gerontology, the volume of research on religion and aging has grown so rapidly that a new periodical, the *Journal of Religious Gerontology,* has emerged, and existing publications have devoted special issues or sections to discussion of the topic. Neal Krause reports that the number of scholarly papers and grant proposals submitted to major journals and funding agencies on this topic has also increased, with the sophistication and high quality of this research making it hard to ignore. "An impressive body of research indicates that elderly people who are involved in religion tend to enjoy better physical and mental health than older adults who are not as religious," according to Krause (1997, S291).

Chapter 2 will show that the data do not confirm claims that religion is often the cause and symptom of psychopathology. Indeed, the new paradigm directly contradicts the postulate that religion is rooted in irrationality.

The Opiate Thesis

That religion is harmful at the level of society is a political, not scientific, claim. Whereas the old paradigm was content to identify religion as the opium of the people, the new paradigm notes that religion is also often the "amphetamine" of the people, in that religion animated many medieval peasant and artisan rebellions (Cohn 1961), generated repeated uprisings among the native peoples of Africa and North America against European encroachment (Wilson 1975), and recently served as a major center of mobilization against the tyrants of eastern Europe (Echikson 1990). Indeed, the whole notion that religion primarily serves to compensate the deprived and dispossessed has become untenable. The consensus among scholars rejects as "imaginary history" Engels's notion that the early Christian movement was rooted in proletarian suffering. The facts force the conclusion that Christianity's greatest early appeal was to the privileged classes (Judge 1960; Scroggs 1980; Stark 1996a). In similar fashion, since the early 1940s, many researchers have attempted to connect religiousness to social class, but their findings have been weak and inconsistent (see chapter 8). Consequently, the need for new theorizing about the role of religion in the political affairs of nations has been recognized (efforts in that direction can be found in Stark and Bainbridge 1985 and [1987] 1996, and we particularly refer the reader to the recent work of Gill 1998.

Against the Secularization Thesis

Chapter 3 is devoted entirely to entombing the secularization thesis beneath a mountain of contrary fact. As a preview: first, there is no consistent relationship between religious participation and modernization (Finke 1992). Indeed, the very few significant, long-term declines in religious participation to be seen anywhere in the world are greatly outnumbered by remarkable increases. What is needed is not a simple-minded theory of inevitable religious decline, but a theory to explain variation. Second, even in nations where religious participation has always been quite low, as in Europe, the overwhelming majority express firm belief in basic religious tenets and describe themselves as religious. It is perverse to describe a nation as highly secularized (as a few of our European colleagues do) when fully two-thirds or more say they are "a religious person," and fewer than 5 percent say they are atheists. These points will be demonstrated fully in chapter 3. Finally, the spread of science cannot result in secularization, because science and religion are unrelated. Indeed, as we shall see in chapter 2, scientists are as religious as anyone else, and the more scientific their fields, the more religious American academics are.

Seeking Religious Causes of Religious Phenomena

Despite their frequent claims that religion is an epiphenomenon, the founders often postulated religious effects, not all of them bad. For example, theorists as diverse as Karl Marx and Herbert Spencer took it for granted that religion reinforced the moral order. Although this placed it in league with the ruling classes, religion was nonetheless credited with sustaining honesty, charity, and temperance. The new paradigm is entirely compatible with the premise that religion has many effects, and a huge empirical literature finds that religious people are more likely to observe laws and norms, and that cities with higher rates of religious participation consequently have lower rates of deviant and criminal behavior (Stark and Bainbridge 1997). Where the old and new paradigms part company is over the causes of religion.

The old paradigm directs social scientists to dig as deeply as necessary in order to uncover the "real" causes of religious phenomena. Thus, religious movements, for example, are always traced back to social causes such as war, financial depressions (or booms), overpopulation, and the like. A successful religious revival campaign is invariably attributed to something that was upsetting people. In contrast, while the new paradigm accepts that religious phenomena may be caused by secular crises, it denies that secular social factors must underlie religious phenomena. Analyzing the basis for the great success enjoyed by George Whitefield's revival meetings in New England in the mid 1700s, those working within the new paradigm stress Whitefield's effective marketing of a standard religious message as the basis for his successes, not "social conditions" (Butler 1982; 1990; Finke and Stark 1992; Lambert 1990; Smith 1983). Nor do proponents of the new paradigm require that religious causes (or secular ones for that matter) be "material" as opposed to ideas and beliefs. Proponents of the new paradigm accept that religious doctrines per se often have consequences. For example, the "root causes" of efforts by the early Christians to nurse the sick during the great plagues that periodically swept the Roman Empire, in contrast to their pagan neighbors, who largely shunned and abandoned stricken family members, were doctrinal: belief that death was not final and in the obligation to be one another's keepers (McNeill 1976; Stark 1996a).

Equally obvious contemporary instances of doctrinal causation can be seen by comparing various religious movements on the basis of their capacity to sustain leaders with sufficient authority. There are many bases for legitimate authority within organizations. However, when organizations stress doctrine, as all religious movements do, these doctrines must define the basis of leadership. Who may lead and how is leadership obtained? What powers are granted to leaders? What sanctions may leaders impose? These are vital matters, brought into clear relief by the many examples of groups that failed (or are failing) for lack of doctrines defining a legitimate basis for effective leadership.

That doctrines can directly cause ineffective leadership is widely evident in contemporary New Age and "metaphysical" groups. If everyone is a "student," and everyone's ideas and insights are equally valid, then no one can say what must be done or who is to do what, when. The result is the existence of virtual nonorganizations—mere affinity or discussion groups incapable of action (Wagner 1983). In similar fashion, some of the early Christian gnostic groups could not sustain effective organizations because their fundamental doctrines prevented them from ever being anything more than a loose network of individual adepts, each pursuing secret knowledge through private, personal means (Pagels 1979; Williams 1996). In contrast, from the start, Christianity had doctrines appropriate for an effective structure of authority inasmuch as Christ himself was believed to have selected his successors as head of the church.

Thus, can one utilize religious doctrine as a causal factor vis-à-vis other religious phenomena, both individual and organizational. It is, of course, logically possible to raise the issue of from whence particular doctrines came and why these, rather than some other doctrines, were adopted. We may grant the legitimacy of such questions without promoting infinite regress or admitting that all fundamental causes are secular.

Finally, to grant causal status to doctrines forces recognition that the most fundamental aspect of any religion is its conception of the supernatural. Many religious doctrines and related practices presuppose supernatural beings with certain characteristics, among them consciousness and virtue. For example, it would seem unavailing to appeal to an impersonal higher power such as the Tao, and quite risky to do so to the undependable and often wicked gods of the Greek pantheon. We expand on this matter in chapters 4 and 6.

Social Approaches

As will be clear throughout the book, many of the most interesting and pressing questions facing the social scientific study of religion require that religion be conceived of as social rather than as psychological, as a property of groups or even of whole societies. It is this emphasis on the social as against the psychological that is the most important feature of the new paradigm. To see more fully what is at issue here, consider the following questions, none of which can be reduced to psychology alone.

> Why is religious participation so low in most European nations and so high in the United States?
> Why are some Roman Catholic religious orders attracting new members, while others are not?
> Why are strict churches so much stronger than those that ask less of their members?
> Why do most sect movements fail?
> Why do cult movements thrive on the West Coast of Canada and the United States, and why are they even more successful in Europe?

We offer answers to these and other such questions in subsequent chapters. In doing so, we of course utilize psychological assumptions and data as appropriate—we do not think psychological states are unimportant or that data on individuals (such as survey studies) are useless. Rather, our concern is not to inappropriately reduce group phenomena to individual traits, or to mistake attitudes for collective activity.

If stressing the social aspect of religion is a hallmark of the new paradigm, its most innovative theoretical feature is to identify religion as a subsystem within the social system: a religious economy (Stark 1983; 1985).

The Religious Economy

Religious organizations do not exist in a vacuum, and they cannot therefore be studied in isolation from their sociocultural environments. Moreover, most of the time, for most religious organizations, a crucial aspect of that environment is religious—aspects of other religious organizations (including their doctrines), and aspects of the rules and norms governing religious activities. To facilitate analysis at this level of abstraction, we shall examine the religious life of societies within an overall conceptual and theoretical model, which we identify as a religious economy. A religious economy is a subsystem of all social systems (see Parsons 1951). It encompasses all of the religious activity going on in any society.

We use the term "economy" in order to clarify that, in terms of certain key elements, the religious subsystem of any society is entirely parallel to the subsystem involved with the secular (or commercial) economy: both involve the interplay of supply and demand for valued products. Religious economies consist of a market of current and potential followers (demand), a set of organizations (suppliers) seeking to serve that market, and the religious doctrines and practices (products) offered by the various organizations. Our application of economic language to things often regarded as "sacred" is meant neither to offend nor as mere metaphor. Rather, we shall show the immense explanatory power that can be gained by applying elementary principles of economics to religious phenomena at the group or social level—an application pioneered by Adam Smith more than two centuries ago.

As Smith recognized, and as we demonstrate at length in part 4, the most significant single feature of a religious economy is the degree to which it is unregulated and therefore market-driven, as opposed to being regulated by the state in favor of monopoly. Herein lies the key to explaining variations in the "religiousness" of societies, for the founders of the social sciences were entirely wrong about the harmful effects of pluralism and religious competition. Rather than eroding the plausibility of all faiths, competition results in eager and efficient suppliers of religion, just as it does among suppliers of secular commodities, and with the same results: far higher levels of overall "consumption."

This conclusion rests on the most basic assumption of all social science: that people try to select the most beneficial line of action. In this instance, they are most apt to respond to religions that make the most effective efforts to enlist them. In all other areas to social science, this first assumption is so taken for granted that it often goes unstated. But when it is applied to religious behavior it arouses the most militant rearguard action in defense of the old paradigm (Bruce 1993; Chaves 1995; Demerath 1995; Marwell 1995; Spickard 1997). Therefore, to conclude this chapter, we shall attempt to clarify what is at issue and to dispel any doubts that people are as rational in their religious behavior as they are in any other area of life.

On Rationality

All of the leading approaches to social theory share a common first premise or proposition. It has been stated in a great many ways, but each variant asserts the same insight: that when faced with choices, humans try to select the most rational or reasonable option. Some advocates of "Rational Choice Theory," especially economists, limit their definition of rationality to the elegantly simple proposition that humans attempt to maximize—to gain the most at the least cost (see Becker 1975; 1996; Iannaccone 1995b). One of the greatest virtues of this version is that it lends itself so well to inclusion in mathematical models, but that virtue may also be its primary shortcoming, for in their daily lives, humans tend to fall well short of its fulfillment. Of course, being sophisticated theorists, economists fully acknowledge human frailties such as "imperfect memories," "erroneous calculations," and "drugs" (Becker 1996, 22). But even if these qualifiers are made explicit, the principle of maximization strikes us as too precise.

We prefer a formulation of the rationality axiom that softens and expands the maximization assumption. Just as those working in the area of artificial intelligence have turned to models based on what they call "fuzzy logic" (Kosko 1992), we acknowledge that human reasoning is often somewhat unsystematic and "intuitive," and that maximization is often only partial and somewhat half-hearted. Indeed, aspects of laziness probably ought to be considered in the calculation of maximization. In any event, we shall adopt the more subjective and bounded conception of rationality, the one John Ferejohn (1991) identified as the "thick" model that has sustained a substantial theoretical literature going back at least as far as Max Weber (Simon 1957; March 1978; 1988; Boudon 1993; Hechter and Kanazawa 1997). It seems worthwhile to consider some of the virtues of this approach.

First of all, this conception of rationality recognizes that humans pursue a variety of rewards or goals and confront an array of potential costs. It is obvious that many of the things human seek tend to be somewhat mutually exclusive, and "maximization" must consequently consist of the best fit among these conflicting ends. For example, some people's best fit would be partial maximizations of the satisfactions of parenting and those of career achievement. It was mainly to deal with the complexities of the pursuit of multiple and somewhat conflicting goals that Herbert Simon (1957) coined the word "satisficing" as a substitute for "maximizing." That is, Simon combined the words "satisfy" and "suffice" to identify the tendency of humans to settle for a sufficient level of satisfaction. In addition to facing conflicting goals, humans also must function within limits, often quite severe, on their information and their available options. Consequently, we feel it excessive to use the maximizing proposition. But, being equally reluctant to resort to a neologism such as satisficing, we shall adapt Simon's later (1982) formulation of subjective rationality. As summed up by Raymond Boudon (1993, 10), subjective rationality applies to all human actions that are based on what appear to the actor to be "good reasons," reasons being "good" to the extent to which they "rest upon plausible conjectures." But, whatever the good reasons for making choices, the imputation of rationality always assumes the presence of subjective efforts to weigh the anticipated rewards against the anticipated costs, although these efforts usually are inexact and somewhat casual.

The subjective approach to rationality is entirely consistent with the axiom of symbolic interactionism that in order to understand behavior, we must know how an actor defines the situation (Mead 1934; Blumer 1969), for only from "inside" can we assess the rationality—that is, the reasonableness—of a choice. As James S. Coleman has put it: "[M]uch of what is ordinarily described as nonrational or irrational is merely so because observers have not discovered the point of view of the actor, from which the action is rational" (1990, 18).

These considerations lead us to this formulation of the principle of human rationality: *Within the limits of their information and understanding, restricted by available options, guided by their preferences and tastes, humans attempt to make rational choices.*

Let us analyze this sentence to see precisely what it does and does not mean. The first part of the sentence—*within the limits of their information*—recognizes that we can neither select choices if we do not know about them nor select the most beneficial choice if we have incorrect knowledge about the relative benefits of choices. The second part—*within the limits of their ... understanding*—acknowledges that people must make choices based on the set of principles, beliefs, or theories they hold about how things work. These may, of course, be false, as the history of science demonstrates, but the rational person applies his or her principles, because these are, for the moment, the most "plausible conjectures." Finally, it is self-evident that people may only select from among *available options,* although the full range of choices actually available may not be evident to them.

However, if humans all attempt to make rational choices, why is it that they do not always act alike? Why don't people reared in the same culture all seek the same rewards? Because their choices are *guided by their preferences and tastes.* Preferences and tastes define what it is that the individual finds rewarding or unrewarding. Consequently, people may differ in what they want and how much they want it (Hechter 1994). This helps us understand not only why people do not all act alike but why it is possible for them to engage in exchanges: to swap one reward for another.

Of course, not all preferences and tastes are variable—clearly, there are some things that virtually everyone values, regardless of their culture: food, shelter, security, and affection being among them (Aberele et al. 1950). Obviously, too, culture in general, and socialization in particular, will have a substantial impact on preferences and tastes. It is neither random nor a matter of purely personal taste whether someone prays to Allah or Shiva, or indeed, whether one prays at all. Still, the fact remains that even within any culture, there is substantial variation across individuals in their preferences and tastes. Some of this variation is also at least partly the result of socialization differences—for example, we probably learn our preferences concerning highly liturgical services as children. But, a great deal of variation is so idiosyncratic that people have no idea how they came to like certain things. As the old adage says, "There's no accounting for tastes." Moreover, differences in tastes and preferences both facilitate exchanges, as already noted, and explain what often are rather remarkable differences in behavior, as we shall see.

Finally, as already mentioned, the phrase that "humans attempt to make rational choices" means that *they will attempt to follow the dictates of reason in an effort to achieve their desired goals.* Within the limits noted, this will involve some effort to maximize the net of rewards over costs. The word "attempt" is included to note that people don't *always* act in entirely rational ways. Sometimes we act impulsively—in haste, passion, boredom, or anger ("I really didn't stop to think about what I was doing"). But, most of the time normal human beings will choose what they perceive to be the more reasonable option, and whenever they do so, their behavior is fully rational, even if they are mistaken. For example, people buy stocks hoping to profit. If their stocks decline in value, it does not mean that they acted irrationally, only that they were wrong about which stocks to buy.

This formulation also leaves explicit leeway for people to act in ways others would define as "unselfish" choices, but it leaves no leeway for altruism, if that term is defined as intentionally selecting a negative cost/benefit ratio purely for the benefit of others. Such a claim usually produces tales of heroism, of soldiers who held out to the end or about parents who rushed into burning buildings to try to save a child. Or, you may wonder, what about people like Mother Teresa who forgo a comfortable life to aid the sick and the poor? How are such people acting reasonably, let alone to maximize their personal rewards and minimize their personal costs? "The people who act out of a sense of duty or friendship, it is said, cannot be accounted rational and cannot be brought within the scope of [the] rational choice [proposition]," the British sociologist Anthony Heath comments. "Of all the fallacies [about rationality], this is the least excusable. Rationality has nothing to do with the *goals* which [people] pursue but only with the *means* they use to achieve them. When we ask whether someone is behaving rationally we ... are not asking whether he [or she] is choosing the 'right' goal" (Heath 1976, 79).

As Heath implies, social scientists are fully aware of people such as Mother Teresa. But we also recognize that their behavior violates the principle of rationality only if we adopt a very narrow, materialistic, and entirely egocentric definition of rewards and ignore the immense variety of preferences and tastes. Human life and culture are so rich because of the incredible variety of our preferences and tastes, of things we perceive as rewarding. There is no need to suggest that a parent has acted against his or her self-interest by rushing into a burning building. Rather, let us recognize that the ability of humans to regard the survival of a child as more rewarding than their own survival is a credit to the human spirit and to our capacity to love. To call that altruism and place it in opposition to rationality is to reduce noble behavior to crazy, irrational action. In fact, the "selfish" premise of rationality is humanistic in the fullest sense. It acknowledges our capacity to find rewards in our dreams, hopes, loves, and ideals.

It is all the more amazing that social scientists have refused to extend the rationality axiom to religion in light of the fact that religious teachers have always stressed maximizing behavior as the justification for faith—that belief is the most rewarding (and hence most reasonable) option. Blaise Pascal stated the maximizing axiom with an enthusiasm that not even an economist would dare: "All men seek happiness. There are no exceptions. However different the means they employ, they all strive towards this goal.... This is the motive of every act of every man, including those who go and hang themselves" (*Pensée* no. 148; [1670] 1966, 45). Most of the world's religious scriptures abound in the language of exchange:

> O Indra ... may plentiful libations of the people, and singing sages' holy prayers rejoice thee ... thus may we be made partakers of the new favours that shall bring us profit." (Rig Veda 10.89)

> Make for Me an altar of earth and sacrifice on it your burnt offerings and your sacrifices of well-being, your sheep and your oxen; in every place where I cause My name to be mentioned I will come to you and bless you. (Torah, Exod. 21:21)

> Verily, Allah helps one who helps Him. (Qur'ān, sura 22:40)

> But to those men who honour me, concentrating on me alone, who are constantly disciplined, I bring gain and security (Bhagavad Gita 9.22).

> He that believeth and is baptized shall be saved. (Mark 16:16)

> And give glad tidings, O Muhammad, unto those who believe and do good works; that theirs are Gardens underneath which rivers flow. (Qur'ān, sura 2:25)

As this last quotation suggests, however, the major world religions not only promise rewards for devotion and belief in God, they also promise rewards for doing good to others. The best-known religious commands—including the Five Pillars of Islam and the Ten Commandments—offer explicit guidelines for action toward others as part of the obligation of the faithful, including actions that others might describe as altruistic: to sustain the needy and to avoid actions that may bring harm to others. And here, too, the language is that of exchange. In his remarkable analysis of the "commercial-theological" terms in the Qur'ān, Charles Torrey emphasizes the prevalence of promises concerning moral equity:

> Allah is in standing account with every man. Each good work is counted in man's favor, each bad deed is a debt. This reckoning is generally allowed to run during man's lifetime, but must at last be settled, by full payment of all balances.... Allah is of course the readiest of all reckoners. He not only keeps each man's account with the greatest exactness, in preparation for the day of judgment, but is ready at any moment to confront believer or unbeliever with his standing. (Torrey 1892, 8, 12) [1]

Torrey goes on to note that Muslim historians commonly assume that it is an entirely adequate explanation of someone's action to say "he did a thing ... counting on the future reward" (ibid., 13). In short, rational choosing is built into the very fabric of Islam, as it is with the other great world religions. We therefore concur with Max Weber's observation that "religiously or magically motivated behavior is relatively rational behavior.... It follows rules of experience.... Thus, religious and magical behavior or thinking must not be set apart from the range of everyday purposive conduct" ([1922] 1993, 1).

Recognize, too, that the rationality proposition is *only the starting assumption* of most modern social science. Thus, while of immense importance, it offers very little in the way of theory. To say, for example, that people try to be rational even when making religious choices is little more than a slogan when we confront the real explanatory tasks. Suppose we wish to explain why people select one church over another, or why they drop out of a religious movement following an initial period of enthusiasm. The rationality premise tells us to look for variations in payoffs or satisfactions, but no more than that, leaving the social scientist in the same position as a detective seeking motives in a murder case. The real work is yet to be accomplished.

Moreover, in constructing theories of many aspects of religion, we ourselves have rarely mentioned rationality. Consequently, we object to being identified as "Rational Choice Theorists," as if we were initiates of some theoretical "sect" of crypto economists unable to deal with the subtleties of religious realities. We find nothing subtle in such hallowed fixtures of the old paradigm as the "irrational choice" theory of religion that traces everything to ignorance or psychopathology. Nor, as should have been clear from the preceding discussion, do we shrink from the obvious influences of socialization and culture as necessary aspects of any social theory. Indeed, this book can be classified as a work in the rational choice tradition to the same extent that the work of James S. Coleman, George Herbert Meade, Karl Marx (see Boudon 1993), or Talcott Parsons (see Johnson 1996) can be so identified, but not more. Although we do not give an inch in our assumption that religious choices are guided by reason to as great an extent as are secular choices, neither do we mistake the rationality premise for an adequate explanation even of individual behavior, let alone of large social processes.

CONCLUSION

These, then, are the elements of the new paradigm. In the chapters that follow, we pursue these fundamental assumptions to a great variety of conclusions, many of them not at all obvious. We are under no illusions that we have gotten everything right. There undoubtedly will be many revisions and a great many extensions to come—some from us, most from our colleagues and successors. But there is nothing illusory about a basic paradigm shift in the social scientific study of religion. A mountain of fact bars any return to the simple certitudes of the past.

CHAPTER 2

Rationality and the "Religious Mind"

The notion that humans are essentially rational creatures underlies the mainstream of modern social science, except when religion is the object of study. When it comes to religion, many social scientists still cling to the doctrine, originated by the founders of their fields, that because the "religious mind" is fundamentally irrational, "choice" plays little or no role in religious behavior. Again and again we have been told that people are unable to balance the costs of religious commitment against its benefits. Instead, to explain why Mormons, for example, are willing to tithe, we are directed to investigate how their childhood socialization leaves them virtually without choice in the matter.

For more than three centuries, the standard social scientific wisdom was that religious behavior must be irrational precisely because people do make sacrifices on behalf of their faith—since, obviously, no rational person would do such a thing. We agree that no rational atheist would do so, but surely such behavior is entirely rational for anyone who believes that the gods reward those who sacrifice. However, given their certainty that no truly rational person would believe in religion, let alone willingly make religious sacrifices, social scientists committed to the old paradigm assume that socialization reduces most religious calculations to tautological "decisions" to choose what one has been trained to choose. And effective religious socialization, in turn, is attributed to ignorance, superstition, false consciousness, "brainwashing," or primitive culture. Indeed, as we shall see later in this chapter, many social scientists—including some of the most famous founders of the field—have attributed sincere religious commitment to that most fundamental form of irrationality: psychopathology.

The underlying issue comes down to this: Does it make sense to model religion as the behavior of rational, reasonably well informed actors who choose to "consume" religious "commodities" in the same way that they weigh the costs and benefits of consuming secular commodities? We believe it does and have made it the starting point of our work.

As we use it, the rationality assumption is an axiom in theories that produce empirical predictions. To construct a proper theory, one postulates or assumes the axioms and then logically deduces propositions, some of which have empirical implications. One tests the theory, and thereby the axioms, by testing empirical predictions deduced from the propositions (Hume [1748] 1962; Reichenbach 1959; Popper 1959; 1962). As Peter Blau has noted:

> The [deductive] theorist's aim is to discover a few theoretical generalizations from which many different empirical propositions may be derived. Strange as it may seem, the higher level [axioms] that explain the lower-level propositions are accepted as valid purely on the basis that they do explain them, in the specific sense that they logically imply them, and without independent evidence; whereas acceptance of the lower-level propositions that need to be explained is contingent on empirical evidence. (Blau 1970, 202)

Beginning in chapter 4, we present a theory of religion based on the rationality assumption. To the extent that we succeed, the case for religious behavior being as rational as are other forms of human behavior is demonstrated. Nevertheless, objections to approaching religion with an axiom postulating rational actors threaten to divert attention away from the results of using such an assumption. Hence, it is necessary to address the matter directly. We cannot, of course, inductively "prove" our rationality axiom (or any axiom), but we believe we have been able to assemble evidence that is sufficient to shift the burden of proof to those who would assert that religious behavior is fundamentally irrational or nonrational.

To proceed, we briefly sketch the recent history of the doctrine that religion is rooted in irrational choice, contrasting it with the rationalist tradition, and showing how the latter dominates social scientific theorizing on matters not involving religion. Against this background, we turn to pertinent data, including fieldwork and surveys involving members of various "costly" religious groups to see if they regard their costs in a way incompatible with the rationality assumption. Next, we examine survey data on the value individuals place on money and time to see if members of strict (costly) religious bodies are distinguishable from others in this regard. Additional survey data are analyzed to see if there are grounds for claiming that when people are willing to pay high costs for their religion, they do so because they think these are offset by substantial benefits. Shifting our focus, we conclude the chapter by examining whether religion and science really are incompatible commitments.

RELIGION AS IRRATIONAL CHOICE

From the beginning, social scientific studies of religion have been shaped by a single question: *What makes them do it?* How could any rational person make sacrifices on behalf of unseen supernatural entities? The answer: because, when it comes to religion, apparently reasonable beings are unreasonable—religion is rooted in the irrational. Keep in mind that claims about the irrationality of religious sacrifices have not been limited to great sacrifices such as asceticism or martyrdom. At issue are such ordinary activities as prayer, observance of moral codes, and contributions of time and wealth.

Whether it be the imputation of outright psychopathology, of groundless fears, or merely of faulty reasoning and misperceptions, the irrational assumption has dominated the field. As noted in the introduction, the notion that normal, sophisticated people could be religious has been limited to a few social scientists willing to allow their own brand of very mild religiousness to pass the test of rationality—as in Gordon W. Allport's concept of "intrinsic" religion. A variation of the proposition that religion is irrational is what might be best called the "ignorance and poor reasoning theory" of religious belief. This view has been especially popular among social scientists with liberal religious views. Thus, in book after book, J. Paul Douglass (see, e.g., Douglass and Brunner 1935) identified the "emotional sects" as "a backwash of sectarianism" found only "in certain quarters," especially "the more backward sections of the nation." Edmund Brunner, Douglass's colleague at the Institute of Social and Religious Research, described one evangelical congregation as "a poor class of mixed blood and of moronic intelligence" (1927, 75–76). And Warren Wilson, another member of the Institute, blamed the growth of evangelical Protestant groups in rural America on the fact that "among country people there are many inferior minds" (1925, 58). He further explained that revivalism was bound to persist in these regions "until we can lift the administration of popular institutions that are governed by public opinion out of the hand of the weak brother and the silly sister."

More typically, however, the ignorance and poor reasoning theory of religious belief is posed only in an implicit way, as the writer stresses the benefits of education in overcoming the illusions of faith. "The college experience, particularly at the better colleges, stimulates free inquiry, encourages the questioning of dogma, and undermines the force of tradition and authority, all of which combine to shake fundamentalistic religious belief," according to David Caplovitz and Fred Sherrow (1977, 127). (In fairness, we should note here that early in his career, the senior author of this book also advocated the view that education frees the mind of religious fetters [Stark 1963]). In any event, despite this immense body of theory and the enormous weight of learned opinion that created and sustained it, the irrationalist position recently has fallen upon hard times, beset by contrary evidence.

THE RATIONAL TRADITION

Ironically, aside from the area of religion, rational models have always dominated social science. As noted in chapter 1, the notion that people weigh the anticipated rewards of a choice against its anticipated costs is fundamental to all mainstream social scientific traditions.

In 1776, Adam Smith made rational self-interest the basis of his *Inquiry into the Nature and Causes of the Wealth of Nations,* and economists have followed in his footsteps. Even sociology has been dominated by this assumption. George Homans and the exchange theorists have, of course, emphasized rationality, but as noted in chapter 1, a belief in human rationality also fully underlies the work of symbolic interactionists, structural functionalists, and Marxists. Furthermore, as pointed out in chapter 1, the rational actor axiom is only the starting point of theorizing. No one proposes to settle for theories that human behavior is the product of "pure reason," unconstrained by norms and culture. We know perfectly well that whether one is a Hindu, Muslim, Jew, or Christian cannot be explained solely by reference to the fact that one is a rational actor. However, that is precisely why we begin our theorizing with an actor free of all such constraints: we want to explain how norms arise, how they constrain behavior, how culture is discovered and accumulated (as the senior author attempted to do in extended, deductive form in Stark and Bainbridge [1987] 1996). These matters can only be theorized about if one starts with an actor not already equipped in these regards—an actor in a vacuum (Coleman 1990, 31–32). We also must note that the nearly universal use of the rationality proposition by the social sciences is not really a matter of taste or preferences, but of utility. That is, it is possible to fashion far more powerful and parsimonious theories by using this proposition than by attempting to do without it. Indeed, even Steve Bruce concedes that "were social action not minimally rational, one would not be able to identify, comprehend, and explain it" (1993, 203). Exactly! Yet, it is precisely this image of people weighing their options vis-à-vis religious costs and benefits that has been scorned by generations of social scientists, including Bruce. Were they justified?

RELIGION AS PSYCHOPATHOLOGY

Despite frequent, confident claims that religiousness is rooted in psychopathology, the data have been uncooperative. In a study based on a sample of persons diagnosed as in need of immediate psychotherapy and a matched sample of the population, the senior author found that those diagnosed as mentally ill were far less likely to attend church or to score high on an index of religious orthodoxy; and neither did the published empirical research support the claim that religious people are more prone to authoritarianism (Stark 1971b).

Subsequently, in a survey of all published, empirical studies on the subject, Allen Bergin (1983) found that most reported a positive, rather than a negative, relationship between religiousness and mental health, and that the studies that did report a negative association between religion and mental health were tautological, having included religious items in their psychological measures. For example, five pro-religious items, each of which counted against a person's ego strength, were included in the "Ego Strength Scale" proposed by Barron 1953, which thus "discovered" that religious people had weak ego strength. Christopher G. Ellison (1993) has assembled an imposing empirical literature that strongly supports the conclusion that religious belief and practice greatly improve self-esteem, life satisfaction, the ability to withstand major social stressors, and even physical health. Finally, Melvin Pollner (1989) showed that prayer, especially to a god conceived of as "king," "judge," or "master," has very powerful positive effects on life satisfaction and on overall happiness, as well as on marital happiness.

THE PHENOMENOLOGY OF SACRIFICE

A number of years ago, the senior author did field observations among the first American members of the Unification Church—popularly known as the Moonies. During what was one of the most instructive moments of the entire experience, a young male convert reflected:

> You know, sometimes at night I wonder what if none of this is true. What if Rev. Moon is not inspired by God? Maybe all of this is for nothing. But then I say to myself, if it's true then I'm in on the ground floor of the greatest event in history. And if it isn't, so what? I was probably going to spend the rest of my life working in that plywood plant anyway.

What "all of this" that might be for nothing consisted of was the total dedication of his life and property to missionary activity. In those days, there was no room in the Unification Church for part-time lay members. It was all or nothing. All of the Unificationists observed by Stark were fully aware that membership was very costly, and, like the young man quoted above, they openly discussed this and frequently balanced the costs and benefits of belonging. Often they reached the conclusion that the benefits offset the costs—adding such things as the great warmth and family feeling of the group, and a busy, often exciting, life to the benefit side of the ledger, along with such religious benefits as the possibility of playing key roles in bringing about the Second Advent. But they also were candid about costs in the shape of long hours, lack of privacy, disruption of family life, and even too-frequent Korean menus. Moreover, members often reached the conclusion that for them, the benefits no longer outweighed the costs and dropped out. Contrary to the image of "cultists" as brainwashed captives of faith, such a large majority of Unificationist converts eventually did quit, especially when it came time to raise a family, that the movement shifted its position and recognized a valid lay membership subject to greatly reduced costs (Barker 1984). How could this happen if Unificationists don't think about the sacrifices they make for their faith as costs?

Of equal significance is the fact that based on Eileen Barker's remarkable field survey (Barker 1984), Unification converts were quite exceptional in terms of their good mental health. Barker was able to get permission to distribute a questionnaire to all those who attended introductory two-day Unification workshops, which were held periodically in London during 1979 and 1980. These people were having their first exposure to the Unificationist teachings, and eventually she obtained data on 1,017 people. In addition to collecting data from all newcomers at their first visit to the group, Barker was able to track their subsequent contacts. Eventually, these data allowed her to chart the eventual recruitment outcomes of each of these potential converts. Hence, Barker could not only describe the entire group of first-time attenders, she could compare those who came once and did not return with those who converted, and among converts she could compare those who remained members for at least two years with those who joined for at least a week but quit within two years of their conversion.

Table 1 compares these three groups in terms of their psychological background and outlook. Keep in mind that these data were collected from people as they arrived to attend their first two-day workshop. Hence, these data were collected *before* anyone had converted and are not subject to retrospective distortions. The first thing to notice is that the group of attenders as a whole were not a bunch of neurotic misfits and malcontents. Few had been in psychiatric treatment, few reported periods of depression, and few were unemployed. The percentage who said they were very happy is only a bit below the 34 percent who gave this response in a national sample of Britain conducted in 1981 (World Values Survey). But an even more important thing to notice is that people who joined and stayed at least two years were substantially *less* likely to have been depressed, unhappy, unemployed or to have had a history of psychiatric treatment than were those who did not join, or who joined but soon quit. Notice the immense differences in the percentage who were very happy.

The number of cases in each group reveals something else of considerable interest. Of those who attended an initial two-day workshop, only 10 percent ended up joining the church for at least a week, and only 5 percent remained

TABLE 1   Persons Attending Unification Church Workshops
in London, 1979–80

	% Non-Joiners (n=915)	% Joiners Who Quit (n=52)	% Joiners Who Stayed (n=50)
Had received prior psychiatric help	8	8	1
Had prior periods of serious depression	15	17	5
Unemployed at the time of the workshop	7	16	3
"Very happy" at the time of the workshop	21	17	52

SOURCE: Barker 1984.

for at least two years. These findings deal a fatal blow to those who claim that the Unificationists use mind control or brainwashing techniques to gain converts. If this is brainwashing, it certainly doesn't work very well.

WITNESS AWARENESS

When we began work on this chapter, we planned to spend time interviewing members of several very high-commitment religious groups, including Jehovah's Witnesses. Initially, we had planned preliminary discussions with a few Witnesses as preparation for a more structured subsequent study. However, after twelve exploratory interviews, we decided that further research was superfluous, as will be clear.

Each interview was conducted in private by one sociologist. After a brief conversation to put each respondent at ease, each was asked: "Let's suppose someone is thinking very seriously about joining your church. What would you say would be the major factors holding them back?" [1]

In all twelve cases, the respondent immediately mentioned the time and energy required of members. As one woman put it: "A lot of people aren't sure about putting in so much time. Being a Witness isn't a matter of just showing up on Sunday for an hour or two. It's a real commitment." The second barrier mentioned by all twelve was the public stigma of membership. "You have to be able to endure a lot of odd looks when people find out your religion," one middle-aged male responded. When asked if they ever found it difficult to witness in public, each seemed to find the question a bit absurd. Wouldn't anyone sometimes find it hard to knock on the doors of strangers?

Jehovah's Witnesses do not pay the high costs of membership in silent ignorance or under the compulsion of fanatical faith. These were very pleasant, reasonable, and interesting people. They knew the costs were high. It was something they talked about openly with outsiders as easily as with one another. And only so long as they think they have good reasons for paying these costs will they do so. Indeed, following the failure of an unofficial, but widely believed, prophesy that Judgment Day would occur in 1975, a significant number of Witnesses did quit and there was a sharp decline in average level of commitment of those who stayed. It took about 5 years for the movement to recover fully (Stark and Iannaccone 1997; Singelenberg 1989).

These interviews with Witnesses are entirely consistent with the results of many other field studies of highly committed (costly) religious groups, including Protestant sectarians (Wagner 1990), Catholic Charismatic prayer groups (Neitz 1987; Neitz and Mueser 1997), and Orthodox Jews (Davidman 1991). Indeed, in her widely quoted study of middle-class female Jewish converts to a very Orthodox synagogue in Manhattan, Lynn Davidman stresses the very overt rationality involved. She notes that the women "were engaged in a process of evaluating their needs against what they saw the institutions offering," and that the rabbis were equally aware of this and made an open appeal to the women's "power of reason." The women Davidman observed were fully aware of the high costs of membership (in ritual observance, dress, choice of a spouse, sex role behavior, etc.). But they found that these were overshadowed by the perceived benefits, such as the great respect given to mothers and wives, the active participation of husbands in child rearing, and a tightly knit, supportive community. Keep in mind that these women did not lack for secular options; nearly all had completed college, and a third had advanced degrees.

MORMON FERTILITY

For more than a century, Mormon leaders have extolled childbearing, and Mormon fertility in the United States and Canada is higher than that of non-Mormons (Bush 1976). What sort of model best explains Mormons' response to their leaders admonitions to be fruitful and multiply?

Two nonrational explanations spring to mind: first, that Mormon socialization dramatically alters members' perceptions of costs and benefits, so that child rearing is no longer perceived as a sacrifice; and second, that socialization and group sanctions overshadow calculations of costs and benefits, thereby also eliminating the element of "choice" from the fertility decision. On the other hand, higher average fertility might be modeled as a purely rational response to a new source of benefits—approval, status, and blessings that the Mormon Church offers in return for family size. The difference here is not merely semantic. For one thing, explanation in terms of socialization and group sanctions invites condemnation of the (manipulative) church and of its (coerced or indoctrinated) members. Much more important, however, the explanations predict different behavior.

If Mormon fertility were nonrational, it would be generally unresponsive to the standard economic predictors of fertility, such as income. If Mormons regarded children as an unmixed blessing, a gift from God to be joyfully welcomed, they would not use birth control, accepting the number that God sends, and the influence of income would be minimal. But if Mormons act rationally vis-à-vis fertility, maximizing their utility over a typical set of preferences and subject to all the standard costs and benefits plus a church-supplied "bonus" for fertility, then we would predict that: (1) Mormon couples will have more children than their non-Mormon counterparts, but (2) they will not maximize family size (and will use birth control); (3) socioeconomic pressures will affect Mormon family size; and (4) over time, changes in Mormon fertility trends will parallel changes in national fertility.

At first glance, the rational model might seem wrong on the face of it. As Lester Bush documented in his historical review of church teachings, "the Mormon leadership has not condoned economic limitation, educational obligations, or 'arbitrary' restrictions of family size as acceptable reasons for the use of any form of birth control" (Bush 1976, 31). But actual behavior, including the behavior of the most devout members and of church leaders, has proved "unmistakably responsive to the pressures that have influence national fertility" (ibid., 33). The vast majority of Mormon couples in the United States do practice birth control (it is not prohibited by church doctrine), thereby averaging about three children per family—more than non-Mormons, but far below their potential maximum. However, unlike their non-Mormon counterparts, higher-income Mormon families average more children. Mormons thus treat children as a "normal" good, and they are demanded in greater numbers by those households that can better afford them, so that Mormon professionals average significantly larger families than do Mormon laborers (Thornton 1979; Heaton 1986a; 1986b).

Finally, consider the history of American fertility trends. For nearly a century, Mormon fertility in the United States has moved in tandem with non-Mormon fertility. Both Mormon and non-Mormon fertility dropped throughout the 1920s and the Great Depression, rose rapidly during the Baby Boom, and subsequently resumed a long-run decline. The difference, of course, is that Mormon families have averaged about one to two children more than non-Mormon families, and Mormon leaders have averaged still more (Bush 1976, 230). The Mormon "preference" for larger than average families has thus remained constant, but the actual size of Mormon families has risen and fallen in response to general social trends.

Mormon fertility thus provides an excellent illustration of what we mean by "rational religious behavior." On the one hand, religion does make a difference: the Mormon Church has managed to maintain an effective system of social and psychic rewards for fertility, thereby increasing member fertility. This is no small achievement—indeed, it is one of the most striking behavioral outcomes achieved by any American religion. Even so, the fertility of Mormon couples functioning within this system is best explained as cost/benefit analysis, responsive to all of the standard, secular costs and benefits and "deviant" only insofar as additional church-supplied benefits enter into the calculations.

WHAT DO FUNDAMENTALISTS VALUE?

Recently, an anonymous journal reviewer condemned claims about rational religious choices on grounds of what he or she took to be the self-evident fact that followers of high-commitment (costly) churches don't count things the way others do. Thus, when "fundamentalists," for example, give a lot of time and money to their church, they do so without any significant sense of sacrifice because they have a different basis for calculating value. In our judgment table 2 constitutes a nearly definitive rejection of such claims. The data for the top portion of the table were collected from a national sample of Americans in January 1992 by the Barna Research Group (Barna 1992), and the remainder of the

TABLE 2   Perceived Costs of Participation in Religion

	% Fundamentalists* (n=279)	% Other Americans (n=889)
How important is your time to you?		
Very Important	81	78
How important is your free time to you?		
Very Important	70	63
How important is living comfortably to you?		
Very Important	63	58
How important is your career to you?		
Very Important	53	52
How important is money to you?		
Very Important	40	38
How important is your community to you?		
Very Important	62	55

SOURCE: Calculated from Barna 1992.

	(n=454)	(n=1122)
How important to you is:		
Being financially secure?		
Very Important	75	69
Having nice things?		
Very Important	25	26
Having a fulfilling job?		
Very Important	73	78

SOURCE: Calculated from the General Social Survey, 1993.
*Members of Evangelical Protestant denominations.

table is based on the General Social Survey of 1993. American "fundamentalists" are even slightly more likely than other Americans to rate their time, money, career and a comfortable living as very important.[2] Clearly, when religious people give time and money, they must be fully aware of the costs, because they value these things as much or more than anyone else. Why then do they do it?

PERCEIVED COST/BENEFIT RATIOS

In subsequent chapters, we demonstrate that people will only accept high religious costs if these result in such high levels of religious benefits that the result is a favorable exchange ratio. That is, people attend not only to cost, but to value in making their decisions. Table 3 offers preliminary support for this position.

TABLE 3   The Contributions and Satisfaction of Church Membership

	Percentage who contributed $2,000 or more to their church in the past year	GPA* of the religious group, graded by members
Roman Catholics (n=386)	2	2.3
Liberal Protestants (n=372)	3	2.3
Conservative Protestants (n=338)	14	3.1
Mormons (n=30)	48	3.8

SOURCE: Calculated from the General Social Survey, 1989.
*Grade Point Average: 4.0 is the highest possible grade; 0 is the lowest.

Clearly, based on table 3, members of some denominations are far more likely to give generously than are others. Only 2 percent of Catholics and 3 percent of liberal Protestants contributed more than $2,000 to their church during the year. However, 14 percent of conservative Protestant members, and 48 percent of Mormons gave that much. Keep in mind that members of the high-contribution groups tend to have lower incomes than do members of the liberal Protestant bodies. Now, look at the second column in the table which shows how members of each group graded their church: A through F. Here we see that church members are fairly tough graders. Based on a standard GPA (A=4.0), Catholics and liberal Protestants ranked their churches at just over a C (2.3). Conservative Protestants gave their denominations a B (3.1), while Mormons graded their church very highly at 3.8. The correlation between level of giving and GPA is very high. Moreover, it holds within these groups—there are dissatisfied conservative Protestants, for example, and they give less.

These findings are entirely consistent with our claim in chapter 6 that members of strict churches give more because they receive more, but seem inconsistent with the claim that religious people do not consider their church contributions to be costs. It might be argued, of course, that religious "fundamentalists" grade their denominations highly out of fanatical loyalty. But why are only some of them like this? Substantial numbers of their co-religionists gave the groups lower grades. Moreover, what made Catholics and liberal Protestants give their churches low grades? Can we make any headway in answering such questions if we reject the reasonable person axiom?

RELIGION AND SCIENCE

Ultimately, the alleged deficiencies of the "religious mind" derive from the presumed limitations of religion itself—specifically, its prescientific, unscientific, and anti-scientific character. A fundamental incompatibility between scientific and religious worldviews is usually taken for granted, but the empirical literature on the topic is surprisingly mixed and generally unsupportive (Wuthnow 1985). For present purposes, it suffices to summarize the central findings of our ongoing study of the religious beliefs and behavior of scientists.

The Carnegie Commission conducted a massive survey of more than 60,000 professors—approximately one-fourth of all the college faculty in America—in 1969, by far the largest survey of its kind. The survey centered on academic issues and sociopolitical attitudes, but also included questions about religion: "How often do you attend religious services?" "What is your present religion?" "How religious do you consider yourself?" and "Do you consider yourself religiously conservative?"

Table 4 summarizes responses to these items across major areas of science. Two rather striking findings challenge claims about the incompatibility of religion and science. First, levels of religiousness were found to be relatively high. Second, social scientists were substantially less religious than those in the "hard" sciences.

In most fields, a substantial majority thought of themselves as deeply or moderately religious—only among social scientists (45%) was this the minority response. Nor did scientists restrict themselves to tepid faiths—40 percent of faculty in mathematics and statistics characterized themselves as "religiously conservative," as did 34 percent of physical scientists and 36 percent of those in the life sciences. Moreover, scientists attended church at the same level of regularity as the general population—47 percent of mathematicians and statisticians reported attending two or three times a month, or more often, as did 43 percent of physical scientists and 42 percent in the life sciences. The 1973 Gen-

TABLE 4   Religiousness by Scholarly Field, 1969

	% *Religious Person*	% *Regular Attend*	% *Never Attend*	% *Religious Conservative*	% *No Religion*
Mathematics/statistics	60	47	35	40	27
Physical sciences	55	43	38	34	27
Life sciences	55	42	36	36	29
Social sciences	45	31	48	19	36
Economics	50	38	42	26	30
Political science	51	32	43	18	30
Sociology	49	38	43	16	36
Psychology	33	20	62	12	48
Anthropology	29	15	67	11	57

SOURCE: Calculated from the Carnegie Commission Survey of 60,028 American academics, 1969.

eral Social Survey (only four years later than the faculty survey) found that 44 percent of Americans attended at least two or three times a month. Scientists are, however, a bit more likely than the general population to report that they never attend church—about a third in most areas, and about half of all social scientists, compared with 21 percent in the 1973 GSS. And scientists surpass the general population in the percentage stating their religious preference as "none." Nevertheless, outside the social sciences, only about one in four gave this response in the Carnegie Commission survey.

But perhaps the most striking finding is that on each of these measures, faculty in the "hard" sciences turned out to be far more likely to be religious than were their counterparts in the "softer" social sciences: they attended church more regularly, were more likely to describe themselves as "deeply" or "moderately" religious, or to say they were "religiously conservative," and they were far more likely to claim religious affiliation. These patterns are evident, not only in the simple cross-tabulations we report here, but in complex regressions: differences between the social and the natural and physical sciences are extremely robust and withstand controls for individual attributes such as age, gender, race, or religious upbringing. Moreover, these differences across scientific areas have been replicated in other samples of college professors (Leuba [1916] 1921; 1934; Thalheimer 1973), and even in samples of graduate and undergraduate students (Feldman and Newcomb 1970). Furthermore, longitudinal data show that professors and students do not become less religious as they progress through their scientific training; rather, those enrolling in the social sciences are less religious than the general population before entering college and graduate school (Wuthnow 1985, 191).

Table 4 also breaks down the social sciences into specific fields. Here we see an additional feature, not previously noted in the literature. It is above all faculty in psychology and anthropology who stand as towers of unbelief. The other social sciences remain relatively irreligious, but these two fields—the two most closely associated with the "primitive" and "religious" mind theses—are true outliers. Compared to faculty in the physical sciences, psychologists and anthropologists are almost twice as likely to not attend church, to not describe themselves as religious persons, and to say that they have no religion. These differences are of such magnitude that one can scarcely imagine their not influencing the tone of conversation, instruction, and research in these two fields. Indeed, these data suggest to us why efforts to base theories of religion on the rationality premise generate so much antagonism.

What are we to make of these results? The central question, posed by Robert Wuthnow, is "why the most irreligious persons [should] be found in the *least scientific* disciplines." Wuthnow proposed an intriguing solution, claiming in effect that certain disciplines lean toward irreligion precisely because they have such a weak claim to be developed sciences: "[T]hese disciplines [tend] to rely on boundary-posturing mechanisms such as irreligiosity (the same patterns prevail, incidentally, on traits such as political radicalism, nonconventionality, and alienation from the public)" (Wuthnow 1985, 197).

We think there is merit in Wuthnow's suggestions, and in future work, we shall pursue issues concerning the religiousness of scientists and professors in detail. Here it suffices to have demonstrated that a very substantial share of faculty engaged in doing science—intelligent and highly educated people, well socialized into that sphere of modern rationality that has been expected to sweep religion away—are quite comfortable with religious faiths.

CONCLUSION

As noted in the introduction, for most of its existence, the social scientific study of religion has been nothing of the sort. Despite the immense antagonism it expresses toward "faith," the truth is that the discipline has not been pursued as a science, but has rested almost entirely on faith. To be sure, this faith consists of secular doctrines, but it is faith in the sense that its fundamental premises are of the type ridiculed by Michael Scriven as "a belief which goes beyond the evidence ... [or] belief in something which is contrary to well-established laws" (quoted in Plantinga 1993, 136).

Claims about the makeup and functioning of the religious mind go far beyond the evidence—indeed, they are contrary to a very formidable body of evidence. Moreover, claims about the fundamental irrationality of religion, and therefore of the religious mind, are clearly "contrary to well-established laws." That is, religious behavior is the only area in the social sciences where the rational actor axiom has been excluded—and without it, all major theories of economics, sociology, political science, and experimental psychology are nullified. Why this exception? Because religion is not regarded as something to explain in the same way that one might attempt to explain fertility, suicide, crime, or inequality. Rather, as discussed in the introduction and chapter 1, religion is seen as *the enemy*. Jeffrey Hadden has noted:

> The founding generation of sociologists were hardly value-free armchair scholars, sitting back and objectively analyzing [religion]. They believed passionately that science was ushering in a new era which would crush the superstitions and oppressive structures which the Church had promoted for so many centuries. Indeed, they were all essentially in agreement that traditional forms of religion would soon be a thing of the past. (Hadden 1987, 590)

Out of this atheism and antagonism came the once-dominant social scientific view that religion is false, and unique theoretical principles had therefore to be invoked to explain it, inasmuch as no rational actor, in a modern situation, could accept false beliefs lacking scientific verification. That this claim was itself a belief lacking scientific verification has been ignored. Moreover, social scientists have been content to cite the relative lack of religiousness among themselves as proof that faith cannot survive scientific enlightenment (a point noted by Greeley 1988), while ignoring the persistence of religion among those involved in the more mature sciences.

One need not be a religious person in order to grasp the underlying rationality of religious behavior, any more than one need be a criminal in order to impute rationality to many deviant acts (as the leading theories of crime and deviance do). In saying this, we do not suppose that religious behavior is the rational choice for every actor—which is why irreligiousness or at least religious indifference is rather common—nor do we propose that just any religious behavior justifies its cost. What we are saying is that religious behavior—to the degree that it occurs—is generally based on cost/benefit calculations and is therefore rational behavior in precisely the same sense that other human behavior is rational.

From this perspective, the full theoretical resources of social science can be utilized to understand religion.

CHAPTER 3

Secularization, R.I.P.

For nearly three centuries, social scientists and assorted Western intellectuals have been promising the end of religion. Each generation has been confident that within another few decades, or possibly a bit longer, humans will "outgrow" belief in the supernatural. This proposition soon came to be known as the secularization thesis, and its earliest proponents seem to have been British, as the Restoration of the monarchy in 1660 led to an era during which militant attacks on faith were quite popular among fashionable Londoners (Durant and Durant 1965).

As far as we are able to discover, it was the English divine and freethinker Thomas Woolston (1670–1731) who first set a date by which time modernity would have triumphed over faith. Writing in about 1710, he expressed his confidence that Christianity would be gone by 1900 (Woolston 1735). Half a century later, Frederick the Great thought this was much too pessimistic, writing to his friend Voltaire that "the Englishman Woolston ... could not calculate what has happened quite recently.... It [religion] is crumbling of itself, and its fall will be but the more rapid" (quoted in Redman 1949, 26). In response, Voltaire ventured that the end would come within the next fifty years.

Widespread press reports about the second "Great Awakening" did nothing to deter Thomas Jefferson from predicting in 1822 that "there is not a young man now living in the United States who will not die a Unitarian" (Healy 1984, 373). Of course, a generation later, Unitarians were as scarce as ever, while the Methodists and Baptists continued their spectacular rate of growth (Finke and Stark 1992).

An earlier version of this chapter was published as Rodney Stark, "Secularization, R.I.P.," *Sociology of Religion* (1999) 60:249–73.

Subsequent prophets of secularization have been no less certain, but they have been somewhat more circumspect as to dates. In France, Auguste Comte (1798–1857) announced that, as a result of modernization, human society was outgrowing the "theological stage" of social evolution and a new age was dawning in which the science of sociology would replace religion as the basis for moral judgments. But Comte did not say exactly when all this would be accomplished. In similar fashion, as often as Frederich Engels gloated about how the socialist revolution would cause religion to evaporate, he would only say that it would happen "soon."

"Every day, every week, every month, every quarter, the most widely read journals seem just now to vie with each other in telling us that the time for religion is past, that faith is a hallucination or an infantile disease, that the gods have at last been found out and exploded," Max Müller complained in his 1878 Hibbert lectures (1880, 218). "[T]he opinion is everywhere gaining ground that religion is a mere survival from a primitive ... age, and its extinction only a matter of time," A. E. Crawley noted early in the twentieth century (1905, 8). But a few years later, when Max Weber explained why modernization would cause the "disenchantment" of the world, and when Sigmund Freud reassured his disciples that this greatest of all neurotic illusions would die upon the therapist's couch, they too would be no more specific than "soon."

More recently, however, "soon" became "under way" or "ongoing." For example, the distinguished anthropologist Anthony F. C. Wallace explained to tens of thousands of American undergraduates that "the evolutionary future of religion is extinction." Although he admitted that it might require "several hundred years" to complete the process, he claimed that it already was well under way in the advanced nations (Wallace 1966, 264–65). Bryan Wilson, too, has throughout his illustrious career described secularization as "a long term process *occurring* in human society," saying that "the process implicit in the concept of secularization concedes at once the idea of an earlier condition of life that was not secular, or that was at least much less secular than that of our own times" (Wilson 1982, 150–51)

In contrast to all this intellectual pussyfooting around, Peter Berger told the *New York Times* in 1968 that by "the 21st century, religious believers are likely to be found only in small sects, huddled together to resist a worldwide secular culture" (Berger 1968, 3). Unleashing his gift for memorable imagery, Berger said that "the predicament of the believer is increasingly like that of a Tibetan astrologer on a prolonged visit to an American university." In light of the recent lionization of the Dalai Lama by the American media and his cordial welcome to various campuses, Berger's simile now admits of rather a different interpretation. In any event, when his prediction had only three years left to run, Berger gracefully recanted his belief in secularization (as is discussed later). We quote his statements during the 1960s only because they so fully express the mood of the times.

Notice five things about all of these secularization prophesies.

First, there is universal agreement that modernization is the causal engine dragging the gods into retirement. That is, the secularization doctrine has always nestled within the broader theoretical framework of modernization theories, it being proposed that as industrialization, urbanization, and rationalization increase, religiousness *must* decrease (Hadden 1987; Finke 1992).

Keep in mind that modernization is a *long, gradual, relatively constant process.* Wars, revolutions, and other calamities may cause an occasional sudden blip in the trend lines, but the overall process is not volatile. If secularization is the result of modernization or, indeed, is one aspect of it, then secularization is not volatile and, rather than proceeding by sudden fits and starts, it too will display a long-term, gradual, and relatively constant trend of religious decline, corresponding to similar upward trends in such aspects of modernization as economic development, urbanization, and education. In terms of time series trends, modernization is a long, linear, upward curve, and secularization is assumed to trace the reciprocal of this curve, to be a long, linear, downward curve. Indeed, since modernization is so advanced in many nations that "postmodernism" is the latest buzzword, it must be assumed that secularization is at least "ongoing" to the extent that a significant downward trend in religiousness can be seen.

The second thing to notice about the secularization prophecies is that they are *not* directed primarily toward institutional differentiation—they do not merely predict the separation of church and state or a decline in the direct, secular authority of church leaders. Their primary concern is with *individual piety,* especially *belief.* Thus, Jefferson predicted that the next generation would find Christian beliefs, and especially faith in the divinity of Jesus, implausible and would limit themselves to the minimalist conception of God sustained by Unitarians. It was not bishops but the religious "fantasies" of the masses that most concerned Engels. Freud wrote about religious illusions, not about church taxes, and Wallace asserted that "belief in supernatural powers is doomed to die out, all over the world" (1966, 265) because, as Bryan Wilson explained "[t]he rational structure of society itself precludes much indulgence in supernaturalist thinking" (1975, 81).

In recent years, secularization has been defined in several ways (Hanson 1997; Tschannen 1991; Dobbelaere 1987; Shiner 1967), which unfortunately permits proponents of the thesis to shift definitions as needed in order escape inconvenient facts (see Dobbelaere, 1987; 1997; Lechner 1991; 1996; Yamane 1997). One definition, often referred to as the macro version (Lechner 1996), identifies secularization as deinstitutionalization (Dobbelaere 1987; Martin 1978). This refers to a decline in the social power of religious institutions, enabling other social institutions, especially political and educational institutions, to escape from prior religious domination.

If this were all that secularization meant, and if we limited discussion to Europe, there would be nothing to argue about. Everyone must agree that, in contemporary Europe, Catholic bishops have less political power than they once possessed, and the same is true of Lutheran and Anglican bishops (although bishops probably never were nearly so powerful as they now are thought to have been). Nor are primary aspects of public life any longer suffused with religious symbols, rhetoric, or ritual. These changes have, of course, aroused scholarly interest, resulting in some distinguished studies (Casanova 1994; Martin 1978). But the prophets of secularization theory were not and are not merely writing about something so obvious or limited. At issue is not a narrow prediction concerning a growing separation of church and state. Instead, as we have seen, from the start, the prophets of secularization have stressed personal piety, and to the extent that they have expressed macro interests, it has been to claim that they are so linked that a decline in one necessitates a decline in the other. Thus, if the churches lose power, personal piety will fade; if personal piety fades, the churches will lose power. Indeed, Peter Berger, long the most sophisticated modern proponent of the secularization thesis, was entirely candid on this point. Having outlined the macro aspects of secularization, Berger noted:

> Moreover, it is implied here that the process of secularization has a subjective side as well. As there is a secularization of society and culture, so there is a secularization of consciousness. Put simply, this means that the modern West has produced an increasing number of individuals who look upon the world and their own lives without the benefit of religious interpretations. (Berger 1969, 107–8)

As noted, recently Berger (1997) gracefully withdrew his support for the theory of secularization. We quote this passage from his earlier work not to emphasize our previous disagreement with Berger, whose work we always have much admired, but as a contrast to the recent tactic by other proponents of secularization, who seek to evade the growing mountain of contrary evidence by pretending that the theory merely pertains to deinstitutionalization, and that any trends in personal piety are irrelevant. Let us note Karel Dobbelaere's breathtaking recent evasion, "the religiousness of individuals is *not* a valid indicator in evaluating the process of secularization" (1997, 9). Such revisionism is not only historically false, it is insincere. Those who employ it revert to celebrating the demise of individual piety whenever they see a fact that seems to be supportive or whenever they believe they are speaking to an audience of fellow devotees. Thus, at a conference in Rome in 1993, Lilliane Voyé and Karel Dobbelaere explained that because science is "a thoroughly secular perspective on the world" and has come to dominate educational curricula, this has resulted in "desacralizing the content of learning and the world-view of students." Citing earlier essays by Dobbelaere, they went on to claim that "the successful removal by science of all kinds of anthropomorphisms from our thinking have transformed the traditional concept of 'God as a person' into a belief in a life-force, a power of spirit and this has also gradually promoted agnosticism and atheism—which explains the long-term decline of religious practices" (Voyé and Dobbelaere 1994, 95).

Exactly! That is precisely what the secularization thesis has always been, and Voyé and Dobbelaere's empirical claims, if true, would fully satisfy Woolston's prophesy—albeit a bit late. But, as will be seen, it is not so. What *is* so, is that secularization predicts a marked decline in the religiousness of the individual.

The third thing to notice about the secularization thesis is that, implicit in all versions, and explicit in most, is the claim that of all aspects of modernization, it is science that has the most deadly implications for religion. For Comte and Wallace, as for Voyé and Dobbelaere, it is science that will free us from the superstitious fetters of faith. Or, in the odd formulation by Bryan Wilson, "Christianity, with the impact of scientific and social scientific hindsights, has lost general theological plausibility" (1968, 86). If this is so, then scientists must be a relatively irreligious lot. But, as was seen in chapter 2, scientists are about as religious as anyone else, and the presumed incompatibility between religion and science seems mythical. Additional evidence is examined later in this chapter.

Fourth, secularization is regarded as an absorbing state, which once achieved at is irreversible, instilling mystical immunity. However, events and trends in eastern Europe and the nations of the former Soviet Union do not support these expectations. Instead, as Andrew Greeley so aptly put it, after more than seventy years of militant efforts by the state to achieve secularization, "St. Vladimir has routed Karl Marx" (Greeley 1994, 272).

Fifth, and finally, while most discussions of secularization focus on Christendom, all leading proponents of the thesis apply it globally. Thus, it is not merely belief in Christ that is "doomed to die out," but, as Wallace explained in the passage quoted above, "belief in supernatural powers," and this is going to happen "all over the world." Hence, Allah is fated to join Jehovah as only "an interesting historical memory." However, no one has bothered to explain this to Muslims, as will be seen.

Now for specifics.

THE MYTH OF RELIGIOUS DECLINE

Many scholars appear to believe that if rates of individual religious belief and participation for most nations of northern and western Europe were graphed, they would indeed be reciprocal to the trends in modernization. Beginning with high levels of faith and practice at the end of the eighteenth century, the master trends are assumed to have been ever downward, culminating in very low current levels of religiousness. And the latter are regarded as but insignificant residuals, soon to disappear too (Wilson 1966; 1982; Bruce 1995; Lechner 1991; 1996). For evidence in support of these claims, we are directed to note a steep decline in church attendance in much of Europe and to infer from this an erosion of individual faith as well, on the grounds that participation is low because of a lack of the beliefs needed to motivate attendance. These views are wrong in all respects.

David Martin (1965) was the first contemporary sociologist to reject the secularization thesis outright, even proposing that the concept of secularization be eliminated from social scientific discourse on the grounds that it had served only ideological and polemical, rather than theoretical, functions and because there was no evidence in favor of any general or consistent "shift from a religious period in human affairs to a secular period" (Martin 1991, 465). Several years later, when Andrew Greeley (1972b) presented survey data refuting the secularization thesis, he was concerned that he might be labeled as a "conservative" because he dared to doubt the "demise of religion." He argued, however, that his debate with other scholars was not ideological, it was empirical: "If I don't believe Martin Marty, Peter Berger, Ramon Echarren, John Cogley, and Eugene Fontinell, it is not because I have ideological differences with any of them but simply because they do not offer evidence that convinces me" (Greeley 1972b, 7).

Astounding as it may seem, the secularization thesis has been inconsistent with plain facts from the very start. For example, having noted the popularity of the secularization doctrine among eighteenth-century philosophers, Alexis de Tocqueville commented: "Unfortunately, the facts by no means accord with their theory. There are certain populations in Europe whose unbelief is only equalled by their ignorance and debasement; while in America, one of the freest and most enlightened nations in the world, the people fulfill with fervor all the outward duties of religion" (Tocqueville [1835–39] 1956, 319).

In the more than 150 years since Tocqueville made those observations, not only has American religiousness not gone into decline, but the rate of church membership has actually doubled (Finke and Stark 1992), while other indices of commitment have held steady or have risen modestly (Greeley 1989; Finke 1992).

Moreover, although the American case continues to offer a devastating challenge to the secularization doctrine, the secularization thesis fails in Europe too. First, there has been *no demonstrable long-term decline in European religious participation*. Participation has probably varied from time to time in response to profound social dislocations such as wars and revolutions, but the far more important point is that religious participation was very low in northern and western Europe many centuries before the onset of modernization.

The second reason to reject claims about the secularization of Europe is that current data do not reveal the arrival of an age of "scientific atheism." *Levels of subjective religiousness remain high*—to classify a nation as highly secularized when the large majority of its inhabitants believe in God is absurd. Indeed, the important question about religion in Europe is, as Grace Davie has put it, not why people no longer believe, but why they "persist in believing but see no need to participate with even minimal regularity in their religious institutions?" (Davie 1990b, 395). Of these two major bases for rejecting claims about the secularization of Europe, the claim that religious participation was never very high in northern and western Europe is the one that must strike most readers as dubious.

THE MYTH OF PAST PIETY

Everyone knows that once upon a time the world was pious—that in olden days most people exhibited levels of religious practice and concern that today linger only in isolated social subcultures such as those of the Amish, ultra-orthodox Jews, or Muslim fundamentalists. But, like so many once-upon-a-time tales, this conception of a pious past is mere nostalgia; most prominent historians of medieval religion now agree that there never was an "Age of Faith" (Morris 1993; Duffy 1992; Sommerville 1992; Bossy 1985; Obelkevich 1979; Murray 1972; Thomas 1971; Coulton 1938). Writing in the eleventh century, the English monk William of Malmesbury complained that the aristocracy rarely attended church, and that even the more pious among them "attended" mass at home, in bed: "They didn't go to church in the mornings in a Christian fashion; but in their bedchambers, lying in the arms of their wives, they did but taste with their ears the solemnities of the morning mass rushed through by a priest in a hurry" (in Fletcher 1997, 476).

As for the ordinary people, during the Middle Ages and the Renaissance, they rarely heard mass *anywhere*, most entering a church only for weddings, funerals, and christenings (if then), and their private worship was directed toward an array of spirits and supernatural agencies, only some of them recognizably Christian (Gentilecore 1992; Schneider 1990; Delumeau 1977; Thomas 1971). Alexander Murray's assessment of medieval Italian religious life is typical: "[S]ubstantial sections of thirteenth-century society hardly attended church at all." The Dominican prior Humbert of Romans, in his handbook *On the Teaching of Preachers*, advised his friars that "reaching the laity involves catching them at markets and tournaments, in ships, and so on," which Murray interprets as "a fair enough sign that they were not to be caught in churches." Indeed, Humbert frankly acknowledged that the masses "rarely go to church, and rarely to sermons [when they do attend]; so they know little of what pertains to their salvation." Finally, Humbert admitted that the regular clergy were so involved in gambling, pleasure, and "worse things," that they, too, "scarcely come to church." In similar terms, the Blessed Giordano of Rivalto reported that, upon arriving in Florence to preach, he suggested to a local woman that she take her daughter to church at least on feast days, only to be informed, "It is not the custom" (Murray 1972, 92, 93–94). The anonymous English author of *Dives and Pauper* complained that "the people these days ... are loath to hear God's Service. [And when they must attend] they come late and leave early. They would rather go to a tavern than to Holy Church" ([ca. 1410] 1976:, 189).[1] In about

1430, St. Antonino, later archbishop of Florence, noted that Tuscan peasants seldom attended mass, and that "very many of them do not confess once a year, and far fewer are those who take communion.... They use enchantments for themselves and for their beasts ... being ignorant, and caring little for their own souls or for keeping God's commandments, which they know not" (quoted in Coulton 1938, 193). Antonino went on to blame most of this on "the carelessness and evil conscience of their parish priests."

In further support of these reports, an extensive survey of surviving parish churches in various parts of Europe reveals them to be too small to have held more than a tiny fraction of local inhabitants (Brooke and Brooke 1984). Indeed, it was not until the late Middle Ages that there even were more than a few parish churches outside of the cities and larger towns (not counting the private chapels maintained for the local nobility), at a time when nearly everyone lived in rural areas (Morris 1993). This was no more than a continuation of the anti-rural outlook of the early Christian movement. Not only were the first Christians urban, as Wayne Meeks (1983) demonstrated, but they regarded peasants with disdain. Richard Fletcher explains:

> The peasantry of the countryside were beyond the pale, a tribe apart, outsiders. Such attitudes underpinned the failure of the urban Christian communities to reach out and spread the gospel in the countryside.... For them the countryside did not exist as a zone for missionary enterprise. After all, there was nothing in the New Testament about spreading the Word to the beasts of the field. (Fletcher 1997, 16)

Indeed, the word *pagan* comes from the Latin word for countryman (*paganus*).

Even when rural parishes did appear, they suffered from neglect and many, perhaps most, lacked a pastor much of the time. Eamon Duffy has estimated that during the sixteenth century, for example, at least 25 percent of the parishes in the diocese of Strasbourg and up to 80 percent in the diocese of Geneva had no clergy. To make matters worse, even where there was an assigned pastor, "[a]bsenteeism was rife" (Duffy 1987, 88). The bishop's visitation of 192 parishes in Oxfordshire during 1520 found 58 absentees (Coulton 1938, 156). "Bishops who never visited their sees were not unknown," too, in northern Europe, P. H. Sawyer notes (1982, 139). Indeed, many bishoprics were given to papal protégés without any obligation to reside (Coulton 1938).

That religious participation was lacking even in the cities is not very surprising when we realize that going to church in, say, the fifteenth century, required the average person to stand in an unheated building to hear a service conducted entirely in incomprehensible Latin; in fact, the priest may not have been speaking Latin at all, but simply mumbling nonsense syllables, for many priests were profoundly ignorant. In 1222, the Council of Oxford described the parish clergy as "dumb dogs" (Coulton 1938, 157).

The Venerable Bede advised the future bishop Egbert that because so few English priests and monks knew any Latin, "I have frequently offered translations of both the [Apostle's] Creed and the Lord's Prayer into English to many unlearned priests" (Bede [730] 1955, 340). More than a thousand years after Bede's efforts to at least teach clergy the Lord's Prayer, however, nothing had changed. William Tyndale noted in 1530 that hardly any of the priests and curates in England knew the Lord's Prayer or could translate it into English. This was confirmed when the bishop of Gloucester systematically tested his diocesan clergy in 1551. Of 311 pastors, 171 could not repeat the Ten Commandments, and 27 did not know the author of the Lord's Prayer (Thomas 1971, 164). Indeed, the next year, Bishop Hooper found "scores of parish clergy who could not tell who was the author of the Lord's Prayer, or where it was to be found" (Coulton 1938, 158).

Across the Channel, St. Vincent de Paul discovered in 1617 that his local priest knew no Latin, not even the words of absolution (Delumeau 1977). Similarly, in 1547, Archbishop Giovanni Bovio of the Brindisi-Oria diocese in southern Italy found that most of his priests "could barely read and could not understand Latin" (Gentilcore 1992, 42).

Clerical ignorance is not surprising when we recognize that "there were virtually no seminaries," and that most priests "learned rubrics" and a "smattering of Latin" as an apprentice to "a priest who had himself had little or no training" (Duffy 1987, 88). In the fifteenth century, St. Bernardine of Siena observed a priest "who knew only the Hail Mary, and used it even at the elevation of the Mass" (Duffy 1987, 88). Eamon Duffy (1992) has effectively demonstrated the ignorance of the parish clergy from the contents of the very first "primers" for clergy that began to be distributed in the fourteenth and fifteenth centuries. That these booklets, most of them written in the local language rather than in Latin, and prepared for those who already were serving as clergy, were limited to the most elementary aspects of doctrine and practice—for example, simple lists of the sacraments and of the sins that should be confessed—shows that church officials thought most serving clergy knew considerably less than a modern 10-year-old attending parochial school.

Given such clerical ignorance, it is no wonder that the masses knew next to nothing in terms of basic Christian culture. The Lateran Council of 1215, in addition to requiring all Catholics to confess and to take communion at least once a year during the Easter season, proposed that a massive campaign of elementary religious instruction of the laity be undertaken. Thus, at the Council of Lambeth in 1281, the English bishops responded by adopting the *aim* of teaching the laity the Lord's Prayer, Hail Mary, and the Apostle's Creed. Later this was expanded to include the Ten Commandments, the Seven Works of Mercy, the Seven Sacraments, and the Seven Deadly Sins (Duffy 1992). Similar plans to catechize the laity were adopted throughout Europe. Despite these very modest goals, it seems unlikely that many of the laity, other than members of the educated elite, ever mastered these simple lessons—since so many priests did not. Ignorance of the formal content of faith was general," writes Colin Morris (1993, 232), recounting the story of a village priest who managed to teach many in his congregation to recite the "Our Father" in Latin, although they had not the slightest idea of what it meant (possibly the priest didn't either). Other examples come from investigations of scores of incidents involving religious apparitions (mostly of Mary) in Spain during the fourteenth and fifteenth centuries. These hearings revealed that most parishioners reporting such visions were ignorant of the Ten Commandments and the Seven Deadly Sins. It was not merely that they could not recite them, but that they were entirely ignorant of their contents. A typical instance involved a man who claimed frequent visions of Mary and who, during an interrogation in 1518, was asked if he knew the Ten Commandments and the Seven Deadly Sins. "He said he did not know any of these in whole or in part.... He was asked if pride or envy or lust or killing a man or insulting someone with offensive words was a sin, to each of these he replied that he did not know. He was asked if theft was a sin, and he said that, God preserve us, theft was a very great sin" (quoted in Christian 1981, 154).

It must be noted, too, that even when medieval people did go to church, they often did so unwillingly and behaved very inappropriately while there. "[I]t is problematical as to whether certain sections of the population [of Britain] at this time had any religion at all," and "many of those who did [go to church] went with considerable reluctance," writes the eminent historian Keith Thomas (1971, 159). When the common people did show up in church, often under compulsion, they often so misbehaved "as to turn the service into a travesty of what was intended" (ibid., 161). "Members of the population jostled for pews, nudged their neighbours, hawked and spat, knitted, made coarse remarks, told jokes, fell asleep, and even let off guns," according to presentations before ecclesiastical courts and scores of clerical memoirs (ibid.). Church records tell of a man in Cambridgeshire who was charged with misbehaving in church in 1598 after his "most loathsome farting, striking, and scoffing speeches" had resulted in "the great offence of the good and the great rejoicing of the bad" (quoted in ibid., 162). A man who issued loathsome farts in church today surely would not draw cheers from part of the congregation in any British church, not even if he accompanied his efforts with scoffing speeches.

People often did gather regularly and eagerly within churches, but it was for entirely unreligious purposes. The archbishop of Florence, St. Antonino, denounced the Tuscan peasants of his diocese because "in the churches themselves they sometimes dance and leap and sing with women" (quoted in Coulton 1938, 193). Indeed, through the centuries there was a constant flow of injunctions to local parishes, and, often enough, even to those in charge of cathedrals, to cease using them primarily as indoor marketplaces and for storage of crops and sheltering livestock. For example, between 1229 and 1367, in England alone, there were eleven episcopal "fulminat(tions) against holding markets ... in churches" (Coulton 1938, 189). Letters survive in which the bishops of Augsburg and of Rheims warned their priests against pawning their vestments and church vessels (Fletcher 1997, 480–81).

Summing up his survey of popular religion in thirteenth-century Italy, Alexander Murray disputes "the notion of an Age of Faith," saying: "The friars [of that era] were not typical figures in a freakish age, but, morally, freakish figures in a typical age. Their mendicant life was a lasting wonder to contemporaries. They were a small minority: 'Virgins are few, martyrs are few, preachers are few,' said Fra Giordano" (Murray 1972, 83, 106). To be sure, there were periodic explosions of mass religious enthusiasm in medieval times as new sectarian movements—including the Waldensians and the Albigensians—attracted large followings (Lambert 1992). However, as we shall see in chapter 8, such outbursts are not to be expected where conventional religious organizations are strong, but only where religious apathy and alienation are widespread. That is, religious rebellions during medieval times offer additional testimony against images of widespread involvement in *organized* religion.

As Europe passed out of medieval times, religious participation seems not to have improved—although the statistics on religious behavior do. Some of the best of these can be found in the reports written by various Anglican bishops and archbishops following visitations of their parishes. Thus, the Oxford Diocesan Visitations report that 30 parishes in Oxfordshire drew a *combined total* of 911 communicants in 1738, based on the four "Great Festivals"—Easter, Ascension, Whitsun, and Christmas. This turnout amounted to far less than 5 percent of the total population of these parishes taking communion during a given year. Other visitation reports yield similarly low rates of participation in communion over the remainder of the eighteenth century (Currie, Gilbert, and Horsley 1977). Indeed, Peter Laslett (1965) reports that only 125 of 400 adults in a particular English village took Easter communion late in the eighteenth century and notes "much smaller attendances" in other villages. Incredibly, Laslett uses these data to demonstrate the unanimity of faith in this era[2]—the title of his book is *The World We Have Lost*. Were these twentieth-century statistics, they would be cited routinely as proof of massive secularization.

If we use 1800 as the benchmark, then church membership in Britain is substantially higher today than it was then. In 1800, only 12 percent of the British population belonged to a specific religious congregation. This rose to 17 percent in 1850 and then stabilized—the same percentage belonged in 1990 (Stark and Iannaccone 1995). In his remarkable reconstruction of religious participation in the British communities of Oldham and Saddleworth, Mark Smith (1996) found there had been no change between 1740 and 1865—a period of intensive industrialization. As will be noted, Laurence Iannaccone (1996) has reconstructed a time series that does show a modest decline in church attendance in

Britain during the twentieth century. This finding is offset both by the lack of similar declines in most other European nations, as well as by studies suggesting recent increases in church participation in lower-class British urban neighborhoods long noted for their very low rates of attendance (G. Smith 1996). Indeed, according to a report issued in 1996 (*Signs of Life*), during the past decade, the decline in membership and attendance in the Church of England has halted, and there has been a very substantial rise in per capita weekly contributions (Cimino 1996, 5). The "market" theory of religiousness developed in chapter 8 is compatible with religious *variation*, that is to say, with increases as well as decreases in religiousness; indeed, its usual prediction is for relatively stable levels of religious commitment in societies. In contrast, the secularization thesis is incompatible with either stability or increase: it requires a *general, long-term pattern of religious decline*. It makes no provision for reports such as Gabriel La Bras's (1963) that French Catholics today participate more willingly and frequently, with far greater comprehension of what they are doing, than was the case 200 years ago.

The evidence is clear that claims about a major decline in religious participation in Europe are based in part on very exaggerated perceptions of past religiousness. Participation may be low today in many nations, but not because of modernization, and the secularization thesis is therefore irrelevant. But what about *very* recent times? Perhaps the secularization theorists' predictions were simply premature? As mentioned, Laurence Iannaccone (1996) has been able to use survey data to reconstruct church attendance rates for 18 nations (most of them European) beginning in 1920. In 15 of the 18, Iannaccone could detect no trends even vaguely consistent with the secularization theses: only in East Germany, Slovenia, and Great Britain did he observe downward trends that could possibly be claimed as support for secularization, and, as mentioned, the British trend may already have been reversed, while the declines in Slovenia and East Germany began with the imposition of Communist regimes.

Little wonder, then, that historians have long expressed dismay at "unhistorically minded sociologists" for clinging to the myth of Europe's lost piety, complaining that "not enough justice has been done to the volume of apathy, heterodoxy and agnosticism that existed long before the onset of industrialization" (Thomas 1971, 173). For, as Andrew Greeley put it so crisply, "There could be no de-Christianization of Europe ... because there never was any Christianization in the first place. Christian Europe never existed" (1995, 63).

THE FAILURE TO CHRISTIANIZE

This raises a most significant question: Why wasn't the Christianization of Europe accomplished? At the start of the fourth century, Christianity was an immense *mass* movement sweeping over the Roman Empire, and by the middle of the century, a majority of the population probably had been converted (Stark 1996a). What happened then? The failure of the early church to Christianize the outer reaches of the empire and the rest of Europe is entirely in keeping with the market model of religiousness developed in chapter 8. The Christianity that triumphed over Rome was a mass social movement in a highly competitive environment. The Christianity that subsequently left most of Europe only nominally converted, at best, was an established, subsidized state church that sought to extend itself, not through missionizing the population, but by baptizing kings (Davies 1996, 275) and then canonizing them as national saints (Vauchez 1997). That is, the Christianity that prevailed in Europe was an elaborate patchwork of state churches that settled for the allegiance of the elite and for imposing official requirements of conformity, but that made little sustained effort to Christianize the peasant masses (Duffy 1987; Greeley 1995). Thus, it is not merely that the state churches of Scandinavia and northern Europe currently lack the motivation and energy to fill their churches. They have *always been like this*. The "Christianization" of a Norse kingdom, for example, often involved little more than the baptism of the nobility and legal recognition of the ecclesiastical sovereignty of the church. This left the task of missionizing the masses to a "kept" clergy whose welfare was almost entirely independent of mass assent or support, with a predictable lack of results.

Indeed, corruption and sloth, as well as power struggles and enforced conformity, became prominent features of the Christian movement in the fourth century, almost immediately upon its having become the official state church (Johnson 1976). Thus, for example, Christian bishops no longer were leaders of a stigmatized, if rapidly growing, sect, but were "rapidly assimilated as quasi civil servants into the mandarinate which administered the empire" (Fletcher 1997, 22). House churches were replaced by resplendent public buildings, sustained by imperial largess. Contrary to the received wisdom, the conversion of Constantine did not cause the triumph of Christianity. Rather, it was the first, and most significant step, in slowing its progress, draining its vigor, and distorting its moral vision. Most of the evils associated with European Christianity since the middle of the fourth century can be traced to establishment.

The "conversion" of Scandinavia is instructive. Denmark was the first "Christian" nation in the north, as a succession of kings accepted, rejected, or were indifferent to Christianity, culminating in the ascension of the devout Christian Knut the Great in 1016 (Sawyer 1982; Roesdahl 1980; Jones 1968; Brøndsted 1965). This now is regarded as the "official" date of the Christianization of Denmark. However, most historians do not equate this with the Christianization of the Danish people, writing instead that this followed only "gradually" (Brøndsted 1965, 310) and noting that the conversions of the monarchs were "[n]ever the result of popular demand" (Sawyer 1982, 139).

Next came the "Christianization" of Norway. Olaf Tryggvason, an English-educated Christian convert, seized the throne of Norway in 995, whereupon he attempted to covert the country by force, killing some who resisted and burning their estates. These and other repressive measures aroused sufficient opposition to defeat him in the battle of Svolder (about the year 1000), during which he died. Fifteen years later, Olaf Haraldsson, who had been baptized in France, conquered Norway. He too used fire and sword in an effort to compel Christianization. And he too provoked widespread hatred, leading to rebellion, and was driven into exile. When he attempted to return leading a new army raised in Kiev, he was defeated and killed at the battle of Stikklestad in 1030. Despite this, he was soon canonized as St. Olaf and is credited with the Christianization of Norway, which seems to have consisted primarily of the reimposition of Olaf's official policies of intolerance (Sawyer 1982; Jones 1968).

The conversion of Iceland followed a somewhat similar pattern as both Norwegian Olafs successively extended their efforts at forced conversion upon their colony. At a meeting of the Althing in 1000, the Icelanders yielded to Norwegian pressure by adopting the law "that all people should become Christian and those who here in the land were yet unbaptized should be baptized." But, the law read on: "people might sacrifice to the old gods in private" (Byock 1988, 142). Although paganism was subsequently outlawed, aspects of it still linger in Iceland, whose Christianization never resulted in more than the most minimal participation in the church.

The Swedish court remained pagan into the twelfth century, and Finland remained officially pagan until the thirteenth (Sawyer 1982; Brøndsted 1965). It seems revealing as to the lack of effort to Christianize the general population that no missionaries were even sent to the Lapps until the middle of the sixteenth century (Baldwin 1900). In reality, it is not clear when popular paganism actually began to wane in Scandinavia, and, as in the case of Iceland, there is reason to suppose that it never did entirely disappear (Sawyer and Sawyer 1993). Indeed, it seems to have been typical for the Norse to "convert" by including Christ and various Christian saints (especially Olaf) in the pagan pantheon. Thus, it was written in the Icelandic *Landnánabók* that Helgi the Lean "was very mixed in his faith; he believed in Christ, but invoked Thor in matters of seafaring and dire necessity" (quoted in Brøndsted 1965, 306). Johannes Brøndsted has noted that "a change of gods at the summit of society might occur easily enough; but lower down on the scale there was a natural resistance." Indeed, Brøndsted suggests that the conversion of Scandinavia occurred "only ... when Christianity took over old [pagan] superstitions and useages and allowed them to live under a new guise" (ibid., 307). Thus, the popular Christianity that eventually emerged was a strange amalgam, including a great deal in the way of pagan traditions and celebrations, some of them only thinly Christianized (Davies 1996).

Consequently, as Andrew Greeley has pointed out, Christian commitment in northern Europe was neither deep enough to generate much mass attendance nor "deep enough to survive changes in the religious affiliation of their political leaders during the Reformation, sometimes back and forth across denominational lines" (Greeley 1996, 66).

Both of Greeley's points are easily demonstrated quantitatively. We began with the sixteen nations of western Europe.[3] For each, we calculated the number of centuries since their supposed Christianization (20 minus the century), with values ranging from 16 for Italy down to 7 for Finland (Davies 1996; Barrett 1982; Sawyer 1982; Roesdahl 1980; Shepherd 1980; Jones 1968; Brøndsted 1965). This variable is based on the assumption that the more recent the Christianization, the more superficial. Turning to the 1990–91 World Values Surveys, we created a variable based on the rate of church attendance. As would be predicted, the duration of Christianization is extremely highly correlated with contemporary rates of church attendance (.72). In similar fashion, the most plausible measure of participation in the Reformation (since some of these modern nations include many areas that were independent states in the sixteenth century) is the percentage of Catholics, which we took from the 1996 *Catholic Almanac*. Again, as predicted, this variable is very highly correlated (.89) with the duration of Christianization.

SUBJECTIVE RELIGIOUSNESS

Steve Bruce of the University of Aberdeen has long been one of the most diehard proponents of the secularization thesis. Recently, even he admitted (1997) that, in terms of organized participation, the Golden Age of Faith never existed. Indeed, Bruce now proposes that the medieval church was not even especially concerned to bring the people to mass as "was clear from the very architecture of churches and forms of service" (1997, 674). But, rather than giving up on the secularization thesis, Bruce now claims that the Golden Age of medieval religiousness was subjective, that people strongly embraced supernatural beliefs, Christian or otherwise. Put another way, Bruce now claims that even if the medieval masses seldom went to church, most people in this era still must be regarded as religious because they believed. We quite agree. Certainly most people in medieval times seem to have held religious beliefs, even if these were somewhat vague and included as much magic and animism as Christianity. Thus, through belief, if not through practice, these were *religious* societies (see Duffy 1992), keeping in mind, of course, that a substantial proportion of medieval populations did not take their religious beliefs very seriously. Nor must we forget that a significant number, probably about the same as today, rejected religious beliefs. As Franklin Baumer has put it, "Contrary to popular supposition there was plenty of scepticism in the Middle Ages, and some of it was quite radical" (1960, 99). Judging from the prevalence of blasphemous graffiti on the walls of Pompeii, the same must be said of the Greco-Roman era (Macmullen 1981; Stark 1996a).

Nevertheless, we also accept that belief was widespread, and we interpret the prevalence of religious beliefs as representing a potential demand for organized religion in these societies—a potential in the sense that it awaited activation by aggressive suppliers such as the Waldensians. However, rather than this restoring a benchmark of past piety against which to demonstrate the secularization of modern-day Europe, the same observation applies with equal force today. That is, while rates of religious participation are far lower in Europe than in the United States, differences are small when comparisons are based on subjective measures of faith (Stark and Iannaccone 1994; Stark 1998c).

We are hardly the first to notice this phenomenon. There is a substantial British research literature on "believing without belonging," as Grace Davie calls it (1990a; 1990b; 1994). "What is clear is that most surveys of religious belief in northern Europe demonstrate continuing high levels of belief in God and some of the more general tenets of the Christian faith but rather low levels of church attendance," Michael Winter and Christopher Short sum up, adding: "[W]e have revealed a relatively, and perhaps surprisingly, low level of secularization" (Winter and Short 1993, 635, 648). It is perhaps for that reason that their work has not been much cited by other European social scientists, but what they say is nonetheless true: subjective religiousness remains high in the nations most often cited as examples of secularization, places where it is claimed that people have outgrown religion for good. It seems useful to examine one case in greater detail.

Because Iceland has been proposed as the first fully (or nearly fully) secularized nation on earth (see Tomasson 1980), it seems an appropriate test case. The claim that Iceland is extremely secularized is taken as self-evident on the basis of its empty churches—about 2 percent attend weekly. Nevertheless, on the basis of extensive fieldwork, William Swatos (1984) reported high levels of religion in homes in Iceland today; there are high rates of baptism, nearly all weddings occur in church, and "affirmations of personal immortality are typical" in newspaper obituaries, which usually are written by a close friend of the deceased rather than by a journalist. It is hardly surprising, therefore, that the 1990 World Values Surveys report that 81 percent of Icelanders express confidence that there is life after death, 88 percent say they believe humans have a soul, and 40 percent believe in reincarnation. And when asked, "How often do you pray to God outside of religious services?" 82 percent said they prayed sometimes, and one of four said they did so "often." Moreover, only 2.4 percent of the population of Iceland say they are "convinced atheists." Surely this is not what usually is meant by a "secularized society." Moreover, that 4 in 10 believe in reincarnation serves to remind us that the secularization theory never has been limited to Christianity; all beliefs in the supernatural are pertinent, and even a massive shift from belief in Jesus to the worship of the goddess Kali would not constitute secularization. It is worth noting, therefore, that spiritualism is also extremely widespread in Iceland, where it is popular even among leading intellectuals and academics (Swatos and Gissurarson 1997).

RELIGION AND SCIENCE

If secularization is to show up anywhere, it *must* show up among scientists. In chapter 2 we examined evidence that the conflict between religion and science is largely fictional, and that scientists are not notably irreligious. But, you may wonder, aren't some scientists militant atheists who write books to discredit religion—the late Carl Sagan being an example? Of course, but their numbers are few compared with those employed in ostensibly religious occupations: it is theologians (see Cupitt 1997), professors of religious studies (see Mack 1996), and clergy (see Spong 1998) who are by far the most prolific sources of popular works of atheism.

Recently, quite amazing time series data on the beliefs of scientists were published in *Nature*. In 1914, the American psychologist James Leuba sent questionnaires to a random sample of those listed in *American Men of Science*. Each was asked to select one of the following statements "concerning belief in God" (all italics in the original):

1. I believe in a God to whom one may pray in the expectation of receiving an answer. *By "answer," I mean more than the subjective, psychological effect of prayer.*
2. I do not believe in God *as defined above.*
3. I have no definite belief regarding this question.

Leuba's standard for belief in God is so stringent it would exclude a substantial portion of "mainline" clergy,[4] and that obviously was intentional on his part. He wanted to show that men of science were irreligious. To his dismay, Leuba found that 41.8 percent of his sample of prominent scientists selected option one, thereby taking a position many would regard as "fundamentalist." Another 41.5 percent selected the second option (many of whom, as Leuba acknowledged, no doubt believed in a somewhat less active deity), and 16.7 percent took the indefinite alternative.

Clearly, these results were not what Leuba had expected and hoped for. So he gave great emphasis to the fact that, as measured, believers were not in the majority and went on to express his faith in the future, claiming that these data demonstrated a rejection of "fundamental dogmas—a rejection apparently destined to extend parallel with the diffusion of knowledge ..." (Leuba 1916, 280).

In 1996, Edward J. Larson and Larry Witham (1997) replicated Leuba's study exactly. They found that nowadays 39.3 percent of eminent scientists selected option one, which is not significantly different from the 41.8 percent who did so in 1914. This time 45.3 percent chose option two, and 14.5 percent took option three. Thus, over an 82-year period, there has been no decline in a very literal belief in God among scientists.

Eastern Revivals

The collapse of Soviet Communism had many remarkable consequences, not the least of which was to reveal the abject failure of several generations of dedicated efforts to indoctrinate atheism in eastern Europe and the former Soviet Union. "Never before in human history has there been such a concerted effort to stamp out not merely *a* religion, but all trace of religion," Andrew Greeley observes. "Atheistic Communism thought of itself as pushing forward the inevitable process of secularization in which religion would disappear from the face of the earth—a process which, in perhaps milder form, is an article of faith for many dogmatic social scientists" (Greeley 1994, 253).

And the results? Atheists are few in the countries of the former Soviet Bloc, not more prevalent than in western Europe, or, indeed, in the United States. In most of these countries, the majority of people pray, and by 1990 church attendance already had recovered to levels comparable to those in western Europe. Moreover, church attendance continues to rise, as do other forms of religiousness. In Hungary, for example, monthly church attendance rose from 16 percent in 1981 to 25 percent in 1991, while the percentage attending less than once a year fell from 62 percent to 44 percent! Meanwhile, the percentage of Hungarians who said they were "convinced atheists" fell from 14 to 4. In Russia, 53 percent of respondents said they were not religious in 1991. In only five years, this fell to 37 percent.

By any measure, major religious revivals are under way during these early days of the postcommunist era in the old Soviet Bloc. This seems to have taken most social scientists entirely by surprise (as have all recent signs of religious vitality). As Mary Douglas pointed out as long ago as 1982:

> No one, however, foresaw the recent revivals of traditional religious forms. According to an extensive literature, religious change in modern times happens in only two ways—the falling off of traditional worship in Christian churches [or whatever the traditional churches of a society are], and the appearance of new cults, not expected to endure. No one credited the traditional religions with enough vitality to inspire large-scale political revolt.... But the explicitly Catholic uprising in Poland, which evokes deep Western admiration, was as unpredicted as the rise of the fundamentalist churches in America. (Douglas 1982, 25)

It would be needlessly vindictive to quote various social scientists who once were certain that "enlightened" educators in "socialist" nations were "freeing children" from the grip of superstition and launching a new era of permanent secularity. But our willpower does not go so far as to prevent a bit of crowing, hence we quote a paper initially presented at a conference in 1979:

> [S]ecular states cannot root out religion, and ... to the extent that they try to root it out, they will be vulnerable to religious opposition.... Lenin's body may be displayed under glass, but no one supposes that he has ascended to sit on the right hand, or even the left hand, of Marx.... dams along the Volga do not light up the meaning of the universe. Moreover, repressive states seem to increase levels of individual deprivation and, in so doing, to fuel the religious impulse. In making faith more costly, they also make it more necessary and valuable. Perhaps religion is never so robust as when it is an underground church. (Stark 1981, 175)

And so it was.

Islam

The evidence examined thus far has been limited to Christian nations. Now let us turn to religious trends in Islam. In extraordinary contradiction to the secularization doctrine, there seems to be a profound compatibility between the Islamic faith and modernization—several studies from quite different parts of the world suggest that Muslim commitment increases with modernization.

In studies of Muslims in Java, Joseph Tamney (1979; 1980) found that religious commitment there was positively correlated with education and with occupational prestige. That is, people who had attended college or held high-status occupations were substantially more likely to pray the required five times a day, to give alms, and to fast in accord with orthodox Islamic practice than were Muslims with little education or low-status occupations. Tamney also recognized that his findings implied that Muslim practice would increase as modernization proceeded. In a subsequent work, Tamney (1992) has analyzed the "resilience" of religion: how it has been able to adjust to challenges of modernity.

A study of the leading Muslim "fundamentalist" movement in Pakistan found that the leaders are highly educated (all having advanced degrees) and supporters of the movement are drawn overwhelmingly from "the new middle class" (Ahmad 1991). This is confirmed by data on Turkish students based on an actual time series. Since 1978 there has been a remarkable increase in the proportion of students at the University of Ankara who hold orthodox Islamic beliefs, and in 1991 the overwhelming majority of students held these views. In 1978, 36 percent of students expressed firm belief that "there is a Heaven and a Hell," whereas in 1991 three-fourths held this view. Faith in "the essential elements of Islamic beliefs is becoming widespread among the university students i.e., the prospective elites, in Ankara," Kayhan Mutlu writes (1996, 355). These students are the future political and intellectual leaders of the nation, including its future scientists and engineers. Moreover, Turkey is, by most measures, the most modernized of Islamic nations and, beginning in the 1920s, experienced decades of official state secularity and semi-official irreligion, although these policies have waned in recent times (for reasons entirely clear in the data).

In similar fashion there have been dramatic shifts toward Islamic piety among university students in Nigeria, France, and Senegal, where branches of the Association of Muslim Students are said to have "quickly filled the place left vacant by Marxism in the student consciousness" (Niandou-Souley and Alzouma 1996, 253).

Of course, these Islamic data are fragmentary. On the other hand, no informed observer even needs data such as these to detect the thunderous vitality of contemporary Islam and to realize that it is in direct proportion to modernization.

Asian "Folk" Religions

Following World War II, all observers expected rapid and profound religious changes in Asian religions, especially in Japan and in the rapidly westernizing

Chinese enclaves of Taiwan, Hong Kong, and Malaysia. More specifically, it was assumed that the traditional, and highly magical, "folk" religions found in these settings would rapidly give way to modernity (Chen 1995; Chee-Beng 1994).

"Shinto religious practices would seem a highly likely candidate for extinction within Japan's hightech consumer society," John Nelson suggested, summing up the scholarly consensus (1992, 77). But that was not what has happened. Shinto remains very vigorous. "[I]t is commonplace that new cars be blessed at a [Shinto] shrine, that new residences, offices, or factories be built after exorcism ceremonies purify and calm the land and its deity, that children are dedicated there" (ibid.). Indeed, Shinto rituals seem to play a more prominent role in Japan today than in the pre–World War II days, when the emperor was thought to be divine and Shinto was the state religion. That Shinto was strengthened by being disestablished is entirely in accord with the market theory of religion.

In Taiwan today, there are likewise proportionately more folk temples than there were a century ago, and a larger proportion of the population (about 70 percent) frequent these temples than ever before (Chen 1995). In Hong Kong, traditional Chinese folk religion also flourishes, with the Temple of Wong Tai Sin, "a refugee god" imported from China in 1915, having the largest following (Lang and Ragvald 1993). And in Malaysia, too, Chinese folk religion "continues to thrive" (Chee-Beng 1994, 274).

In Japan, Taiwan, Hong Kong, and Malaysia alike, then, "old fashioned," traditional faiths have thus come to be seen as especially suitable for modern life. Shinto and Chinese folk religion do not so much linger on among elderly, uneducated peasants as flourish among successful, educated young urbanites (Chen 1995; Chee-Beng 1994; Lang and Ragvold 1993; Nelson 1992).

MODERNITY, DOUBT, AND THE UNAFFILIATED

But, perhaps the proponents of secularization merely claimed too much too soon. Although religion has shown no terminal symptoms, it is nevertheless true that even in societies where the churches flourish, such as the United States, many people are not active in a religion, and even many of those who are active often harbor religious doubts. If these are the results of modernity, then it might be possible to salvage the secularization theory in modified form. However, considerable evidence shows that there is nothing modern about the primary reasons for religious doubt, and that the overwhelming majority of people who deny any religious preference are religious.

The prophets of secularization have always stressed the incompatibility between religion and science and argued that this cannot help but cause religious doubt. It must be recognized, however, that there is nothing modern about doubt per se: "Lord, I believe; help thou mine unbelief" (Mark 9:24). Indeed, for millennia, religious thinkers have stressed the problems of evil and tragedy as the primary sources of doubt. Why does God permit evil to flourish in the world; why do bad things happen to good people? When Christian Smith and his colleagues (1998, 163) asked Americans why they "often" doubted their religious faith, the overwhelming majority of those who reported doing so cited traditional reasons: "personal tragedies and heartaches, evil and suffering in the world, human hypocrisy, the daily troubles of life ... human universals ... not problems that particularly afflict modern people." Few made any mention of science. "We have no sound basis for believing, then, that anything particular to modernity itself has become the cause of a significant decline in the plausibility of religious belief." These findings were based on a sample of churchgoing Americans, but very similar results turn up in the general population. Respondents in the 1988 General Social Survey were asked to place themselves on a scale of one through seven on the basis of their degree of doubt concerning their religion. About one American in four (27.4%) is "completely free of doubts." Most expressed a very low level of doubt, 61.4 percent ranked themselves at three or below. Only 7.2 percent ranked themselves at seven ("My faith is mixed with doubts"), and another 5 percent placed themselves at six. Of even greater interest is that concerns about religion and science came in a distant third when people were asked *why* they experienced doubts. Fifty-five percent attributed their doubts to personal suffering; 50 percent said that "evil in the world" contributed to their doubts; only 30 percent agreed that a "conflict of faith and science" caused them doubt. This rank order held among those with the most doubts as well as those with the least. Moreover, very few respondents thought that doubt was a significant problem for them, even if they did experience it from time to time.

But what about that "hard core" of American skeptics who, in national surveys, say they have no religious affiliation? Anywhere from 5 to 10 percent (frequently referred to as "religious nones") give this response. Although several social scientists have claimed that this percentage has risen over the past fifty years, it turns out that any variations over time are because of variations in the wording of the question (Smith 2000). Far more significant is the fact that very few of those who report their affiliation as "none," are irreligious. For example, data from the 1996 General Social Survey show that 85 percent of the "nones" pray! It would seem that most who give their religious preference as "none" mean "none of the above," not "I am irreligious."

Thus, even the weakest version of secularization fails to find support.

WHAT ABOUT CHANGE?

Recently one of us spoke to a group of Christian historians, some of whom found it very difficult to accept that secularization is not far along. One historian mentioned that religiousness rose very sharply in Germany in the latter half of the nineteenth century, only to fall precipitously in the twentieth. Another went on at length about doctrinal changes over the past several centuries, and yet another chided us for failing to see secularization in the decline in belief in witchcraft. At first it was difficult to see how some of this related to the secularization thesis, until it became clear that these remarks came from people who somehow believed that we were proposing that there is no such thing as religious change! But of course religion changes. There is more religious participation and even greater belief in the supernatural at some times and places than in others, just as religious organizations have more secular power in some times and places than in others. So too do doctrines change—Aquinas was not Augustine, and both would find heresy in the work of Avery Dulles. But change does not equate with decline. If next year everyone in Canada became a pious Hindu, there might be many interpretations, but secularization would not be among them. Indeed, what is needed is a body of theory to explain religious variation, to tell us when and why various aspects of religiousness rise and fall, or are stable. In that regard, the secularization theory is as useless as a hotel elevator that only goes down.

CONCLUSION

Let us emphasize that no one can prove that one day religion will not wither away. Perhaps the day will come when religion has been relegated to memory and museums. If so, however, this will not have been caused by modernization, and the demise of faith will bear no resemblance to the process postulated by the secularization doctrine. Let us therefore, once and for all, declare an end to social scientific faith in the theory of secularization, recognizing it as a product of wishful thinking. As a requiem, we offer final remarks by three distinguished scholars: an anthropologist, a medieval historian, and a sociologist.

Mary Douglas has argued forcefully and persuasively against the secularization doctrine as having "been constructed to flatter prejudged ideas" that will need to be discarded "when religious sociology modernizes." It is simply not true, Douglas notes, that modern life contrasts sharply with life in simple societies when it comes to the prevalence of religious belief. With Clifford Geertz (1966), she recognizes that unbelief is not uncommon in preliterate societies, and, indeed, was not uncommon in Old Testament times: "Uncritical nostalgia for past ages of faith being out of place in religious studies, let us note at once that there is no good evidence that a high level of spirituality had generally been reached by the mass of mankind in past times.... Nor does [anthropology] teach that modern times show a decline from ancient standards of piety" (Douglas 1982, 29).

Where did the notion of an Age of Faith come from? Alexander Murray asked, having demonstrated that the original sources are nearly unanimous in their admission of widespread irreligiousness in medieval times. "The scientific enlightenment was tempted to conceive faith not as a virtue, but as an original sin, from which the Messiah of knowledge came to rescue it," he concluded. "It follows from that view that, in the olden days, men must have believed all the Church told them" (Murray 1972, 106).

And, finally, interviewed in 1997, Peter Berger admitted:

> I think what I and most other sociologists of religion wrote in the 1960s about secularization was a mistake. Our underlying argument was that secularization and modernity go hand in hand. With more modernization comes more secularization. It wasn't a crazy theory. There was some evidence for it. But I think it's basically wrong. Most of the world today is certainly not secular. It's very religious. (Berger 1997, 974)

After nearly three centuries of utterly failed prophesies and misrepresentations of both present and past, it seems time to carry the secularization doctrine to the graveyard of failed theories, and there to whisper, "Requiescat in pace."

PART TWO

The Religious Individual

CHAPTER 4

The Micro Foundations of Religion

The origins of religion are not to be found through historical or archaeological research. As William J. Goode remarked, "[H]ow, under what conditions, [humans] began to believe in divine beings nearly a million years ago must remain sheer speculation," for "the data are irrevocably gone" (1951, 22, 230). Consequently, the only feasible way to discover the fundamental sources of religious expression is, not to seek data on early humans, but to examine elementary theoretical principles about what humans are like and how their aspirations exceed their opportunities.

This chapter resumes our theoretical quest to understand religion (Stark and Bainbridge 1980c; 1985; [1987] 1996; Finke and Stark 1988; 1992; Stark 1996b; 1998a; 1998b). Since religion did not first appear in cathedrals, we begin with "bedrock" propositions that are universally applicable to humans regardless of their circumstances. Once we have assembled these, in the remainder of the book, we explain more complex manifestations of religious expression—including cathedrals.

In earlier versions of the theory, the micro foundations are a mixture of cognitive and interactional (social exchange) elements and processes. Unfortunately, too little explicit attention was given to the emotional and expressive components of religion, nor was sufficient scope given to the typical elements of religious practice such as ritual, sacrifice, prayer, and the like. Indeed, the earlier version of the theory failed to address the question of why these aspects of religion *are* typical. With the luxury of hindsight, we have greatly extended the approach to the micro foundations of religion and this time, in addition to improving the clarity of the cognitive aspects of the theory, we have paid close attention

An earlier version of this chapter appeared as Rodney Stark, "Micro Foundations of Religion: A Revised Theory," *Sociological Theory* (1999) 17:264–89.

to emotional and expressive aspects of what is a particularly emotional and expressive phenomenon—to in some measure capture the sense of "religion as poetry" (Greeley 1995). Specific provision is made for religious emotions, and for ritual, prayer, sacrifice, miracle, mystical experiences, for bargaining with the gods, and even for religious procrastination. Our aim is to construct a theory in which both phenomenologists and rational choice theorists can take comfort.

For the sake of those familiar with the earlier version, let us note that, with four exceptions, we have only added to the theory, not made significant changes in the original. As for changes, the most important probably is that we have dispensed with the concept of religious compensators, having discovered that an adequate understanding of otherworldly rewards was sufficient. Second, consistent with dropping the concept of compensators, it was necessary to remove that term from the definition of religion, with results that will be clear in the new definition. Third, parallel to the revised definition of religion, we have redefined magic to permit a far more efficient distinction between the two. Finally, we discarded the very "thin" formulation of rational choice, replacing it with a far more "sociological" version, as is discussed at length in chapter 1 and in a subsequent section.

In addition to trying to more fully capture the emotional and expressive aspects of the subject matter, this version of the theory makes far more use of the work of anthropologists. One reason is that it often is claimed (mostly incorrectly) that because sociology began as an effort to understand modernization, its theories are largely inapplicable to premodern societies, or to non-Western societies, or, in the case of religion, to societies other than the United States (see Carroll 1996; Bruce 1995; Murphy 1994). Consequently, we shall be careful to show that the propositions are entirely consistent with the anthropological record—that the propositions apply as appropriately to the beliefs of Buddhists in the Burmese highlands, and to pig sacrifices among the Tsembaga in New Guinea, as to a Catholic wedding in Rome, or concerts by the Mormon Tabernacle Choir. A second reason to feature anthropologists is that they have paid far more attention to religion than have sociologists—what ethnographer's account of a preliterate or traditional society fails to include a chapter on religion? And while most of these accounts are little more than descriptions of religious doctrines and rituals in a particular society, very insightful fragments of theorizing are scattered throughout. If we often compare these fragments very favorably to the more extensively theoretical offerings of sociologists, it is probably because immersion in concrete details has often imposed needed discipline on anthropological theorizing, the lack of which caused Paul Radin to object to the theories of "members of the Durkheim school" because "most of what they say is strangely unreal and largely beside the point ... an unconscious falsification of the record" ([1937] 1957, 77). Nevertheless, we are entirely on the side of sociology in recognizing the need for general theories of social phenomena. We do not admire anthropology for its circumspect approach to theorizing— Durkheim's theory may be mostly wrong, but he was right to try.

As the title indicates, in this chapter we mostly ignore the more macro aspects of religion, taking our theorizing only to the point where we can explain why religion generates organizations. We begin with the assumption that people make religious choices in the same way that they make other choices, by weighing the costs against the benefits. But what are the benefits; why do people want religion at all? They want it because religion is the only plausible source of certain rewards for which there is a general and inexhaustible demand. In the remainder of the chapter, we construct a theory around this simple insight. For the sake of clarity, we state the most important steps in the theory as formal propositions and definitions. As will be clear, we have not attempted to present a fully deductive theoretical system, but the logical connections among the propositions are clear. For ease of reference, the formal portions of the theory are re-listed separately in the Appendix.

REWARDS AND EXPLANATIONS

To begin:

PROPOSITION 1. Within the limits of their information and understanding, restricted by available options, guided by their preferences and tastes, humans attempt to make rational choices.

As explained in chapter 1, our formulation of the rationality axiom softens and expands the economists' version that humans attempt to maximize, allowing for a more "natural" view of human behavior, which often involves relatively "fuzzy" logic as well as impulse. Keep in mind, however, that actions are not irrational simply because the actor has inadequate or faulty information or has miscalculated—intention is everything (Boudon 1993; Hechter 1983; 1997). Thus, an effort to increase wealth by investing in commodities is rational even if the deal goes bad. The same applies to many efforts to obtain rewards through religious means. It would be irrational for Canadians to seek manufactured goods by means of the religious methods developed by cargo cultists, because Canadians know how such goods really are made and obtained. But, as I. C. Jarvie (1970, 61) demonstrated so clearly, it is not irrational for South Sea Islanders to construct crude docks or landing strips in order to "attract" ships and planes loaded with cargo. Given their explanations of the source and distribution of "cargo," they are doing the reasonable thing—it appeared to them that this was how Allied forces obtained cargo during World War II. Jarvie brilliantly makes the point that rationality and ignorance are independent, and that the cargo cultists are "just as rational" in their "ignorance" as the observing anthropologists are (it may be hoped) in their greater knowledge.

Given these limits on our definition of rationality, we nevertheless must acknowledge that rationality *usually to some extent involves the subjective weighing of anticipated rewards and costs when making choices.* Consequently, we must note that rewards and costs are complementary, in that a lost or forgone reward is a cost (the latter is often referred to as an opportunity cost), while an avoided cost is a reward. It also must be recognized that rewards and costs vary in kind, value, and generality. A reward or cost is more general to the extent that it includes other rewards or costs. Happiness is a more general reward than having a nice day. Poor health is a more general cost than having the flu.

We shall not attempt to characterize rewards (or costs) as to kind, although obviously they include psychic, and even intellectual, as well as material "commodities." As will be obvious throughout, we assume that culture and socialization do substantially account for taste, culture providing the general outlines of what people seek (and seek to avoid), and socialization filling in many of the details. Nevertheless, all normal individuals in all societies retain a substantial leeway for idiosyncrasy, innovation, and deviance. Specifically, religious doctrines and practices do change,[1] and irreligion is common,[2] not only in modern societies, but in traditional and preliterate societies as well. However, we agree with Gary Becker that social scientists should resist the "temptation of simply postulating the required shift in preferences" to explain changing patterns (Becker 1976, 5). Thus, for example, when confronted with major changes in religion, as when Buddhism swept through the Chinese upper classes in the fourth century, the usual approach has been to ask: Why did people's preferences change? The assumption is that events like this occur because people suddenly develop new, unmet, religious preferences, or "needs." A far better explanation of such events can usually be found by postulating changes in supply and other constraints, however, rather than prior changes in preferences—that is, in religious "demand" (see Finke 1997a; 1997b; Stark and Iannaccone 1994; Finke and Iannaccone 1993; Finke and Stark 1992; Stark 1985; 1996a). When people change churches or even religions, it is usually not because their preferences have changed, but because the new church or faith more effectively appeals to preferences they have always had (Sherkat 1997; Sherkat and Wilson 1995). Indeed, even when changes do occur in preferences, this is usually the consequence, rather than the cause, of variations in choices.

Humans not only reason; as thinking and feeling creatures, we *wonder*. We do not blindly repeat actions merely because we have been reinforced for doing so. Rather, humans attempt to understand their circumstances. Early hunters were not content to know that if they approached game from the downwind direction, they would not be able to get very close to their prey; they wanted to know *why* this happened. And their answers took the form of what are called "stories" in the recent merger of the conceptual and analytical tools of literary criticism with those of the neural and cognitive sciences (Turner 1996). Stories distill thought and experience and provide it to others secondhand in the form of accounts about how the world works. If we ask a computer why it is calculating a regression equation, it remains silent. But the human using the computer will answer with a story explaining his or her behavior. Constructing, telling, and comprehending stories are the most basic human mental processes, and while the "cultural meanings" embedded in a particular story may be peculiar as to time and place, "the mental processes that make these meanings possible are universal," Mark Turner has noted (1996, 11).

PROPOSITION 2.   Humans are conscious beings having memory and intelligence who are able to formulate **explanations** about how rewards can be gained and costs avoided.

Definition 1.   **Explanations** are conceptual simplifications or models of reality that often provide plans designed to guide action.

Because explanations help humans to maximize, in and of themselves explanations constitute rewards and will be sought by humans.

Explanations differ on a number of dimensions. First, they differ in the value and generality of the rewards they aim to produce. Second, they differ in their expected ratio of costs to benefits. That is, there usually are many ways by which a particular reward could be obtained, some of them more efficient than others. Third, explanations vary in the duration required for them to yield the desired rewards. Finally, and most important, explanations differ in terms of their apparent adequacy—their reliability or fallibility. Obviously, "true" explanations usually will be more reliable than "false" ones, but not always. Moreover, truth and falsity are slippery criteria, often difficult to assess. Most of the time, what matters is whether an explanation suffices for the users' needs. For example, some early hunters might have concluded that the spirits of game always congregated to the windward, and that when hunters approached downwind, the spirits saw them and warned the game. Others might have attributed this behavior of game to scents carried by the breeze, so that when hunters approached downwind, their scent preceded them, warning the game to flee. Both explanations would direct hunters always to approach into the wind, and they would thus work equally well. However, only the explanation based on scent can be expanded to account for the ability of carnivores to track game.

PROPOSITION 3.   Humans will attempt to evaluate explanations on the basis of results, retaining those that seem to work most efficiently.

Humans persist in efforts to find ways to gain rewards, to find procedures or implements that will achieve the desired results. Those that don't seem to work will be discarded; those that appear to work, or those that work better than some others, will be preserved. As a result of this process, humans *accumulate culture.* Other things being equal, through the process of evaluation, over time the explanations retained by a group will become more effective. It also must be recognized that it is far more difficult to evaluate some explanations than others, and that this also may change as culture becomes more complex. Not only were the ancient Greeks, for example, unable to evaluate many explanations we know to be false today, they also could not evaluate many we take to be true.

More important, we possess many more, and more general, explanations than did the ancient Greeks.

PROPOSITION 4.   Rewards are always limited in supply, including some that simply do not exist in the observable world.

People always want more rewards than they can have, and the supply of any given reward (to the extent that it is available at all) will vary by time and place. In addition to variations in the supply of rewards, there exist substantial differences in the relative ability of individuals to gain rewards—some will have much, while others have little. That is, *stratification* is a given and those with less will always seek means to obtain more.

If that weren't bad enough, some of the most intensely desired rewards are unavailable, here and now, to anyone. The most obvious of these is the desire to overcome death. In addition, people generally seem to want their existence to have meaning, for there to be reasons behind reality. No such reasons can be fully verified in this life.

PROPOSITION 5.   To the degree that rewards are scarce, or are not directly available at all, humans will tend to formulate and accept explanations for obtaining the reward in the distant future or in some other nonverifiable context.

Such explanations are difficult if not impossible to evaluate, and to accept them requires a substantial level of trust or faith. The mention of faith is not meant to suggest that only religious explanations have this aspect; in fact, most explanations of this sort are secular. When a child wants a bike and a parent explains that the bike can be obtained next year if certain conditions (such as getting good grades) are met, the child must take this explanation on faith. There is no way to verify it, at least not before the due date. What distinguishes religious from secular explanations of this variety, aside from the immense value and scope of the rewards that are plausible through religious explanations, is the capacity to postpone the delivery of the rewards to an otherworldly context. As we shall see, religions also offer many rewards here and now, but the truly potent religious resource is *otherworldly rewards*.

Definition 2.   **Otherworldly rewards** are those that will be obtained only in a nonempirical (usually posthumous) context.[3]

Such rewards are plausible through religious means because the postulated source is not a parent or a bank, but a supernatural being. However, the significant point here is the context within which the rewards are to be realized—one in which it is at least extremely difficult, if not impossible, for living humans to discover whether or not the rewards arrive as promised. In contrast, many other rewards that can be sought from supernatural sources, such as miracles, are not otherworldly, inasmuch as they entail delivery in an empirical context. As will be seen, empirical rewards from the gods play a very significant role in generating and sustaining faith. But the most valuable of all religious rewards are otherworldly.

THE SUPERNATURAL

Religion is concerned with the supernatural; everything else is secondary. As Sir Edward Burnett Tylor put it, "a minimum definition of Religion [is] the belief in Spiritual Beings" ([1871] 1958, 2: 8). Or, as Sir James G. Frazer explained, "religion consists of two elements ... a belief in powers higher than man and an attempt to propitiate or please them" (1922, 58). Writing about the "concept of the supernatural," Ruth Benedict noted: "The striking fact about this plain distinction between the religious and the nonreligious in actual ethnographic recording is that it needs so little recasting in its transfer from one society to another. No matter how exotic a society the traveler has wandered, he still finds the distinction made and in comparatively familiar terms. And it is universal" (Benedict 1938, 628).

Emile Durkheim mistakenly rejected this definition of religion because, he asserted, the supernatural is far from being a universal feature of religions: "One idea which generally passes as characteristic of all that is religious is that of the supernatural ... it is certain that this idea does not appear until late in the history of religions; it is completely foreign, not only to those people who are called primitive, but also to all others who have not attained a considerable degree of intellectual culture" (Durkheim 1915, 24–25).

Durkheim went on to argue that there even are "great religions from which the idea of gods and spirits is absent" (ibid., 30), identifying Buddhism as among those lacking a supernatural element. Because of his a priori claim that religion exists in *all* societies, being the source of social integration, he thus felt it necessary to omit a supernatural component from his definition in order to salvage the generalization, hence his famous definition: "A religion is a unified system of beliefs and practices relative to sacred things" (ibid., 47). Although Durkheim was explicit that sacred did not imply "supernatural," we don't really know what sacred did imply for him, because he never defined it, beyond saying that it referred to "things set apart and forbidden." Sir Edward Evans-Pritchard dismissed this criterion as "vague and ill-defined" (1960, 12), as have many other prominent anthropologists (see Firth 1959; Horton 1960; Goody 1961; Spiro 1966a).

Ironically, Durkheim's exclusion of the supernatural was quite unnecessary. As Alexander A. Goldenweiser pointed out in his 16-page review of the original French edition (1912) of Durkheim's *The Elementary Forms of the Religious Life* in the *American Anthropologist:* "In claiming that primitive man knows no supernatural, the author fundamentally misunderstands savage mentality.... [Here] Durkheim commits his initial error, fatal in its consequences" (Goldenweiser 1915, 720–21). It was one thing for Durkheim to claim that when people worship the gods, they are really worshipping society, but it was rather too much to conclude that they don't even know what gods are. As for his remarkable claims about Buddhism, apparently Durkheim confused the Buddhism of a small intellectual elite with Buddhism in general, and seemingly was unaware that popular Buddhism is particularly rich in supernatural beings. This blunder has long been cited by anthropologists as among Durkheim's many shortcomings (for definitive treatment, see Spiro 1966a). Nevertheless, Durkheim's claim about Buddhism and the corresponding idea that supernaturalism cannot be included in a universal definition of religion was accepted by sociologists for decades and was routinely used as a basis for ridiculing Tylor and other early social scientists (see Goode 1951). Amazingly enough, while claiming adherence to the Durkheimian tradition, Talcott Parsons (1951, 369–70) made the "supernatural" the central aspect of his definition, substituting it for Durkheim's term "sacred."

Definition 3.   **Supernatural** refers to forces or entities beyond or outside nature that can suspend, alter, or ignore physical forces.

When available natural means are of no avail, humans search for other means to achieve their goals. The supernatural, as conceived of by human beings, holds the potential for gaining rewards unobtainable from any other source.

PROPOSITION 6.   In pursuit of rewards, humans will seek to utilize and manipulate the supernatural.

This is not a flight into irrationality. The consensus among anthropologists is that efforts to use and control the supernatural are exceptional for their hardheaded rationality, as one might suppose, given that efforts to invoke the supernatural mostly involve matters of importance. Nor do humans resort to the supernatural capriciously. "No savage tries to induce a snowstorm in midsummer.... He dances *with* the rain," Suzanne Langer noted (1942, 129). Recall Bronislaw Malinowski's ([1925] 1992, 28–29) profound observation that the Trobriand Islanders he studied resorted to supernatural means *only* as a *last* resort. They did not employ supernatural means in an effort to rid their gardens of weeds or to repair fences. They did turn to the supernatural to try to influence the weather. Thus, a limiting proposition must be added:

PROPOSITION 7.   Humans will not have recourse to the supernatural when a cheaper or more efficient alternative is known and available.

GODS

As defined above, the supernatural is a rather vague and impersonal concept. It refers to forces and entities, not to "beings." This is because in many contexts the supernatural is only a vague idea, a virtual background assumption, as will be clear in the subsequent discussion of magic. But humans also hold more elaborate conceptions of the supernatural.

For the sake of clarification, let us offer a hypothetical account of cultural evolution. Early humans believed themselves to be surrounded by supernatural forces capable of causing them great harm, and thereby capable of providing great rewards, if only by sparing them from harm. Since it often seemed as if there were intentions behind supernatural activity, these early humans concluded that while some supernatural forces might well be impersonal, others must be conscious beings. Having no experience with conscious beings having no desires, these early humans also assumed that bargains could be struck with the supernatural, if only they were able to discover the right terms of exchange.

Definition 4.   **Gods** are supernatural "beings" having consciousness and desire.

As defined, the word "god" implies no gender, and even when we mention female members of the Greek pantheon, we shall identify them as gods, not as goddesses. As will be discussed, there is immense variation among conceptions of gods' temperaments, character, and scope, but it is universally believed that gods have desires, and that they can therefore be enlisted on behalf of human desires.

In defining gods as beings, we reject the frequent practice by many scholars of comparative religions of stretching the definition in order to apply it to unconscious essences such as the Tao, Immanuel Kant's "First Cause," or Paul Tillich's "ground of our being." We reject the pretense that any system of thought that addresses existential or ethical concerns is a "religion," and that any sufficiently ambiguous psychological structure is a "god"—even essences or structures having an aura of supernaturalism. As we define it, therefore, the Tao is not a god, while the pantheon of supernatural beings that thrive within popular Taoism are gods (Eichhorn 1959; Shahar and Weller 1996).

PROPOSITION 8.   In pursuit of rewards, humans will seek to exchange with a god or gods.

Finally, we are able to define the fundamental subject matter:

Definition 5.   **Religion** consists of very general explanations of existence, including the terms of exchange with a god or gods.

It is important to see that this definition does not reduce religion merely to a set of commandments or divine demands. Terms of exchange with the gods provide the foundation for much religious thought, but as the words "explanations of existence" indicate, there will be an extensive collection of ideas, principles, myths, symbols, images, and other elements of religious culture built upon this base. In addition to clarifying what the gods want, religious explanations specify the fundamental meaning of life: how we got here and where we are going (if anywhere). Religion is first and foremost an intellectual product, and *ideas* are its truly fundamental aspect.

Because this definition is rooted in the relationship between humans and divinity, it returns, in its essentials, to that offered by Tylor more than a century ago. Indeed, Tylor attributed early religions to the reflections and inferences of "ancient savage philosophers" and described religion as "a fairly consistent and rational primitive philosophy." Moreover, as he explained,

> nor, because the religions of savage tribes may be rude and primitive compared with the great Asiatic[4] systems, do they lie too low for interest and even for respect.... Few who will give their minds to master the general principles of savage religion will ever again think it ridiculous, or the knowledge of it superfluous to the rest of mankind. Far from its beliefs and practices being a rubbish-heap of miscellaneous folly, they are consistent and logical in so high a degree as to ... display principles of their formation and development; and these principles prove to be essentially rational. (Tylor [1871] 1958, 1: 22–23)

It seems fitting that Tylor's position came to be known (and condemned) as "rationalism" by Durkheim and several generations of functionalists. William J. Goode thus thought it quite devastating to reveal that in Tylor's work "religious doctrines and practices are treated as theological systems created by human reason" (1951, 243). Similarly, William Lessa and Evon Z. Vogt claimed that as anthropology gained sophistication, it no longer could condone Tylor's attempt to make "primitive man into a kind of rational philosopher who tried to find answers to [life's] problems" (1972, 63).

Why has it been thought absurd to suppose that "primitive man" wonders about life's many mysteries and tries to understand them? Initially, as discussed in chapter 2, the answer given was that "primitives" can't think very well—that the "primitive mind" is incapable of intellectual speculation. Quite aside from being racist nonsense, the claim that "primitives" can't reason about the supernatural is absurd. As Andrew Greeley puts it, the ancient "mythmaker may be a poet but he is not a superstitious fool" (1989a, 189). Granted that preliterate societies do not produce the equivalent of the *Summa Theologica*, but neither are they lacking in systematic bodies of religious ideas. In the concluding chapter of *Nuer Religion*, regarded by many as the finest ethnography ever written about the religion of a preliterate society, Evans-Pritchard noted: "The Nuer are undoubtedly a primitive people by the usual standards of reckoning, but their religious thought is remarkably sensitive, refined, and intelligent. It is also highly complex" (1956, 311). And so it should be. Unlike the sciences, religious thought does not depend upon centuries of accumulation of physical and natural facts. What it mainly requires is curiosity and inspiration, and these seem to be in ample supply in all human groups. Summing up his own fieldwork and that of others, Clifford Geertz concluded that humans are incapable of simply looking at the world "in dumb astonishment or bland apathy," but always seek to explain what is going on. Geertz added that the villagers he studied in Java behaved fully in accord with Tylor's claims about primitive philosophers, "constantly using their beliefs to 'explain' phenomena" (1966, 15).

In any event, following World War II, Tylor's claim that religion is about belief in supernatural beings reemerged as the preferred definition of religion by a distinguished list of anthropologists: Monica Hunter Wilson (1957, 9), Raymond Firth (1959, 131), Robin Horton (1960, 211), Jack Goody (1961, 157), David G. Mandelbaum (1966, 1174), Anthony F.C. Wallace (1966, 5), and Melford Spiro (1966a, 96–98). Even Mary Douglas, who always has been reluctant to accept *any* general definition of religion, wrote: "I am not especially fond of the one based on belief in spiritual beings, but at least it defines the field without begging any questions about the integrative power—moral, intellectual, or social—of religion" (1982, 29).

Unfortunately, as Douglas noted, it was not merely a contempt for primitive thinking that led many early social scientists to exclude the gods from definitions of religion, but also their conviction that social life is shaped by large, impersonal forces that go unnoticed by the uninitiated. These, not the reasons cited by individuals, are the real causes of social phenomena. Applied to religion, what this often has meant is that its "real" cause is its contribution to social integration. Indeed, the inability of religious people to explain their behavior in these terms has often been cited as good reason to ignore them. Thus, Durkheim and his followers seemed to take considerable satisfaction in revealing that people are deluding themselves when they say they are worshipping a god, for they actually are worshipping their own reflection: gods are society, and social integration is the truly divine miracle.[5] Hence, as they embraced the doctrines of functionalism, many anthropologists reported that humans persist in giving "incorrect" answers when asked why they perform religious rituals and ceremonies. Malinowski reported that if asked to explain the purpose of a religious ceremony, a "native" will merely "narrate an explanatory myth" ([1925] 1992, 38). A.R. Radcliffe-Brown agreed, noting that it is a "grievous error" to believe the reasons groups give for performing religious rites (1939, 25). Both men actually claimed that only sophisticated outsiders[6] can identify the true cause of ritual activities, which, of course, has nothing to do with god but with generating social solidarity and integration. Hence their emphasis on rite and ritual rather than belief.

Why is the "correct" explanation for the ringing of church bells all over America on August 14, 1945, that it contributed to social integration, rather than the reason that would have been given by those who rang the bells: that they did it "to thank God for peace"? Indeed, on what grounds can social scientists claim to know better than the Apa Tanus when they explain that the purpose of their Korlang-uni rite is to honor Mokum and thus to ensure a healthy rice crop? The rite may indeed *also* contribute to group solidarity among the Apa Tanus, just as the World Series may do so for the two American or Canadian cities whose teams are taking part, but surely solidarity is not the "real" cause of either activity.

We propose to take people at their word when proximate causes are involved and to credit even early humans with the capacity to base their religious rites on explanations that are recognizable as "philosophy." Here too, we are in good company. Melford Spiro spoke for many of his peers when he noted:

> The most obvious basis for religious behavior is the one which any religious actor tells us about when we ask him—and, unlike some anthropologists, I believe him. He believes in superhuman beings and he performs religious ritual in order that he may satisfy [them] ... despite [Robert K.] Merton's incisive analysis of functional theory, it is highly questionable if the persistence of Hopi rain ceremonies is to be explained by the social integration to which *he* (Merton) thinks their performance is conducive ... rather than by the meteorological events to which the *Hopi* think they are conducive. [Spiro's italics]
>
> The Hopi belief in the efficacy of their rainmaking ritual is not irrational—although it is certainly false[7]—because the conclusion, rain ceremonies cause the rain to fall, follows validly from a worldview whose major premise states that the gods exist, and whose minor premise states that the behavior of the gods can be influenced by rituals. (Spiro 1966a, 112–13)

At least Merton made social integration a *latent* function of the Hopi rain dance. In contrast, anthropologists committed to symbolist theory make this the *manifest* function by absolutely denying that religious rituals are performed in pursuit of any tangible results. That is, despite the fact that most prayers in all societies make specific requests of the gods (for health, good weather, safe travel, abundant crops, or the soul of a loved one), we are asked to accept that this is not why people do it. Thus, Clifford Geertz denies that healing ceremonies among the Navaho are performed to cure the afflicted, contending that they are merely to provide "the stricken person a vocabulary" to relate his or her distress "to the wider world" (1966, 19–20). Never mind that the ceremony consists almost entirely of the chant "may the patient be well." Dan Sperber (1975, 5) offers the extraordinary claim that because it is self-evident that supernatural beings do not exist, it is impossible to interpret religious rituals as efforts to enlist the gods on one's behalf. That is, since people don't actually believe in the gods, their prayers are not to be taken literally as attempts at exchange. S. R. F. Price (1984) has gone so far as to claim that religious "belief" is a purely Christian invention, and that when Romans prayed, they didn't really mean it, in the sense that they thought prayers were heard. In response, one can only ask what Cato thought he was doing when he prayed:

> Father Mars, I beg and entreat you to be well disposed toward me and toward our house and household. I have ordered an offering of pigs, sheep and bulls ... on account of this request, so that you may prevent, ward off and remove sickness ... and damage to crops and bad weather.... Preserve my shepherds and flocks un-

harmed and give good health and strength to me, my home, and our household. For this purpose ... Father Mars ... you shall be increased by these offerings of suckling pigs, sheep and bulls. (*On Agriculture* 141, trans. Charles King)

Indeed, why did Cato publish this prayer in a book meant to instruct others on good farming methods? Was it because, although he knew full well that there is no Father Mars, he thought saying so would be good for the morale of his live-stock?

We would not belabor the matter were there not so many well-received books advocating the symbolic theory position. Among them is Rodney Need-ham's *Belief, Language, and Experience* (1972), wherein he explicitly rejects the exis-tence of any "interior state" that might be called belief. From this, Needham deduces that belief cannot be essential to ritual, and that worship is not directed toward ends other than the socio-emotional. Requests concerning fields, flocks, health, and fortune be damned! In similar fashion, Sperber is certain that it is so obvious that supernatural beings do not exist that even the rudest tribal priests must realize this "fact," and that they therefore cannot really be attempting to exchange with the gods. Rather, they accept the reality of what is being symbol-ized by various rituals, and *that* always turns out to be some representation of the group and its well-being. Put another way, the proponents of symbolist the-ory do not argue, as the functionalists have done, that these symbolisms are an *additional* set of meanings and interpretations of religious rituals, but that they are the *entire basis* for such activities. The statements made by those who per-form the acts are not merely dismissed as in error (à la Durkheim), but are re-jected as fundamentally insincere, for those doing the praying, or performing the rituals, or offering the sacrifices know better, or at least *they ought to* (see Tooker 1992). In this regard John Beattie is entirely candid:

> If a Nyoro tells me that his sacrificial ritual is effective ... because it is a means of coercing gods or spirits to do what he wants ... by what conceivable right do we assert that these informants are mistaken, that we know better than they do what they "really" think, and that even though they do not know it, what underlies their behaviour is a belief in the power of the symbolic expression itself? ... [My] hy-pothesis that ritual has an essentially expressive quality, and that its causal efficacy is thought (when it is deeply thought about) to reside in this very fact, is not re-futed by the observation that it is not thought to be thus effective when it is not deeply thought about, as it rarely is. (Beattie 1966, 69–70)

Hence, the only reason informants tell anthropologists the wrong reasons for their religious undertakings is lack of deep thought. Presumably, if they thought about what they were doing more deeply, the Nyoro would agree with Beattie (ibid., 70) that the symbolic theory must be the real explanation of their behav-ior, for "any alternative explanation of the thought which underlies ritual insti-tutions simply does not make sense of people's behaviour." Beattie's claims turn to slush if it is assumed that when people ask the gods for help, they think there

is someone or something to hear them. Indeed, this simple assumption, universally attested by all who do such things, makes perfect sense of their behavior—
"Ask, and it shall be given you" (Matt. 7:7). It seems to us that the urgent need
here is for a theory to make sense of the behavior of the symbolic theorists.

We have no quarrel with the notion that religion can contribute to solidarity.
But rather than asserting this by definition, we propose to allow the *social* aspects of religion to emerge through theorizing and not to assume that religion *is*
the basis of social integration. Indeed, to define religion as integration results in
a theory incapable of dealing with religious sources of social disorganization
and conflict.

Many of the definitions of religion offered by the anthropologists cited
above mention actions as well as beliefs. Since religious explanations define the
terms of exchanges with the gods, they obviously do have implications for behavior, but religious action per se is excluded from our definition, because we
think it worthwhile to separate the two. As W. G. Runciman pointed out: "It
also is well to emphasize at the outset that the explanation of putatively 'religious' *actions* raises problems which are quite separate from those of explaining
beliefs ... an answer to the question of why people hold the beliefs that they do
does not depend on answering the question why they perform the actions they
do" (1969, 150–51).

Indeed, in the religious sphere, people often believe without acting—Grace
Davie describes the religiousness of the average European as "believing without
belonging" (1994, 2). The utility of a purely cognitive definition of religion is
that it facilitates study of this link. Indeed, later in this chapter, it enables us to
formulate a proposition concerning religious procrastination.

TERMS OF EXCHANGE

It follows from our definition of religion that the primary religious question is:
What do the gods want? Rather than pausing here to categorize the variety of
goods and services that have been offered to the gods, its seems more significant
to focus on the matter of cost or price. That is, there are limits on how much
even divine beings can charge for their favor, and this will vary depending on a
number of factors. One of these is competition.

PROPOSITION 9.   The greater the number of gods worshipped by a group,
the lower the price of exchanging with each.

This is self-evident, as well as being widely observed. In polytheistic settings,
people "shop around" from god to god and temple to temple. In ancient Egypt,
there were thirty-one primary gods, each with temples (Barrett 1996), and in
Rome, when the Pantheon ("[temple] of all the gods") was reconstructed by
Hadrian in the year 119, there were fifteen major gods and scores of minor
ones, not including the gods of various ethnic groups that had temples dedi-

cated to them at Rome (MacMullen 1981). Other things being equal, the availability of many alternative gods will exert downward pressures on price. Of course, even within a pantheon as elaborate as that sustained by the ancient Egyptians, other things were not equal, and while competition kept down prices in general, in the religious marketplace, some gods could demand higher prices than others. That is, some gods seemed to be more valuable and reliable exchange partners. These same principles also apply across societies.

PROPOSITION 10.   In exchanging with the gods, humans will pay higher prices to the extent that the gods are believed to be more **dependable.**

Definition 6.   **Dependable** means the gods can be relied upon to keep their word and to be consistent in their orientations towards humans.

Undependable, wicked, mischievous gods are legion. There is a huge anthropological literature on "trickster" gods and spirits (see, e.g., Radin 1956; Evans-Pritchard 1967; Hynes and Doty 1993). Trickster gods are unusually frequent in the religions of Native North Americans, but are common all around the world. In Dahomey, people never know what to expect from "the lecherous, mischievous, but sometimes humanly helpful god Legba" (Norbeck 1961, 79), while Japanese Shinto includes the misbehaving Susa-no-o, who is "divine yet subject to the most infantile of human passions" (Ellwood 1993, 142). As conceived of by the ancient Greeks, *most* of the gods were quite undependable, being capricious and amoral. Sometimes they kept their word, and sometimes they provided humans with very valuable rewards. But sometimes they lied, and they often did humans great harm for very petty reasons. It may have been worthwhile periodically to offer such gods a sacrificial animal or two (especially since the donors feasted on the offering after the ceremony), but they were not worth more.

To the extent that they regard the gods as dependable, humans will tend to separate them into two classes, good and evil. This distinction arises because gods are more dependable, and hence are more suitable exchange partners, to the extent that their intentions toward humans are either benign or hostile, as opposed to gods who unpredictably shift orientations (Stark and Bainbridge [1987] 1996, 113–16). This division is, of course, true of all the "world" religions. But it is very common in the religions of preliterate societies too. For example, the Yakö in West Africa distinguish "several distinct categories" of "supernatural beings," according to Daryll Forde. One category consists of "protective tutelary spirits," while another is made up of "spirits capable of inflicting sickness, sterility and death" (Forde 1958, 166). Gladys Reichard (1950) reported that the Navaho distinguish their gods according to their dependability in giving help.

Definition 6a.   **Good gods** are those who intend to allow humans to profit from their exchanges.

Definition 6b. **Evil gods** are those who intend to inflict coercive exchanges or deceptions on humans, resulting in losses for human exchange partners.

Definition 6c. **Inconsistent gods** are those who alternate unpredictably between benign and evil orientations toward humans.

It will be evident that humans will prefer to exchange with good gods, especially with good gods who will protect them from evil gods, although sometimes humans will be forced to accept losses in order to propitiate evil gods. But whether explanations involve the terms of exchange with benign or evil gods, the definition of religion is met. That is, even Satanic worship is a form of religion, not something else.

Gods may be dependable without being especially responsive or sympathetic. Unlike most Greek gods, Zeus was depicted as a consistent "good god," but he also was seen as remote and not very concerned about human affairs. Greeks did not talk about having experienced the love of Zeus.

PROPOSITION 11. In exchanging with the gods, humans will pay higher prices to the extent that the gods are believed to be more **responsive.**

Definition 7. **Responsive** means the gods are concerned about, are informed about, and act on behalf of humans.

We have selected "responsive" as the most appropriate term to sum up many similar attributes ascribed to the gods, including "personal" (impersonal), "caring," "loving," "merciful," "close," and "accessible," all of which can be summed up as the belief that "there is somebody up there who cares." The Nuer often refer to God as their father and themselves as "'*gaatku*,' thy children," not meaning these terms literally, but to indicate a relationship that involves "the sense of care and protection parents give to a child," and they commonly acknowledge God's care with the remark "God is present" (Evans-Pritchard 1956, 8–9) This same sense of divine responsiveness is found in the orthodox conception of God presented by Judaism, Christianity, and Islam. Such a God makes an extremely attractive exchange partner, who can be counted on to maximize human benefits.

The ancient Sumerians could only appeal to their high gods through a divine bureaucracy beyond Franz Kafka's worst nightmare, consisting of an incredible number of levels, because the gods on the lower levels had insufficient scope to "fulfill all the wishes of the petitioner" (von Soden 1994, 176).

PROPOSITION 12. In exchanging with the gods, humans will pay higher prices to the extent that the gods are believed to be of greater **scope.**

Definition 8. The **scope** of the gods refers to the diversity of their powers and the range of their influence.

Having more diverse powers, a god of weather is of greater scope than a god of wind or a god of rain. A god who controls weather everywhere is of greater scope than a god who controls weather only in a small tribal territory. At one extreme are the minor gods and godlings that abound in preliterate societies or on the peripheries of pantheons, and at the other extreme is the omnipotent God of the Jewish-Christian-Islamic tradition.

Gods of greater scope can provide far more valuable rewards, and can therefore require more in return. Indeed, only gods of great scope offer rewards so valuable that they can be obtained only in another world.

PROPOSITION 13.   The greater their scope (and the more responsive they are), the more plausible it will be that gods can provide otherworldly rewards. Conversely, exchanges with gods of smaller scope will tend to be limited to worldly rewards.

None of the gods in polytheistic pantheons offer immortality. Indeed, being immortal was the primary distinction the Greeks and Romans made between being a god or being a mere human. Like the Greeks and Romans, many cultures conceive of the afterlife as an unattractive, shadowy existence that is not a gift of the gods. And, also like the Greeks and Romans, groups with many gods go to them for worldly benefits: for health, for success in love, for victory, for good harvests, for financial success. These are to be achieved here and soon, not later and elsewhere.

PROPOSITION 14.   In pursuit of otherworldly rewards, humans will accept an **extended** exchange relationship.

Definition 9.   An **extended exchange relationship** is one in which the human makes periodic payments over a substantial length of time, often until death.

In societies where most people patronize many gods, their exchange relations with any given god are infrequent and very short-term. Hsinchih Chen notes that Taiwanese folk religion "is very this-worldly oriented. If one feels that the deity is no longer efficacious and cannot satisfy the individual's requests, then that person will switch his or her worship to other deities. In some extreme cases like lottery gamblers, some losers destroy the images of deities, just because they are furious with the gods that fail them on the lottery" (Chen 1995, 1).

Christians, Jews, and Muslims find such behavior sacrilegious, accustomed as they are to seeing faith as a lifelong undertaking, involving obligations and duties that must be met and performed from cradle to grave. Indeed, in the case of Buddhists, it may prove necessary to extend an exchange relationship over several lifetimes, as with the Burmese Buddhists studied by Melford Spiro:

> Recognizing that their future welfare can best be achieved through saving and investment, the Burmese *do* save and invest extensively. Their investments ... take the form of religious contributions, whose returns are in the form of improved karma. Although these returns cannot be cashed in, so to speak, until some future existence, their accumulation builds up large reserves in the form of merit. It is

from deep concern with their future that the Burmese maintain constant vigil on their reserve balance. Like Weber's puritans, many Burmese keep a merit account book in which all expenditures on merit production are entered, and the units of merit thus achieved can be compared with the units of demerit attendant upon violation of the Buddhist precepts. In this way it is possible to compute the reserve balance in one's present merit bank and thereby come to some rough assessment of the contribution of one's present existence to one's future security. (Spiro 1966b, 1171–72)

Differences in the duration of exchange relationships with the gods rest on what people anticipate in return from the gods—a winning lottery ticket, a better next life, or life everlasting.

PROPOSITION 15. In pursuit of otherworldly rewards, humans will accept an **exclusive exchange relationship.**

Definition 10. An **exclusive exchange relationship** is one in which the human may exchange only with one specific god (and approved subordinate gods, such as angels).

Not only must Jews, Muslims, and Christians engage in long-term religious exchange relations, they must do so with only one God. This is, of course, the First Commandment.

While otherworldly rewards can generate extended commitments, the fact that they are only to be realized in the distant future has implications for commitment. Other things being equal:

PROPOSITION 16. People will seek to delay their payment of religious costs.

Just as people often delay their investments in a retirement plan, they often delay bringing their afterlife arrangements up to date. We might refer to this as the *principle of religious procrastination.* Evidence of it shows up in the tendency for people to raise their levels of religious commitment as they age (Argyle and Beit-Hallahmi 1975) and in the frequency of fox-hole and deathbed conversions. It also is consistent with the new literature on risk aversion and gender differences in religious commitment (Miller and Hoffmann 1995).

We have seen that religious costs will vary depending on certain aspects of the gods, on the amount of competition among them, and according to their dependability and scope. But from the other side of the exchange relationship, the principle that humans attempt to maximize gains leads to the conclusion that, in addition to delaying their payments:

PROPOSITION 17. People will seek to minimize their religious costs.

Based on the assumption that religion is irrational and not amenable to calculation, many social scientists have stressed that people, especially in traditional societies, gladly (and blindly) bring their offerings to the gods. Royden Keith Yerkes claimed, for example, that in ancient times in the Near East, "Sacrifices were always as large as possible; the larger they could be made, the greater the accompanying joy and festivity" (1952, 4). Indeed, a substantial theoretical literature grew up around sacrifice to explain why people would act in ways so contrary to rational economic self-interest. Turning a deaf ear to unanimous testimony that "we give to the gods in order to gain their favor," various scholars have offered several more profound explanations (Smith [1889] 1907; Freud [1912–13] 1950; Durkheim 1915; Frazier 1922; Money-Kyrle 1929). There is absolutely no room in any of these schemes for rational economic behavior. *Au contraire,* to these scholars sacrifice epitomized the irrationality of religious expression—being a never-ending reenactment of the Oedipus conflict, according to Freud and Money-Kyrle. If sacrifice is irrational, then proposition 17 is quite unrealistic. However, the charge of being unrealistic is better directed at these same "theorists," none of whom "had ever been near a primitive people," according to Evans-Pritchard (1965, 6).

In contrast, anthropologists who actually have gone into the field report abundant examples that the sharp practices, the endless haggling, and the raw self-interest we expect in even the most rudimentary bartering systems turn up in exchange relations with the gods as well. C. M. Doughty, who lived among the Bedouin, reported that although a ritual would call for the sacrifice of a camel, they often substituted a sheep or a goat or a decrepit camel. On one occasion, when a young suckling camel was sacrificed, there were protests that it was much too valuable, and that a sheep or goat should have been substituted. The answer given was that "she refuses the teat" and would have died anyway (Doughty 1926, 1: 451–52). Evans-Pritchard found that among the Nuer, although a ritual may require that a certain number of oxen be given in sacrifice, they usually sacrifice fewer oxen than are called for, and often will sacrifice none, making all manner of cheaper substitutions. In fact, in lieu of an ox, the Nuer sometimes offer a wild cucumber *(Cucumis prophetarum),* which "is treated as though it were an animal victim. It is presented and consecrated, an invocation is said over it, and it is slain by the spear, being cut in half along its edge.... In a sacrificial context Nuer also always speak of a cucumber-victim as '*yang*', 'cow'" (Evans-Pritchard 1956, 202–3). In his brilliant essay on economic aspects of sacrifice, Raymond Firth remarks that substituting a cucumber for a cow, "is a most economical way of meeting one's ritual obligations" (1963, 20).

A somewhat similar practice among the Swazi is a form of "bait and switch." Each priest secures "a particularly fine beast" and dedicates it to his ancestors, making it a *licabi* animal. When time comes for a sacrifice, the *licabi* animal is placed in an enclosure with a much inferior animal, which, by association, acquires the ritual qualities of the *licabi.* The inferior beast is then used in the ritual, and "the *licabi* itself serves the role many times; it is not killed until it becomes too old to serve as the display animal" (Firth 1963, 21).

Lest it be thought such calculating religious behavior is somehow limited to traditional societies, note the Catholic tendency to "shop" for a confessor who imposes the mildest penances. At the collective level, the well-known transformation of sects into churches is primarily a process of minimizing religious costs. Thus, although nineteenth-century American Methodists did not feel obligated to sacrifice camels or oxen, they were obligated not to gamble, dance, drink alcoholic beverages, or go to the theater. These rules were dropped precisely because new generations of more affluent Methodists no longer desired so costly a faith.

Implicit in each of these examples of calculation in exchanging with the gods is the answer to the question of why people exchange with the gods at all. They do so not because they don't know better, or can't help themselves, but because they want what the gods have to offer—even if they cannot resist seeking the best possible terms. "One may serve God without losing touch with Mammon," Firth comments (1963, 23).

INTERCESSION

However it is that humans conceive of the gods, few individuals formulate their own religious explanations or attempt to discover on their own what it is that the gods want.[8] That is, religious expression does not consist primarily of interaction between a lone individual and a god, but is anchored in social groups and in the division of labor.

Since humans will retain explanations (conceptual simplifications or models of reality) (proposition 3), other things being equal, human cultures will over time become more extensive and complex. Indeed, from very early in prehistory, any given culture has been so extensive and complex that no single person could master it all. At that point, cultural specialization (or a division of labor) occurred, whereby individuals mastered parts of their culture and relied on exchanges with others in order to have the benefits of other parts. The order of emergence of specialists reflected the importance of a particular cultural "bundle" and the particular qualities required to master and sustain it. Thus, it is not surprising that political leadership seems to have been the earliest specialization. It is indicative of the importance given religion that priesthood was perhaps the second specialization to emerge (Spencer 1896, vol. 2; Lenski 1966). Not surprisingly, societies lacking religious specialists also are relatively deficient in terms of their religious culture (Holmberg 1950; Norbeck 1961). Among the Chenchu nomads in the jungles of the Indian state of Andhra Pradesh, there "are no priests or other religious experts ... and the structure of Chenchu religions is thus one of extreme simplicity" (Parrinder 1983, 37). As with the fine arts, so too with religion: creative talent is uncommon, and it benefits from training and practice.

Definition 11. An **ecclesiastic** is anyone who specializes in religion—in explaining, supervising, and/or conducting exchanges with a god or gods.

We have followed Herbert Spencer (1896, vol. 2) in using the term "ecclesiastic" to identify religious specialists. Its advantages are several. It does not impute gender and seems sufficiently generic to transcend cross-cultural variations in a way that terms such as "priest" or "cleric" do not.

Definition 12.   **Religious organizations** are social enterprises whose primary purpose is to create, maintain, and supply religion to some set of individuals and to support and supervise their exchanges with a god or gods.

People may participate in religious organizations for all sorts of secular reasons (fun and friendship are common motives), but the raison d'être of all organizations to be identified as religious has to do with relationships with a god or gods.

PROPOSITION 18.   A religious organization will be able to require extended and exclusive commitments to the extent that it offers otherworldly rewards.

This is a simple extension of propositions 13–15. As a direct result of the capacities attributed to the god or gods they serve, religious organizations will differ in the extent to which they can bind members in a long-term, exclusive relationship. As noted, these relationships involve a great variety of worldly rewards, but these too are proportionate to the scope of the god or gods.

Definition 13.   **Religious commitment** is the degree to which humans promptly meet the terms of exchange with a god or gods as specified by the explanations of a given religious organization.

Generally speaking, religious organizations will distinguish two forms of commitment, *objective* (behavior) and *subjective* (beliefs and feelings). This distinction is consistent with our decision to limit the definition of religion to cognitive elements, in that these definitions also facilitate examination of the link between faith and practice.

Definition 14.   **Objective religious commitment** refers to all behavior in accord with the explanations sustained by a religious organization.

Such behavior includes all forms of religious *participation* or practice (taking part in rites and services, for example), *material offerings* (sacrifices, contributions, and donations), and *conformity* to rules governing actions (not sinning).

Definition 15.   **Subjective religious commitment** involves belief in, and knowledge of, the explanations sustained by a religious organization and having the appropriate emotions.

That religion involves belief and knowledge is obvious and needs no additional discussion here, although it will be given fuller treatment later. But, some discussion is required of the immense literature on the emotional aspects of religion. Some have argued that religion consists primarily of emotions, even to such an extent that religion is an entirely subjective phenomenon that can only be apprehended through experience, and then only described, not analyzed. Early in his famous work *The Idea of the Holy*, Rudolph Otto asked readers to recall a moment of deeply felt religious feelings; anyone who could not do so was "requested to read no further." His point was that the essence of religion is "inexpressible" and therefore cannot be discussed intelligibly with those who lack direct experience of the "mental state" he called "numinous," which "is perfectly *sui generis* and irreducible to any other" (Otto 1923, 7–8).

No one could deny that emotions are of very great importance in religious life, and that people often seem to have some difficulty in describing these feelings. But there is no evidence whatever that there exist *uniquely religious* emotions. Rather, humans experience all of the normal emotions in response to religious stimuli. No one put this better than William James. In the second lecture of the set making up *The Varieties of Religious Experience*, James announced his intention to have done with the notion that "religious sentiment" was "a single sort of mental entity" (James [1902] 1958, 39–40). "There is religious fear, religious love, religious awe, religious joy, and so forth," James agreed. But these are only ordinary, natural emotions "directed to a religious object." Later in this chapter, we discuss mystical experiences—incidents of perceived direct contact with a god. These do seem to be uniquely religious in *form*, but the emotions and feelings involved are those of ordinary experience. Put another way, it is the *object* of emotions and feelings that determines whether an episode is religious or secular. Were we to accept claims that religion consists of feelings per se, such as awe, reverence, or depth of commitment, we would be forced to expand the category of religion to include the belief systems of groups such as the Communist and Nazi parties, Greenpeace, and even some fan clubs, as well as activities such as sex and drug use, or contemplation of the starry sky, all of which are, for some people, the object of such feelings. A subjective definition appeals to many intellectuals (particularly those employed in seminaries or in departments of religion) who wish to claim to be religious while rejecting all aspects of supernaturalism, but ignores the profound differences between secular and supernatural assumptions.[9] To adopt such a definition would require that we immediately introduce a distinction between "religions" that do and do not assume the supernatural, in which case nothing has been accomplished—apart from making "religion" a superfluous concept (Stark 1965; 1981).

In terms of religious commitment, what typically is required is that people feel and exhibit the appropriate emotions concerning their religious actions and undertakings. The gods may require that their altars be approached in awe, or that prayers be said sincerely. And, as countless millions of children have learned through the ages, one does not giggle during solemn rites.

RELIGION AND MAGIC

Sociologists have had a very difficult time distinguishing religion from magic, mainly because they have favored much too broad a definition of religion. Indeed, many sociological definitions of religion are so general that they not only are unable to separate magic and religion, but, as in the case of subjective definitions, they can neither differentiate religion from wholly secular philosophies, such as those that animate radical political movements, nor efficiently separate magic from science (see Luckmann 1967; Bellah 1970; Yinger 1970; Beyer 1994). However, all secular philosophies, including science, are excluded if the supernatural is made part of the definition of religion and magic. To distinguish religion from magic, we would note two distinctions: magic neither includes a general account, or explanation, of existence nor invokes gods.

All religions offer some universal existential statements, while magic tends to focus on specific and immediate results and to ignore matters of meaning—it usually even fails to include explanations of why or how its own mechanisms work (Kieckhefer 1976, 6). As Durkheim put it, magic seeks "technical and utilitarian ends, it does not waste its time in pure speculation" (1915, 42).

Both religion and magic are based on supernatural assumptions, but while religion deals primarily with the gods, magic is *limited to impersonal conceptions of the supernatural.* "[T]he realm of magic is that in which human beings believe that they may directly affect nature and each other, for good or for ill, by their own efforts (even though the precise mechanism may not be understood by them), as distinct from appealing to divine powers by sacrifice or prayer," John Middleton pointed out, summing up more than a century of anthropological studies of magic (1967a, ix). Of course, Middleton did not mean to place in the magical realm just any or even most human efforts to affect nature or one another. He assumed his readers understood that, just as rain dances differ from irrigation projects, only efforts involving a resort to supernatural means constitute magic. Hence:

Definition 16.   **Magic** refers to all efforts to manipulate supernatural forces to gain rewards (or avoid costs) without reference to a god or gods or to general explanations of existence.

When a Catholic wears a St. Christopher's medal to ensure a safe journey, that is not magic, because the power of the medal is attributed to the patron saint, whose powers, in turn, are granted by God. The medal is intrinsic to an exchange with God. But, when a devotee of the New Age places "mystic" crystals under his or her pillow in order to cure a cold, it *is* magic, because no appeal has been made to a god. That is, magic deals in impersonal supernatural forces, often in the belief that such forces are *inherent properties* of particular objects or words—especially written or spoken formulae and incantations. Ruth Benedict was among the first to distinguish religion and magic in this way, when she proposed, in a nearly forgotten essay, that the former involves "personal relations with the supernatural," while the latter deals with "mechanistic manipulation of the impersonal" (1938, 637).

Anthropologists often use the Melanesian word *mana* to identify these impersonal supernatural forces or properties. More than a century ago, R. H. Codrington defined mana as "a force altogether distinct from physical power which acts in all kinds of ways for good and evil and which it is of the greatest advantage to possess and control" (1891, 118–19). Ruth Benedict offered a more precise definition: "[T]his supernatural quality [is] an attribute of objects just as color and weight are attributes of objects. There [is] just the same reason that a stone should have supernatural power as one of its qualities as there [is] that it should have hardness. It [does] not imply the personification of the stone" (1938, 631–32).

Admittedly, magic sometimes involves supernatural forces a bit more animate than mana. That is, sometimes magic does involve attempts to compel certain primitive spiritual entities to perform certain services (often to harm someone). Thus, some magical incantations are believed to summon minor demons or various other supernatural entities and bend them to the will of the magician. The key concept here is "compel" as opposed to "exchange," or as Benedict put it: "*Magic* is mechanical procedure, the compulsion of the supernatural" (ibid., 637) Later in her essay, Benedict explained that there are "two techniques for handling the supernatural—at the one extreme compulsion and at the other rapport" (ibid., 647). Compulsion of spiritual entities remains within the realm of magic, but exchange (which implies rapport) shifts the activity into the realm of religion.

Finally, because magic promises worldly rewards to be realized in the short term, magic is unable to form its clients into organizations.

PROPOSITION 19.   Magic cannot generate extended or exclusive patterns of exchange.

PROPOSITION 20.   Magicians will serve individual clients, not lead an organization.

Thus, we give more formal expression to Durkheim's famous assertion: "There is no Church of magic. Between the magician and the individuals who consult him, as between these individuals themselves, there are no lasting bonds.... The magician has a clientele and not a church" (1915, 44).

CONFIDENCE AND RISK

Although otherworldly rewards are impervious to disproof, by that same token, they cannot be demonstrated to exist. Therefore, exchanges involving long-term expenditure of tangible costs here and now, in hope of otherworldly rewards, involve risk.

PROPOSITION 21.   All religious explanations, and especially those concerning otherworldly rewards, entail risk.

The universal problem of religion is one of confidence. No exchanges with the gods will occur until or unless people are sufficiently confident that it is wise to expend costs. Like all investors, people contemplating religious commitments will seek assurance. Not surprisingly, they are able to obtain it in a number of ways, both secular and sacred.

PROPOSITION 22.   An individual's confidence in religious explanations is strengthened to the extent that others express their confidence in them.

As Darren Sherkat put it, "Religious goods are not simply 'experience' goods which must be consumed in order to be evaluated; rather, these goods must be experienced in communities which direct us on how to evaluate them" (1997, 68). Throughout our lives, we rely on the wisdom and experience of others to help us make good choices. The proposition can no doubt be qualified by noting the additional tendency for people to assess what others tell them on the basis of their evaluation of each as a source. That is, we learn to place greater faith in the testimony of some people than in that of others.

The next two propositions examine ritual and prayer as sources of confidence in religious explanations. We do not suggest that this is the primary reason why people engage in these religious activities—we think they do so mainly because they are believed to be proper forms of exchange with the divine. But neither do we suggest that the confidence that these activities provide is an unconscious "function" that escapes individual notice. It is very common for people to pray for strengthened faith—"Lord, I believe; help thou mine unbelief" (Mark 9:24)—and to believe that they have received it. The "peace of mind" that comes from this has been widely remarked.

PROPOSITION 23.   Confidence in religious explanations increases to the extent that people participate in **religious rituals.**

Definition 17.   **Religious rituals** are collective ceremonies having a common focus and mood in which the common focus is on a god or gods, while the common mood may vary.

Here we respond to Randall Collins's (1997) suggestions that the previous version of the theory gave insufficient attention to the ritual aspects of religion. Our definition of religious rituals was informed by his (1998) definition of social or interaction rituals.

It is quite astonishing that, although "ritual" is one of the most frequently used terms in social scientific writing on religion, it is a concept badly lacking in definitional efforts. Durkheim, for example, regarded ritual as *the* elementary form of the religious life, and claimed to know what it did, but never said what it was. Nor did Malinowski. A collection of outstanding anthropological studies was published under the title *Gods and Rituals* (Middleton 1967b), but the term "ritual" does not appear in its index (although there are eleven entries under the heading "chickens, sacrifice of"). Worse yet, various definitions are all-inclusive synonyms for religion. A.R. Radcliffe-Brown, being averse to any definitional mention of supernatural beings, and unable to restrict his subject matter by use of the principle of social integration alone, chose to use the term "ritual" rather than "religion." Within a page, however, he was driven to speak of "ritual value" to distinguish things that are included in or excluded from ritual (1952, 136–39). Radcliffe-Brown never was able to say what constitutes ritual value, other than it has nothing whatever (heaven forfend!) to do with the gods.

In contrast, Monica Wilson identified ritual as "a primarily religious action … directed to secure the blessing of some mystical power" (1957, 9). She proceeded to define religious ceremonials as an "elaborate conventional form for the expression of feeling."

We have chosen to define ritual as collective or social activities, and to further restrict the class to ceremonies, which are formal acts, usually based on custom, with a preset pattern or script. By limiting ritual to collective activities, we have excluded private, personal "rituals," as will be clear in our definition and discussion of prayer. By referring to *religious* rituals, we eliminate magical activities of a similar patterned form. We have also omitted Wilson's clause about securing blessings, not because the benefits to be gained from faith are not always implicit, but because they are not always explicit. That is, rituals may be experienced primarily as celebrations and festive occasions, rather than as a time for submitting petitions. For example, among the Dinka of the southern Sudan, even when "the occasion for a sacrifice may be a sad one … the ceremony itself is regarded by the Dinka as essentially a happy one, and they behave at such ceremonies as though they enjoyed themselves, and indeed attend in order to do so. Every sacrifice has a festive atmosphere" (Lienhardt 1961, 281). Similarly, Christmas services held in most Christian churches celebrate the birth of Jesus without reference to the blessings of faith, and the feast upon the breaking of the fast of Ramadan is an occasion of joy and thanksgiving in Muslim communities, as is the Passover seder among Jews.

However defined, social scientists are unanimous that participation in rituals builds faith. "Ritual actions … [give] the members of a society confidence" is how George Homans put it as a young functionalist (1941, 172). "Ritual helps to remind the individual of the holy realm, to revivify and strengthen his faith in this realm," Kingsley Davis advised (1949, 534). Even Durkheim admitted that the "*apparent* function [of ritual] is to strengthen the bonds attaching the believer to his god," although he quickly added, of course, that what ritual "*really*" does "is strengthen the bonds attaching the individual to society, since god is only a figurative expression of society" (1915, 226; emphasis added).

We are entirely willing to give Durkheim and the functionalists their due with respect to the observation that social rituals do generate group solidarity and, in that sense, social integration. But a crucial element of solidarity is commitment to the central ideas and ideals of the group. Indeed, propositions 22 and 23 are legitimate extensions of George Homans's (1974) propositions concerning how interaction results in agreement among group members. And what religious social rituals produce is agreement about the value of religious explanations. For example, Christmas services affirm the truth of all Christian teachings by affirming that Jesus was born the "son of God." In that sense, affirmation becomes integration.

PROPOSITION 24.   **Prayer** builds bonds of affection and confidence between humans and a god or gods.

Definition 18.   **Prayer** is a communication addressed to a god or gods.

Prayers may be silent or spoken out loud, impromptu or regular, formulaic (ritualistic) or spontaneous, mandatory or voluntary, and they may express need, praise, hope, joy, or even despair. People may pray in private, in small groups (formal, as in the case of the Jewish minyan, or informal, as in the case of the family devotion), or as part of a collective ceremony. But, in all cases, prayers are meant to be *heard.* As Firth puts it, "prayer is ostensibly a manifestation of a personal tie with the transcendent ... [and] constitutes an act of faith or hope that it will reach its mark" (1996, 169). As in the case of ritual, people *do not* always pray *for* something; often prayer is an experience of sharing and emotional exchange, much as goes on between humans having a long, intimate relationship, for in fact many people have come to regard their prayer relationship as long and loving (Poloma and Gallup 1991). This is entirely to be expected. Homans's (1974) law of liking reads that the longer people interact, the more they will come to like one another. Prayer, then, can have many purposes, but an important result is to reassure humans that religious phenomena are real.

Granted that we may not assume that prayer really is interactive, that there really is a second party. But, that doesn't matter provided the human experiences prayer as a two-party affair, if the divine seems to hear and to care. Hjalmar Sundén developed an elegant role-taking model of how people come to experience a divine exchange partner ([1959] 1966; 1987). And, in the well-worn words of W. I. Thomas, "If men define situations as real, they are real in their consequences" (quoted in Merton 1995, 380). Thus, when the Nuer address their god as *madh* "a word which has for them the sense of intimate friendship" (Evans-Pritchard 1956, 8–9), this reflects a relationship established and experienced through prayer. When Christians speak of "knowing the love of Christ," they do not do so as a figure of speech, but as an accurate description of their devotional life. Indeed, in the early 1990s, 79 percent of Americans reported feeling the "strong presence of God" during their prayers, and 72 percent acknowledged having received a "definite answer to a specific prayer request" (Poloma and Gallup 1991, 47).

PROPOSITION 25.   Confidence in religious explanations will increase to the degree that **miracles** are credited to the religion.

Definition 19.   **Miracles** are desirable effects believed to be caused by the intervention of a god or gods in worldly matters.

Miracles vary from the quite limited (a specific person's recovery from alcoholism, or survival of a seemingly fatal event) to the immense (the parting of the Red Sea, or the sinking of the Chinese invasion fleet by a "divine wind" during its voyage to Japan in 1281). However, unlike results sought through magic, miracles are regarded as problematic. That is, the results of a magical procedure are thought to be certain if it is properly conducted, but religions merely regard miracles as possible. For example, when they offered prayers for victory, Roman priests did not assure the results of an impending battle. They merely sought the support of the gods, fully acknowledging that the gods retained their autonomy and could freely choose whether or not to grant the request.

Even religions with an omnipotent God, such as Islam and Christianity, do not guarantee miracles. Allah or Jehovah may or may not respond. All religions assume that, in deciding to grant a miracle, gods must consider the consequences for their larger plans or concerns. It is also believed that gods consider the motives and moral worthiness of the beneficiaries of requested miracles, as well as possible unanticipated consequences of the meeting of their request for the supplicants. Thus, the saying, "God answers all prayers, but often the answer is 'no.'" In this way, even those religious explanations involving worldly rewards are relatively immune to disproof.

Nevertheless, miracles happen in *this* world. If people observe desirable effects that seem not to have naturalistic explanations, and if they attribute these effects to a god, confidence is increased in *all* explanations offered by the religion (and therefore in the reality of otherworldly rewards). Thus, for example, during the two great plagues that swept the Roman empire during the second and third centuries, Christians had a much lower death rate than did their pagan neighbors. Today we attribute that to the fact that Christians nursed the sick while the pagans generally did not. At the time, however, Christians (and many pagans) attributed these results to miracles and their faith in other Christian doctrines was strengthened thereby—they had objective proof that Christianity "worked" (McNeill 1976; Stark 1996a).

PROPOSITION 26.   Confidence in religious explanations will increase to the degree that people have **mystical experiences.**

Definition 20.   **Mystical experiences** are some sense of contact, however fleeting, with a god or gods.

This addition to the theory was proposed by Lawrence Young, who noted that a "religious experience [may be] understood to demonstrate unobservable realities such as the existence of God or of life beyond the grave," and to thereby offset the potential "risk" involved in religious promises (1997, 142).

Events qualifying as mystical experiences differ greatly according to the intensity and intimacy of the contact (Stark 1965), and they vary correspondingly in their impact on confidence. But even the least intense mystical experience constitutes a "small miracle" and provides recipients with personal confirmation of their religious explanations (Neitz and Spickard 1990; Howell 1997). For example, during his encounter with the "Madonna of O'Hare," Andrew Greeley did not ever believe that the young woman and child he saw in the Chicago airport *were* the Madonna and Child, but seeing them evoked a flood of memory and emotions involving the Christmas story in a powerful reaffirmation of faith (1995, 27–28). Consider the impact on individual faith when people believe they are encountering the actual Madonna (see, e.g., Zimdars-Swartz 1991).

Although mystical experiences do occur among the mentally ill and are sometimes caused by fasting or drugs, the overwhelming majority happen to normal, sane, sober people (Stark 1965; 1971; 1992b; Stark and Bainbridge 1997). Indeed, there is an immense body of evidence suggesting that quite ordinary mental phenomena can be experienced as some sort of mystical or religious episode involving contact with the supernatural being (Hood 1985) and that many (perhaps even most) people in most societies have such experiences (Greeley 1975; Gallup International 1984; Yamane and Polzer 1994). More dramatically, trances, seizures, glossolalia, and other remarkable symptoms of contact with the divine occur, not only in simple, preliterate societies (Norbeck 1961, 83–100), but even among well-educated members of advanced industrial societies (Neitz 1987; Poloma 1987; Yamane and Polzer 1994; Goldman 2000). Not surprisingly, such occurrences are taken as direct evidence of the truth of religious explanations. As a young Catholic student said during a class discussion, "How do I know Mary hears my prayers? I've seen her!"

The testimonial is a primary means by which people communicate their confidence in religion. In addition to asserting their personal certainty about otherworldly rewards, people often enumerate miracles—how they recovered from cancer, overcame alcoholism or drug abuse, became reliable and faithful spouses, survived a catastrophic accident, or had their prayers for a dying child answered—to demonstrate that a religion "works," that its promises come true. And like the young Catholic student mentioned above, they also testify about their own mystical experiences as proof that religious explanations are valid. In the case of groups that engage in various forms of collective "ecstatic" experiences, they offer one another direct *demonstrations* of the existence of a god or gods (Neitz 1987; Poloma 1987).

Testimonials are especially effective when they come from a trusted source. Thus, friends are more persuasive than acquaintances, and testimonials are even more persuasive when those testifying have little to gain (and perhaps much to lose) thereby. For this reason, laity are often more persuasive than ecclesiastics, since the latter often have a vested interest in promoting religious commitment. Indeed:

PROPOSITION 27.   Confidence in the explanations offered by a religion will be greater to the extent that its ecclesiastics display levels of commitment greater than that expected of followers.

There are several ways in which ecclesiastics can demonstrate superior commitment. They can *do more* or they can *do without* more. Ecclesiastics do more by excelling in objective forms of commitment. For example, spirit baptism (speaking in tongues) is required in order to become an Assemblies of God minister, but is not required of members (Poloma 1989). Of perhaps even greater impact is the extent to which ecclesiastics do without by making personal sacrifices. Celibacy and poverty are common forms of sacrifice, and to the extent that ecclesiastics are known to pay these costs on behalf of their faith, they will have more influence.

This conclusion may seem inconsistent with the general prevalence of rich priests serving opulent temples. But what has too long been overlooked is that when this is the case, there tends also to be a relatively low level of mass commitment and a quite high level of antagonism to ecclesiastics. The clergy in modern Scandinavia and Germany are probably the most highly paid in the world, and nowhere is organized religious participation lower, although subjective commitment, in terms of belief in basic religious concepts, remains high. Public antagonism to priestly luxury surely played an important role in both the Reformation and the Counter-Reformation. And while we still admire the luxurious beauty of Greek and Roman temples, it should be remembered that they did not reflect widespread, positive public sentiments, as the many blasphemous graffiti uncovered on the walls of Pompeii demonstrate (MacMullen 1981). Or, to shift to very different settings, in his classic study *Primitive Religion*, Paul Radin remarked on "the average man's … jealousy of the shaman's economic security … [and] his resentment at the fees he is forced to pay" ([1937] 1957, 105).

The practice of burnt offerings arose as a way of assuring people that their sacrifices went to the gods, not to priests who ate the sacrificial animals on behalf of the gods. Indeed, other things being equal, well-paid clergy are never a match for lay preachers or impoverished ascetics in head-to-head credibility contests. As Walter Map observed, after seeing Waldensian representatives who appeared in Rome in 1170: "They go about two by two, barefoot, clad in woolen garments, owning nothing, holding all things in common like the Apostles.... [I]f we admit them, we shall be driven out" (in Johnson 1976, 251). Indeed, proposition 27 explains why a powerful ascetic current persists in all religious traditions—it offers competitive advantages vis-à-vis credibility. This does not mean that ecclesiastics cannot effectively motivate their flocks unless they sacrifice, but those who do not must be able to offset this by demonstrating a high level of commitment in other ways—often by very effective displays of *subjective* commitment.

Finally, this entire line of theorizing leads to this proposition:

PROPOSITION 28. Vigorous efforts by religious organizations are required to motivate and sustain high levels of individual religious commitment.

When religion is anchored in stable social groups, people are able collectively to maximize their confidence in religious explanations and in the security of otherworldly rewards, and also effectively to reinforce one another's commitment. Put another way, as we define it, a stack of books or a few pamphlets in the library qualify as a religion, but these systems of explanations only come to life when they are embodied in collective activity.

CONCLUSION

Nowhere in this chapter do we suggest that religion is a universal aspect of human societies. Obviously, belief in the supernatural is very common, and Ruth Benedict may well have been correct in claiming it to be present in all known cases. However, having rejected the circularity of the functionalist claim that religion is whatever integrates societies, and is therefore universal, we are quite willing to leave open the possibility that irreligious societies could exist. We entirely agree with Melford Spiro (1966, 89) that it might be of immense scholarly value to find atheistic societies. Indeed, Mary Douglas (1975, 76–77) has suggested that in fact some premodern societies may not have had religion, but that reports of this have been discarded as incompetent by an anthropology committed a priori to the axiom that all societies do have religions.

A theory of religion based on reason and choice stands in opposition to the long-held social scientific view that such a theory makes no sense, because the phenomenon itself is irrational. In chapter 1, we examined evidence to the contrary. Here we would like to also note that many studies based on field observations in a modern context note the rationality of religious people (Warner 1988; Barker 1984; Neitz 1987; Poloma 1987; Davidman 1991; Howell 1997; Goldman 2000). This is surely not to say that religion is true, for that is as beyond science as is proof that religion is false. But, it is to say that people go about being religious in much the same way that they go about everything else.

We have attempted to demonstrate that point by showing that it is possible to produce an adequate micro theory of religion based on rational assumptions. The single difference we acknowledge between exchanges involving only humans and exchanges when one of the partners is a god is that the latter can involve far more valuable payoffs. Aside from that, in their dealings with the gods, people bargain, shop around, procrastinate, weigh costs and benefits, skip installment payments, and even cheat. Blind faith indeed!

CHAPTER 5

Religious Choices
Conversion and Reaffiliation

Even in tiny, preliterate societies, people have religious choices. The most obvious of these is whether to be religious at all, and some people in all societies opt for irreligion. But even people who do choose to be religious must select a mode of religious expression from the available options. In complex societies, the range of possible religious choices is usually very substantial, but even in preliterate groups, religious factions are common and new religious movements often arise, hence people must decide whether to shift their commitment or stick with tradition.

In this chapter we attempt to explain why and how these sorts of religious choices are made. To do so, we must identify two basic varieties of choice: *conversion* and *reaffiliation*.

Definition 21. **Conversion** refers to shifts across religious traditions.

We reserve the term "conversion" for "long-distance" shifts in religious allegiance, those involving a shift across traditions, as from Judaism or Roman paganism to Christianity, from Christianity to Hinduism, or from the religion of the Nuer to Islam.

Definition 22. **Reaffiliation** refers to shifts within religious traditions.

Usually, when people switch from one religious group to another, nothing so dramatic as conversion is involved. Rather than shifting their religious tradition, most of the time, people merely join a new group within their prior tradition, as when Baptists become Catholics, or Sunni Muslims become Shi'ites.

As we shall see, the process of reaffiliation is very similar to the process involved in conversion—although it is far more frequent and much less disruptive than conversion in terms of the costs to the individual and the group. However, even if it occurs far more often than does conversion, in most places and at most times, there is relatively little reaffiliation taking place either. Even in the extremely diverse, unregulated, and very competitive American religious economy, most people remain within the religious organization into which they were born, and most of those who do shift from one organization to another remain within the religious tradition into which they were born—even including conversions across the Christian-Jewish divide, fewer than 1 percent of Americans convert. But, even if conversions are relatively rare, it is these shifts across traditions that are the more dramatic and generate the greater amount of conflict. And those infrequent times when rates of conversion are high also are times of immense social and culture upheaval. So, to begin this chapter we focus on the question: Why and how do people sometimes choose to embrace a new faith?

DOCTRINAL APPEAL

The explanations of conversion that dominated social science until recently all share with the explanations favored by religious scholars the assumption that people convert primarily because they are attracted to particular new doctrines—disagreement concerns the role of rationality in this attraction. Social scientists have often traced the appeal of religious doctrines to the irrational and frequently subconscious deprivations and fears said to afflict converts. Religionists stress the role of reason when converts recognize the theological virtues of one doctrine over another.

In similar fashion, both social scientists and religionists have relied on doctrinal appeal to explain spontaneous, mass conversions. Here too the split is over rationality, inasmuch as social scientists have asserted the essential irrationality of such collective behavior (see Turner and Killian 1987), often stressing "herd instincts" (Trotter 1919) "contagious crowd psychology" (Le Bon 1896) the "collective consciousness" (Durkheim, 1915), or the "collective unconscious," which Sigmund Freud (1922) believed to be the source of "psychical epidemics, of historical mass convulsions" (in Jones 1953, 184). In contrast, religionists attribute mass conversions to an effective prophet or preacher who exposes people to the light of truth and logic. For example, for Christian scholars, the oldest and still dominant explanation of the rise of Christianity is that the Greco-Roman world was saved by mass conversions in response to public preaching that led reasonable people to draw reasonable conclusions (Eusebius [ca. 325] 1965; Harnack 1908; MacMullen 1984).

Later in this chapter, we analyze mass conversions more carefully and suggest that they are mythical. Before doing so, however, we shall begin by assessing the role of rationality in conversion by summarizing what social scientists actually know about this phenomenon, as opposed to what is claimed about it by those who have never seen it happen.

NETWORKS AND CONVERSION

In the early 1960s, John Lofland and Rodney Stark were the first social scientists actually to go out and watch people convert to a new religious movement (Lofland and Stark 1965; Lofland 1966). Up to that time, the most popular social scientific explanation of conversion involved the pairing of deprivation with ideological (or theological) appeal. That is, one examined the doctrines of a group to see what kinds of deprivation they addressed and then concluded— *mirabile dictu!*—that converts suffered from those deprivations (see Glock 1964). As an example of this approach, since Christian Science promised to restore health, it was argued that its converts must disproportionately be drawn from among those with chronic health problems, or at least those who suffer from hypochondria. Of course, one might as plausibly argue the reverse: that only people in excellent health could long hold to the Christian Science doctrine that illness is mental. Such a debate cannot be settled in a library.

Consequently, Lofland and Stark were determined to watch people go through the process of conversion and try to discover what really was involved. Moreover, they wanted to watch conversion, not simply reaffiliation or an increase in an individual's level of commitment. That is, they wanted to look at people who were making a major religious shift, as from Christianity to Hinduism, rather than examine how Episcopalians became Presbyterians or how lifelong Christians got themselves born again. Although of considerable interest, the latter questions were not Lofland and Stark's interests at the time.

Lofland and Stark also wanted a group that was both small enough for two observers to provide adequate surveillance and new enough to be in an early and optimistic phase of growth. After sifting through many deviant religious groups in the San Francisco Bay Area, they came upon a group of about a dozen young adults who had just moved to San Francisco from Eugene, Oregon. The group was led by Dr. Young Oon Kim, a Korean woman who had once been a professor of religion at Ewha University in Seoul. The movement she served was based in Korea, and in January 1959, she had arrived in Oregon to launch a mission to America. Dr. Kim and her young followers were the very first American members of the Unification Church, who later came to be widely known in the mass media as the "Moonies."

Although the Unificationists assert that they are fully within the Christian tradition, many of their teachings are based on new revelations received by the Reverend Sun M. Moon. Among these are doctrines concerning the role of Moon as the Lord of the Second Advent, as the new messiah sent to complete the tasks of full human redemption left undone by Jesus. Consequently, the Unificationists are perceived by most Christian leaders as representing a new, heretical religious tradition, and Christians who join thus qualify as converts.

As Lofland and Stark settled back to watch people convert to this group, the first thing they discovered was that all of the current members were united by close ties of friendship *predating* their contact with Dr. Kim. Indeed, the first three converts had been young housewives who were next-door neighbors who became friends of Dr. Kim's after she rented a room in the home of one of them. Subsequently, one of the husbands joined, followed by one of his friends from work. When Lofland and Stark arrived to study them, the group had never yet succeeded in attracting a stranger.

The sociologists also found it interesting that although all the converts were quick to describe how empty and desolate their spiritual lives had been prior to their conversion, many claimed that they had not been particularly interested in religion before. "If anybody had said I was going to join up and become a missionary I would have laughed my head off," one young man reported. "I had no use for church at all."

Lofland and Stark also found it instructive that during most of her first year in America, Dr. Kim had tried to spread her message directly by talks to various groups and by sending out many press releases. Later, in San Francisco, the group also tried to attract followers through radio spots and by renting a hall in which to hold public meetings. But these methods yielded nothing. As time passed, however, Lofland and Stark were able to observe people actually become Unificationists. The first few converts were old friends or relatives of members who came from Oregon for a visit. Subsequent converts were people who formed close friendships with one or more members of the group.

Eventually, Lofland and Stark realized that of all the people the Unificationists encountered in their efforts to spread their faith, the only ones who joined were those *whose interpersonal attachments to members overbalanced their attachments to nonmembers.* In part this is because, as noted in Proposition 22, social networks make religious beliefs plausible and *new* social networks thereby make *new* religious beliefs plausible. In addition, social networks also reward people for conforming—in this case by converting. In effect, conversion is seldom about seeking or embracing an ideology; it is about bringing one's religious behavior into alignment with that of one's friends and family members.

This is simply an application of the highly respected control theory of deviant behavior, which is based on the rational actor premise (Toby 1957; Hirschi 1969; Stark and Bainbridge [1987] 1996; Gottfredson and Hirschi 1990). Rather than asking why people deviate, why they break laws and norms, control theorists ask, why does anyone ever conform? Their answer is posed in terms of *stakes in conformity.* That is, rather than arguing that people are driven to deviance to compensate for various deprivations, control theory postulates that people conform when they believe they have more to lose by being detected in deviance than they stand to gain from the deviant act. Some people deviate, while others conform, because people differ in their stakes in conformity. That is, some people simply have far less to lose than do others.

A major stake in conformity consists of our attachments to others. Most of us conform in order to retain the good opinion of our friends and family. But some people lack attachments. Their rates of deviance are much higher than are those of people with an abundance of attachments.

Becoming a Unificationist today is an act of deviance, as was becoming a Christian in the first century. Such conversions violate norms defining legitimate religious affiliations and identities. Lofland and Stark saw many people who spent some time with the Unificationists and expressed considerable interest in their doctrines, but who never joined. In every instance these people had many strong attachments to nonmembers who did not approve of the group. Of those who did join, many were newcomers to San Francisco whose attachments were all to people far away. As they formed strong friendships with group members, these were not counterbalanced, because distant friends and families had no knowledge of the conversion in process. In several instances, a parent or sibling came to San Francisco intending to intervene after having learned of the conversion. Those who lingered eventually joined up too. Keep in mind that becoming a Unificationist may have been regarded as deviant by outsiders, but it was an act of conformity for those whose most significant attachments were to Unificationists.

During the three decades since Lofland and Stark first published their conclusion that attachments lie at the heart of conversion, and that conversion therefore tends to proceed along social networks formed by interpersonal attachments, many others have found the same to be true in an immense variety of religious groups all around the world. A study based on Dutch data (Kox, Meeus, and t'Hart 1991) cites twenty-five additional empirical studies supporting the initial finding. And that list is far from complete.

Let us analyze these findings more closely and formulate some propositions about religious choices.

CHOICE AND CAPITAL

The first proposition in our theory (chapter 4) notes that people attempt to make rational choices, which substantially expands the principle of micro economics that people attempt to maximize gain. As used in economics, maximization usually involves capital and the attempt to acquire the most while expending the least. Here we shall expand upon this usage to examine far more general forms of capital: the social and the religious.

Definition 23.   **Social capital** consists of interpersonal attachments.

The word "capital" is used to note that our relationships with others represent very substantial investments of time, energy, emotion, and even material. Moreover, we can draw upon this capital in times of need—our friends will rally to our support. Put another way, most people, most of the time, have accumulated a network of relationships that they regard as valuable. When people base their religious choices on the preferences of those to whom they are attached, they conserve (maximize) their social capital—they do not risk their attachments by failure to conform, and therefore they do not face the potential need to replace their attachments. This principle can be stated thus:

PROPOSITION 29.   In making religious choices, people will attempt to conserve their **social capital.**

Variations in the religious composition of their individual social networks and relationships influence what religious choices individuals select (Ellison 1995, 91). Generic variations in social capital result in the following propositions:

PROPOSITION 30.   Under normal circumstances, most people will neither convert nor reaffiliate.

Here we see why children usually adhere to the faith of their parents and relatives. By doing so, they protect their kinship ties. By remaining within the faith of those to whom one is attached, one maximizes social capital by retaining the good opinion of others. Research shows that most people do remain within the religious organization in which they were raised (Stark and Glock 1968; Kluegel 1980; Sherkat and Wilson 1995; Sherkat 1998a). The qualifying phrase "under normal circumstances" is included to recognize that social crises can greatly alter social networks so that most people are deficient in social ties. For example, the two great plagues that swept the Roman Empire in the second and third centuries left large numbers of people relatively unattached, their families and close friends having died or fled. This made conversion to Christianity not only less expensive in terms of social capital, but profitable for those who replaced their lost social ties to pagans with new ones to Christians (Stark 1996a).

PROPOSITION 31.   To the extent that people have or develop stronger attachments to those committed to a different version of their traditional religion, they will reaffiliate.

PROPOSITION 32.   To the extent that people have or develop stronger attachments to those committed to a religion in a different tradition, they will convert.

Marriage and migration are major factors tending to produce shifts in attachments. Newcomers must make new friends. Marriage tends to attach each spouse to a new kinship network. Age also plays a role, because people are more apt to marry or migrate when they are young, and many people shift their social networks upon leaving their parents' homes. Consequently, reaffiliation and conversion will be more prevalent among the geographically mobile, teenagers and young adults, at marriage and following a divorce. Each of these generalizations is supported by a wealth of research (Beit-Hallahmi and Argyle 1997; Wuthnow 1978; Tamney and Condran 1980; Tamney and Hassan 1987; Iannaccone 1990; Stark and Bainbridge 1985; 1997).

Thus far we have minimized the importance of religious factors in religious choices in order to emphasize the importance of social capital. But, in fact, selecting a religion is not exactly like joining a secular club. Belief is the central aspect of religion, and therefore one's beliefs do matter, but in a more subtle fashion than has been assumed by those who attribute religious choices to doctrinal appeal. To understand this point, it will be necessary to introduce the concept of religious capital (Iannaccone 1990).

The term "culture" refers to the complex pattern of living that directs human social life, the things each new generation must learn, and to which eventually they may add. That is, culture consists of the sum total of human creations—intellectual, technical, and moral. To become normal humans, all newborns must master the cultural package deemed essential in their society. As defined in chapter 4, religion is a purely cultural phenomenon, a set of very general explanations that justify and specify the terms of exchange with a god or gods. Hence, among the things each newborn needs to master is the cultural "bundle" composed of the religion of his or her parents. The process of acquiring culture is known as socialization. And when we are being socialized into our culture, we also are *investing* in it—expending time and effort in learning, understanding, and remembering cultural material. For example, persons raised to be Christians have accumulated a substantial store of Christian culture: not only doctrines, but prayers, hymns, rituals, history, and personal memories. The French sociologist Pierre Bourdieu (1984) coined the term "cultural capital" to identify the investments or sunk costs that culture represents to each individual. Thus, people tend to stay put and to not migrate or emigrate, not only to protect social capital, but also to protect their cultural capital. For example, if one is already proficient in French, one maximizes one's cultural capital by remaining within a French-speaking community rather than moving and having to invest in learning a new language and all of the other essential parts of a new culture. By the same token, if one is already proficient in Roman Catholicism, one maximizes religious capital by remaining within the bosom of the Catholic Church (Iannaccone 1990).

Definition 24.   **Religious capital** consists of the degree of mastery of and attachment to a particular religious culture.

Religious capital has two parts, which can be roughly identified as culture and emotions. To participate fully in any religion requires mastery of a lot of culture: how and when to make the sign of the cross, whether and when to say Amen, the words to liturgies and prayers, passages of scripture, stories and history, music, even jokes. Moreover, through practice (especially with others), one ordinarily infuses religious culture with emotions, such as in the common expression "It just wouldn't be Christmas without...." Over time these emotional bonds tend to become intrinsic to one's biography. Indeed, as stressed in chapter 4, the effects of religious activities such as prayer, rituals, miracles, and mystical experiences build up over a lifetime, not only increasing confidence in the truth of a religion, but strengthening emotional ties to a specific bundle of religious culture. It is these emotional and cultural investments built up over time that constitute religious capital.

It is impossible to transfer all of one's religious capital, and quite difficult to transfer many portions of it. That is what gives stability to the religious life.

PROPOSITION 33.   In making religious choices, people will attempt to conserve their religious capital.

When faced with making religious choices, people will attempt to save as much of their religious capital as they can and to expend as little investment in new capital as possible.

A number of additional propositions follow:

PROPOSITION 34.   The greater their religious capital, the less likely people are either to reaffiliate or to convert.

Generally speaking, the greater their commitment to their original religious heritage, the greater the store of religious capital people will have amassed. Hence, the more they have invested in a faith, the more they have at risk should they change faiths. Looking at this from a slightly different direction, Darren Sherkat (1997) has noted that the more actively and the longer people practice a religion, the stronger their preferences for that religion—preference deepens with additional consumption. Thus, people who are deeply committed to any particular faith do not go out and join some other faith. For example, Mormon missionaries who called upon the Unificationists were immune to conversion, despite forming warm relationships with several members. Indeed, the Unificationist who previously had "no use for church at all" was typical. Converts were not former atheists, but they were essentially unchurched, and many had not paid any particular attention to religious questions. Unificationists quickly learned that they were wasting their time at church socials or frequenting denominational student centers. They did far better in places where they came in contact with the uncommitted.

Research confirms that converts are overwhelmingly recruited from the ranks of those lacking a prior religious commitment or having only a nominal connection to a religious group (Stark and Bainbridge 1980a; 1985; [1987] 1996). The same holds for reaffiliation. Thus, in the United States, the single most unstable "religion" of origin is "no religious preference." Whereas the great majority of those raised with a religious affiliation retain that affiliation, the great majority of those who say that their family had no religion join a religion as adults (Kluegel 1980; Sherkat and Wilson 1995; Stark 1998d). In his long-term study of a Mexican millenarian colony of "traditional Catholics" (who reject the Vatican II reforms), Miguel C. Leatham (1997, 299) found that those who joined had been "quite marginal Catholics at the time of recruit-

ment," with "extremely low mass attendance"; some had not even been baptized. Thus, a basis for these conversions and reaffiliations is that a lack of prior
religious commitment makes it inexpensive (in terms of religious capital) to take
up a new faith.

This explanation contradicts the more conventional interpretation that it is a
"felt need" for religion that impels the unaffiliated to faith. In fact, converts very
seldom are religious seekers, and conversion is seldom the culmination of a conscious search—most converts do not so much find a new faith as the new faith
finds them. Had social scientists not gone out and watched people as they converted, this point might well have been missed entirely, because when people
retrospectively describe their conversions, they tend to put the stress on theology. Many studies of conversion have noted that one of its primary aspects is
the "reconstruction" of the convert's "biography" to show how conversion was
the end result of a self-conscious search for truth. This is neither duplicitous nor
irrational. Rather, having embraced a new faith, people look back over their
prior lives and reinterpret various past events and thoughts in light of the present (Beckford 1978; Snow and Phillips 1980; Snow and Machalek 1983; Greil
and Rudy 1984; Staples and Mauss 1987; Machalek and Snow 1993). For example, when asked why they converted, Unificationists invariably noted the irresistible appeal of the Divine Principles (the group's scripture), suggesting that
only the blind could reject such obvious and powerful truths. In making these
claims, converts implied (and often stated) that their path to conversion was the
end product of a search for faith. But Lofland and Stark knew better, because
they had met them well before they had learned to appreciate these doctrines,
before they had learned how to testify to their faith, back when they were not
seeking faith at all—when most of them regarded the religious beliefs of their
new set of friends as quite odd. Research by Hsing-Kuang Chao (in press) helps
to clarify how doctrine retrospectively becomes the central factor in conversion.
He studied a small Taiwanese Protestant sect group in Los Angeles whose
members are converts from the ranks of Chinese non-Christians. The group
publishes a very lengthy church bulletin, which for a number of years gave detailed accounts of each new convert's journey to faith, invariably emphasizing
the role of doctrine, but also offering much secondary information about the
social relations by which the person was recruited. Eventually, however, the flow
of converts became too large for such lengthy published accounts. In editing
them down, the bulletin editors excised all mention of social relations, leaving
only doctrinal appeals. They did so, not to deceive, but to save space for what
they believed to be the more important factor. When converts "reconstruct"
their biographies, the same principles come into play. That is, because the
essence of religion is a belief system, adherents really have little choice other
than to make doctrine the explicit center of attention. But that doesn't prevent
outside observers from recognizing that converts typically have a great deal still
to learn about doctrines subsequent to their initial professions of faith.

Indeed, this prompted Leatham (1997, 295) to distinguish two stages in the process of taking on a new religious identity: recruitment and conversion. Based on several years of fieldwork in the Mexican millenarian colony mentioned above, he discovered that doctrine was "a minimal or negligible" factor in "decisions to join." Rather, people were drawn to the group through their network ties to members, thus becoming recruits, a stage of belonging prior to knowing much about what the group believed. Leatham defined conversion as the process of mastering the group's religious culture. The path to full membership thus began with recruitment and passed through conversion.

PROPOSITION 35.   Reaffiliation will be far more prevalent than conversion (under normal conditions).

This reflects that fact that reaffiliation is far less costly in terms of religious capital.

PROPOSITION 36.   When people reaffiliate, they will tend to select an option that maximizes their conservation of religious capital.

People raised in one Jewish Hasidic body are more apt to shift to another Hasidic group than to join a Conservative Synagogue, are more likely to join a Conservative than a Reform Synagogue, and are far more apt to become Reform Jews than Unitarians.

The empirical literature is entirely supportive of this proposition. When they do shift their affiliations, most people switch to a religious body very similar to the one in which they were raised. That is, people raised in an evangelical Protestant denomination tend to switch to another, a process that Reginald Bibby and Merlin Brinkerhoff (1973) have described as "the circulation of saints." Many subsequent studies have found that the tendency to select a new church that very closely resembles one's previous affiliation holds across the theological spectrum, for that is the choice that maximizes the conservation of religious capital (Ellison and Sherkat 1990; Sherkat 1993; Sherkat and Wilson 1995; Sherkat 1998a). We pursue this in chapter 8.

PROPOSITION 37.   When people convert, they will tend to select an option that maximizes their conservation of religious capital.

It may be helpful to imagine a young person from a Christian background and living in a Christian society who is deciding whether to join the Mormons or the Hare Kishnas. By becoming a Mormon, this person retains his or her entire Christian culture and simply adds to it. Noting that the person has copies of the Old Testament and the New Testament, Mormon missionaries will suggest that an additional scripture, the *Book of Mormon*, is needed to complete the set. In contrast, Hare Krishna missionaries note that the person has the *wrong* scriptures and must discard the Bible in exchange for the Bhagavad Gita. The principle of the conservation of religious capital predicts (and explains) why the overwhelming majority of converts in a Christian context will select the Mormon rather than the Hare Kishna option (see Stark 1996b).

Similarly, in a study of evangelical Chinese Christian churches in the United States, Fenggang Yang (1998) found the "churches emphasizing the compatibility of Confucianism and Protestantism" and in this way helping converts preserve their cultural capital. "Because most Chinese regard Confucianism not as a religion, but as a traditional philosophy of life, evangelical Chinese Christians can integrate Confucian moral values without falling into a stigmatized syncretism," Yang writes (1998, 253). This allowed the Chinese churches to retain cherished Confucian values about family and ascetic ethics and still incorporate Christianity's teachings on the supernatural. Evangelical Christianity provided a new foundation for a long-standing morality and allowed a substantial conservation of cultural capital.

Our final propositions concern marriage and religious choices. On the basis of the conservation of both cultural and religious capital:

PROPOSITION 38.   Most people will marry within their religious group.

This is especially the case in social settings where there is a great deal of conflict among religious groups, and for individuals where none of the available alternative choices closely resembles his or her religion of origin—a limiting factor for Roman Catholics as compared with Protestants, for example.

PROPOSITION 39.   In mixed religious marriages, spouses usually will be of very similar religious backgrounds, belonging to groups within the same religious tradition.

Thus, in rising order of frequency: Baptists will marry Nazarenes, and Presbyterians will marry Episcopalians; Protestants will marry Protestants; Christians will marry Christians. These patterns are well known on the basis of research in both the United States and Canada (Johnson 1980; Lehrer and Chiswick 1993). Also pertinent here is the literature on divorce and intermarriage, which shows that marital instability increases with the dissimilarity of the initial religions of the spouses (Becker, Landis, and Michael 1977; Lehrer and Chiswick 1993). For example, a marriage between a Mormon and a non-Mormon is three times more apt to end in divorce than is a Mormon's marriage to another Mormon.

PROPOSITION 40.   Mixed religious marriages are more likely to the degree that one or both spouses lack religious capital.

In one sense this is simply a variant on proposition 39, in that religious *similarity* can be approached through *lack* of religion. An uncommitted Jew is more similar to an uncommitted Episcopalian than committed members of these two groups are to one another. Similarly, if one spouse is uncommitted, he or she is less different from a religious partner than is a potential spouse who is committed to a very different religion. Finally, then:

PROPOSITION 41.   When mixed religious marriages occur, the couple maximize their religious capital when the partner with the lower level of commitment reaffiliates or converts to the religion of the more committed partner.

This is a restatement of what has come to be known as Greeley's Law: "[T]here is a tendency for religious change ... to take place in association with marriage, so that at least denominational homogeneity is guaranteed to the family. Normally the change is in the direction of the denomination of the more devout partner" (Greeley 1982, 127). So far as we are able to determine, no actual research has been done on this proposition.

This entire discussion of social, cultural, and religious capital investments provides a compelling explanation of why ethnicity and religion frequently combine to form religious organizations that seem impervious to reaffiliation and conversion. These overlapping investments frequently make an investment in one an investment in all. When members make heavy investments in their group's religious and cultural capital (e.g., language, rituals, saints, and songs specific to their religio-ethnic group) and their interpersonal attachments are primarily with others holding the same investments, any attempts to abandon either the religion or the ethnicity will result in heavy personal losses. Moreover, in many environments, these ethnic and religious commitments are also wedded to strong political positions forming an allegiance that lasts for centuries.

International and historical examples of the durability and intensity of these allegiances abound. Indeed, even a cursory understanding of recent events in the Middle East and eastern Europe requires an awareness of the social, cultural, and religious capital investments of the people concerned.

These overlapping allegiances also help to explain why religious reaffiliation and conversion will increase for ethnic congregations when the members' investments in religious and cultural capital decline. Over the past century, this has been especially evident in ethnic congregations in the United States when second and third generations abandon the use of their native tongue, give less attention to their unique rituals or patron saints, and move out of the ethnic neighborhood. Each of these changes increases contacts and affiliations outside the group and reduces the investments members make in the religious and cultural capital of past generations. "First they leave the party, then they leave the faith!" Irish American Catholics would lament when hearing of a fellow member becoming a Republican in the early twentieth century.

MASS CONVERSION

Within the subfield of the social sciences dealing with "collective behavior," there is an extensive literature that attempts to explain why mass conversions occur, why people in substantial numbers suddenly take up a new faith without any apparent prior period of preparation. This entire approach suffers from two equally fatal defects. First, what are called theories are little more than ugly imputations. What was explained by Gustave Le Bon when he wrote that riots occur when "the mind of the crowd" takes over? Two leaders in the field of collective behavior, Ralph H. Turner and Lewis M. Killian (1987, 5), note the contribution made by Everett Martin (1920) when "he coined the memorable saying that the crowd consists of 'people going crazy together.'" Memorable perhaps, but utterly uninformative. The second defect is that while many people have seen riots, no one has seen a mass conversion—or at least we have no credible firsthand accounts.[1] All we really have are conclusions that mass conversions *must have* taken place. The most famous of these conclusions credits mass conversions as playing a major role in the rise of Christianity. Let us pause and evaluate this conclusion.

From earliest days, mass conversions are central to the Christian story: crowds gathered, listened, marveled, and were saved. Thus, Acts 2:41 reports that after Peter preached to a multitude "there were added that day about three thousand souls." Writing in about 325, Eusebius (3.37.3) tells us that "at first hearing whole multitudes in a body eagerly embraced in their souls piety towards the Creator of the universe."

That mass conversions built Christianity has seemed obvious. Adolf von Harnack put it plainly: how else can we understand the "inconceivable rapidity" of Christian growth and "astonishing expansion" of the movement (1908, 2: 335–36)? Indeed, Harnack (ibid., n. 335) reminded his readers of St. Augustine's insight that the greatest miracle of all would have been for Christianity to grow as rapidly as it did without the aid of miracles. In his distinguished study *Christianizing the Roman Empire,* Ramsay MacMullen also stresses the arithmetical necessity for mass conversions. Because "very large numbers are obviously involved," Christian growth could not have been limited to an individual mode of conversion, but obviously required "successes en masse" (1984, 29).

This is all very troublesome, because informed social scientific opinion dismisses the possibility of spontaneous mass conversions and rejects doctrinal appeal as the primary cause of conversion (Machalek and Snow 1993). That is, from the perspective of the new paradigm, the kind of mass conversions described by Eusebius and accepted by historians ever since would indeed be miraculous. And if the rise of Christianity can be explained only by resort to miracles, then social science would seem to have little to contribute.

Fortunately, the "facts" justifying the miraculous assumption are wrong. The only reason people believed that there was an arithmetical need for mass conversion was because until recently (Stark 1996a), no one had ever bothered to do the actual arithmetic. A brief summary suffices here.

There is general agreement among scholars that Christians in the Greco-Roman world numbered somewhere between five and seven million in the year 300. How this total was reached from a tiny starting point of, say, 1,000 Christians in the year 40 is the arithmetical challenge. At first glance, growth of this magnitude might seem a miraculous achievement. But suppose we assume that the Christian rate of growth during this period was similar to that of the Mormon rate of growth over the past century, which has been approximately 40 percent per decade (Stark 1984; 1996b). If the early Christians were able to match the Mormon growth rate, then their "miracle" was fully accomplished in the time history allows. That is, from a starting point of 1,000 Christians in the year 40, a growth rate of 40 percent per decade (or 3.4 percent per year) results in a total of 6,299,832 Christians in the year 300. Moreover, because compounded rates result in exponential growth, there is a huge numerical increase from slightly more than a million Christians in the year 250 to more than six million in 300. This creates further confidence in the projections, because historians have long believed that a rapid increase in numerical growth occurred at this time (see Gager 1975). Clearly, then, the rise of Christianity could easily have been accomplished in accordance with our current understanding of why and how conversion takes place, and social science is sufficient unto the task at hand.

This account of the rise of Christianity is, of course, based on a rather sparse historical record. In contrast, the rise of Mormonism has been very carefully documented from the beginning. It too has grown very rapidly, and some have supposed that at least one mass conversion took place in Kirtland, Ohio, in 1830. It will be helpful, therefore, to pause here for an examination of the early days of Mormon growth. In doing so, we shall not merely show that what took place in Kirtland was not a mass conversion but examine how the Mormon experience illustrates and conforms to many of the propositions developed above.

THE NETWORK BASIS OF MORMON GROWTH

In 1823, in a farm home just outside Palmyra, New York, lived Joseph Smith, Sr., his wife Lucy Mack Smith, their six sons, Alvin (25), Hyrum (23), Joseph, Jr. (18), Samuel (15), William (12), and Don Carlos (7), and their three daughters, Sophronia (20), Catharine (11), and Lucy (2). They were by all accounts a close and loving family, greatly given to religious discussion and experimentation, having switched denominations repeatedly (Smith [1853] 1996; Bushman 1988; Berrett 1988; Backman 1988). In September 1823, Joseph Smith, Jr., had a vision during which the Angel Moroni revealed to him the existence of a set of golden plates on which was written a "Record" of events concerning Christ's visit to the New World, known today as *The Book of Mormon: Another Testament of Jesus Christ*. According to Joseph Smith, Jr., the next day he found the plates in the place identified by Moroni. But, having done so, he then disobeyed Moroni's injunction not to look directly upon the plates and suffered a severe physical shock. At this point, the angel reappeared, rebuked him for touching the plates, and told him he was forbidden from "bringing them forth" until he had demonstrated his willingness "to keep the commandments of God." Four years later, Smith finally was able to secure the plates, bringing them home inside a locked trunk, which could not be opened, because, as he reminded everyone, to look directly upon the plates could be fatal. He also claimed to be able to read the plates through the trunk and to translate them from reformed Egyptian by looking through two transparent stones, known as the Urim and Thummim. Smith thus began to translate the *Book of Mormon,* usually doing so orally in front of the family, which now included his wife Emma.

From his first report of meeting the Angel Moroni, the Smith family embraced young Joseph's revelations. Once the translation began, the family responded enthusiastically, and everyone was eager to hear each new installment. As the translated manuscript began to pile up, Joseph and Emma established their own household, and others outside the family began to learn about his activities. Among them were Joseph's longtime friend, neighbor, and sometime employer Martin Harris and Oliver Cowdery, a young schoolteacher who was rooming in the home of the senior Smiths and who learned about the ongoing translation process from long conversations with the prophet's mother, Lucy. Having been introduced to Joseph Smith, Jr., Cowdery volunteered to serve as his scribe to write down the translation as Smith dictated it.

Soon after meeting Joseph Smith, Jr., Cowdery formed a close friendship with David Whitmer. As work on the translation progressed, Cowdery sent Whitmer "a few lines of what they had translated" (Porter 1988, 75). David Whitmer shared these with his entire family, who responded with very great interest. Subsequently, Smith and Cowdery, and Smith's wife Emma, moved into the Whitmer home, where the manuscript was completed late in 1829. During this stay, Cowdery got to know Elizabeth Ann Whitmer, whom he later married. Figure 1 depicts the first 23 Mormons at the start of 1830, just before the official founding of the church. Counting in-laws, there were 11 Smiths, 10 Whitmers, Martin Harris, and Oliver Cowdery. This was, of course, only the start. By the end of the year, there were 280 Mormons. At the end of 1831, they numbered 680, and the next year, 2,661. By 1840, there were almost 17,000. But, this rapid growth was not less dependent on networks of kinship, neighbors, and friends. The first recruits beyond those listed in figure 1 consisted of "a few friends and neighbors" (Arrington and Bitton 1979, 21), including six members of the Jolly family, five Rockwells, and many relatives of the Smith family. As Richard L. Bushman notes, the Mormons "spread mainly along family lines. Not just brothers and sisters but cousins, in-laws, and uncles listened and believed.... The most remarkable collection of kin was the offspring and relatives of Joseph Knight, Sr., and his wife Polly Peck Knight" (1984, 151).

Joseph Knight's son Newell was a boyhood friend of Joseph Smith's, and the prophet enjoyed warm relations with the entire Knight family, who lived in nearby Colesville. Newell Knight attended the first meetings of the Mormon Church (initially called the Church of Christ) after it had been officially organ-

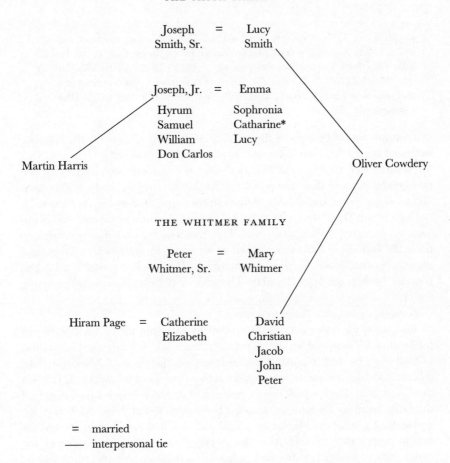

THE SMITH FAMILY

Joseph   =   Lucy
Smith, Sr.   Smith

Joseph, Jr. = Emma

Hyrum   Sophronia
Samuel   Catharine*
William   Lucy
Don Carlos

Martin Harris   Oliver Cowdery

THE WHITMER FAMILY

Peter   =   Mary
Whitmer, Sr.   Whitmer

Hiram Page = Catherine   David
               Elizabeth   Christian
                                 Jacob
                                 John
                                 Peter

=   married
———   interpersonal tie

* Also spelled Catherine and Katherine in some recent sources, but this is how her mother spelled it.

Figure 1. The First Mormons, 1830

ized at the start of April 1830, and in May he was baptized by David Whitmer. Then, in June:

> Joseph Smith, Oliver Cowdery, and John and David Whitmer went to Colesville, where Oliver baptized several people, including ... Joseph Knight, Sr., and his wife, Polly Peck Knight, Newell's parents ... Polly's brother, Hezekiah, and his wife, Martha Long Peck, were also baptized that day.... Also baptized at about that time was Emily Coburn, a sister of Newell Knight's wife, Sally. (Allen and Leonard 1992, 60)

Within nine months following the printing of the *Book of Mormon*, the Knights' extended family "accounted for sixty baptisms" (Bushman 1984, 151).

Nevertheless, all Mormon histories stress the immense significance of the conversion of more than 100 people in Kirtland, Ohio, an event said to have taken only several days and that seemed to come out of the blue. As Leonard J. Arrington and Davis Bitton describe it, "One of the most significant early conversions occurred in late 1830 when four missionaries who had been sent to meet the Indians in Missouri stopped at Kirtland, in northeastern Ohio, and there recruited Sidney Rigdon—a prominent Campbellite preacher who had recently broken off from the main Disciples of Christ movement—together with part of his congregation" (1979, 21).

Now, let us see what really took place.

Early in 1830, Parley P. Pratt signed over his farm outside Kirtland, Ohio, to his brother William and set out to preach the gospel. Trusting the Holy Ghost to lead him, he and Thankful, his bride of less than a year, boarded a lake schooner for Buffalo and there transferred to a canal boat bound for Albany via the Erie Canal. On the way, the 23-year-old Pratt suddenly felt called to get off the boat. Sending his wife on ahead, he disembarked at Newark, New York, and walked around until he found a local pastor who was willing to arrange for him to preach that evening. After the meeting that evening, a member of the congregation told Pratt he had acquired a strange volume, the *Book of Mormon,* that had just been published in nearby Palmyra. Pratt's religious background was ardently pre-millennial, and the reason he felt called to preach was because he was eagerly awaiting new prophesies. So he borrowed the book. Pratt was sufficiently impressed by what he read that he walked thirty miles to Palmyra to meet Joseph Smith (Pratt [1873] 1985).

Upon his arrival, he discovered that for the moment Smith was living in Harmony, Pennsylvania, so he began discussing the *Book of Mormon* with Smith's older brother Hyrum—they talked all night. Then Pratt walked back to Newark, where he was scheduled to preach again that night and the next. Meanwhile, he read the *Book of Mormon* during the day. On the third day, he decided he could preach no more, as he was not commissioned to preach this new faith. So he walked back to Hyrum Smith's house and requested baptism. Hyrum arranged for a gathering of the local community of saints the next evening in the home of Peter Whitmer, Sr. Pratt was deeply impressed to be in the very place where the translation had been completed and among persons whose names appeared in the front of the book as witnesses to the plates. He found the gathering to be "full of joy, faith, humility and charity" (Pratt [1873] 1985, 24), and the next day Pratt was baptized in Seneca Lake by Oliver Cowdery.

Although it is quite unnecessary for social theories to fit every single individual case, it will be useful to pause here and consider the case of Parley Pratt in light of our propositions about conversion. Pratt began preparing for his conversion long before he ever encountered the *Book of Mormon*. Under the guidance of his local pastor, Sydney Rigdon (of whom more later), he had felt called to go out to preach and to search for signs of the second advent. Unlike most converts, he was, in fact, a seeker. Moreover, his large stock of religious capital was contingent on his discovery of new tidings concerning the arrival of the millennium. But even with this expectation, he was not converted by a book. Had no one been home at the Smith residence when he arrived, he would not have become a Mormon, or at least not at this particular time. It was crucial that he formed a relationship with Hyrum Smith and subsequently was immersed (even if briefly) in the tightly knit network of Mormon founders. Moreover, it also was essential that this encounter came at a moment when Pratt was, at least situationally, very deficient in social capital. He had uprooted himself from Kirtland. Then he had sent his new wife off to her family, while he wandered among strangers in western New York. His meeting with Hyrum Smith thus offered the prospect, not only of enhanced religious capital, but of an immediate and very substantial increase in his social capital too.

Soon after Pratt's baptism, Joseph Smith had a revelation that it was time to dispatch missionaries to the Indians in Missouri. The missionary party was led by Oliver Cowdery and included Peter Whitmer, Jr., Ziba Peterson, and Parley Pratt. Before their departure, Pratt convinced the group that a fertile missionary opportunity awaited them along the way in Kirtland, where they were sure to get a favorable hearing from the local minister, and Pratt's mentor, Sidney Rigdon.

Sidney Rigdon was one of the most colorful characters in nineteenth-century American religious history (Van Wagoner 1994). An extraordinary preacher, he was equally extraordinary in his pursuit of religious novelty.[2] He began as an itinerant Baptist preacher, established congregations in Mentor and in Kirtland (neighboring towns in Ohio), and then was expelled by the Baptists in a dispute over infant damnation. After several years of working as a tanner with his brother-in-law, Rigdon became infatuated with the teachings of Alexander Campbell and resumed his ministry, managing to quickly rebuild his following in Mentor and Kirtland. When the Mormon party arrived in Kirtland, however, Rigdon had recently been expelled by Campbell because of his "organization of a communal society" (Bushman 1984, 174), the result of having met Robert Owen and being very taken with his New Harmony commune.

Although now without any denominational sanction, Rigdon still led a congregation made up of those who had followed him from the Baptists, and then into the Campbellites and out again—a testament to the strength of Rigdon's leadership. Lydia Partridge undoubtedly spoke for many of her fellow congregants when she explained that although she had joined the Campbellite Church, "she was in reality a 'Rigdonite'" (R. Anderson 1971, 490).

On October 28, 1830, Cowdery and Pratt called at the Rigdon home. "You brought truth to me, now I ask you as a friend to read this for my sake," Pratt told him (Van Wagoner 1994, 59). After reading for about an hour, Rigdon threw down the book, pronouncing it a "silly fabrication." But then he picked it up again and read all night. The next morning, Rigdon dropped in on a neighboring family during breakfast and told them he had been reading a fascinating book that might very well be a discovery of great importance that would usher in the Millennium (ibid., 49–64).

At this point, Rigdon agreed to let Pratt and Cowdery preach to his congregation. There was a very large turnout to hear these two young men, who claimed to be "special messengers of the Living God, sent to preach the gospel in its purity, as it was anciently preached by the Apostles" (ibid., 59). When they had finished, they asked Rigdon if he would like to comment. He told the congregation that this was information "of an extraordinary character" that "demanded their most serious consideration," as he was giving it his (ibid., 59; R. Anderson 1971, 483).

During the next few days Rigdon continued to read the *Book of Mormon* and to discuss it with Pratt and Cowdery. Cowdery took this opportunity to explain how he and others had been present during the translation process, and that Smith's behavior had been that of a reader, not a writer. The dictation came smoothly without false starts or long pauses (Bushman 1984, 98).[3] When Rigdon learned that Joseph Smith was not yet 25 and had had "hardly a common school education," he remarked, "[I]f that was all the education he had, he never wrote the book." It took another two weeks, but Rigdon eventually accepted the new faith as "of God" (R. Anderson 1971; Pratt [1873] 1985; Van Wagoner 1994; K. Anderson 1996).

Following some discussion of whether or not he needed to be rebaptized, Rigdon agreed to do so (R. Anderson 1971, 480). But first, he gathered his followers and devoted an emotional two-hour sermon to explaining why he was going to make a new commitment—he was so eloquent that many in the audience "melted into tears" (Pratt, quoted in R. Anderson 1971, 487). Then, the next morning, November 15, 1830, as a crowd looked on, Rigdon and his wife Phebe were baptized by Oliver Cowdery. Emerging from the river, Rigdon explained that he had never been able to satisfy his religious yearnings until that moment. Finally, he asked if anyone else would like to come forward. One man did and was baptized immediately. Rigdon called for more converts, and a few others came forward. There were even more baptisms the next day. Isaac Morley,[4] leader of "The Big Family," the utopian commune Rigdon had initiated and that had caused his dismissal from the Disciples of Christ, brought all seventeen members to be baptized (Van Wagoner 1994, 50; Allen and Leonard 1992, 64). This was a "family" in more than just name, inasmuch as it included Morley's wife Lucy and his three older daughters, his sister Diantha, her husband, Titus Billings, and several of their older children, and Lyman and Harriet Wight and several of their children. Other members of Rigdon's congregation also accepted baptism that day and the next—most of them coming forward in kinship clusters (Grandstaff and Backman 1990; Backman 1983). Before long there were about 130 Mormons in tiny Kirtland, amounting to about half of all the Mormons in the world (R. Anderson 1971, 478). It must be noted that Rigdon was not the only link to the congregation. Parley Pratt had many friends and relatives among them too, including his brother William (Pratt already had baptized his brother Orson before leaving New York).

Soon Sidney Rigdon went east and met Joseph Smith. They hit it off extremely well, and out of their conversations came the decision to consolidate the movement in Kirtland. Martin Harris led about 50 members from Palmyra, Newel Knight led about 70 of his kinfolk from Colesville, and the prophet's mother, Lucy Mack Smith, led a third group of about 80 from the Waterloo/Fayette area. Upon her arrival in Kirtland, Lucy lived for a time in Isaac Morley's communal dwelling. In 1833, the Mormons built their first temple in Kirtland.

By gathering in Kirtland, everyone maximized their social capital. Newcomers arrived as closely knit social networks, and by merging with the network of local converts and becoming part of the dominant social group in the Kirtland vicinity, they escaped the social disapproval they had suffered back home. The spate of marriages that took place during the next year suggest how rapidly social bonds intensified in the new Mormon community. Indeed, all subsequent Mormon migrations, culminating in the trek to Utah, aimed at preserving this level of community and local dominance. But, it was not just social capital that prompted and sustained conversion. For pre-millenarian Protestants, which most of them were, conversion involved only a modest investment in new religious capital, and we should not fail to recognize that sometimes people can find it very rewarding to make such investments. Here, finally, they possessed the eagerly awaited new tidings, and as it turned out, these included an exciting new history of the Western Hemisphere.

Even as the Mormon network became increasingly far-flung and their numbers grew rapidly, the importance of kinship ties did not decline. Rather, the underlying structure remained a conglomeration of various kinship networks, often interlocking, through which the church spread, as it had from Palmyra to Kirtland. It is worth considering several typical examples.

In April 1830, at about the same time that Parley Pratt was being baptized by Hyrum Smith and Oliver Cowdery, Samuel Smith met Phinehas Young in Mendon, New York, a town fifteen miles from Palmyra. Phinehas was a

Methodist circuit rider whose home was in Mendon. When Samuel Smith attempted to interest him in a copy of the *Book of Mormon*, he accepted, because he had heard about its contents from his sister Rhoda and her husband, John Greene, also a Methodist circuit rider. Rhoda had received a copy from Samuel Smith during a previous visit to Mendon. Phinehas wanted a copy so that he could prepare himself to refute it among his fellow Methodists, especially since the Greenes thought it had merit. Phinehas studied it for a week and could not find the errors he had anticipated. So he lent it to his father Joseph Young, who thought it "the greatest work ... he had ever seen," and then he gave it to his sister Fanny, who called it "a revelation" (Arrington 1985, 19–20). But nothing happened. The Youngs remained Methodists.

This underlines the principle that, by themselves, *scriptures do not make converts*. Despite their very positive reactions to the *Book of Mormon*, it required two more years of interacting with committed Mormons before the Youngs were ready to join. Then, in April 1832, John Young and his wife Hannah, four sons, three daughters-in-law, two daughters, and two sons-in-law were baptized as Mormons. A month later, two more of Joseph Young's daughters and their husbands were baptized. The next year, another Young son, daughter, and son-in-law were baptized. By building strong friendship ties to several members of one family, the Mormons thus gained twenty converts, including their eventual leader Brigham Young.

But there's more. Fanny Young's husband Roswell Murray's sister Vilate was married to Heber C. Kimball, who was also Brigham Young's closest friend; indeed, the Youngs and the Kimballs were cousins. The day after the first group of Youngs were baptized, all the Kimballs were too (Arrington 1985, 16, 28–32), and Brigham Young and Heber Kimball went on to lead the Mormon Church through its crucial first decades in Utah, Young as Smith's immediate successor and Kimball as his First Counselor. Not only were Brigham Young and Heber Kimball cousins, but both were distant cousins of Joseph Smith's, kinship ties of which they all were well aware (Quinn 1997, 165).

In 1837, Joseph Smith directed that missionaries should be sent to Great Britain. The British mission was so successful that for a period, beginning in the late 1840s, there were more Mormons in the British Isles than in the United States, despite large-scale Mormon immigration from Britain. In fact, the combination of Mormons in Britain and first-generation British Mormon immigrants made up the majority of all Mormons from 1845 until 1895 (Stark 1998a). Many have suggested that economic and social conditions in Great Britain at this time created a receptive audience for the Mormon message (Arrington 1985; Allen, Esplin, and Whittaker 1992; Stark, 1998a), but our interest is limited to the network aspects. How did the missionaries get started? Who would listen? Who had reason to trust them?

After landing in Liverpool, the Mormon missionary party went directly to the textile-manufacturing city of Preston in Lancashire. There they were given access to the pulpits of three nonconformist churches, from which for several weeks they freely preached the Mormon doctrine, to great effect. Joseph Fielding was the missionary who had made these arrangements well in advance of their departure. The three English pastors who opened their pulpits to the Mormon missionaries were Fielding's brother and his two brothers-in-law (Allen, Esplin, and Whittaker 1992).

Even today, when there are more than ten million Mormons worldwide, networks are the basis of conversion, as revealed in records kept by a Mormon mission president in 1981–82. When Mormon missionaries make cold calls, when they knock on the doors of strangers, this leads to a conversion once out of a thousand calls—and never immediately, only after a long series of contacts as a friendship is established. However, when missionaries make their first contact with a person in the home of a Mormon friend or relative of that person, this results in conversion 50 percent of the time (Stark and Bainbridge 1985). What is really going on in such instances is that the missionaries offer religious instruction to persons whose network ties already have inclined them to join. This pattern is not peculiar to Mormons; it is how all successful movements spread.

CHOICE OR COMPULSION?

Some readers, and especially social scientists devoted to the irrationality of religion, may wish to interpret the centrality of network relations for conversion as demonstrating that conversion is not based on rational choices. Evidently, then, most people do not convert as the end process of a search for a suitable faith, having carefully weighed the benefits of potential alternatives. Converts fail to realize the direction in which their continued association with members is leading. Conversion is really a matter of resocialization, rather than choice, and in that sense, converts are more or less passive victims of social processes beyond their grasp and control. Indeed, don't many religious groups use techniques known as "thought reform," "mind control," or "brainwashing" to compel conversions? It would be irresponsible of us to ignore these claims, especially since we regard them as the worst sort of spurious "science."

The term "brainwashing" was introduced in the 1950s to describe the indoctrination methods that Chinese and Korean communists used to elicit false confessions and political repudiations from prisoners of war. The method involved extreme and long-term coercion of prisoners—deprived of food, water, and sleep, often tortured, threatened with death, they were forced to act, speak, and *perhaps* even think in ways that bore little relationship to their original beliefs and commitments. It is very significant that fewer than 50 of more than 3,500

American servicemen exposed to "brainwashing" in Communist prison camps actually gave in, and of those who did, it is not clear that any actually came to believe the doctrines their captors tried to pound into them (Scheflin and Opton 1978; Anthony 1990).[5] However, brainwashing soon became a popular media concept and added to the plot possibilities of spy novels and movies, culminating in John Frankenheimer's *The Manchurian Candidate* (1962).

In the 1970s, Margaret Singer (1979) and several other scholars (see Robbins 1988, 72) reintroduced the term "brainwashing" to describe the recruitment practices of the so-called "cults"—religious groups outside of or somewhat marginal to the conventional American Judeo-Christian tradition, groups such as the "Moonies," the Hari Krishnas, the Children of God, or the Mormons. For reasons that had much to do with politics but little to do with practices, brainwashing was viewed as the special province of cults. Priests, nuns, and other devotees of "legitimate" (which is to say, more influential) religions were almost never accused of having created brainwashed automatons, no matter how much formal training, family encouragement, or hellfire-and-brimstone preaching preceded their vows. A spate of lurid books, articles, and media reports painted the Moonies, in particular, as masters of mind control who duped, and sometimes even kidnapped, unsuspecting youth to attend indoctrination seminars at isolated locations where, locked up, sleep-deprived, and "buzzed" on high-sugar diets, they were subjected to mind-numbing lectures, repetitive chanting, "love bombing," and other insidious practices that deprived them of judgment, individuality, or personal will and turned them into "robots, glassy eyed and mindless, programmed" to serve the organization and person of the Reverend Moon (Barker 1984, 121).

The truth, however, turned out to be far less diabolical or extraordinary. Numerous studies of cult recruitment, conversion, and retention have turned up virtually no evidence of "brainwashing." The Moonies and other new religious movements did indeed devote much energy to missionizing, but they employed conventional methods and enjoyed very limited success. In the most comprehensive study to date, described by Thomas Robbins (1988, 77) as "an empirical and theoretical tour de force," Eileen Barker (1984) could find no evidence that Moonie recruits were ever kidnapped, locked up, or subjected to physical coercion (although some anti-cult "deprogrammers" did kidnap and confine converts to "rescue" them from the movement). Those who attended Unification Church orientation seminars were not deprived of sleep; the food was "no worse than that in most college residences"; the lectures were "no more trance-inducing than those given everyday" at many colleges; and there were no drugs or alcohol, very little chanting, and little that could be termed "frenzy" or "ecstatic" experience (Barker 1984, 141–44). People were free to leave and did leave, in droves. Barker's comprehensive enumeration showed that starting "from the number of those who get as far as visiting a [Moonie] Unification centre, a generous estimate suggests that no more than 0.005 per cent [or 5 out of 1,000] will be associated with the movement two years later" (ibid., 146). Even among the relatively small number of recruits who went so far as to attend the two-day, full-time Moonie workshops that were the object of most "brainwashing" claims, fewer than 25 percent joined the group for more than a week, and only 5 percent remained full-time members one year later (see chapter 2). With failure rates this high, it is perhaps no wonder that the number of full-time members of the Unification Church in the United States never exceeded a few thousand. Although Barker was unwilling to characterize the Moonie conversion process as "a calculated decision ... consciously taking into account all the relevant details," she did conclude that "the evidence would seem to suggest that the answer lies considerably nearer the rational-choice pole of the continuum than it does to the irresistible brainwashing pole" (ibid., 250–51, 254).

In short, despite all the media attention it has received, and all the fear it inspired among parents, "brainwashing" has been thoroughly discredited by careful research—so much so that the Society for the Scientific Study of Religion and the American Sociological Association stated this fact in an *amicus* brief to the United States Supreme Court (Richardson 1985).

CONCLUSION

Who is to say that it is more "rational" to convert on the basis of doctrinal appeal than to accept a doctrine initially because of the testimony of family and friends? Would we suggest that people would be more rational if they put more faith in advertising than in the firsthand experiences of their family and friends when buying a car? Keep in mind, too, that we do not suggest that doctrine is not important. As we shall see in chapter 6 and again in chapter 8, doctrine matters a great deal when it comes to generating and sustaining commitment, and thus, among others things, in *retaining* converts and reaffiliates. Here we have argued only that doctrine usually plays a secondary role when people initially make their choices. Subsequently, doctrine often becomes a central aspect of commitment. It should also be recognized that although the process of conversion is sometimes quite rapid, as it was in the case of Parley Pratt, it is rarely sudden. Rather, people who have encountered a new religion through their friends or family usually resemble the Youngs, who went through a gradual process of learning and listening and questioning before finally embracing the new Mormon faith. Moreover, people usually take a quite active role in this process. Indeed, a decade after the original Lofland and Stark theory of conversion appeared, John Lofland (1976; 1977) criticized the theory for projecting a too-passive image of converts. Further fieldwork had convinced him that people play a major role in "converting themselves" (Lofland 1977, 817). People do not simply succumb to missionary efforts, for conversion not only involves interaction, it quite clearly involves introspection. People question, weigh, and evaluate their situations and options. Nor does the introspective process end with the initial profession of faith. As noted, members of religious groups continue to assess their choices—to such an extent that many recant. Since Lofland published his conclusions concerning the active role played by converts, similar observations have been made by other field researchers (see, e.g., Bainbridge 1978; Barker 1984; Richardson 1985).

But neither Lofland's second thoughts nor subsequent field research have suggested any revision of the essential insight concerning the conservation of social capital: people adjust their religious choices to coincide with what is going on around them. In the next chapter, we shall see that this same principle determines their level of commitment.

PART THREE

The Religious Group

CHAPTER 6

Religious Group Dynamics

Imagine a Protestant church where every Sunday seems like Christmas. The turnout is huge—everyone always attends and helps "make a joyful noise unto the Lord." The collection plates come back overflowing, and there are far more volunteers than needed to perform all of the necessary congregational tasks. And because members actively seek to share their faith, the group is growing so fast that it will soon need to build a larger church or split into two congregations.

At the end of chapter 4, we proposed that individual religious commitment is rooted in social support and reinforcement—that the high levels of involvement exhibited by participants in some religious groups are generated by the group itself, that enthusiasm engenders enthusiasm. It is easy to see how this would be accomplished among newcomers to the congregation just described. But there are many congregations that fall far short of this level of collective enthusiasm, and religious groups therefore vary immensely in their capacity to generate and sustain commitment. Why? What makes religious groups enthusiastic and effective?

In this chapter we first attempt to explain how religious groups generate high levels of commitment. Then we shall see how groups are able to translate high levels of commitment into resources enabling them to grow. Finally, we examine threats to the effectiveness of religious organizations that arise from success, especially from growth. Keep in mind, our focus will not be on religious individuals, but upon religious groups, as we attempt to identify their most fundamental dynamics.

EXCLUSIVITY

Chapter 4 explained that there can be no church of magic. Because magic deals in short-term rewards to be realized here and now, it cannot engage its consumers in either an extended or an exclusive relationship. Consequently, magic cannot generate a stable group of lay "members." As noted, the same point applies to religions based on many gods of limited scope. They, too, will lack for otherworldly rewards, specializing instead in relatively immediate payoffs. Consequently, exchanges with any given god will be short-term (even if they occur repeatedly) and nonexclusive. Indeed, in a polytheistic setting, the sensible investor would not risk all on any given god, preferring instead to spread the risk across a number of options (Iannaccone 1995a). For example, in Chinese cultures, it is assumed that the prudent petitioner will make offerings in several different temples and exchange with many different gods, while in Japan today, total religious "preference" statistics exceed 200 percent of the population (Miller 1995).

To understand strong, effective religious organizations, then, is to understand *exclusive* religious organizations—all nonexclusive organizations being inherently weak.

We may summarize this in a proposition:

PROPOSITION 42.   Among religious organizations, there is a reciprocal relationship between the degree of lay commitment and the degree of exclusivity.

Exclusivity is not merely a dichotomy but a matter of degree. That is, not only are some religious groups exclusive, but some are more exclusive than others. For example, many Protestant bodies claim belief in the same God, but they differ greatly about what God is like and what is required to be a good Christian. The most exclusive Protestant groups recognize only one road to salvation, require a life-changing "conversion" experience, and impose many nonnegotiable demands on behavior. Others are less absolute and less demanding. And some appear to be so open that even clergy can believe and do pretty much anything they wish. When we pursue these contrasts, we discover the primary conceptual basis for distinguishing religious groups.

CHURCH AND SECT

Nearly a century ago, Ernst Troeltsch identified two kinds of religious groups ([1911] 1991; [1912] 1931). A church, according to Troeltsch (1931, 331), is a very conventional religious organization that "accepts the secular order" to such an extent that it "becomes an integral part of the existing social order." That is, the church does not impose moral demands substantially more excessive than the prevailing moral code. A sect, on the other hand, "does not give in to the general state of sinfulness," but "demands the actual overcoming of sin, the living up to the divine commandments" (ibid., 325). Moreover, to "the sect, the religious community is not a general, all-inclusive institution." Put another way, the orientation of churches is more worldly and less otherworldly, while sects reverse the emphasis.

Obviously, Troeltsch did not coin the words "church" and "sect." Rather, as social scientists often do, he took terms in common usage and refined their definitions somewhat in order to give them sufficient precision for use in social science theorizing. Troeltsch's friend and colleague Max Weber also used both terms at about this same time, but did not bother to define "the church-sect distinction at any length" (Demerath and Hammond 1969, 69). Unfortunately, the same was not true of subsequent users. For the next several generations, social scientists devoted endless effort to constructing increasingly elaborate definitions of church and sect, designating subtypes of each—especially of sects. Thus, Bryan Wilson (1959) proposed four varieties of sects: "conversionist sects," "adventist sects," "introversionist sects," and "Gnostic sects." This proliferation of types reflected the common error of mistaking definitions for theories (Stark and Bainbridge 1979; Stark 1985b). But names explain nothing. To classify a religious group as a sect (of whatever subtype) tells us nothing about how it formed or what to expect it to become. It was, therefore, of considerable importance when Benton Johnson proposed a clear and parsimonious conceptualization of churches and sects. He began by postulating a single axis of variation fully in accord with Troeltsch's original insight: religious bodies "range along a continuum from complete rejection to complete acceptance of the environment." He went on to note that "a sect tends to be in a state of tension with its surroundings," and concluded: "A church is a religious group that accepts the social environment in which it exists. A sect is a religious group that rejects the social environment in which it exists" (Johnson 1963, 542–44).

Although people sometimes refer to political sects (O'Toole 1977), such groups are excluded from this definition, as are all *non*religious groups. Having a clear axis of variation, Johnson's definition allows unambiguous comparisons, making it possible to say that one group is more sectlike or churchlike than another, that during the nineteenth century, the Catholic Church was far more sectlike in the United States than in Spain, and, most important, that a given group is more or less sectlike (or churchlike) than it used to be. Indeed, later in this chapter, and in chapter 8, we theorize about the movement of religious bodies into increased or decreased tension. To state Johnson's contribution a bit more formally:

PROPOSITION 43.   All religious groups can be located along an axis of **tension** between the group and its sociocultural environment.

Definition 25.   **Tension** refers to the degree of distinctiveness, separation, and antagonism between a religious group and the "outside" world.

At the high end of the tension axis, serious antagonism exists, sometimes erupting into bloody conflict. At the low end, there exists such compatibility between a group and its environment that it is hard to distinguish between the two.

Definition 26.   **Churches** are religious bodies in relatively lower tension with their surroundings.

Definition 27. **Sects** are religious bodies in relatively higher tension with their surroundings.

Note that here we ignore the distinction between cults and sects, which classifies higher-tension groups on the basis of whether their religion is rooted in the dominant religious traditions of the society in which they are being observed (sects), or whether they represent a novel or alien religious tradition (cults). Although this distinction is important for some purposes such as analyzing conversion, here it suffices to distinguish groups only according to their tension with their sociocultural environment.

Earlier we assessed the capacity of religions to generate *extended* and *exclusive* commitments. Now we add two additional aspects of commitment that follow directly from the degree of tension with the group's environment: *extensive* and *expensive* commitments.

Tension is equivalent to subcultural deviance (Stark and Bainbridge 1985). Subcultures are cultures within a culture, groups having norms and values different from those of the surrounding society. To the degree that a religious organization sustains norms and values different from those of the surrounding culture, it is deviant (Stark and Bainbridge 1980b; 1985). To the degree that a subculture is deviant, the more it will influence all aspects of the lives of its adherents.

PROPOSITION 44. The higher its level of tension with its surroundings, the more **extensive** the commitment to a religious organization.

Definition 28. As applied to religious commitment, **extensive** refers to the range and depth of religious effects on the individual.

The higher the tension of their religious group, the less distinction people draw between religious and secular matters: religious doctrines and practices impinge on everything else, defining with whom they associate, how they spend their leisure time, sometimes even how they dress and speak. Examples such as Hasidic Jews, Mennonites, or Sikhs demonstrate the point. But even among groups in less tension, there is variation in the extensiveness of commitment. For an American to be an Episcopalian or for an Italian to be a Catholic has far more limited consequences than to be a Jehovah's Witness or a Mormon in either nation.

PROPOSITION 45. The higher its level of tension with its surroundings, the more **expensive** it is to belong to a religious group.

Definition 29. As applied to religious commitment, **expensive** refers to the material, social, and psychic costs of belonging to a religious group.

An easy way to measure the expensiveness of a group's commitment is the length of the list of things members are required to do and not to do. Thus, by their strict observance of the Law, Orthodox Jews pay far higher religious costs than do Reform Jews. For example, their social relations are restricted, because they must refuse invitations to meals in homes of those who do not keep kosher. In similar fashion, practicing Mormons observe a lengthy list of "do nots," and their "do" list includes the obligation to tithe. In calculating religious expenses, we also must count the many psychic costs imposed on members of higher-tension groups by outsiders, as reflected in nouns such as "cultists," "heretics," and "fanatics."

To sum up:

PROPOSITION 46. The higher its level of tension with its surroundings, the more exclusive, extensive, and expensive is the level of commitment required by a religious group.

Clearly it follows that, to the degree that they manage to attract and to hold members:

PROPOSITION 47. The higher a group's level of tension with its surroundings, the higher its average level of member commitment.

We now confront one of the most important and disputed issues in the social scientific study of religion. *Why do they do it?* Why are people willing to make the very high levels of sacrifice required by higher-tension religious organizations? Traditionally, social scientists have answered this question in terms of irrationality. People pay high prices for their religion because they do not recognize an alternative, having been socialized to regard a high level of commitment as normal and necessary. However, in previous chapters, we have seen compelling evidence that people *do* weigh the costs and benefits of religious commitment. Indeed, we have postulated (propositions 16 and 17) that, other things being equal, people will seek to minimize and delay payment of religious costs—that they will go so far as to "cheat" the gods. If this is so, why does anyone belong to a sect? Why don't Jehovah's Witnesses, Primitive Baptists, and Nazarenes flock to the far less expensive religion offered by low-tension bodies such as the Presbyterians and Episcopalians?

The answer can be found in elementary economics. Price is only one factor in any exchange; quality is the other, and combined they yield an estimate of *value*. Herein lies the secret of the strength of higher-tension religious groups: despite being expensive they offer greater value, indeed, they are able to do so partly *because* they are expensive.

PROPOSITION 48. Among religious organizations, there is a reciprocal relationship between expense and the value of the rewards of membership.

Since the key to this proposition is the value of rewards, let us pause to examine how and why higher-tension religious groups can offer greater value in return for commitment. Membership in any religious organization involves both religious and social-emotional rewards. That is, in addition to those things prom-ised via religious means are the ordinary pleasures of belonging to a group. On both counts, higher-tension groups excel.

RELIGIOUS REWARDS

The association of religious rewards with tension rests upon differences in the conception of god and of otherworldly rewards. In keeping with the analysis offered in chapter 4, all *exclusive* religious organizations conceive of a *dependable* god of *great scope* and capable of providing *otherworldly rewards*. What differs is the vividness of these conceptions, the confidence generated in them, and the ex-tent to which god is thought to be *responsive*.

As mentioned in chapter 4, the lower their tension, the more that religious groups tend to conceive of god as a distant, impersonal, rather *unresponsive* en-tity. Of course, no mass-based religious organization is entirely godless,[1] and even in the most liberal Western divinity schools, many faculty and students affirm some sort of god. Indeed, many of the rank and file in the most liberal Protestant churches continue to worship more traditional visions of God, re-jecting the modern revisions and resenting the revisionists sent to them as clergy. Nevertheless, compared with a god who notes the fall of every sparrow and is brimming with concern and generosity, the god presented by lower-tension groups is quite unsuitable as an exchange partner. For example, the very influential American theologian Paul Tillich proclaimed that "you must forget everything traditional you have learned about God, perhaps even the word it-self" in order to comprehend that "the word *God* means" the "depth of exis-tence" (1962, 63). No conscious "being" for Tillich. Not surprisingly, most who have followed Tillich's lead have ended with no god of any kind, being or oth-erwise. Hence the title of the Cambridge theologian Don Cupitt's *After God: The Future of Religion* (1997).

But why would a religion without god have a future? Cupitt's prescription strikes us as rather like expecting people to continue to buy soccer tickets and gather in the stands to watch players who, for lack of a ball, just stand around. If there are no supernatural beings, then there are no miracles, there is no sal-vation, prayer is pointless, the Commandments are but ancient wisdom, and death is the end. In which case the rational person would have nothing to do with church. Or, more accurately, a rational person would have nothing to do with a church *like that*.

COST AND COMMITMENT

To the extent that one is motivated by religious value, one must prefer a higher-priced supplier. Not only do more expensive religious groups offer a far more valuable product, but in doing so, they generate levels of commitment needed to maximize individual levels of confidence in the religion—in the truth of its fundamental doctrines, in the efficacy of its practices, and in the certainty of its otherworldly promises. This occurs in two ways: by example and by exclusion.

By Example

People take their cues from the example set for them by typical others. To the extent that most people around them display high levels of commitment and express their confidence that their religion is true and effective, people will conform. That is, just as people join religious groups in response to social influence (chapter 5), their level of participation responds to that of those around them, especially to that of close friends and family members. It follows that the higher the level of commitment expected by the group, as displayed by the average member and justified by the group's doctrines, the higher the average level of confidence and of commitment. This, of course, takes us back to the ideal Protestant church described at the start of the chapter. It would be difficult for most people to maintain a low level of commitment in that environment.

Compare this with a Protestant church where most people fail to attend on the average Sunday, and where those who do attend display little enthusiasm, including the pastor, who devotes his or her sermon to social justice and seems to say as little as possible about Christ. Because no one volunteers, a substantial portion of available church funds must be spent on janitorial and clerical services and on maintenance. Consequently, the church must struggle with budgetary problems, which get worse each year, since membership is declining. Here, if one responded to the example of others, one would attend only occasionally and have little confidence in religion per se.

One way to prevent such a congregation from developing is to eliminate the deadwood, to prevent those of little commitment from setting the example. Here we encounter a growing theoretical literature on the "free-rider problem."

By Exclusion

The initial work on this topic concerned the creation of collective or public goods, those from which everyone benefits. Mancur Olson (1965) noticed that the rational person would withhold his or her contribution to the creation of a public good, enjoying the benefits while avoiding the costs. For example, any given individual is better off if he or she can benefit from flood-prevention dams, highways, or military security without contributing time or money to the collective enterprise. As Michael Hechter has explained: "Truly rational actors will not join a group to pursue common ends when, without participating, they can reap the benefits of other people's activity in obtaining them" (1987, 27). Olson identified such persons as free-riders and explained why societies must protect themselves against being exploited in this fashion, and why governments must therefore coerce citizens to pay their proper share. Of course, the problem is not limited to public works—all collective activities face potential exploitation by free-riders to the degree that benefits created by the group cannot be withheld from nonparticipants.

Returning to our two hypothetical Protestant congregations, we easily can see that the low-commitment congregation is the victim of free-riding. Indeed, religious organizations are especially vulnerable to free-riding, as Mary Douglas (1986) recognized, because some of the most important features of religion are collective goods. They exist only to the extent that some set of individuals pool their resources to provide the physical setting within which religious activities can occur and engage in the collective activities themselves—religious rituals such as worship services, weddings, and funerals are collective "goods." The norms of religious groups, especially of lower-tension religious groups, are such that it is difficult to justify withholding these collective goods from anyone. This, of course, encourages a substantial amount of free-riding. For example, it is a form of free-riding to show up only for services at Christmas and Easter, expecting them to occur despite the fact that you have relied on others to keep things going the remainder of the year. And only free-riders would expect to draw upon the congregation for weddings, funerals, and christenings if they only take part in these ceremonies when they are directly involved. Even if such people do make an appropriate financial contribution, it does not offset the drain upon the average level of group commitment caused by their inactivity. Couched in contemporary jargon, these folks are bad role models.

Considering this state of affairs, Laurence R. Iannaccone noticed that free-riding could be prevented in religious groups by requiring high costs of everyone, so that "potential members are forced to choose whether to participate fully or not at all" (Iannaccone 1992; 1994, 1188) In this way, potential free-riders, those with only low levels of commitment, are excluded and thereby prevented from exploiting the group. Hence, high costs make membership sufficiently unattractive so to chase away the apathetic, and in doing so make the rewards of belonging far more intense. Thus, in our hypothetical high-commitment Protestant congregation, inasmuch as each person pays the high cost of membership, each receives greater religious value because of the increased capacity of the group to create a religious product that is undiluted by low-commitment "members."

Think of a congregation in which individual levels of religious commitment fluctuate on a scale from one to ten. Suppose that there are the same number of people at each level, which yields an average commitment level of 5. Now suppose that this congregation imposes a rule requiring a commitment level of 5 or above in order to remain a member. The immediate result is an average level of commitment of 7.5. Moreover, people who previously had scored 5 and thus had been average members in terms of commitment, now find themselves at the bottom. Many of these are likely to respond by increasing their level of commitment in order to once again become average members. As they do so, the average level of commitment also rises, and the returns on their investments increase correspondingly.

A real-world example of the consequences of eliminating free-riders is provided by the data on Jehovah's Witnesses shown in table 5. All respondents were asked their religious preference. These responses are somewhat inflated, because about 90 percent of Americans will name a specific religious body (10 percent or fewer answer "none"), but only about two-thirds of Americans actually belong to a specific religious congregation. The discrepancy is even greater among self-identified Jehovah's Witnesses, because their church will only count people as members if they qualify as "publishers" by putting in about four hours a week doing missionary work and by attending church meetings several times a week. Thus, in the case of Jehovah's Witnesses, surveys always project nearly twice as many "members" as are claimed by the group in its official statistical reports. Nominal, low-commitment members are free-riders in most denominations, but the Witnesses tend to exclude them from congregational life, and hence they are not lurking on the periphery to serve as bad examples. To see the difference exclusion makes, table 5 separate self-identified Witnesses into "publishers" and "nominal members" on the basis of attending church at least twice a week. The combined column shows what Witness congregations would be like in terms of commitment if the free-riders were not excluded. "Strong identification" with the group would drop precipitously, as would the frequency of prayer. Intermarriage would increase, as would smoking and going to bars (Witnesses do not prohibit drinking). Similar results were obtained when active Mormons were compared with nominal members (Stark 1998a). The immense vitality of the average congregation of both faiths is explained by the high value of religious rewards *and* the screening out of free-riders.

TABLE 5   Jehovah's Witnesses: "Publishers" and Nominal Witnesses

	"Publishers" (n=*105*)	*Nominal* (n=*97*)	*Combined* (n=*202*)	*U.S. population*
"Strong" identification with denomination (%)	93	27	61	39
Pray daily (%)	100	59	83	56
	(n=*74*)	(n=*57*)	(n=*117*)	
Spouse is a Witness* (%)	80	21	61	—
Smoke (%)	0	48	24	35
Drink (%)	76	85	81	71
Go to a bar at least once a year (%)	14	49	30	49

SOURCE: Stark and Iannaccone 1997, General Social Surveys, 1972–94.
*Married persons only.

Obviously, there are limits to this reciprocal relationship between cost and value. It is easy to find religious groups too expensive to grow substantially, as will be considered at length in chapter 8. But costs must be sufficient to exclude potential free-riders.

Of course, active, enthusiastic congregations do not only provide religion. They also produce substantial worldly gratifications. It is a common observation that people in high-tension churches have a lot of fun in church (Miller 1997; Warner 1988). Moreover, these groups offer very substantial levels of emotional and even material security. This is well illustrated by early Christian congregations. Because of their capacity to generate high levels of commitment, the early Christian communities were bastions of mutual aid in a world almost entirely lacking in social services. The early Christians tended the sick and elderly and provided for widows and orphans (Stark 1996a). So too do the Mormons and the Witnesses today, and they are able to do so only because they ask a lot of individual members. For the fact is that commitment provides organizations with resources. Some of these are used to reward members. Some are used to gain new ones.

GENERATING RELIGIOUS RESOURCES

Commitment is energy. Moreover, members of higher-tension churches do not expend all of this energy doing directly religious things. After the worship service is over, after the prayers are said, there is a lot of time and energy remaining for more mundane, but organizationally vital, activities. For example, Mormons are asked not only to tithe in terms of financial support, but to tithe in terms of their time. Indeed, James T. Duke (1997) reports that for each of the local congregations (wards), there are between 150 to 250 positions that are considered "callings" by the church. These callings are not merely "requests to help out" from the local bishop, they are considered callings from God. Using conservative estimates, Duke calculates that the average congregation receives 400 to 600 hours of voluntary labor per week, or the equivalent of ten to fifteen full-time employees. The result is such a huge and talented labor force that all functions necessary for operating the local ward are performed by unpaid volunteers—including the role of bishop (pastor), which typically requires from 20 to 40 hours per week. And after all the clerical, janitorial, and other maintenance jobs are done, there still is a huge supply of labor remaining, which Mormons deploy to perform social services for one another. Volunteers paint and repair the homes of the elderly and disabled. Volunteers do childcare. Volunteers transport people to church, to medical and dental appointments, and to the supermarket. Indeed, Mormon charity and volunteer social services provide for members who otherwise would go onto the welfare roles. In similar fashion, volunteer crews of Jehovah's Witnesses build all of their churches, often over a single weekend, and the Witnesses also rely entirely on volunteers to lead and maintain their congregations. Similar patterns exist in all of the higher-tension religious groups. Indeed, a recent study based on the United States and Canada found that high-tension groups with only a relatively small share of the each nation's church members had huge shares of available human and capital resources (Iannaccone, Olson, and Stark 1995). Not surprisingly, these resources translate into growth.

TENSION AND GROWTH

In recent years much has been written about the decline of America's liberal "mainline" denominations and the rapid and continuing growth of more conservative groups (Kelley 1972). As we demonstrated in our book *The Churching of America, 1776–1990*, it's true, but it's not new. Throughout our history, growth has been concentrated among the higher-tension religious groups, while lower-tension groups have declined. Indeed, the Methodists have displayed the entire pattern, having grown at a spectacular rate during the nation's first century and declined quite dramatically during the second. When they grew, the Methodists were an aggressive sect. As they became a lower-tension denomination, decline set in. And a major factor in both eras was human resources. In keeping with the findings of chapter 5, the early Methodists grew because rank-and-file members brought their friends, relatives, neighbors, and fellow workers into the church. When this ceased, members began to be drawn away by other groups with a missionizing rank and file, and the Methodists began to decline. Table 6 offers evidence of the link between tension and missionizing. In the lower-tension, declining denominations, fewer than half say they have "ever tried to encourage someone to believe in Jesus Christ or to accept Jesus as his or her savior." In the growing, higher-tension denominations, nearly everyone has missionized.

Table 7 displays the remarkable results of these efforts in terms of founding new congregations. Obviously, lower-tension denominations have lost the capacity to plant new churches. The tiny Vineyard Christian Fellowship, with only 305 existing congregations in 1994, managed to plant as many new churches as did the huge United Methodist Church, which had more than 36,000 congregations. That it is tension, not size, that matters is demonstrated by the fact that the Southern Baptist Convention, with nearly 40,000 existing congregations, has a substantial rate of new church starts. In contrast, the rate of new church formation is so low among the lower-tension bodies that it fails to offset the loss of congregations. Indeed, parish consultant Lyle Schaller (1991, 184) has calculated that in the United States today, a denomination needs to found 8 new churches per 1,000 existing churches each year just to stay even. Moreover, new congregations tend to be the more rapidly growing congregations and therefore contribute quite disproportionately to denominational growth.

TABLE 6   Rank-and-File Missionizing and Church Growth

"Have you ever tried to encourage someone to believe in Christ or to accept Jesus as his or her savior?"

	Yes *(%)*	*Gain or Loss* *in Members* *per 1,000* *U.S. Population,* *1960–90* *(%)*
Lower-Tension		
United Presbyterian Church (USA) (*n*=24)	17	−34
United Church of Christ (*n*=15)	20	−48
Episcopal Church (*n*=30)	23	−46
American Baptist Churches in the United States (*n*=28)	43	−50
Evangelical Lutheran Church in America (*n*=27)	44	−28
United Methodist Church (*n*=58)	47	−39
Higher-Tension		
Southern Baptist Convention (*n*=151)	77	+12
Church of Jesus Christ of Latter-day Saints (*n*=31)	84	+109
Pentecostal (All) (*n*=33)	88	+100
Assemblies of God (*n*=21)	100	+214

SOURCE: General Social Survey, 1988, and the *Yearbook of American and Canadian Churches,* 1962 and 1992.

Table 8 expands the perspective to foreign missions. While members gained and new churches started in other nations do not count in a denomination's domestic statistics, missions are indicative of commitment to growth. The low-tension denominations hardly sustain a foreign missionary effort at all. The huge United Methodist Church sustains far fewer missionaries (452) than does the tiny Church of the Foursquare Gospel (780). And when the effort is standardized for size, the differences are enormous. The Episcopal Church sustains 1 missionary for every 50,000 members, while the Church of the Nazarene supports 1 missionary for every 100 members! After having broken away from the low-tension United Presbyterian Church in 1973, the higher-tension Presbyterian Church in America has fielded proportionately 100 times as many foreign missionaries.

TABLE 7   Annual Formation of New Churches, United States, 1995

	Number of New Churches Formed per Year*	New Churches Formed per 1,000 Existing Churches
Lower-Tension		
United Methodist Church	35	1.0
United Presbyterian Church (USA)	30	2.6
Evangelical Lutheran Church in America	50	4.5
Episcopal Church	38	5.1
Higher-Tension		
Southern Baptist Convention**	484	12.1
Jehovah's Witnesses	208	20.2
Assemblies of God	271	23.0
Latter-day Saints	254	24.9
Vineyard Christian Fellowship	34	109.8

SOURCE: For each denomination, we interviewed the official in charge of starting new churches. They provided the data on the number of new churches started per year and information on the procedures followed.

*Annual average based on data for 1993–95, except United Methodists based on one year, the Vineyard is based on two years, and the number of Episcopalian new starts was "estimated" by the denominational official in charge of starting new churches.

**Based on "church starts" statistics.

TABLE 8   Foreign Missionary Efforts of American Protestant Bodies, 1995

	Foreign Missionaries per 10,000 Members
Lower-Tension	
Episcopal Church	0.2
United Methodist Church	0.5
United Church of Christ	0.6
Evangelical Lutheran Church in America	0.6
United Prebysterian Church (USA)	0.7
American Baptist Churches in the United States	1.4
Higher-Tension	
Southern Baptist Convention	8.9
Seventh-day Adventist Church	9.6
Christian Churches and Churches of Christ	10.8
Assemblies of God	11.0
Christian and Missionary Alliance	25.6
Pentecostal Holiness Church	29.0
Church of the Foursquare Gospel	35.0
Presbyterian Church in America*	71.3
Church of the Nazarene	100.5

SOURCES: *Mission Handbook, 1993–95*, and *Yearbook of American and Canadian Churches, 1996*.
* Broke away from the United Presbyterian Church (USA) in 1973 to reaffirm traditional doctrines and practices.

We theorize at length in chapter 8 about how other market forces influence growth and decline. Here it is sufficient to know that church growth is no mystery. It is the direct result of effort:

PROPOSITION 49. There is a reciprocal relationship between commitment and growth.

Commitment results in growth as members bring in new members. Growth, in turn, reinforces commitment. That others can be convinced that a belief is true is strong confirmation of the validity of that belief (Festinger 1959).

Implicit in *all* theoretical propositions is the qualifying phrase, "other things being equal." That is vital here, because there is another force that can greatly offset all commitment gains generated by growth: size. Consequently, growth is a mixed blessing. Indeed, growth has the potential to undo the enthusiasm and effectiveness of religious groups.

THE PERILS OF GROWTH

A generation after Ernst Troeltsch introduced the concepts of church and sect, an American theologian gave them theoretical life by linking them into a process. H. Richard Niebuhr (1929) proposed that over time, successful sects tended to reduce their level of tension with society, being thereby transformed into churches. Niebuhr based his theory on rather crude Marxism, identifying the transformation of sects into churches as the work of the ruling classes. Despite this, his work has lasting value, because he correctly identified a cycle in which sects arise and those that grow eventually turn into churches, wherein dissident members who prefer a higher-tension religion break away and found a new sect—hence the repeated birth, transformation, and rebirth of sect movements. We give close attention to this process in chapter 8, where we attempt to specify adequate explanatory mechanisms to account for it. Here, our focus will be on Niebuhr's most important insight: that growth tends to result in the lowering of a religious group's tension with society and thereby leads to a decline in the average level of member commitment.

PROPOSITION 50. As religious organizations grow, their **congregations** will tend to become larger.

Definition 30. **Congregation** refers to the smallest, relatively autonomous membership unit within a religious organization.

Other terms might have been used,, but it seemed to us that "congregation" was the most useful, because it is restricted to people and implies nothing about physical structures or locations. This is especially important because the secret of the so-called "mega" churches is that they consist of a great many small congregations, which unite for a common worship service but otherwise function as quite autonomous membership units.

When a religious group grows, the actual growth tends to occur within congregations. Denominations only grow on paper. What really grow are specific congregations belonging to the denomination, and there will be a marked tendency for growth to be retained within congregations. At least initially, growth contributes to congregational morale ("Watch us grow!"), and it also results in economies of scale and increased discretionary resources. These may be spent to upgrade worship facilities: a new or better organ, stained glass windows, fancier choir robes, and then, perhaps, a professional choir director and the occasional professional soloist. However:

PROPOSITION 51.   Congregational size is inversely related to the average level of member commitment.

For over 200 years, social scientists have commented on the relationship between the small fellowships and high membership demands of Protestant sects. Adam Smith reported that "in little religious sects, ... the morals of the common people have been almost always remarkably regular and orderly" ([1776] 1981, 317). Max Weber argued that "in principle, only relatively small congregations" can enforce strict standards for membership ([1913] 1946, 316). Ernst Troeltsch wrote that because the sects "aspire after personal inward perfection, and they aim at direct personal fellowship between the members of each group. ... they are forced to organize themselves in small groups" ([1912] 1931, 1: 331).[2] This relationship is not unique to religious organizations. Mancur Olson has argued that "unless the number of individuals in a group is quite small, or unless there is coercion or some other special device to make individuals act in their common interest," there will be substantial free-riding, and that "the larger the group, the farther it will fall short of providing an optimal amount of a collective good" (1965, 2, 34).

Contemporary research on American Protestant denominations supports these views (Alston and Aguirre 1970; Wilken 1971; Pinto and Crow 1982; Hougland and Wood 1980; Finke 1994; Zalenski and Zech 1995). Table 9 demonstrates the effects of size. In all instances, rates of participation decline with congregational size, and the sharpest declines occur when congregations exceed 50 members. Moreover, indicative of its current pattern of growth, the Church of the Nazarene attracts more people to worship services than it has members, and in its smallest congregations, average attendance exceeds membership by 50 percent.

Fully aware of the negative impact of size on commitment, two of the world's fastest growing religious movements, the Jehovah's Witnesses and the Mormons, intentionally limit the size of local congregations. The Jehovah's Witnesses tend to split when the group exceeds 200 (Alston and Aguirre 1970), and the Mormon stake president can choose to split a ward once it exceeds 300.[3] The leadership of each movement is so committed to small local fellowships that they will split the local group into two fellowships even when only one

TABLE 9   Congregational Size and Commitment

		Congregation Size					
	Under 50	50–99	100–149	150–99	200–299	300 and Over
Church of the Nazarene*						
Average Adult Sunday School Attendance per 1,000 Members	613	475	429	411	408	397
Average Sunday Worship Attendance per 1,000 Members	1,504	1,287	1,163	1,153	1,128	1,110
United Methodist Church**						
Average Total Sunday School Attendance per 1,000 Members	516	309	259	234	211	192
Average Sunday Worship Attendance per 1,000 Members	731	529	479	446	421	379
Southern Baptist Convention***						
Average Adult Sunday School Attendance per 1,000 Members	542	380	313	281	260	243

* Rates are based on 1995 data supplied by the Church of the Nazarene Church Growth Center. We would like to thank the Research Program Manager, Richard Houseal, for his assistance.

** Rates are based on 1994 data supplied by the General Council on Finance and Administration of the United Methodist Church. We thank Steve Zekoff for his assistance.

*** Rates are based on 1990 data taken from the *Southern Baptist Handbook, 1991.*

building is available. In areas where land prices are high and membership growth is rapid, it is common practice for two or more fellowships to share the same building. Until recent decades, the Southern Baptists have tended to have smaller congregations, not because of official policy, but owing to the intense competition among pastors for a church of their own. This is caused by an oversupply of pastors, because local congregations retain the right to ordain anyone who seeks it and whom the local members deem fit (Finke and Stark 1992). This same factor is at work in many small sects.

At first glance the new mega-churches would seem to defy the small-group thesis. But, as mentioned above, this is an illusion. What outsiders see are the huge gatherings for worship services—the highly publicized Willow Creek Community Church (Illinois), averages over 14,000 in attendance for weekend worship services and is best known for its "seeker" services offering contemporary music, drama, and anonymity for all who attend.[4] Yet, church leaders describe their small cell groups (approximately ten members) as the "basic unit of church life" (Trueheart 1996, 54) and explain that these groups provide "accountability, instruction, encouragement, and support for each of its members" (Mellado 1991, 12). Likewise, the largest church in the world, the Yoido Full Gospel Church in Seoul, Korea, reports that its small groups provide fellowship, instruction, and discipline for church members. A former staff member of the church described small groups as the "fabric of the church," where the church changes from "an event to attend" to a "community to belong to" (Hurston 1994, 99).[5]

In his book *Prepare Your Church for the Future*, Carl George, a specialist in church growth, provides an outline of this organizational design, in which groups of ten are guided by cell leaders, each cell leader is encouraged and trained by cell coaches, the cell coaches report to subcongregational leaders, and so on (fig. 2). "The model for a healthy and thriving church ... highlights the lay-led small group as the essential growth center. It's so important that everything else is to be considered secondary to its promotion and preservation," George explains (1992a, 41; see also 194–96). His "vision of the future sees each leader as working to develop lay ministers who care for a group of ten" (ibid., 102).

George's vision is also, however, a vision of the past. Early in the nineteenth century, Bishop Francis Asbury's Methodists were based on small fellowships called "classes," guided by a class leader, who was responsible to the lay minister of the local congregation, while the lay minister reported to the full-time traveling minister, or circuit rider. The organizational design (see fig. 3) was nearly identical to that prescribed by George. Like the small cell groups of today's mega-churches, the classes served the dual purpose of holding members accountable and providing an intense fellowship—including prayer, instruction, and social support.[6]

Now we must address the question of *why*—why does size influence commitment? The answer involves several steps. The first has to do with the density of the networks of social relationships.

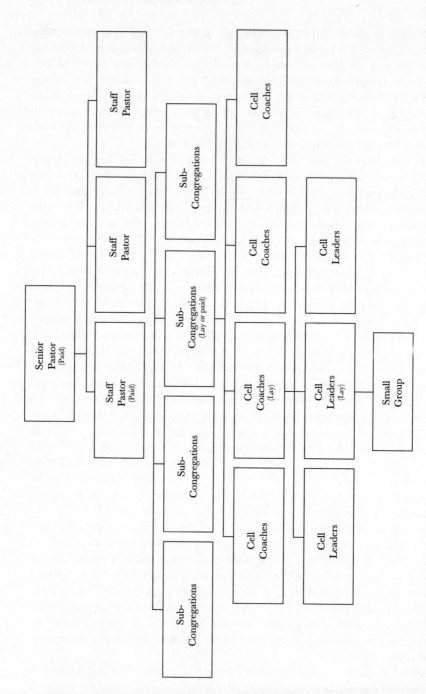

Figure 2. C. F. George's Church of the Future

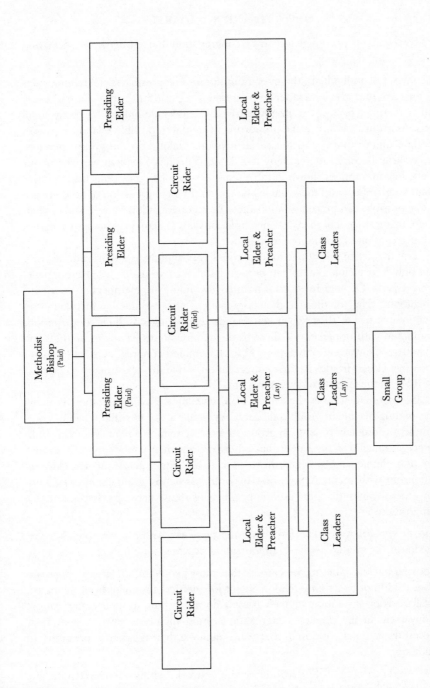

Figure 3. Francis Asbury's Church from the Past

GROWTH AND SOLIDARITY

PROPOSITION 52.   The larger the congregation, the less dense the social networks within the group.

In any set of individuals, the maximum number of possible social relationships is for each and every member to maintain a relationship with each and every other member $[n \times (n - 1)]/2$. Clearly, this is possible only in relatively small sets. As groups get larger, the proportion of actual to possible relationships *must* decline quite rapidly, and the social network making up the group therefore necessarily becomes increasingly less dense. This helps explain why the major shifts in commitment shown in table 9 are between congregations having fewer than 50 members and those having 50 to 100. In a congregation of 50 there are 1,225 possible two-person relationships. In a congregation of 100, rather than there being twice that many possible relationships (2,450) there are 4,950, and in a congregation of 400 there are 79,800.

The density of social networks declines very rapidly as congregations grow, not only in principle but, as can be seen in table 10, in reality too. Respondents were asked, "Of your five closest friends, how many are members of your congregation?" Half of those in the congregations of fewer than 50 members said that four or five of their five closest friends also belonged to their congregation, compared with 15 percent of those in the congregations having more than 400 members. Conversely, only 8 percent in the smallest congregations had none of their five closest friends in their congregation, while this was true of 40 percent of those in the largest congregations.

It is axiomatic that as the density of a social network declines, there is a corresponding decline in group solidarity. In chapter 4, we saw that religious commitment ultimately rests upon group support or reinforcement. We gain confidence in religion to the extent that others express their confidence in it and we are more influenced by what others tell us to the extent that we have a close relationship with them. As networks become less dense, group support or reinforcement wanes, for these are the products of dense networks. Expressed as a proposition:

PROPOSITION 53.   The less dense the networks within a congregation are, the lower the average level of reinforcement provided for commitment.

Looking back at table 10, we can see that most people in the largest congregations could not be gaining reinforcement for their commitment from their closest friends because most of their friends do not belong to their congregation. Conversely, in the smallest congregations, most members have most of their closest friends in a position to share and reinforce their religious expressions. In addition:

PROPOSITION 54.   The less dense the networks within a congregation are, the less efficient the monitoring of member behavior.

TABLE 10   Congregation Size and Social Networks, Northern California, 1963

"Of your five closest friends, how many are members of your congregation?"

	Congregation Size*			
	50 or less (n=69)	*51–200* (n=314)	*200–400* (n=517)	*Over 400* (n=1,787)
4–5 (%)	50	21	22	15
2–3 (%)	33	34	31	27
1 (%)	9	15	13	18
0 (%)	8	30	34	40

"Generally speaking, would you say most of the people you associate with in activities aside from church affairs are or are not members of your congregation?"

Half or more are members (%)	77	42	44	37

"All in all, how well do you think you fit in with the group of people who make up your congregation?"

Very well (%)	66	35	31	24

SOURCE: Stark and Glock 1968.
*Adult members.

Conformity to high standards of commitment are achieved, not only by rewarding conformity, but also by punishing failures to conform. But just as network density determines the flow of positive reinforcement, density also greatly influences the ability of a group to detect and therefore to deter inadequate commitment or improper behavior. Thus it follows:

PROPOSITION 55.   The larger the congregation, the higher the proportion of free-riders.

The obverse of weak intra-group social ties is strong external ties.

PROPOSITION 56.   The less dense the networks within a congregation, the stronger the ties maintained to external networks.

Lacking close ties within their congregation, members of large congregations will tend to be linked to outsiders. This also shows up clearly in table 10: two-thirds of the members of large congregations reported that most of the people they associated with outside of church affairs were not members of their congregations, while in the small congregations, three-quarters reported that their associates were fellow congregants.

Not only are outsiders unable to reinforce commitment, they often express some degree of skepticism. Therefore:

PROPOSITION 57.   The more prevalent member ties to external networks, the greater the pressure on the group to reduce tension.

This is self-evident. Imagine what would happen to the Amish if most members of the community were to have most or all of their closest relationships with people who were not Amish. Indeed, during the early nineteenth century, substantial numbers of European Jews responded to emancipation by becoming involved in non-Jewish networks; the result was the Reform Movement (Steinberg 1965; Stark 1996a). The preponderance of external attachments may be the reason that the overwhelming majority of members of large congregations did not say they fitted in very well with the group making up their congregation, while two-thirds of those in the small congregations felt they did fit in very well (table 10).

GROWTH AND ECCLESIASTICAL POWER

As groups grow, it becomes increasingly difficult to coordinate activities—to make and pursue decisions. As a result, increasing effort must be devoted to administration. Keep in mind that our primary focus is on *congregational* growth— some very large denominations (the Mormons, for example), as well as large corporations (fast food franchisers, for example), have demonstrated that the management sector can be minimized if the essential operating units are kept small, even if the total number of such units becomes quite large (Finke 1994). However, as operating units grow, not only will each need to devote greater resources to management, but usually there will be a corresponding expansion of the trans-unit administrative sector. Growth of the administrative sector of religious organizations has crucial and inherent consequences, which we shall now analyze in detail.

PROPOSITION 58.   As religious organizations grow, their administrative sector grows more rapidly.

We have adopted this proposition from the work of Peter M. Blau (1970; 1972), who has established on both theoretical and empirical grounds that the larger the organization, the greater the proportion of total resources that must be devoted to management or administration.

PROPOSITION 59.   As the administrative sector expands, authority will become more centralized and policies will be standardized.

It is always in the interests of administrators to increase their authority, and power will therefore flow upward and into increasingly fewer hands. Moreover, it simplifies administration if all subordinate units must adhere to common procedures, policies, and standards—that there not be one rule for one group and another for another. That these principles reflect common sense makes them all the more irresistible. But they can be very harmful at the level of the operating unit.

Perhaps the most sensible, yet harmful, principle usually imposed by central religious authorities has to do with avoiding duplication of effort, and they therefore impose limits on competition and proliferation of local units. Frequently this has taken the form of enlisting state support to eliminate "outside" competitors (a matter we discuss at length in chapters 8 and 9). In slightly less extensive form, this occurred when the Grand Itinerant, George Whitefield, attracted unprecedented crowds throughout colonial New England—an episode that came to be labeled the Great Awakening. In the immediate aftermath, Congregational Church officials moved quickly to defend their establishment from "needless duplication." Acting upon their appeal, in 1742, the Connecticut legislature prohibited itinerants "from preaching in any parish without the approval of the minister of that parish" (McLoughlin 1971, 363). But even without state intervention, churches have signed comity agreements to limit competition. The 1801 Plan of the Union was an effort to reduce competition between the Presbyterians and Congregationalists on the western New York frontier.

Less obvious, but no less damaging and far more common, are internal rules of "efficiency," which often weaken denominations, because central administrators place severe restrictions on where and when new churches can form. These restrictions may overtly suppress new churches from starting. Or, more frequently, denominations will withhold subsidies or deny membership to churches that fail to follow set procedures.[7] For example, many "mainline" churches typically provide financial support for new churches that receive approval from the local district, presbytery, diocese, or conference.[8] Such prior approval requires new congregations to meet many criteria, such as be in an area with a growing population and have grassroots support, the support of surrounding congregations, an ordained pastor, and a financial plan for support after the subsidy ends. Seldom are all of these criteria met. If churches shun the financial support and begin without the approval of surrounding congregations, they can be, and often are, denied admission into the denomination. We already have seen the end results of such policies in the extraordinary lack of new church formation in these same denominations.

By contrast, most growing religious movements place few restrictions on the formation of new congregations. From the Pentecostal sects to the growing segment of independent churches, new congregations are the work of religious entrepreneurs—volunteers who felt called to begin a new church. New congregations can also be formed when existing churches choose to split. A frequent theme of the Baptist denominations is that they "multiply by dividing."[9] As already noted in the case of the Mormons and Jehovah's Witnesses, sometimes the split is carefully planned, with one church sponsoring another. But the more common scenario is where the split results from internal factions and the disgruntled group and their leader leave to start their own congregation. The editor of a Texas Baptist newspaper put such congregational in-fighting in perspective when he noted that when you hear a lot of "screaming cats during the night, the result is never a pile of dead cats, but a pile of kittens."

PROPOSITION 60.   As authority becomes more centralized it will tend to be more exclusively in the hands of **professional** ecclesiastics.

Definition 31.   A **profession** is an occupational group claiming sole possession of the training, talent, or other qualifications needed to perform a specific occupational role.

Those who administer a large organization cannot do so after-hours or on weekends. It is a full-time job, it is how they earn their livings, it is a career—a profession. And in religious organizations, a professional is an ecclesiastic. Here we draw upon the enormous sociological literature on professions and professionalization (Abbott 1988; Freidson 1986; DiMaggio and Powell 1983). The first step in the formation of a profession is when members of an occupation are transformed into a reference group and lay exclusive claim to expertise in their field. That is, to become a profession is to succeed in laying exclusive claim to the qualifications to perform some set of services or functions and to seize control over access to the training as well as the right to perform these services or functions. Put more formally:

PROPOSITION 61.   Professional ecclesiastics will seek to define the necessary qualifications for the performance of their role.

PROPOSITION 62.   Professional ecclesiastics will attempt to control entry into the profession.

Whether it is the apprenticeship and initiation rites of shamans or an Episcopalian seminary, the same sociological phenomena are involved. As an anonymous cynic put it, "'All professions are conspiracies against the laity." In the eighteenth century, it was decided at the Harvard and Yale divinity schools that a qualified clergyman would know Latin and Greek. And the Congregationalists and Episcopalians soon withheld ordination from all who lacked a degree from a seminary that required these essential skills. Meanwhile, the Baptists and Methodists remained certain that God understood English. They resisted seminary training and allowed local congregations to ordain any local young man whose character and piety seemed sufficient. The response of professional ecclesiastics to such "unqualified" competitors was amazingly intemperate. For example, being faced with competition from Baptist and Methodist preachers who were without seminary educations and who often served without pay, a Presbyterian pastor wrote to his superiors in 1846: "After a minute examination and mature and prayerful deliberation I have come to the settled conviction that it would be decidedly for the religious interests of Arkansas if every minister and preacher of the above denominations were out of the State" (Sweet 1964, 698).

Elsewhere (Finke and Stark 1992), we have written at length about how, once they gain full control over religious doctrines, professional ecclesiastics often begin to intellectualize them in ways that typically lead to a more distant, less responsive conception of divinity—the suggestion that god is a metaphor or pure subjectivity never comes from the pews, but from the pulpit (or, more accurately, from the seminary). Often, however, ecclesiastics limit these conceptions of the gods to their own inner circle and (sensibly) do not promulgate them to the laity. We are not prepared to include this ecclesiastical tendency among our theoretical propositions, but merely note that it is a frequent aspect of the negative impact of a professional clergy on faith.

Professions are never content merely to control who is allowed to practice. As rational actors, they will exploit their monopoly:

PROPOSITION 63.   Professional ecclesiastics will seek to improve their ratio of rewards to costs.

In the case of professional ecclesiastics, this usually will mean a reduction in their expected level of religious commitment, whether de jure or merely de facto. As the early Christian religious movement was supplanted by an established state church, a very noticeable gap developed between the lifestyles of ecclesiastics and of the rank and file. Of course, in keeping with proposition 27, the ability of affluent clergy to inspire their congregations declined proportionately, as indicated by the low levels of religious participation noted in chapter 3 and by the constant emergence of popular movements led by ascetics.

PROPOSITION 64.   Professional ecclesiastics will favor growth.

Generally speaking, administrators always favor growth, because their sector grows at a proportionately greater rate than the rest of the organization, creating more positions for them and their peers to fill. Also, to the extent that overall growth increases available resources, those in charge will benefit from a higher potential level of reward. This is especially clear at the level of the congregation. Unless the members are wealthy (as in the case of private chapels for members of a noble family), below a certain size, a congregation cannot support a full-time ecclesiastic. For this reason, those involved in the "community church movement" during the 1920s and 1930s used every possible argument to end the "overchurching" of rural America and replace the local proliferation of small congregations with a large, federated church. For these small congregations could only support pastors who usually were "untrained and poorly paid, if paid at all." In contrast, if a standard were adopted of not "more than one church for one thousand," it would be possible to have a well-educated and well-paid full-time pastor (Finke and Stark 1992, 210–15).

The irony is that most efforts directed toward growth have the opposite effect in the longer run. We pursue this point at length in chapter 8. Here, it is sufficient to note the obvious: paying a full-time ecclesiastic increases operating costs for existing congregations and start-up costs for new ones. In the case of the country churches of the 1920s and 1930s, the mainline churches often closed their doors, while the churches of lay-led sectarian groups remained open, because the mainline congregations couldn't afford to pay their full-time pastors. Paying a professional ecclesiastic also reduces a group's ability to start new churches. This is clearly evident in table 7, where all of the denominations with a high rate of new church starts are the higher-tension groups relying on lay ministers for starting new congregations. The professional ecclesiastics of the low-tension groups, who are subsidized by their denominations to start new churches, have secured a far more attractive ratio of rewards to costs, but that does not promote the growth of the movement.

The tendency of professional ecclesiastics to seek greater rewards and/or lower costs is progressive because:

PROPOSITION 65.   To the extent that ecclesiastics enjoy a favorable reward ratio, religious motives will be less important among those entering the position.

This is a matter of immense significance in the careers of religious organizations. No one seeks unpaid, costly religious positions from materialistic motives. Once such positions offer an attractive living, however, the question of why aspirants want to enter the profession arises. Thus, for example, there was little besides religious motivation that could have led people to leadership in the early Christian house churches, but once Christianity became the official, subsidized religion of the Roman Empire, many clearly sought ordination primarily to enjoy the material rewards of office. In similar fashion, given the sacrifices required of their positions, Mormon bishops and Jehovah's Witness elders must be motivated primarily by faith. But when clergy are well-paid and not subject to greater restrictions than regular members, there are many nonreligious reasons to seek entry.

We return to this in chapters 8 and 10, where we look at the conditions under which the reward ratios of ecclesiastics can shift in the less favorable direction, thus restoring the importance of religious motivations. Here it is sufficient to see that:

PROPOSITION 66.   Growth (especially at the congregational level) and the professionalization of their ecclesiastics will tend to shift religious organizations from higher to lower tension—from sects to churches.

Thus, we have partly explained the widely observed phenomenon that sects tend to be transformed into churches. It also is widely observed that the usual outcome of such transformations is to create dissatisfaction and dissent among many followers who prefer higher tension and who place far greater faith in those leaders who continue to display higher levels of commitment. In chapter 8, we present a more complete model of this entire process. Here we merely wish to note how this interacts with the efforts by professionalized ecclesiastics to impose their authority:

PROPOSITION 67.   Professional ecclesiastics will seek to minimize diversity, especially with respect to organizational practices.

Although seminary training encourages the exploration of new beliefs and teachings, often leading to an intellectualized version of the faith, both seminary training and the ongoing professional socialization that follows will promote conformity to acceptable organizational practices. In part this is nothing more than the preference of administrators for uniformity. In part, too, it involves the suppression of all potential challenges to the qualifications for entry and for performance of the professional role. But professional ecclesiastics have a substantial motive for suppressing diversity, because the most threatening diversity comes from the direction of higher tension. Those who want to lower the costs and raise the rewards of the profession can usually pursue these ends effectively within the system. It is those who wish to establish (or reestablish) higher costs or reduced rewards who must challenge those in authority. Thus the history of religious organizations abounds in the expulsion (or worse) of those who have challenged the level of rewards going to the professionals in charge.

It was to maintain control and eliminate diversity that the Presbyterians defrocked Barton Stone and his colleagues for introducing the "camp meeting": that the Congregationalists attempted to force Charles Finney to moderate his revival efforts; that the Church of England ejected the Wesley brothers for their Methodism; that the American Methodists booted out the Holiness Movement; and that the famous and permissive Episcopalian Bishop James A. Pike prohibited his vicars from holding charismatic services.

PROPOSITION 68.   To the extent that tendencies toward greater tension are suppressed, the average level of commitment of a religious group will be reduced by the departure or expulsion of the most highly committed members.

Conflicts over conformity cannot be limited to disciplining or ejecting the occasional rebel, for efforts to silence a heretic often propel the organization of a heretical movement, and when recourse to armed suppression by the state is not available to professional ecclesiastics, a "heresy" may become a very successful mass movement. In any event, when people leave a religious body in pursuit of a higher-tension faith, their departure always leaves behind an organization with a reduced level of commitment.

CONCLUSION

In this chapter we have tried to explain the seeming contradiction that "expensive" religion generates higher levels of commitment and satisfaction. As noted, this is a contradiction only so long as people mistake price for value. If price were the key factor, then we might expect low-tension denominations to bankrupt their higher-tension competitors by stressing how "easy" it is to belong. But fortunately we never see ads such as:

Why Not Try the Easiest Faith in Town?

The Church of Your Choice
Accepts:
Incest, Dope, Liquor, Lies, Embezzlement
and
All Major Credit Cards

CHAPTER 7

Catholic Religious Vocations

Decline and Revival

For the past three decades, a rapid decline in Roman Catholic religious vocations has been under way in North America and most of western Europe. For example, in 1965, there were 181,421 nuns, 12,255 brothers, and 48,046 male seminarians in the United States. Just five years later, in 1970, there were only 153,645 American nuns. During that year, 4,337 Catholic women (most of them young) left the religious life, a defection rate six times higher than in the early 1960s. Meanwhile, the number of seminarians had declined by 40 percent to 28,819, and the number of brothers had dropped to 11,623. By 1995, the number of American nuns had dropped to 92,107, of brothers to 6,578, and of seminarians to 5,083.

Table 11 shows similar drops in Canada and several nations of western Europe. Notice the immense similarity in the percentages of decline in the number of women religious—from 51 percent in the Netherlands to 44 percent in France. The percentage declines in male religious and in male seminarians are even higher than those for women religious but, being based on far smaller numbers of cases, are somewhat more variable across nations.

Understandably, changes of such magnitude have prompted a great deal of concern, and many explanations have been offered. Although we shall present data revealing that some of these explanations are inadequate, we would like to acknowledge the very careful scholarship and concern for objectivity that characterizes the large literature on this subject.

The most popular explanation of the loss of vocations blames the refusal of the Church hierarchy to respond to new generations of Catholics unwilling to accept the traditional sacrifices required of priests and the religious—chief among these being vows of celibacy, obedience, and, in the case of those entering orders, poverty. In support of this explanation, a number of studies conducted during the late 1960s and the 1970s found celibacy to be the most com-

TABLE 11   Percentage Decline in Catholic Vocations, 1965–95

Canada	
Female religious	46
Male religious	77
Male seminarians*	72
France	
Female religious	44
Male religious	68
Male seminarians*	69
Germany (united)	
Female religious	48
Male religious	81
Male seminarians*	54
Netherlands	
Female religious	51
Male religious	78
Male seminarians*	81
Great Britain	
Female religious	43
Male religious	82
Male seminarians*	54

*Diocesan and religious seminarians combined.

mon cause given by ex-priests for having defected (Greeley 1972a; Schoenherr and Greeley 1974). More generally, the decline in vocations has been linked to the intransigence of local bishops in response to the aspirations of the religious for liberal reforms. In particular, the bishops have been blamed for responding "traditionally, sternly, and in a disciplinarian manner" (Seidler and Meyer 1989, 123), thereby reaffirming the traditional demand for obedience rather than allowing the religious greater participation in decision-making.

However, some studies of nuns have not blamed their decline on failures of the Church, instead emphasizing how secular social changes have reduced the attractiveness of the role of nun as a career option for young Catholic women. Specifically, the rapid decline in Catholic women's religious orders is attributed to rapid changes in the secular opportunities of women (Ebaugh 1993; 1977). The argument is made that, faced with greatly increased secular career opportunities, Catholic women—especially in economically developed nations—became less inclined to pursue careers within the confines of religious vows. A recent empirical study (Ebaugh, Lorence, and Chafetz 1996) appeared to clinch the case. Using data for fifty nations, several measures of the extent of secular opportunities for women were found to be quite strongly related to the rate of decline in the number of women in religious orders. In nations where a larger proportion of women in the labor force are managers and professionals, and where a higher percentage of women pursue higher education, there has been a greater decline in religious vocations among Catholic women.

Finally, some propose that the decline in Catholic vocations was caused by the radical revisions in religious roles adopted by Vatican Council II (1962–65). They argue that inasmuch as many of the most central sacred aspects of the religious roles were dismissed or discontinued, the *sacred* gratifications of religious vocations were thereby greatly reduced, as were features of the religious life that sustained and even generated these gratifications. For example, as will be discussed in detail later, the Council withdrew the doctrine that the religious life is morally superior and equated the holiness of the religious and the laity. Moreover, as the orders dispensed with their distinctive dress in response to the Council's directive to modernize, the religious became indistinguishable from anyone else, and thus no longer received special treatment and respect in public. These losses came without any offsetting decreases in expectations concerning the level of commitment needed for the religious life or any increases in its secular rewards. (Finke 1997c; Wittberg 1994; Iannaccone 1994; DiIanni 1993; 1987; Finke and Stark 1992; Greeley 1982; Falk 1980). That the declines began immediately upon the conclusion of the Council has been cited in support of this thesis.

In this chapter, we attempt to bring appropriate data, properly analyzed, to bear on all of these explanations. For reasons that will be clear, we begin with an investigation of the decline in women's religious orders and demonstrate that the "secular opportunity" explanation does not hold. In doing so, we shall demonstrate why it is inappropriate to seek separate explanations of the decline in female and male vocations—that any adequate explanation must include both. We then propose such an explanation and test it with the *principle of reversibility*. That is, if we have correctly identified the factors that caused the decline in religious vocations, then should these factors be reversed, the trend in vocations also should be reversed. Thus, we shall show that our explanation accounts for recent instances of increased vocations. Finally, our most fundamental purpose in this chapter is not to explain this specific historical development, but to test portions of the theory of religious dynamics presented in chapter 6, especially propositions concerning why expensive or costly religious organizations engender higher commitment. Readers are asked to keep in mind that we do not suggest that religious organizations *ought to be* strict or that religious organizations *ought to rely* on very high levels of motivation.

NUNS: OPPORTUNITY AND DECLINE

It is a commonplace in writing about Catholic women's religious orders that at one time, while non-Catholic girls wishing to be teachers, nurses, or social workers could seek these positions through secular education, Catholic girls found these careers linked to the role of nun. This was so, not only because most of these positions within Catholic life were filled by nuns, but because the orders provided educational opportunities appropriate to these occupations. The orders were a primary "avenue of social mobility for Catholic girls, many of them from immigrant, working-class, and/or farm families, who otherwise had virtually no opportunity for upward mobility" (Ebaugh et al. 1996, 174). Moreover, nuns could aspire to executive careers largely denied other women, Catholic or Protestant. Because nuns ran the hospitals, schools, orphanages, and other charitable institutions, nearly all North American and western European women in important executive positions during the nineteenth and early twentieth century were members of Catholic orders (Thompson 1986).

It is implied in much, but not all, of this literature that, although women in religious orders dutifully fulfilled their religious obligations (devoting hours daily to prayer and meditation, observing enclosure rules, being obedient, accepting poverty, wearing distinctive and often extremely impractical habits, and the like), it was primarily the occupational and educational opportunities that drew most of them to the orders. From this perspective, it is no surprise that the immense recent shift in the opportunities for women in the secular world would have a devastating impact on Catholic women's religious vocations. As Helen Rose Ebaugh and her colleagues put it: "As educational and career opportunities expanded for women ... during the last three decades, the unique rewards of upward mobility traditionally provided by religious orders no longer outweighed the costs of membership, namely a celibate life of poverty and obedience to superiors" (Ebaugh et al. 1996, 174). This argument is so elegant and plausible that it seems a shame to challenge it. Moreover, as noted, Ebaugh et al. have offered impressive empirical support for this view, based on cross-national comparisons of fifty nations. But challenge it we must.

Table 12 is based on all nations for which there are data on the number of members of religious orders in 1965, immediately prior to the onset of the decline. Lack of data eliminates nations under communist rule in 1965 and results in a total of 103 cases. Following Ebaugh et al. (1996), we then eliminated thirty-seven nations with fewer than 500 nuns apiece in 1995 (although the results were only slightly weaker when these cases were included), for a final sample of 66 cases.

The primary dependent variable is the decline or increase in the *number* of nuns in each nation from 1965 through 1995. Ebaugh et al. attempted to take cross-national changes and variations in the size of Catholic populations into account by basing their measure of decline or increase on the number of nuns per 1,000 Catholics in 1960 and 1990. This results in a somewhat unreliable measure, because estimates of the size of the Catholic population often are extremely inaccurate, especially in "Catholic nations" (Stark 1992a). Thus, while the statistics on the number of religious are very accurate, this accuracy is gravely compromised if the number of religious is divided by a very unreliable population denominator. An additional source of unreliability is the fact that

TABLE 12   Correlates (*r*) of Rates of Decline in Religious Vocations, 1965–95

	Decline in the Number of Women Religious	*Decline in the Number of Women Religious per 1,000*	*Decline in the Number of Male Religious*
Secular Opportunities			
Gender empowerment			
measure (GEM)	.48* (57)	.31* (57)	.48* (58)
Gender inequalities index			
(GDI)	.40* (61)	.37* (61)	.48* (62)
Economic Development			
Per capita GNP	.60* (63)	.56* (63)	.60* (64)
Per capita electricity			
consumption	.61* (66)	.49* (66)	.50* (66)
Cars per 1,000	.62* (65)	.50* (65)	.63* (66)

*$p < .001$.

Catholic populations, whatever their actual size, also vary greatly in their age composition, and thus in the size of the potential pool of recruits to religious orders, a problem acknowledged, but then ignored, by Ebaugh et al. Use of the absolute numbers of nuns in 1965 and 1995 gets around these measurement problems, since each nation is, in effect, its own control, because our measure is based on the growth or decline in the number of nuns from Time 1 (1965) to Time 2 (1995). However, for the sake of comparison, we also calculated a measure based on nuns per 1,000 Catholics (column 2 in table 12). Overall, the measure of change based on the absolute number of nuns produces results offering far stronger support for the increased secular opportunity explanation, as might be expected when substantial measurement error is eliminated.

The first "opportunity" variable shown in table 12 consists of a gender empowerment measure (GEM) developed by staff social scientists at the United Nations and published in the *Human Development Report, 1995*. This index estimates the relative power of women in societies based on such things as the percentage of females holding political offices and appointments, the percentage of females among managers, professionals, and technicians, and women's share of earned income. The correlation with the decrease (increase) in the number of nuns is strong (.48) and highly significant—the higher a nation's score on the GEM, the greater its decline in the number of nuns. This independent variable also is significantly correlated with the rate of change when the number of nuns is calculated as a rate per 1,000 Catholics, but the correlation is substantially weaker (.31). The second "opportunity" independent variable is a gender development index (GDI), constructed and published by the same source as the GEM. The GDI indexes gender inequalities in both opportunity and achievement, paying particular attention to education, literacy, occupation, and health. As would be predicted by the secular opportunity explanation, this variable also is highly correlated with a decrease in nuns. Both indices are based on data for the 1990s.[1]

Ebaugh et al. reported that the decline in Catholic vocations was limited to the economically more developed nations. The lower half of table 12 strongly confirms this finding: all three measures of development are highly correlated with a decline in vocations. Clearly, it would be appropriate to examine the opportunity effects under controls for development. Table 13 shows that these effects entirely evaporate when per capita GNP and each opportunity measure are entered into regressions—each of the other development measures produced the same results. We must thus conclude that it is economic development that is the real causal factor, and that female opportunity measures have no net effects of their own. Later, we suggest why the declines have not taken place in many less developed nations. An even more compelling reason for dismissing the female opportunity explanation is revealed by these data. The third column in table 12 shows the high, positive correlations between increases in secular female opportunities and declines in membership in male religious orders. These correlations defy the claim that expanded opportunities for women led to a decline in women's religious vocations, for surely increased secular opportunities for women could not plausibly cause men to cease becoming monks. Thus it is necessary to seek an explanation that applies to both male and female vocations. We shall return to this matter in the next section.

AMERICAN VOCATIONS, 1948–95

There is a direct and powerful way to test the thesis that American women ceased to become nuns because of the immense increases in their secular op-

TABLE 13   Controlling for Economic Development

Dependent Variable: Decline in the Number of Women Religious

	Standardized Beta	T Value
$R^2 = .334$		
Index of gender inequalities (GDI)	0.080	0.474
Per capita GNP	0.637	3.789*
$R^2 = .336$		
Gender empowerment (GEM)	0.107	0.595
Per capita GNP	0.493	2.752*

*$p < .001$.

portunities. Consulting *The Official Catholic Directory*, we assembled data on the number of female religious for each year from 1948 through 1995. We also assembled data on female labor force participation rates for the same period.

A glance at figure 4, which graphs the number of American nuns, reveals that most discussions of the decline in female religious vocations in the United States have ignored a vital fact—that following World War II, there were nearly two decades of consistent and substantial growth in the number of nuns: from 141,083 in 1948 to 181,421 in 1965. Only then did the numbers begin the decline. In contrast, the percentage of females participating in the labor force grew slowly and consistently during the entire period. Thus, figure 5 (which graphs both variables on the basis of their Z-scores to take account of their very different magnitudes) shows that the "opportunity thesis" is either strongly rejected or strongly supported by the data, depending upon the era examined. From 1948 through 1965, as female opportunities increased, so did the number of nuns, resulting in a huge *positive* correlation of .92. Anyone who examined this time series in 1966 would probably have concluded that for many Catholic girls, becoming a nun was *their way of participating* in the labor force. But then came the incredible news that number of nuns had dropped by 4,750 during

Figure 4. Number of American Nuns, 1948–95

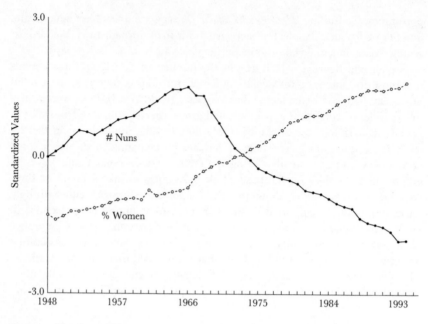

Figure 5. Number of Nuns and Percentage of Women in the U.S. Labor Force, 1948–95

1966, thus beginning a long, uninterrupted decline in membership. Meanwhile, the percentage of women participating in the labor force continued to increase. Consequently, subsequent to 1965, the two rates are *negatively* correlated (−.97). As is obvious to the naked eye, when the entire period is examined (and the curvilinearity of the data is taken into account by removing the quadratic of the trend), there is no significant correlation between female labor force participation and women's religious vocations. These findings were replicated when the percentage of women receiving advanced degrees was substituted for female labor force participation.

Those proposing the secular opportunity explanation probably should have anticipated this outcome, because it was obvious all along that the expansion of secular opportunities for Catholic women was a long, gradual process, whereas the decline in female religious orders was extremely sudden and rapid, and thus that the former could not explain the latter. Moreover, as already noted, an equally obvious shortcoming of the secular opportunity thesis lies in the failure to include men.

The curves for the numbers of male religious and seminarians from 1948 through 1995 are extremely similar to the curve for nuns. All three rise until the mid 1960s, then all three plunge. The only important difference is that once the decline began, the number of males declined more rapidly and further. Changes in the number of female religious is correlated .98 with changes in the number of male seminarians and .88 with changes in the number of male religious. The similarity of the curves precludes all gender-specific causes—and let it be noted that most explanations of the decline in male vocations have been as narrowly gender-biased as those advanced for women. Indeed, the voluminous literature on the decline in seminarians and male religious seldom even mentions the decline in women religious, and vice versa. This seems to be the unintentional result of these studies being dominated by ex-priests and ex-nuns, each seeking to understand his or her biography, and thus failing to examine the larger picture.

However, by far the most important feature of these curves is that together they strongly discourage any explanation based on gradual social changes. The declines are sudden and simultaneous. This very strongly suggests that the explanation lies in a causal event.

VATICAN II AND VOCATIONS

Let us return to October 11, 1962, when Pope John XXIII convened the Second Vatican Council in Rome, a gathering of all of the bishops of the Church to reassess and restructure doctrine and practice. In preparation for the Council, the pope used the word *aggiornamento* (which means updating) so often to describe his intentions to open the Catholic Church to new ideas and influences that for a time it entered the vocabulary of the news media. And "updating" there was. By the time the last session ended on December 8, 1965, an extraordinary set of revisions in basic doctrines and practices had been adopted by the Council, resulting in a period of extremely rapid change. Almost overnight, core doctrines and liturgical practices that had stood for centuries were abandoned or greatly revised. And no one felt these changes more acutely than the religious.

Three documents published by the Council impelled a revolution in the religious life. The first, *Lumen Gentium*, declared that *all* Christians were called "to holiness" simply by having been baptized, and those who pursued a religious vocation could no longer aspire to a superior state of holiness. Previously, the Catholic Church had taught that priests and the religious were in a superior state of holiness. Now, despite their vows, they were just like everyone else. "The importance of this ... statement cannot be stressed enough," Patricia Wittberg notes. "*In one stroke, it nullified the basic ideological foundation for eighteen centuries of Roman Catholic religious life.* The traditional ideology had postulated ... that only vowed members of religious orders could achieve true spiritual perfection" (1994, 214; emphasis in original). This change was especially devastating for women religious. Unlike males, they had never been granted ordination, and now their holiness was reduced to that of all other lay Catholics.

The second document, *Gaudium et Spes* (known as "The Church in the Modern World"), revoked centuries of preference for withdrawal from the "sinful world" and proclaimed that it now was inappropriate for the religious to pursue a cloistered life. Instead, they should become full participants in the secular world. Indeed, this document stressed the need to modernize the entire lifestyle of the orders.

The third document, *Perfectae Caritatis* (usually referred to as the "Decree on the Up-to-Date Renewal of Religious Life") was released in October 1965, just as the Council came to a close. Although it was quite vague on the outcomes to be expected or the methods to be used for renewal, a single sentence opened the door to dramatic revisions by religious orders, most of them by then primed for radical changes: "The manner of life, of prayer and of work should be in harmony with present-day physical and psychological conditions of the members" (quoted in Flannery 1992, 613). At once, all manner of suggestions arose for changing the religious life to harmonize with modern conditions, and an era of extraordinary changes began. Soon entire orders abandoned their convents for a new life as scattered apartment dwellers, often without roommates, and dressed like everyone else.

Such changes, plus the doctrine denying that special holiness attached to religious vocations, transformed the sacrifices of the religious life into gratuitous costs without special standing or significance. Doing the work of a teacher, nurse, or social worker was never seen as having special *religious* rewards. The rewards that had once distinguished nuns who performed these tasks from lay people who also performed them were inherent in those aspects of the religious life that modernization led the orders to abandon: the separated life in a religious community, the daily devotions, the habit that resulted in instant recognition and special treatment by a laity who acknowledged the greater holiness of the religious. Although secular social scientists often have some difficulty comprehending the phenomenology involved, it is quite obvious that many people find the religious life, thus defined, to be deeply rewarding. Moreover, few people (if any) lead religious lives unreflectively—even those who accept martyrdom seem carefully to weigh the costs and benefits of their actions (Stark 1996a; Iannaccone 1994). Entirely consistent with this theoretical view, in the absence of the primary rewards of the religious life, few potential recruits any longer found it an attractive choice. Indeed, many teaching or nursing nuns now compared their circumstances with that of lay women performing the same occupations and asked themselves, "Why?" Why be a nun in addition to being a teacher? What does a woman gain in return for her vows of celibacy, poverty, and obedience if she lives alone in an apartment, where her devotional life is not amplified by collective participation, and who acquires no special holiness thereby, while spending her working hours side by side with married women who now are officially seen as her equals in terms of virtue, but who are free from her obligations?

To sum up our view, many of the most distinctive aspects of Catholic liturgy, theology, and practice abandoned by the Council turned out to have been crucial for generating and sustaining vocations, especially vocations sufficient to meet the high costs of Catholic religious life. "[A]nyone save an academic or a bishop would have anticipated that, when you change that which was unchangeable for 1,500 years, you are going to create a religious crisis," Andrew Greeley observes. "Attempts to put together a new system of religious symbols were half-hearted, unplanned and, most of all, insensitive to the actual religious needs" (Greeley 1982, 88). As it jettisoned many sacred traditions and thereby reduced the rewards of vocations, the church did not adopt positions that would have substantially reduced the *costs* of religious life; instead, it adopted a "worst of both worlds" position, as Laurence Iannaccone puts it (1994, 1204). The rapid decline in Catholic vocations was in response to a cost/benefit ratio that had suddenly gone from positive to negative.

We think that a very crucial factor in favor of our thesis is *timing.* Table 14 shows in rather dramatic fashion that the declines began suddenly and in the immediate aftermath of the Council's pronouncements. Moreover, the exceptions to this generalization offer even more compelling evidence that Vatican II was the causal event.

The data are based on the female religious, because their much larger numbers provide greater statistical stability (but data for seminarians and male religious display similar patterns). Most of the data were taken from the *Catholic Almanac,* and several obvious errors were corrected, as indicated by the asterisks.[2] Italy was omitted because its totals fluctuate so greatly in response to the comings and going of foreign religious.

Now, examine table 14 with care. For the six nations to the left (the United States through Great Britain), membership rose during the early 1960s. Then the era of rapid decline ensued. In the United States, Canada, France, and the Netherlands, the decline registered in 1966, but it did not show up until 1967 in Germany and Great Britain. Once in motion, the decline in the numbers of female religious was very steep in all six nations. But now look at Portugal and Spain to the right of the table. Here, the number of nuns *continued to rise* throughout the remainder of the 1960s! Why? In each nation, an extremely conservative hierarchy refused to endorse or even publicize many decrees of Vatican II, particularly those concerning the religious. The insulation of the national church in both nations was greatly facilitated by authoritarian governments with profound commitments to traditional Catholic piety and power to veto all appointments to bishop (Barrett 1982). With the fall in 1974 of the dictatorship instituted by Antonio de Oliveira Salazar (who ruled Portugal from 1932 until his retirement in 1968) and the death in 1975 of Francisco Franco (who had ruled Spain since 1936), new democratic governments ceased to control appointments to bishop, and both state and church became far more liberal. Under these new conditions, religious orders in both nations began to decline.

TABLE 14 Vatican II and the Decline in the Number of Nuns

	United States	Canada	France	Germany	Netherlands	Great Britain	Portugal	Spain
1962	177,154	47,045	101,665	90,392	32,654	17,773	6,459	67,426
Vatican II begins, October 11, 1962								
1963	180,015	49,352	105,543	89,876	32,667*	18,272	6,872	67,584
1964	179,954	51,725	106,151	90,191	32,680	18,279	7,157	75,280
1965	181,421	52,760	106,810	89,038	31,773	18,115	7,090	77,492
Vatican II ends, December 8, 1965								
1966	176,671	51,770	105,131	89,204	30,776	18,294	6,958	79,704
1967	176,341	50,653	102,103*	87,255	30,194	16,148*	7,150	80,443
1968	167,167	50,565	99,074	87,053	26,740	14,266*	7,036	81,076
1969	160,931	48,111*	96,899*	86,994	23,038	13,195	7,500	88,817
1970	153,645	45,656	94,724*	80,583	24,400	13,215	7,787	89,976
1980	122,653	38,858	87,791	68,782	22,034	11,968	7,818	80,524
1995	92,107	28,498	60,027	46,366	15,463	10,316	6,950	68,750

*Corrected total.

These findings also shed light on the negative relationship between modernization and religious vocations. Just as the hierarchy in Portugal and Spain delayed the decline in vocations by resisting Vatican II changes, vocations continue to increase in some less developed nations where a pre-Vatican II traditionalism still prevails.

It is important to realize that to blame the rapid declines in Catholic vocations on changes in the cost/benefit ratios of the religious life, it *not* to argue that the Catholic Church must adopt a conservative solution to its future staffing needs. Indeed, the most obvious solution for ending the staffing shortage, especially the priest shortage, would be to drop the vow of celibacy. Proponents have long argued that dropping the celibacy requirement for priests would eliminate the shortage without greatly altering the quality of the candidates. After all, Protestant churches have survived for centuries without imposing such high levels of sacrifice on vocations as required by the Roman Catholic Church.

In part, we agree with this remarkably simple solution. Allowing priests to marry, even if the priesthood were still confined to males, would greatly increase the number seeking ordination. But would the candidates seeking ordination be unchanged? We think not. The high costs of entering the priesthood currently serve as a screening mechanism for entry, barring all but the most committed from entering. A recent survey of new seminarians by the Educational Testing Service (ETS) provides a glimpse of the changes that might occur. A national survey of 5,109 incoming seminary students between 1992 and 1994 included 416 who were entering Catholic seminaries—fewer than half (189) of whom had already taken vows of celibacy. The survey was designed to evaluate how students selected a specific seminary, but students were also asked: *"How important were the following in your choice of a profession or calling?"* Each seminarian was given seventeen possible reasons and asked to rank each on a 5-point scale from "of no importance" to "very important." The reasons included the influences of family, church, and friends, intellectual interests, experiencing a call from God, and a desire to serve the church and others.

Table 15 includes the five reasons receiving the highest rankings from new Catholic seminarians. If we assume that seminarians not yet under vows of celibacy are somewhat representative of those who would be drawn to Catholic seminaries should that vow be discarded, the differences shown in the table are quite striking. Catholic seminarians not yet under a vow of celibacy, whether male or female, were two to four times more likely to rate "intellectual interest" and the "opportunity for study and growth" as "very important" than were the celibates. Moreover, among those not yet vowed to celibacy, these two reasons were the ones most frequently rated as "very important." In contrast, the celibates gave the major emphasis to "a call from God" and a "desire to serve others." In short, the celibates seem to see themselves as in transit to the religious life, while the noncelibates seem like students.

TABLE 15   Catholic Seminarians' Reasons for Choosing Profession or Calling,
by Vow of Celibacy
(% responding "very important")

	Male Catholic Seminarians		Female Catholic Seminarians	
	Vow of Celibacy (*n*=137)	No Vow (*n*=106)	Vow of Celibacy (*n*=50)	No Vow (*n*=121)
How important were the following in your choice of a profession or calling?				
Intellectual interest in religious questions	17	44	16	64
Opportunity for study and growth	17	41	19	63
Experienced a call from God	58	41	54	42
Desire to serve others	48	40	46	40
Search for meaning in life	31	40	30	39

SOURCE: The data were collected by the Educational Testing Service (1992–94) and were downloaded from the American Religion Data Archive website (www.arda.tm).

In any event, we conclude that the Roman Catholic Church can revive vocations in *either* of two ways: (1) by *lowering the costs* (and accepting a lower level of commitment), or (2) by *restoring the traditional benefits* of the religious life. We are not advocating either strategy.

However, over the past few years, there have been a variety of attempts to pursue the latter strategy. Pope John II has worked to reassert Catholic traditions and has selected bishops accordingly. In addition, some religious orders have "demodernized," and a number of new orders have been formed—most of them substantially more traditional in terms of their practices. If we are correct about why vocations declined so rapidly, then these developments ought to be followed by increases in vocations.

DIOCESAN CULTURE AND VOCATIONS

Initially, we hoped to identify the prevailing Catholic culture of each American diocese by coding bishops as "traditional" or "progressive." Our intention was to see if variations in culture correlated with ordination rates. However, this proved impossible. First of all, there are no available objective bases for rating bishops, such as voting records on matters brought before the Council of Bishops. Such records are kept, but they are kept secret. Second, when we tried to recruit expert observers to rate the bishops, we discovered immediately that no one knows enough about all of them, or even nearly all of them, to rate them. In part this is because there are so many bishops, few of whom gain much national attention, and in part it is because so many are newly appointed. Indeed, so many bishops have been in their current position for such a brief time that they could hardly have made their presence felt—and not all of them would appear to wish to do so. Thus, to do what we wished, it would have been necessary in many dioceses to rate one or two previous bishops.

In the end, the best we could do was ask a group of expert observers to identify the ten most traditional and the ten most progressive *dioceses*. We explained that we were interested "primarily in the cultural context that has prevailed in the diocese over the past 5 years or so. Consequently, if a bishop is new ignore him in favor of his predecessor since it is dioceses, not bishops, that interest [us]." The ability of the raters to focus on the diocese is evident in the fact that most rated San Francisco as one of the most progressive dioceses, despite the fact that its new bishop is very traditional. Nine of eleven sent back completed rating sheets. Frankly, we were surprised at the very high level of agreement among the raters, particularly since they were only asked to select a few cases from a long list. Not a single case was rated as traditional by one rater and as progressive by another. The only disagreements took the form of being selected to the list of ten of most traditional or most progressive by one or more raters and going unselected by one or more others. To identify our set of traditional and progressive dioceses, we included only those named by six or more of the nine raters. This resulted in the six traditional and eight progressive dioceses shown in table 16. Confidence in the ratings is increased by the fact that the selections are not dominated by the major cities, San Francisco, St. Louis, and Milwaukee being the only exceptions. Instead, the lists are dominated by places such as Lincoln, Nebraska, and New Ulm, Minnesota. Thus, at the very least our raters were well informed (and in agreement) about otherwise more obscure dioceses. In addition to these ratings, data were obtained from *The Official Catholic Directory* on the number of diocesan (secular) priests ordained in each diocese during 1994 and 1995—we merged two years to increase the stability of the rates (Stark 1998b).

Table 16 contrasts the two groups and the differences are quite astonishing. The traditional dioceses are far more successful in attracting young men to the priesthood. Only Saginaw, Michigan, with the highest ordination rate (2.0) among the progressive dioceses, has a rate higher than any of the traditional dioceses. The immense difference between the means is thus a reasonable summary measure—these traditional dioceses are about 4 times more productive of priests. Even if we delete Lincoln, Nebraska, the ratio favors the traditional dioceses by 3 to 1, and there is no obvious reason why this diocese—which has been much in the press because of its bishop's traditional pronouncements—should be dropped. Indeed, Lincoln would seem be the truly compelling example in support of our position.

TABLE 16   Diocesan Culture and Ordinations

	Ordinations per 100,000 Catholics*
Traditional	
Lincoln, Neb.	10.6
Arlington, Va.	5.1
Bridgeport, Conn.	3.1
Scranton, Pa.	2.5
St. Louis, Mo	1.8
Camden, N.J.	1.7
Mean =	4.1
Mean without Lincoln	2.8
Progressive	
Saginaw, Mich.	2.0
New Ulm, Minn.	1.4
Albany, N.Y.	1.2
Milwaukee, Wis.	1.0
Joliet, Ill.	0.6
San Francisco, Calif.	0.5
Rochester, N.Y.	0.3
Richmond, Va.	0.0
Mean =	0.9

* Data for 1994 and 1995.

We hasten to admit that these comparisons of 14 dioceses are a poor substitute for an analysis based on the full set of 174 American dioceses (this total omits the territories, as well as the 14 dioceses following the Eastern Rite). But the cases were selected prior to any examination of their rates. Several colleagues have suggested that these findings are misleading because young men from elsewhere are attracted to seminaries in the traditional dioceses, thus inflating their rates. This might be so. If it is, surely the relative failure of the progressive dioceses similarly to attract outsiders simply supports our argument about the basis of Catholic vocations. Moreover, these findings about ordinations are entirely congruent with data on why priests remain within the fold—that the traditional attractions remain in force for some.

REMAINING IN THE FOLD

We are not the first to discuss the cost/benefit ratio of religious vocations. Reporting on a 1970 NORC survey of 3,045 diocesan priests, Richard Schoenherr and Andrew Greeley (1974) found that when the net balance of costs exceeded rewards, priest resignations resulted. Replicating the survey 15 years later, Mary Jeanne Verdieck, Joseph J. Shields, and Dean R. Hoge (1988, 524) offered similar conclusions. Yet most of the attention has centered on the high cost of celibacy, not on the benefits of religious vocations. Schoenherr and Greeley concluded that the "cost of celibacy is currently a priest's principal consideration in the commitment sequence" (1974, 407). Verdieck et al. found the relationship was weaker in 1985, but concluded that celibacy was still the "principal consideration in determining whether a priest will withdraw or continue" (1988, 524). We would agree that celibacy is the principal cost for many priests, and the desire to marry does lead to resignations, but centering attention on the costs of celibacy tends to ignore the benefit side of the scale. How would anyone find adequate rewards to remain, and what explains the sudden increase in resignations following Vatican II? The costs of celibacy did not sharply increase.

As we noted earlier, the renewal efforts of Vatican II did reduce the benefit side of the ratio, threatening priests' distinctive and exalted position within the church. *Lumen Gentium*, a constitutional document,[3] not only called all Christians to holiness but pronounced that the laity and the priesthood "each in its own way shares in the one priesthood of Christ." Moreover, it went on to add that through the sacrament of matrimony, "married couples help one another to attain holiness in their married life and in the rearing of their children" (Flannery 1992, 361, 362). Although a priest was still required to hear confessions and consecrate the bread and wine at the mass, the clear distinction between the priest and his flock was beginning to blur. The laity had gained some of the privileges of the priesthood without shouldering the burden of celibacy or a direct accountability to the church hierarchy. For many, the priesthood was no longer a good deal following the renewal efforts of Vatican II.

Evidence on how the ratio of costs and benefits is weighed can be seen in a 1993 survey of priests by Dean R. Hoge (Hoge, Shields, and Griffin 1995). Duplicating several of the questions asked in Schoenherr and Greeley's 1970 survey, Hoge asked priests about their "future in the priesthood." The possible responses ranged from (1) "definitely decided to leave" to (5) "definitely will not leave." He also asked three questions about the priest's beliefs on the status of the priesthood. Did ordination provide him with a "new status or a permanent character which makes him essentially different from the laity," is the priest a "man set apart," and is there an "ontological difference between the priest and the laity?"[4] Finally, in an effort to capture the rewards and costs of the priesthood, Hoge also asked a series of questions about the "sources of satisfaction" and the "many problems" facing priests today.

So how do these factors contribute to a priest's decision to continue in the priesthood? It is necessary to consider parish (diocesan) priests separately from priests who belong to religious orders. Among parish priests, regression analysis revealed a fragile balance between the rewards and costs of remaining in the priesthood. As in previous research, celibacy and loneliness, along with the way the church exercises authority, remain the highest costs for diocesan priests—

each strongly predicts the likelihood of leaving. But the strongest single predictor, stronger even than feelings about celibacy, was the belief that priests enjoy a superior religious status to that of the laity. Priests who continue to hold this view do not plan to leave. These results confirm our explanation of why resignation rates rose so suddenly following Vatican II. To the extent that Vatican II pronouncements convinced the religious that they are not set apart and do not hold a special status, they found far less reason to stay.

The cost and benefit situation of priests in religious orders differs significantly from that of parish priests. Being likely to live in a community, they do not cite loneliness as a significant cost, and insulated from the church hierarchy, they do not cite problems with church authority. In sharp contrast to diocesan priests, even celibacy and a belief in the higher status of the priesthood have no significant effects on religious priests. Their problems are focused on confusion over the roles to be played by religious priests, and inadequacies in their communal life. As will be seen, maintaining a strong community and a clarity of mission helps to explain the ability of female religious orders to attract new members as well.

GROWING ORDERS

The renewal efforts of Vatican II initially were viewed as essential for the future growth of religious orders. When older members resisted a "person-oriented" view of religious life, a 1969 report by the Adrian Dominican community posed the question many others were asking: "Are we preserving the Adrian Congregation to provide a tranquil, secure life and retirement for the present membership, or are we building a life style that will provide the vitality and secure the growth of the community in the future?" (quoted in Burns 1992, 139). But the euphoria of renewal soon gave way to the realities of declining membership.

As shown earlier in table 14, the sharp drops in membership came immediately after the conclusion of the Second Vatican Council. Timing alone suggests that Council reforms contributed to this decline. But survey data provide even more evidence that the relationship between renewal and declining membership is more than coincidental. Marcelline Falk's 1978 survey of 300 communities, for example, tied the lack of new recruits to the most visible change following Vatican II. Communities without a "distinctive religious habit" and allowing sisters to wear secular clothes at their "own discretion" had significantly fewer new recruits (Falk 1980). Recently, Eleace King's series of essays in the *CARA Formation Directory for Men and Women Religious* suggest that communities attracting new members have held a "fidelity" to their "spiritual tradition" (King 1993; 1992; 1990). Rather than "secure the growth" of religious communities, renewal efforts of the sort projected by Vatican II have been associated with membership decline and a shortage of new members.

These outcomes have struck some observers as paradoxical. Why should recruitment plummet when religious communities *reduce* the cost of being a member? And why would groups placing more demands on their members attract more recruits? We believe the answers can be found in chapter 6, and especially in propositions 47 and 48. There we theorize a reciprocal relationship between the expense of membership and the value of the rewards of membership, that more expensive and extensive faiths offer a superior cost/benefit ratio to their followers. Specifically, as Vatican II made membership in religious organizations less extensive and expensive, it greatly decreased the rewards of belonging. For example, having dispensed with distinctive dress, the religious no longer were treated with special respect as they went about in public—no one says "Good afternoon, sister," to a stranger dressed like everyone else. Even in their professional circumstances, priests, monks, and nuns not in distinctive garb tend to be treated as laity. Parochial students may address one teacher as "Mrs. Kelley" and another as "Sister Ann," but this is not anything like the difference in treatment involved when "Sister" wears a habit. In similar fashion, when the Council encouraged orders to "update" their rules, it also eliminated the doctrine that the religious have a special claim to holiness and encouraged orders to dispense with those aspects of communal practice that were the primary basis of dense, internal social networks. Indeed, the religious were encouraged to form ties with outside networks.

Despite these changes, it was not the intention of the Council that there no longer be religious orders, and that their roles be taken over by the laity. That is, Vatican II did not propose to shift from a celibate priesthood to the far less costly Protestant clergy model; nor were nuns and monks encouraged to return to ordinary Catholic life as teachers, social workers, or nurses. Rather, the Council assumed that people would still be willing to pay high costs, including celibacy and 24-hour-a-day service, for greatly reduced benefits. Nor could the Council have avoided the collapse of vocations by even greater reductions in the costs. The rewards needed to sustain the sort of high-commitment religious life long associated with Catholic vocations cannot be separated from high costs. Without significant sacrifices, there is no meaningful difference between the religious and the laity, and in such circumstances to claim to be a "nun" or a "monk" would be at best empty words and at worst pure conceit. Nor can the high commitment that characterized centuries of Catholic religious life be purchased for material rewards—$150,000 a year might inspire someone to be a good social worker or even a capable teacher, but not an authentic nun. Above all, it is sacrifice that has defined Catholic vocations. Thus, to revive religious vocations, it would seem necessary to restore primary *religious* rewards of vocations. Indeed, as we clarified in chapter 6, sacrifice and rewards are inextricably linked: only those orders that ask much of members are able to give much. For example, by asking members to concentrate their primary social ties within the group, an order is enabled to provide the rewards of intense attachments and interaction. Thus the hypothesis that *religious orders that retain higher costs will offer more valuable rewards of membership and therefore will be more successful in recruiting new members.*

The 1993 survey of religious orders conducted by the Center for Applied Research in the Apostolate (CARA) allows us to test this conclusion. Requesting detailed information on the number of members in formation programs and those who have taken final vows, the survey allows us to compute a rate of new members in formation. The survey also asked a series of questions about the order's support and involvement in some of the most common post–Vatican II changes. These items included the order's support for living arrangements stressing physical proximity and religious houses, a change in their spirituality (identity and mission) since Vatican II, and whether an order uses an intercommunity formation program or conducts its own training. Each item measures the order's adoption (or resistance to) of changes prompted by Vatican II.

Table 17 offers strong support for the hypothesis. Religious orders abandoning the more traditional demands have far fewer members in formation programs. Orders that still emphasize the importance of religious houses and physical proximity have a new member rate over four times higher than those giving less emphasis to these aspects of community (107 to 23). The new member rate for orders that changed their spirituality since Vatican II was only 41 per 1,000 full members (active members who have taken their final vows), compared to a rate of 95 for those that hadn't changed. Orders participating in intercommunity formation programs also attracted far fewer novices than those who did their own training (40 to 120).

Note that we do not suggest that potential recruits are attracted to the high costs of community life, as if shopping for the most "expensive" order available. Rather, recruits tolerate these costs because they are attracted to the wealth of social and religious rewards provided by a stable community of "religious life." Moreover, higher costs select for those most able and willing to contribute to overall communal satisfaction, while screening out the less committed (both initially and later). Some who at first were attracted to the distinctive lifestyle and community will undoubtedly have second thoughts as they progress through formation programs and the full costs of membership become apparent. Hence, we would expect communities requiring more from their members also to sustain higher rates of attrition from their formation program.

Although the survey did not provide retention rates, it did ask for the number of new members entering in 1992 and the number of members taking final vows in 1992. This gives us the chance to look at a single year and compare the number recruited with the number taking final vows. These comparisons also are shown in table 17 where we can see that the high-commitment communities do have a higher rate of attrition. For example, communities reporting religious houses and physical proximity as extremely important have a rate of 48 new re-

TABLE 17   Recruitment and Commitment to "Tradition" among
531 Catholic Women's Religious Orders
(per 1,000 members)

	Yes	*No*
Life in religious houses and in physical proximity rated as "extremely important."		
Number of novices in formation	107	23
Number of novices entering in 1992	48	6
Number taking final vows in 1992	22	5

	Yes	*No*
Order has changed its "spirituality" since Vatican II		
Number of novices in formation	41	95
Number of novices entering in 1992	15	43
Number taking final vows in 1992	6	22

	Yes	*No*
Novices are trained only by their own community		
Number of novices in formation	120	40
Number of novices entering in 1992	56	13
Number taking final vows in 1992	21	10

SOURCE: 1993 survey of religious orders conducted by the Center for Applied Research in the Apostolate (CARA).
All differences are significant beyond .01.

cruits per 1,000 members, but a rate of only 22 taking final vows, for a dropout rate of 26 per 1,000. By contrast, communities supporting renewal efforts had a dropout rate of only 1 per 1,000.

However, as anticipated, the higher levels of attrition sustained by the more traditional communities were offset by far higher rates of new members taking final vows. Even after the attrition, the rate of members taking final vows was still two to four times higher than that of orders that had embraced the Vatican II changes. The data clearly support the thesis that to the degree that religious orders provide an intense communal life, they will be more successful in recruiting new members.

Yet support for this thesis does not suggest that *all* demands will increase the benefits provided to members. First, religious orders can limit too many activities, just as they can limit too few. The optimal level is high for religious orders, because they must generate community supports that justify the vows of poverty, obedience, and chastity, but it is not unlimited. Second, supporting the tradition of high demands does *not* mean that the most effective strategy is a return to the religious life as it existed just prior to Vatican II. Indeed, religious orders are constrained to maintain an institutional awareness that an uncompromising embrace of tradition can be quite as harmful as laxity—orders can become too rigid to be attractive to new members.

A new generation of religious communities seem aware of this need to balance tradition and adaptation to changing times, for they emphasize the need for *innovative returns to tradition*. Thus, as one founder of a new religious order put it, "[O]ur traditions don't go back to 1953; our traditions go back to 1253. Or 453" (Wittberg 1996, 155). These new orders are demonstrating that they can return to tradition even though the limits they place on their membership vary from those of the pre-Vatican II Church. Thus, for example, while Patricia Wittberg found that the successful new religious communities have restored distinctive habits, "most also wear secular clothes as needed" (ibid., 153).

Like most new movements, many of these new orders will struggle to survive even one generation, often stagnating with only two or three members. But a few are thriving and seem poised for success, and these offer us a glimpse of the possible. A key element, as Albert DiIanni has noted, is that "members are bound together closely and maintain this closeness through communal practices or a structured way of life, a rule" (1993, 747–48).

CONCLUSION

We believe the data are conclusive that the collapse of Catholic vocations was self-imposed, not merely incidental to the process of modernity. It was the assembled bishops of the Catholic Church who, after collective deliberations, withdrew many of the most compelling motivations for the religious life, while retaining the most costly aspects of vocations. Perhaps orthodox Freudians and other proponents of irrational choice theories might have expected that Catholics would still flock to the religious life out of neurotic need. The fact that the "flocking" went in the other direction testifies that humans subject even their most intense forms of religious commitment to reasoned evaluation. This point is additionally confirmed by the exceptions: some dioceses still generate vocations, and some religious orders still attract new members—those able to revivify perceptions of a positive ratio between the costs and rewards of the religious life.

We do not propose that the Catholic Church ought to retain its reliance on costly religious vocations—on a church staffed by a corps of what Max Weber called "religious virtuosi." Centuries of Protestant experience demonstrate the adequacy of less costly vocations. What we do suggest is that to generate and sustain religious virtuosi requires constant reinforcement from an equally committed community of peers, firm belief in divine appreciation of the relevant sacrifices, and special levels of worldly recognition of virtue.

PART FOUR

The Religious Economy

CHAPTER 8

A Theoretical Model
of Religious Economies

Within all social systems there is a relatively distinct subsystem encompassing religious activity. It is useful to identify this subsystem as a religious economy (Stark 1983; 1985).

Definition 32. A **religious economy** consists of all of the religious activity going on in any society: a "market" of current and potential adherents, a set of one or more organizations seeking to attract or maintain adherents, and the religious culture offered by the organization(s).

Just as a commercial economy can be distinguished into elements of supply and demand, so too can a religious economy. Indeed, it is the emphasis on the supply side that so distinguishes the new from the old paradigm, for the latter has stressed demand as the primary dynamic propelling religious change. To illustrate the truly fundamental character of the shift in emphasis, consider that when confronted with major changes in the religious composition of societies— as when the Methodists churched America—proponents of the older paradigm usually pose the basic question as: Why did people's religious preferences change? Why did they abandon one religious institution (or set of institutions) for another?

That seems an entirely reasonable question. Yet, when posed this way, we are directed to seek our answer in shifting demand—to conclude that such changes occur because people suddenly develop new, unmet religious needs and turn to or produce new religious institutions able to meet these needs. Not only do we think this is the wrong answer, we think it answers the wrong question. We shall suggest that religious demand is very stable over time and that religious change is largely the product of supply-side transformations. Hence, we would pose the fundamental question this way: Why do religious organizations change so that they no longer enjoy mass appeal?

In what follows, we construct a model of the structures and processes of religious economies in which the supply side provides the dynamic and the demand side is the basis of stability. Briefly, we begin by identifying a set of relatively stable market niches (or shared preferences) to be found in any society. We then analyze the interplay between religious organizations and market niches under various conditions of regulation by the state. This model has been evolving for more than a decade (Stark 1983; 1985b; 1996b; 1998b; Stark and Bainbridge 1985; [1987] 1996; Finke and Stark 1988; 1992; Finke 1997a; Stark and Iannnaccone 1993; 1994). However, because the version presented here is far more extensive than those previously published, we ask readers who are familiar with our earlier work to take time to examine each step carefully even if they think they are covering familiar ground.

As is obvious from the cumulative numbers given to propositions and definitions across chapters, the theory of religious economies assumes and builds upon all of the more micro elements assembled in previous chapters.

To begin, our focus in this chapter will be on religious economies dominated by exclusive religious organizations:

PROPOSITION 69. Because exclusive religious organizations offer more valuable and apparently less risky religious rewards, when exclusive firms appear in religious economies previously dominated by nonexclusive groups, the exclusive firm(s) become dominant.

A religious portfolio can serve individuals well enough when full-service religious firms are unavailable, but history suggests that when nonexclusive firms are challenged by exclusive competitors, in a relatively unregulated market, the exclusive firms win. The rise of Judaism, of Christianity, and of Islam are classic instances. Each appeared in an economy dominated by nonexclusive firms, and each won because it was the better bargain, despite requiring higher costs. The very rapid growth of Sōka Gakkai in Japan is a contemporary example. Unlike most other Japanese religions, it demands exclusive commitment from its followers and has grown from fewer than six thousand households in 1951 to more than eight million in 1995. Indicative of things to come, a study of students in Singapore by Joseph B. Tamney and Riaz Hassan (1987), found that the overwhelming majority of students from nonexclusive religious backgrounds (Buddhists and various traditional Chinese folk religions) had converted to Islam or Christianity, while virtually no students raised in the latter groups had left their original faith.

In what follows we ignore economies consisting of nonexclusive firms. However, as discussed at length in Chapter 6, there is considerable diversity even among exclusive religious groups and, in the theorizing to come, we pay particular attention to the interplay and competition (actual or potential) among religious groups differing in their degree of tension with their sociocultural environments: churches and sects.

Recall that churches are religious bodies in relatively lower tension with their surroundings while sects are religious bodies in relatively higher tension. Tension consists of differences in norms and values: to the degree that a religious organization sustains norms and values different from those of the surrounding culture, it is deviant. Put another way, the higher the tension between a religious group and its surroundings, *the more expensive it is to belong.*

If religious firms come in a variety of degrees of tension, one reason is because people differ greatly in their religious preferences and tastes. Put more formally:

PROPOSITION 70.   All religious economies include a set of relatively stable market **niches.**

Definition 33.   **Niches** are market segments of potential adherents sharing particular religious preferences (needs, tastes, and expectations).

To postulate the existence of stable preferences is a hallmark of the rational choice approach to social theory.[1] As Gary S. Becker pointed out:

> The preferences that are assumed to be stable do not refer to market goods and services, like oranges, automobiles, or medical care, but to underlying objects of choice.... The assumption of stable preferences provides a stable foundation for generating predictions about responses to various changes, and prevents the analyst from succumbing to the temptation of simply postulating the required shift in preferences [as the explanation of the events or behavior in question]. (Becker 1976, 5)

The growing literature on niches and voluntary associations (Blau 1977; 1994; McPherson 1981; McPherson and Smith-Lovin 1987; McPherson, Popielarz and Drobnic 1992; Popielarz and McPherson 1995) stresses the "homophily principle"—that people tend to associate with people similar to themselves and that voluntary organizations are rooted in specific homophilous niches. This literature stresses "sociodemographic characteristics" as the basis for niche homophily. As will be seen, religious niche homophily does involve such characteristics, but these are much less significant than a *homophily of preferences.*

To the degree that a religious economy is unregulated and market forces prevail, these niches will be quite visible, and each will sustain a set of specialized religious bodies. However, even in highly regulated religious economies limited to a single monopoly faith, these niches will exist, if less distinctly. Under these conditions, some major niches will lack suitable religious options, and will thus serve as a current basis for religious apathy and resentment and as a potential basis for change.

Pamela Popielarz and J. Miller McPherson have proposed that voluntary organizations remain relatively fixed in social space because they "lose members at the edge of the niche faster than in the center. This differential loss of members at the edge of the niche keeps groups from spreading unchecked in social space" (Popielarz and McPherson 1995, 702). But that "rule" has limited application to religious organizations, precisely because they *do not* remain fixed in social space. It is not church-switching that is the primary dynamic in religious economies. Rather, it is *the shifting of religious firms from niche to niche* that has the greatest impact on the overall religious economy, with the consequence that the primary religious suppliers change over time. Thus, rather than ask why so many people abandoned Congregationalism (and did so long before it changed its name to the United Church of Christ), we shall try to explain why the Congregational Church abandoned a relatively large market niche, progressively shifting to smaller niches notable for the lukewarm commitment of their consumers.

We also shall attempt to explain that the stability and dynamics of religious economies are interdependent. Stability consists of the durability of niches in terms of their relative size and the character of their demand. Within free market religious economies, the dynamic of niche-switching by firms ensures that each niche is effectively supplied.

BASIC NICHES

Suppose we ranked people according to the intensity of their religious desires and tastes, and hence by the degree of tension between their religious body and the surrounding society that they would accept. We think the results would somewhat approximate a bell-shaped curve, in that people would cluster towards the center of the axis in the area of medium tension (see fig. 6). Of course, the real world is undoubtedly somewhat lumpier than is shown, but it seems reasonable to assume that to the extent that people prefer levels of intensity that are higher or the lower than medium, the less numerous they will be.

In every known society, people have differed in how much religious intensity they prefer. Max Weber recognized this sort of variation, but explained it in terms of personal abilities or charisma. "That people differ greatly in their religious capacities was found to be true in every religion ... [but] not everyone possesses the charisma that makes possible the continuous maintenance in everyday life of the distinctive religious mood," Weber wrote ([1922] 1993, 162). We can avoid the implicit circularity that often mars Weber's use of the term "charisma" if we distinguish people on the basis of their preferences rather than in terms of some imputed semi-magical or psychic power. That is, rather than focus on religious capacities, it seems far more efficient to settle for the observation that some people always want the religious rewards available only from high-tension (strict) religion and are willing to pay high costs to obtain them, others want very low intensity and inexpensive faith, and some want no religion at all, while most people want religion that maintains some moral reservations vis-à-vis secular life, but not too many.

As we shall see, this variation in demand is obvious in an unregulated religious economy with highly developed competition and specialization. It is less

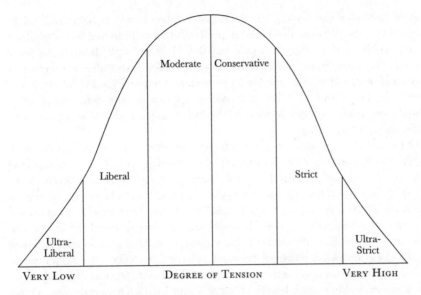

Figure 6. Hypothetical Distribution of Tension across Religious Niches

obvious in highly regulated and monopolized religious economies, where the preferences of many niches go unmet. But even in these societies, niches for those seeking higher- and lower-tension options are provided by the never-ending line of heretical challengers to the monopoly, some offering higher-tension faith and some proposing more worldly faiths. Put another way, in monopoly situations, religious deviants seem to have little trouble finding receptive consumers.

Patterns of religious mergers and of sect formation strongly suggest that the number of religious bodies that the American religious economy needs and can sustain is quite stable, according to a study by André Nauta, who writes:

> I believe that the available evidence supports the premise that there is a critical number of religious organizations necessary to supply the diverse demands of the American population. When the number of denominations drops below this "critical number," then the demand side of the religious economy drives the market to create new alternatives. Conversely, when the number of denominations exceeds this "critical number," then the supply side kicks in, limiting the duplication of services provided by organizations serving the same target market by encouraging religious organizations to merge. (Nauta 1994, 48–49)

NICHE COMPOSITION

It is far easier to describe the array of market niches than it is to explain why they exist. Sociologists have mostly been content to attribute diversity in religious taste to social class. Class undoubtedly plays a role, it being well established that the privileged will tend to prefer a lower-tension and less costly faith than will the less privileged (Argyle and Beit-Hallahmi 1975; Iannaccone 1988; 1990). As Adam Smith put it, religious groups offer "two different schemes or systems of morality," one the "strict or austere; the other the liberal, or, if you will, the loose system." The strict system appeals to "the common people," while the liberal system is adopted by "what are called people of fashion" (Smith [1776] 1981, 794).

Even if class serves as a basis for niches, however, it is not the only, or even the most important, basis. For one thing, novel religions (cult movements) tend to overrecruit the privileged, even if these groups are relatively costly (Stark 1996a). Moreover, overwhelmingly upper-class and lower-class religious organizations, of the sort that most "qualitative" studies of church and sect have taken for granted,[2] simply don't exist. It is past time that we accepted the unanimous results of more than fifty years of quantitative research that show that although class does somewhat influence religious behavior, the effects are very modest, and most religious organizations are remarkably heterogeneous in terms of social status (Bultina 1949; Burchinal 1959; Cantril 1943; Demerath 1965; Dynes 1955; Lenski 1953; Stark 1971a; 1984).

There are many other factors besides class that influence religious preferences, many of which cross-cut (Sherkat 1991; Wallace 1975). Indeed, socialization effects tower above those of class (Sherkat and Wilson 1995). In addition, women seem more inclined than men to favor higher-tension faiths (Argyle and Beit-Hallahmi 1975; Cornwall 1988; Miller and Hoffmann 1995; Thompson 1991). A similar preference for higher tension is typical of disadvantaged racial and ethnic minorities (Argyle and Beit-Hallahmi 1975; Ellison and Sherkat 1995; Fauset 1944; Yinger 1957). Nor should one overlook existential factors stemming from particular life events (Ellison 1991; 1993; Wallace 1975; Yinger 1957; 1970). For example, some people have their religious tastes intensified by crises and subsequently attribute many positive benefits to their faith (Iannaccone 1988). Others develop a preference for a particular niche on the basis of experiences such as participating in secular social movements (Sherkat 1998b).

In any event, we postulate the existence of a stable distribution of diversity of religious demand and identify clusters of persons with shared preferences as market niches. The importance of these niches for the overall religious economy lies in the fact that they make it impossible for one religious organization to satisfy demand. The following propositions now become pertinent.

PROPOSITION 71.   To the degree that a religious economy is unregulated, it will tend to be very **pluralistic.**

Definition 34.   **Pluralistic** refers to the number of firms active in the economy; the more firms there are with significant market shares, the greater the degree of pluralism.

PROPOSITION 72.   The capacity of a single religious firm to monopolize a religious economy depends upon the degree to which the state uses coercive force to regulate the religious economy.

These propositions can easily be deduced from the existence of diverse market niches within an economy dominated by exclusive firms. Variations in demand result in the inherent inability of a single religious product line to satisfy divergent tastes. More specifically, pluralism arises in unregulated markets because of the inability of a single religious firm to be at once worldly and otherworldly, strict and permissive, exclusive and inclusive, expressive and reserved, or (as Adam Smith put it) austere and loose, while market niches will exist with strong preferences on each of these aspects of religion. Thus, no single religious organization can achieve monopoly through voluntary assent—religious monopolies rest upon coercion.

By the same logic, it becomes clear that religious economies can never be fully monopolized, even when backed by the full coercive powers of the state. Indeed, even at the height of its temporal power, the medieval church was surrounded by heresy and dissent (Lambert 1992). Of course, when the repressive efforts of the state are sufficiently intense, religious firms competing with the state-sponsored monopoly will be forced to operate underground. But, whenever and wherever repression eases, pluralism will begin to develop. And this pluralism will be sustained by specialized religious firms, each anchored in a specific niche or a complementary set of niches.

PROPOSITION 73.   To the degree that a religious firm achieves a monopoly, it will seek to exert its influence over other institutions, and the society will thus be **sacralized**.

Definition 35.   **Sacralized** means that there is little differentiation between religious and secular institutions and that the primary aspects of life, from family to politics, are suffused with religious symbols, rhetoric, and ritual.

Sacralization is precisely the social phenomenon so often mistaken for universal piety. The Age of Faith attributed to medieval Europe, for example, is based on the fact that religion was intertwined with other institutions, especially politics and education, and because the presence of religion was so impressively visible. Traveling across Europe today, one's attention is constantly drawn to the magnificent churches and cathedrals that dominate local landscapes. Because all these buildings were built many centuries ago, they seem to offer undeniable proof that faith was once universal and robust enough to erect these marvelous structures. The truth is quite different. These structures were, in effect, extracted from an unwilling and sullen populace whose members seldom crossed their thresholds—at least not for religious purposes. It was because of the piety (and interests) of the medieval ruling classes that religion was so omnipresent and visible on all public occasions. For example, all ceremonies were religious in character, especially political ceremonies such as coronations. Indeed, in sacralized societies, political leadership per se typically has a vivid religious hue, as in claims of the "divine right" of kings and emperors. Close ties between religious and political elites are inherent in religious monopolies, because without such ties religious monopolies are impossible. Sacralization of the political sphere is the quid pro quo by which a religious firm enlists the coercive powers of the state against its competitors.

PROPOSITION 74.   To the degree that deregulation of the religious economy occurs in a previously highly regulated economy, the society will be desacralized.

When the state, for whatever reasons, no longer underwrites the monopoly faith's claims to exclusive legitimacy, desacralization must ensue. Where a plurality of religious firms exists, no one of them is sufficiently potent to sustain sacralization.[3] Nor can sacralization be sustained by some coalition of competing religious firms, for any statements emitted by such a group must be limited to vague generalizations to which all can assent. Such may be the stuff of "civil religion" (Bellah 1967), but it is not the stuff of sacralization. But then neither is it necessarily a symptom of religious decline.

Desacralization, as we define it, is identical to what many scholars have referred to as the macro form of secularization. So long as this definition of secularization is limited to the differentiation of religious and other primary social institutions, we accept it. However, few who apply the term "secularization" to institutional differentiation are able to resist linking desacralization to a general decline in individual religious commitment (the micro version of secularization), because they are convinced that only religious monopolies can sustain belief. We take the entirely opposite position. Our model of religious economies holds that the demise of religious monopolies and the deregulation of religious economies will result in a general increase in individual religious commitment as more firms (and more motivated firms) gain free access to the market.

Keep in mind that there will be a lag between the onset of desacralization and the rise of a vigorous religious pluralism. Thus, for example, although the Roman Catholic Church has been stripped of its monopoly standing and much of its temporal power in many parts of Europe and Latin America, this did not immediately create unregulated religious economies filled with eager firms competing for souls. Considerable desacralization will tend to occur before there is sufficient pluralism to greatly increase religious participation. Thus, over the short term, desacralization can give the appearance of secularization. We must emphasize, however, that this sort of "secularization" is temporary and largely limited to a decline in religious participation—it is never the "extinction" of religion proposed by the standard theories of secularization.

Many factors can slow the development of vigorous pluralism. For one thing, as we explore at length in chapter 9, deregulation of a religious economy often is more apparent than real. The government may announce a policy of religious freedom, or at least of religious toleration, but continue to grant special privileges and financial aid to the traditional monopoly firm, while imposing many hindrances upon new firms. Fully developed pluralism can thus be distorted and delayed by de facto establishment.

In addition, cultural inertia (tradition) will delay the acceptance of new firms as normal and legitimate. The stigmas attached to its competitors by the old monopoly faith will linger, sustaining various forms of prejudice and discrimination against new firms, as will be seen in chapter 9.

Another cause of delay in the development of pluralism is that, to the extent that new firms are branches of outside firms, their success must await the development of social ties between missionaries and locals, for, as noted in chapter 5, network ties must exist or be created in order for religious firms to attract members. Thus, for example, American evangelical Protestant missionaries have been active in Latin America for decades, but growth was extremely slow until after World War II, when the primary missionary work was progressively taken over by local converts. Subsequently, growth has been so rapid that by now evangelical Protestant bodies claim very substantial followings throughout most of the continent—in many nations, Protestants now make up the majority of those actually in church on Sunday (Gill 1998; Stoll 1990; Martin 1990).

Finally, it must be recognized that much of the "decline" in consumer commitment that accompanies desacralization is illusory. Monopoly churches always manage to appear vastly more popular and pervasive than they actually are. A major effect of desacralization in Europe and Latin America was to reveal widespread apathy, rather than to reflect a decline in piety. Keep in mind, too, that monopolists always claim that should they be dislodged, religious life will suffer (and social scientists have been too quick to believe them).

PROPOSITION 75. To the degree that religious economies are unregulated and competitive, overall levels of religious participation will be high. (Conversely, lacking competition, the dominant firm[s] will be too inefficient to sustain vigorous marketing efforts, and the result will be a low overall level of religious participation, with the average person minimizing and delaying payment of religious costs.)

Notice our theoretical emphasis on competition. Religious pluralism (the presence of multiple suppliers) is important only insofar as it increases choices and competition, offering consumers a wider range of religious rewards and forcing suppliers to be more responsive and efficient. A society whose religious economy consists of a dozen rigid castes, each served by its own independent, distinctive religious firm, would be highly pluralistic, but utterly lacking in religious competition. Functionally, the situation of any given individual in such a society would be identical with the situation of an individual in a society with only one, monopoly religious firm. And our prediction would be the same: that within each caste there would be the same low levels of religious commitment expected in monopolized religious economies. Pluralism and competition are usually linked, but when they are not, it is competition that is the energizing force. Misunderstanding of this point seems to have arisen because, lacking direct measures of competition, we often have used measures of pluralism as proxy measures of competition—as we often do in the next chapter.

However, we now must recognize that sometimes *conflict can substitute for competition* as the basis for creating aggressive religious firms able to generate high overall levels of religious commitment.

PROPOSITION 76.   Even where competition is limited, religious firms can generate high levels of participation to the extent that the firms serve as the primary organizational vehicles for social conflict. (Conversely, if religious firms become significantly less important as vehicles for social conflict, they will be correspondingly less able to generate commitment.)

Consider the example of the society noted above in which a dozen rigid castes each has its own religious firm. Now suppose there is a high level of conflict among these castes, and that the religious firms serve as the organizational basis for these conflicts. Perhaps the temples serve as the gathering place for planning all political action, protest demonstrations begin at the temples, and religious symbols are used to identify caste solidarity. In such situations, religious commitment would be inseparable from group loyalty, just as high levels of Catholic commitment in Ireland and Quebec both symbolized and sustained opposition to the English ruling elites in both societies. For generations, Catholic piety was inseparable from Irish and French-Canadian nationalism. The same principle applies to Islamic "fundamentalism." Opposition to political, economic, and cultural colonialism has found its firmest institutional basis in the mosque. We shall pursue these matters in greater detail in chapter 9.

Three additional propositions conclude this portion of the theory:

PROPOSITION 77.   Societies with low levels of religious participation will be lacking in effective religious socialization.

Simply put, where parents are lax religiously, children will be too. And where the dominant religious firm(s) are inefficient and lack vigor, they will fail effectively to socialize the young. Recall the religious ignorance of people in medieval times.

PROPOSITION 78.   Where large numbers of people receive ineffective religious socialization, subjective religiousness will tend to be idiosyncratic and heterodox but far more widespread than organized religious participation.

Recall that medieval peasants worshipped a jumble of supernatural beings, only some of them Christian, but that belief in such supernatural beings was far more widespread than was mass attendance.

PROPOSITION 79.   The capacity of new religious firms to enter relatively unregulated markets successfully is inverse to the efficiency and variety of existing religious firms.

Other things being equal, new firms can enter any market only to the extent that opportunity exists either because of weak competition from firms already in place or because of unserved or underserved niches in the market. Anything that results in inefficiency among existing religious firms, or in an unserved market niche, will ease the entry of new firms. The reference to relatively unregulated markets is to call attention to the fact that start-up costs for new religious firms will be high when the state represses challengers to an established faith. But the larger point is that entry will also be difficult (albeit usually less dangerous) when the market is saturated with efficient firms. The relationship between the degree of regulation of a religious economy and start-up costs for new religious firms is thus curvilinear, declining as the state exerts less coercion on behalf of a monopoly firm, but rising again as fully developed pluralism results in a crowded marketplace of effective and competitive firms.

In chapter 9 we summarize and assess an immense body of research pertinent to these propositions. But many more aspects of religious economies remain to be examined. For example, if pluralism is the natural state of religious economies, where do all of these competing religious organizations come from?

SUPPLY-SIDE MOVEMENT: THE SECT-TO-CHURCH PROCESS

As discussed in chapter 6, H. Richard Niebuhr (1929) gave theoretical life to the terms "sect" and "church" by linking them in a process. According to Niebuhr, sects arise to meet the religious needs of the "masses." However, over time, the more successful sects tend to be transformed into churches and no longer adequately serve the needs and tastes of the proletariat. Consequently, dissidents break away to found a new sect. This gives rise to an endless cycle of birth, transformation, and rebirth of sect movements.

Chapter 6 gave extended attention to the ways in which growth, in and of itself, can cause the transformation of sects into churches by diluting the density and effectiveness of social networks. Although Niebuhr did recognize that growth was involved, his model rests on the assumption that sect transformation is caused by a shift in the social class composition of the sect—that when a sect includes a sufficient number of middle- and upper-class members, they will successfully initiate reductions in the tension between the organization and secular society. However, Niebuhr said very little about how or why a sect would develop a middle- and upper-class membership.

Subsequently, a number of obvious mechanisms have been identified to explain the upward shift in the class composition of sects. Each shares the assumption that, once in control, the privileged will seek to lower a sect's tension with the world, because *the privileged pay a higher cost for strictness.*

That strictness is more costly for the privileged seems obvious. At the turn of the twentieth century, it was rich Methodists who bore the heaviest burden of rules such as those against drinking, gambling, dancing, card-playing, and theater-going (Finke and Stark 1992)—for these rules hindered their association with others of their class. In similar fashion, the emancipation of Jews in most of Europe during the middle of the nineteenth century presented wealthy Jews with intolerable temptations to shed the very distinctive appearance of Orthodoxy (yarmulkes, side curls, and shawls) and to abandon kosher dietary restrictions, as these greatly limited their ability to associate with non-Jews. Reform Judaism was the organizational result (Steinberg 1965).

Clearly, too, it is the privileged who join with the clergy (see chapter 6) to transform sects into churches—there is a very substantial literature on the relationship between class divisions and sectarian schisms (Stark and Bainbridge 1985; 1987). But where do privileged sect members come from?

First of all, despite the fact that the privileged often favor reduced tension, privileged persons also usually play a leading role in forming sects. It is unlikely that any sect movement (or at least any modestly successful one) has been entirely the work of the dispossessed. Most sects begin with a significant number of more privileged persons who, for a variety of idiosyncratic reasons, prefer intense religion. Thus, for example, early Christianity is now known not to have been a proletarian movement, but was based primarily on more privileged classes (Stark 1996a). Privileged founders do not typically seek subsequently to reduce the tension of the group (although that occurred in Christian Science), but their children often do play such a transformative role. In addition, major changes often occur in the initial class composition of sects because many people who join or who are born into the sect become successful. Simple regression to the mean would account for some of this shift in class composition (Stark and Bainbridge 1985). It also has long been recognized that sect membership often engenders financial success. In his much neglected *The Theory of Moral Sentiments,* Adam Smith noted ([1759] 1982, 170–74) that sects socialize people to act in disciplined and responsible ways, which causes them to achieve. In addition, Smith noted, sect members are regarded as exceptionally trustworthy, and this gives them advantages in financial transactions. More than a century after Smith wrote about these aspects of sectarians, Max Weber ([ca. 1913] 1946) made the same points following his visit to America. Subsequently, Benton Johnson (1961) found strong empirical support for this thesis in a study of members of holiness sects. And David Martin (1990) has offered similar observations about Latin American converts to Protestant sects, that they gain an economic advantage, both because they become more reliable employees and because employers are aware of this and give them preference in hiring.

Finally, when a religious body has shifted from a higher- to a lower-tension niche, its class composition will change because of a shift in who joins, as well as because of the departure of less privileged members.

In any event, often it does not require a large proportion of privileged members to transform a sect into a lower state of tension. Studies repeatedly have found that church contributions are extremely skewed—most of the funds come from a few large donors (Hoge 1994; Hoge and Yang 1994). Laurence Iannaccone (1997) has shown that this is necessarily the case in all instances when members of a religious body vary substantially in terms of both commitment and wealth, and when commitment and wealth are little correlated. The wishes of the few who provide the funds are bound to matter, and this will be especially the case when a new generation of seminary-trained clergy have their own motives for wishing to make the sect more "respectable" (Finke and Stark 1992; Stark and Bainbridge 1985).

It is important to realize that sect transformation is gradual—religious firms don't jump from one niche to another; rather, they slowly proceed down the tension dimension. Internal conflicts arise as they begin to pass out of range of a higher-tension niche, causing people in that niche to begin to display sectarian discontents.

To sum up this discussion more formally:

PROPOSITION 80.   Religious organizations mainly originate through sect formation.

Note that this proposition does not mention schisms, leaving open the possibility of sects forming to serve high-tension niches without having actually broken away from a lower-tension religious organization. Thus, in addition to Niebuhr's mechanism whereby new sects are created via schisms as sects are transformed into churches, this proposition can be derived otherwise, as shown in proposition 91 below.

PROPOSITION 81.   Sect movements that endure and grow will tend to reduce their tension with the sociocultural environment, thereby moving away from the market niche(s) in which they originally were based (a process referred to as the sect-to-church transformation).

This is the central proposition in Niebuhr's theory. At the beginning of this process, reduction in tension will be reinforced by results:

PROPOSITION 82.   As sects initially lower their tension, they become more appealing to larger niches and will therefore grow.

The recent history of the Seventh-day Adventists offers an instructive example (Lawson, 1995). Not only will growth confirm the wisdom of modest reductions in tension, it will begin to draw members with a preference for less tension.

PROPOSITION 83.   As religious groups move into range of the largest niches and abandon their original market niche(s), they tend to suffer schisms as sect movements break away to serve members with higher-tension preferences.

This helps explain why larger religious groups are substantially more subject to schisms (Liebman, Sutton, and Wuthnow 1988).

Propositions 80 though 83 can be found in Niebuhr, at least implicitly. However, if this line of theorizing is pursued, additional results come to light.

ADDITIONAL IMPLICATIONS OF SECT-TO-CHURCH MOVEMENT

PROPOSITION 84.   Where free market conditions prevail, given the relative size of niches, at any given moment, religious bodies based on medium-tension niches will enroll the larger portion of the population.

This is obviously true in the United States, where free market conditions prevail, but may be distorted in societies where the religious economy is highly regulated and where there may be no religious options for the largest preference niches. Thus, in European nations with state churches, in terms of actual participation the higher-tension niches claim a larger membership, while apathy characterizes most of those in the medium niches.

PROPOSITION 85.   As moderate religious bodies continue to reduce their tension, they move away from the larger niches and cease to grow.

Propositions 80 through 85 explain the rise and subsequent decline of many American religious bodies (also see chapter 6).

PROPOSITION 86.   At any given moment, religious growth will therefore be limited primarily to somewhat higher tension bodies.

There is an abundance of evidence on this point, summarized in chapter 6.

PROPOSITION 87.   Because of the transformation of sects into churches, there will tend to be an oversupply of lower-tension religious bodies.

As bodies move from higher- to lower-tension niches, they will tend to accumulate at the liberal end of the spectrum, and growing numbers of organizations will thus attempt to serve a relatively static number of potential members. Consequently:

PROPOSITION 88.   Low-tension bodies will typically have declining memberships and will tend to disappear via mergers.

From examination of many church mergers, André Nauta concluded that "mergers seem to be primarily related to supply. In particular, there is a recognition on the part of adherents in two (or more) denominations that their organizations are serving the same type of consumers, that they are offering essentially the same product" (Nauta 1994, 46)

PROPOSITION 89.   Because of the transformation of sects into churches, there will tend to be an undersupply of religious bodies serving the medium-tension niches, creating an opportunity for new bodies, most of which will migrate from stricter niches.

This adds to the opportunity for growth noted in proposition 82. Now let us see more clearly where the seeming abundance of sects comes from.

PROPOSITION 90.   Religious organizations are easier to form to the extent that they can be sustained by a small number of members.

There are two reasons why this is the case. First, the smaller the number needed, the easier it will be for a founder or founders to attract the necessary number—to attract 20 followers, rather than, say, 2,000. Second, as noted in chapter 6, small groups can much more easily reduce free-riding by better monitoring of members' contributions and by being better able to motivate those contributions, hence the smaller the group, the greater the proportional per capita contributions. Consequently, it takes amazingly few people to sustain a sect, if they are sufficiently committed. In the late 1970s, of 417 American-born sects, about 30 percent had fewer than 500 members, and more than half had fewer than 2,000 (Stark and Bainbridge 1981a). There are many sects able to own a church building despite having fewer than two dozen members. Such groups can exist only if each member makes a substantial contribution of both time and money. Therefore:

PROPOSITION 91.   Most religious groups will begin in a relatively high state of tension.

Thus, we have rederived proposition 80. Strict groups are strong because only they can inspire very high levels of commitment in their followers. However, people who can be motivated to the extent required to sustain the birth of a sect make up a relatively small market niche. Thus, as noted, the subsequent success of a sect will require eventual relaxation of tension, thus enabling the group to appeal to a larger niche. Despite the small size of the highest-tension niche, however, it seems fairly easy to recruit a founding nucleus of members from within this niche if a group displays sufficient intensity of purpose, particularly a group that is just forming and aspires to great accomplishments. Perhaps this is because some people are especially receptive to what might strike others as minor differences in theology or worship style. That surely is consistent with the immense amount of diversity be found among the very strict sects and the emphasis each gives to these differences.

PROPOSITION 92.   Most sects do not reduce their initial level of tension and do not grow, and the high-tension end of the church-sect spectrum will therefore abound in small, unsuccessful religious organizations.

That most sects are not transformed into lower-tension religious groups has been derived formally (Iannaccone 1988), and this necessarily results in the existence of a large number of sects. Here we depart from Niebuhr's classic thesis that sects naturally evolve into mainstream denominations, for the evidence is overwhelming that most sects never amount to much. Most are dead ends. They start small, remain small, and slowly wither away.

There are many reasons why most sects fail. As with all organizations that must face the marketplace, sects often fail for want of a sufficiently attractive or distinctive product. Others fail because of ineffective marketing. Still others fail because of internal faction fights or lack of effective leadership. Sometimes sects begin with a level of tension that virtually precludes much recruitment. Many sects are created by the efforts of one person—they form around a leader with exceptional interpersonal skills (some call this charisma). In many such instances, initial growth ceases as the leader becomes smothered in intra-group relationships and loses the capacity to form new attachments with out-siders (Stark and Roberts 1982). Finally, the success or failure of many sects stems from lack of a sufficient market opening. As a result of the overproduc-tion of sects, they face fierce competition.

Thus, for every sect movement that achieves great things, there are scores that amount to very little. Only one of the many Bible student groups that formed in response to the teachings of Charles Taze Russell went on the be-come the Jehovah's Witnesses. The others were (and some remain) small and obscure. In our judgment, Niebuhr was fully aware of this, but focused his theo-rizing on the fate of "successful" sects, because these are the ones that change religious history. Yet because sect formation occurs so frequently, especially in an unregulated religious economy, it is important to include the failures as well as the rare successes in any general model.

DEMAND-SIDE MOVEMENT: SWITCHING NICHES

Although it is true that some people do move from religious niche to niche in response to various factors, most do not. Most Americans who switch churches select a new church that is very similar to their old one in terms of the church-sect continuum. As noted in chapter 5, most church-switching occurs within niches, and what switching across niches does occur tends to be intergenera-tional. Niche-switching is mildly related to status attainment, because, as al-ready noted, higher-tension religion is more costly for the more privileged. People who have achieved a status well above the average level of their niche will tend to shift to a lower-tension faith. Conversely, the downwardly mobile will tend to switch toward higher tension. But keep in mind that these are not strong effects. Class is far from the primary determinate of religious prefer-ences. Socialization is many times more important, which is why niches are so stable and why so few people switch. Even socialization effects are far from be-ing determinative, however, and there remains substantial latitude for people to formulate religious preferences on the basis of quite idiosyncratic life experiences and influences (Sherkat 1991; 1996; Sherkat and Wilson 1995; Stark and Glock 1968; Stolzenberg, Blair-Loy, and Waite 1994).

It also should be noted that a major mode of demand-side niche-cycling does not show up in church-switcher statistics, because the people don't switch. Instead, they move to a lower-tension niche along with their religious body— indeed, they propel that body into lower tension. This was how genteel Congregationalists shifted niches without shifting affiliation.

NICHE CHARACTERISTICS: A CLOSER LOOK

Let us pause to characterize what we believe to be the primary religious niches. Although most of the examples will be from the American religious economy, let it be clear that we propose that a set of demand niches, differing in terms of the degree to which they seek high levels of religious rewards and will accept high costs to gain them, exist in all religious economies. Keep in mind that variation in demand, as we define it, is probably a continuous variable, and it is therefore somewhat arbitrary to impose distinct boundaries on this continuum. By identifying distinct sectors along this continuum, however, we are able to clarify the analysis without too greatly distorting the underlying reality. The number of distinct niches along the continuum of demand will undoubtedly be influenced by the size of the society and its social complexity. Thus, some small, premodern societies might contain only three niches, consisting of those wanting their religion to be intense, not so intense, or permissive (Geertz 1966). In contrast, we identify six primary niches in the American religious economy. We think the American pattern is basic, but for it to fully develop requires that a free market religious economy have been functioning for a substantial time. In regulated economies, such as European nations with state churches, the niches will be more latent than in the American case. Moreover, just as regulation distorts a religious economy by suppressing pluralism, so, too, it may produce some shifts in the relative size of niches—especially the most liberal. This is likely because, if the dominant religious firm(s) is lax, popular religious tastes are apt to be affected (as is implied in proposition 28). Regulation also may increase the proportion of the population whose religious indifference or even antagonism places them entirely outside of the religious market.

The Ultraliberal Niche

Let us begin with the most liberal or lowest-tension end of the spectrum, at the very boundary between religion and "philosophy." Here we find people who barely want religion at all. It is significant that they are not quite willing to be atheists or agnostics, but they will accept only a very remote and inactive conception of the supernatural ("I can conceive of some sort of higher power in the universe, but not a personal god.")

Organizations serving this niche include the Unitarian Universalists, many New Age groups, some of the early Christian Gnostic groups (Williams 1996), and (at least until recently) Reform Judaism. In addition, the most liberal wing of the Episcopalian Church and the United Church of Christ appeal to this niche.

Many of these groups were not created by sect transformation, but were created from scratch. Others were born as church movements. Whereas sect movements often break off from churches (or from sects moving in the churchlike direction) to provide a new organization for members of a niche that is being abandoned, church movements break off from medium- and higher-tension organizations.

PROPOSITION 93. **Church movements** are formed by dissidents wishing to shift to a lower-tension niche who lack the power to shift the organization.

Definition 36. **Church movements** are schismatic movements that break away to enter a lower level of tension.

In a sense, church movements break off from the front edge of a higher-tension organization, whereas sect movements break off from the trailing edge. When the Unitarians abandoned (or were ejected from) Congregationalism, they were a church movement (Stark and Bainbridge 1985). Another important example is, of course, Reform Judaism when it broke with Orthodoxy. Michael Allen Williams has identified several groups of Christian Gnostics, including the Valentinians and the Basilideans, as "church movements" (1996, 109–13).

Religious bodies based on the ultraliberal niche are not often subject to schisms. For all that they may have begun as church movements or have spawned sect movements earlier in their histories, when they were in higher tension, they now hardly have sufficient member interest to sustain themselves, and no one cares enough to launch a sect. This accounts for the fact that the more liberal the denomination, the less likely it is to undergo a schism (Liebman, Sutton, and Wuthnow 1988).

Groups in this niche typically have little intergenerational stability and must recruit new members each generation. In part this seems to be because they serve as a sort of halfway house on the route to irreligion. And in part it is because, like most of the offspring of the irreligious, their children so often opt for a relatively high-tension faith (Kluegel 1980). These groups also suffer from low levels of participation and an oversupply of free-riders and therefore tend not to be durable. The ultraliberal and ultrastrict niches probably "each lose about as many members as they gain [in the niche-shifting process, but] the liberals gain the least committed, while the more committed choose the conservative denominations," Darren Sherkat notes (1997, 72).

The Liberal Niche

People in this niche want real religion, but they want it to be very permissive in terms of sacrifices. Many of them entered this niche as adults, often as a result of upward social mobility. They believe in an active supernatural, but conceive of it in very diffuse and agreeable ways. Among Christians, for example, people in this niche tend to believe in heaven, but to reject hell. They do not desire their religion to impose moral prohibitions much more rigorous than those of the secular world. They also typically prefer a money-intensive as opposed to a labor-intensive organization, and the actual time they devote to religious activities is thus low compared to their church contributions (see chapter 6).

Among groups primarily serving this niche are the Episcopalians and United Church of Christ, while the Presbyterians and Methodists are currently based in both this and the moderate niche. Aside from the Episcopalians, each of these groups was once a vigorous sect, but today all are denominations in decline, because this niche is considerably smaller than the niches each left behind, and there is a substantial oversupply of groups available.

The Moderate Niche

Here, in one of the two largest niches, are people who prefer a more demanding faith but generally wish to limit their "religiousness" to specific times, places, and functions. They are regular worshippers and experience a sense of relatively close relations with the supernatural, which they define in active, aware, personal terms. They pray frequently and in specific terms. They do not, however, want an especially strict faith—one that involves many duties and prohibitions.

Bodies serving this niche include most Lutheran groups, American Baptists, the more liberal wing of the Southern Baptist Convention (Ammerman 1990), and some congregations of Conservative Jews. As noted above, too, the Methodists and Presbyterians still serve this niche to some extent. There is still some room for growth within this niche, but because it will tend to have an oversupply of groups, rates of growth will be far lower than in the conservative niche.

The Conservative Niche

Here are people who take their religion quite seriously and are willing to endure some degree to sacrifice and stigma on its behalf. For example, they observe significant behavioral prohibitions, such as against drinking, dancing, gambling, or eating certain foods. They tend to devote considerable time to religious activities and they often refer to their religion to guide them in daily life.

Examples of organizations based on this niche are most congregations within the Southern Baptist Convention, the Seventh-day Adventists, Missouri Lutherans, and Conservative Jews. Most of these groups are growing.

The Strict Niche

These are the people Niebuhr had in mind when he wrote about the birth of sects in response to the transformation of religious bodies into more worldly organizations. Being the liberal intellectual that he was, however, Niebuhr could not praise their "emotional fervor" without sneering at their theology and modes of worship; their "power of abstract thought has not been highly developed," he wrote, and the result is "a simple, often crude symbolism" and an "intellectual naïveté," which leads to millenarianism (Niebuhr 1929, 30).

In point of fact, there is no lack of intelligence and sophistication in this niche. The most famous sect founders in history—including the Wesley brothers and John Calvin—stood firmly within it. What is characteristic of people in this niche, which so often puts off outsiders, is a determination to let their lives be fully guided by their religious convictions. This always involves substantial sacrifices and stigmas. That is, people in this niche tend to do a lot for their religion, including missionary activity, and many people will regard them as fanatics for doing so much.

Two of the most rapidly growing religious movements in the world serve this niche: the Jehovah's Witnesses and the Mormons. In addition, most Pentecostal groups, including the Assemblies of God and the Nazarenes, also serve this niche, as do the many Churches of Christ, and some Orthodox Jewish groups. This niche tends to be overproductive of religious organizations, and competitive forces are thus severe, but this ensures the vigor and market appeal of those bodies that emerge from the pack.

The Ultrastrict Niche

Here are people for whom this world is of limited interest, who attempt to focus on the supernatural to the fullest extent possible, and who find frequent means to demonstrate their devotion, often by rejecting worldly joys and pleasures. Max Weber identified these "religious virtuosi who work methodically at their salvation" in a variety of different religious traditions:

> In India all the sacred laws concerned themselves with the ascetic in this sense, since most of the Hindu religions of salvation were monastic. The earliest Christian sources represent these religious virtuosi as comprising a particular category, distinguished from their comrades in the community, and they later constituted the monastic orders. In Protestantism they formed the ascetic sects or pietistic conventicles. In Judaism they were the *perushim (Pharisaioi)*, an aristocracy with respect to salvation which stood in contrast to the *am haarez*. In Islam they were the dervishes, and among the dervishes the particular virtuosi were the authentic Sufis. (Weber [1922] 1993, 162–63)

Organizations serving this niche are notable for their degree of separation or encapsulation from secular society. Often this separation is sustained by visible stigmas that clearly mark their religious identity as Amish, Benedictine monks, Hare Krishnas, or Hasidim. In addition, actual physical separation is often maintained, as in the case of many religious orders and rural communes (the Shakers, for example). This niche also abounds in obscure, tiny, unsuccessful religious organizations.

Let us pause here to reconsider the distribution of demand. Figure 6 depicts it as a bell-shaped curve, and we justified that assumption on the grounds that demand probably would cluster around the mean. After having postulated that distribution and even after having associated various denominations with particular market niches, we undertook a quantitative assessment of this assumption. Unfortunately, no direct measures of demand are available. No items have assessed underlying religious preferences, and nearly all measures of religious belief and behavior are extremely skewed. Most Americans believe in God, attend church, pray, read the Bible, say grace, and give money to a church, and such data do not therefore distinguish niches. The best approximation of niche membership must be inferred from denominational affiliation.

Table 18 is based on all years of the General Social Surveys from 1972 through 1994 (GSS). We coded Christians[4] according to the location of their religious group[5] along the tension dimension, assuming that this reflected the primary niche bases of the various bodies: that Unitarian Universalists, for example, mainly represent the ultraliberal niche, while members of Holiness sects belong in the ultrastrict niche. Because the Catholics make up such a large group, and because the church clearly straddles the conservative and moderate niches (see the next section), we assigned Catholics to a niche on the basis of their responses to the question: "Would you call yourself a strong Catholic or not a very strong Catholic?" The 39 percent of Catholics who said they were "strong Catholics" were assigned to the conservative niche, and the rest were assigned to the moderate niche.

Notice that the distribution of cases does roughly trace a normal curve. Notice too that our coding is in extraordinary agreement ($r = .83$) with the three-category coding assigned by the staff of the National Opinion Research Center (NORC) where the data were collected. Finally, the data strongly suggest that niche preferences are quite stable, in that most people are in a denomination similar to the one to which they belonged at age 16.

NICHE-STRADDLING

We have noted that the Methodists and the Presbyterians are currently based in both the liberal and the moderate niches; the Episcopalians and the United Church of Christ straddle the ultraliberal and liberal niches; and some Southern Baptist congregations serve the moderate niche, even though most serve the conservative niche. Niche-straddling is not uncommon, because the move toward lower-tension niches is usually gradual. However, some bodies are better

TABLE 18   American Demand Niches

	% Ultraliberal (n=132)	% Liberal (n=2,957)	% Moderate (n=5,059)	% Conservative (n=5,623)	% Strict (n=2,066)	% Ultrastrict (n=200)
	0.8	18.4	31.5	35.1	12.9	01.3
NORC denominational coding						
Liberal	100	92	0	0	0	0
Moderate	0	8	94	57	2	3
Fundamentalist	0	0	6	43	97	98
Denomination at age 16 (NORC codes)						
Liberal	50	67	5	6	12	10
Moderate	35	20	87	55	18	18
Fundamentalist	15	13	8	39	70	72

SOURCE: General Social Surveys, 1972–95

suited than others for straddling niches. For example, the immense autonomy of local congregations facilitates the ability of the Southern Baptists to serve two niches and perhaps even three, given the recent doctrinal pronouncements of the Southern Baptist Alliance—a liberal faction that still remains within the Convention. The remarkable internal diversity of the Baptists has escaped those who characterize religion in the American South as monolithic because of the high proportion of Baptists. In many southern towns, there is as much diversity among the four Southern Baptist congregations as would be found in a town whose four congregations were affiliated with the Episcopalians, Methodists, Nazarenes, and Assemblies of God. Indeed, a remarkable degree of competition in the form of "sheep stealing" often exists among local Southern Baptist congregations. Indeed, no denominational approval is required in order to found a new Southern Baptist congregation or for it to be welcomed into full affiliation.

For rather different reasons, the Roman Catholic Church is especially capable of serving several niches. One important factor is that parishes are geographically defined, and niches often have distinctive geographic patterns too. Consequently, Catholic parishes in different parts of a city often attempt to serve rather different niches and therefore vary their worldliness accordingly. Catholic religious orders have played a major role in helping the church serve diverse niches. First of all, the orders serve as a substitute for sects, allowing Catholics who seek a very high-tension religious life to have it (Stark and Bainbridge 1985; Finke and Wittberg in press). Second, the orders provide the church with the equivalent of sectarian preachers and revivalists to appeal to the conservative and strict niches (Dolan 1978; Finke and Stark 1992).

In recent years, however, the Catholic Church has emphasized its appeal to the liberal niche, with many of the expected consequences, such as massive losses to Protestant sects in Latin America and in the American Southwest (Martin 1990; Stoll 1990; Gill 1998). These losses may have been somewhat limited because Catholicism is a "high church," one in which ritual plays a major role in worship services. Thus, while many Protestant groups have gradually omitted most traditional religious language and references from their worship services, this cannot happen in high churches (Episcopalians and Lutherans in addition to Catholics) because traditional Christian doctrine is firmly embedded in the liturgies. Catholics who want a vigorous faith can find it in the liturgy and rituals, while liberals can treat the ritual as poetry and theater, taking comfort from the lack of high-tension passages in the sermons. This makes sense of Darren Sherkat's (1998a) finding that at the liberal end of the American denominational spectrum, the high churches are doing better than the low churches.

However, although niche-straddling frequently occurs, it is limited even for high churches. There is no way that a single organization can straddle niches from the liberal through the conservative, to say nothing of the liberal to the strict niches.

CHURCH-TO-SECT MOVEMENT

Niebuhr denied that it was possible for churches to shift in the direction of higher tension. And, although Benton Johnson pointed out in a footnote that a shift in this direction "is at least conceivable" (1963, 543), that possibility has been ignored. Probably because so many social scientists have such a pronounced preference for low-tension religion (or for none at all), it has been all but unthinkable that once a denomination was well along the road to liberalism, anything could cause it to move back up the tension dimension. Yet, as the Counter-Reformation demonstrated, this is entirely possible.

PROPOSITION 94.   If the secular rewards of religious vocations decline, then religious rewards must play an increasing part in the motivation of those who pursue such vocations.

PROPOSITION 95.   To the extent that religious rewards motivate religious leaders, they will prefer a relatively higher level of tension for the group.

These propositions are the subject of chapter 10, where we shall see that precisely these changes already are under way in many American religious groups.

PROPOSITION 96.   As a religious body in a low state of tension moves to a higher state of tension, it moves from smaller to larger niches and has an increased opportunity for growth.

PROPOSITION 97.   In an unregulated religious economy, where the survival of all religious groups rests on market processes, growth will facilitate the efforts of clergy to move a group into lower or higher tension.

Chapter 10 also documents these developments.

Thus, the circle is closed. If growth tempts sects to reduce their strictness, it may likewise tempt declining liberal groups to increase their tension with society. The implication of both kinds of shifts occurring simultaneously greatly complicates the model. That is, the onset of church-to-sect movement by firms that have found the liberal niche too small and too uncommitted may cause an oversupply of firms appealing to the medium-tension niches. What then? It may be that if religious firms begin to enter the medium-tension niches from the left, this will reduce the opportunities for groups entering from the right. Will this eventually lead former liberal groups to shift back to the state of lower tension they previously occupied? Could offsetting tendencies to move toward the center stabilize the religious marketplace, with firms coming to rest within specific niches, thereby conforming to the "rule" whereby voluntary organizations become fixed in social space, as proposed by Popielarz and McPherson (1995)? If so, then the dynamic forces would be found on the demand side, inasmuch as church-switching would become the primary form of religious change. Because America has the first fully unregulated religious economy, and it has not been functioning very long, we may have yet to see the full range of processes inherent in it. That fact also should remind us that shifting from church to sect is likely to occur only to the extent that the religious economy is unregulated and individual firms are therefore fully market-dependent.[6] In regulated economies, although the state-supported churches draw their members only from the moderate-to-liberal niches, they will not benefit from growth, because they are not at the mercy of the market. On the contrary, when clergy are civil servants (as they are in Germany and Scandinavia), they have more to gain from empty churches (which make no demands on their time) than from full ones, as will be described in chapter 9.

CONCLUSION

H. Richard Niebuhr wrote *The Social Sources of Denominationalism* in order to explain the "evils of denominationalism" (1929, 21). In recognizing the existence of a cyclical process by which sects are born, transformed, and born again, he made a most important (if grudging and often vituperative) contribution to social theory. Here we have attempted to take Niebuhr's parsimonious little model and embed it in a larger system wherein many additional processes and relationships can be seen and explained. Our expanded model reveals the "whys" of many things we already knew as facts, such as why most religious movements begin as sects; why liberal churches have been prone to mergers, as well as to declining membership; why growth is concentrated in the higher-tension sector. The model also prompts awareness of things not previously obvious: for example, that clergy of liberal denominations may turn conservative, and that religious organizations may move from lower to higher tension. Time will tell.

CHAPTER 9

Religious Competition and Commitment

An International Assessment

When it was first introduced (Stark 1983; 1985), some social scientists seemed offended by the phrase "religious economy," and the very idea that competition strengthens religion was greeted with considerable derision. Only a true Philistine would attempt to apply crass economic principles to the sacred. And doesn't everyone know that competition corrodes religious plausibility? Fortunately, in addition to all this heat, there were frequent glimmers of light in the form of research. So now, more than a decade later, only a few recusants continue to claim that religious phenomena are exempt from principles such as supply and demand. As ought to be the case, most social scientists changed their minds about these matters on the basis of a very large and still-growing empirical literature supporting the new approach, a literature notable for its diversity as to time and place.

In this chapter, we summarize and interpret this body of research in order to assess our claims about religious competition. Unfortunately, competition is one of those concepts that is very difficult to measure, except indirectly. In the pertinent research literature, competition often has been inferred from the degree of pluralism, the number of independent religious organizations having a significant market share (often estimated by the Herfindahl Index). It must be noted that in some circumstances, pluralism does not result in competition and thus will not be associated with higher levels of religious commitment. For example, in multicultural caste systems where each caste has its own religion, there is much pluralism but no competition. In several other studies, competition has been inferred from the degree of state regulation of the religious market. And, in fact, variations in pluralism and competition typically are the result of variations in regulation. However, this measure can be distorted by the substantial lag that occurs between decreases in regulation and the rise of religious competition. Thus, it was several generations after Latin American regimes began to condone Protestant activity before substantial pluralism developed.

As the model was refined to recognize demand niches, it became clearer that an important aspect of competition was, not merely to force religious firms to be energetic and efficient, but to ensure market diversity. That is, to the extent that efficient and energetic firms seek to mobilize all of the basic variations in demand, overall levels of participation also will be higher. We assume that in relatively unregulated markets with an abundance of firms, market forces will ensure diversity. Hence, competition and diversity are both aspects of pluralism.

Most efforts to test the model have concentrated on the following hypotheses:

1. To the extent that pluralism or regulation are adequate inferential measures of competition, the overall level of religiousness will be higher where pluralism is greater or where regulation is lower.
2. Under special circumstances, conflict can substitute for competition in generating high levels of religiousness. For example, when a church serves as the organizational basis for ethnic conflict (as might be the case in the example of the caste system noted above) or provides the rallying point for resistance to external repression (as was the case in Poland), a "monopoly church" can generate immense support.
3. Individual religious groups will be more energetic and generate higher levels of commitment to the degree that they have a marginal market position—lack market share. That is, other things being equal, small religious minorities will be more vigorous than will firms with a large local following. Thus, for example, Roman Catholics will be more active the less Catholic their community.
4. Above a certain level, pluralism becomes redundant. In principle, maximum diversity is not reached until everyone in a given population belongs to her or his own individual congregation of one. Not surprisingly, we have discovered that there is a "ceiling effect"—that beyond a certain point, the market is saturated and additional competition and diversity do not increase the overall level of religious participation.
5. From the point of view of the individual, religious diversity is a very local phenomenon. This becomes important if effects of diversity are examined in larger areal units that are more diverse than the local units within which people actually have options. For example, a county might consist of eight towns, each having only one denomination. Hence, the county might appear to be quite diverse, with eight denominations, when in fact no resident has more than one convenient option.
6. In the absence of effective state repression of competition, the success of new religious firms will be proportionate to "market" opportunities provided by unserved niches and the inefficiency of existing firms.

This chapter is organized not only in terms of the above hypotheses but also in terms geocultural "blocs." We begin with the obvious case: Why is religious participation so high in the United States? Then we examine western Europe.

Next, we consider instances when conflict substitutes for competition: Quebec, Poland, the Netherlands, and Ireland. Then, because Catholicism presents some special issues, we devote a section to competition and Catholicism. Returning to Europe, we examine the character and probable futures of the religious revivals that have attended the fall of communist regimes. We briefly apply the model to Islam, paying particular attention to its recent revitalization. Finally, we shift our focus slightly to explore when and where new religious movements are more successful, giving special attention to the prevalence of deviant religious movements in Europe and to the rapid growth of Protestantism in Latin America.

General theories need to be tested in as great a variety of times and places as possible, but to do so always taxes one's comprehension. It is impossible to grasp the details and subtleties of ten nations as fully as can be achieved by specialization in any one of them. On the other hand, specialists frequently mistake the general for the specific.[1] In any event, while we cannot claim expertise even on the religious aspects of the many instances we discuss in this chapter, we have confidence that if we have made mistakes that have significant interpretive implications, specialists will make them known.

AMERICAN RELIGIOUS EXCEPTIONALISM

For more than 150 years, European visitors have remarked on the popularity of religion in the United States, and especially on the immense level of voluntary support Americans give to their churches. Thus, in 1818, William Cobbett wrote home to his neighbors in the English town of Botley about the density of churches in America and how well supported they were:

> Here are plenty of Churches. No less than three Episcopal (or English) Churches; three Presbyterian Churches; three Lutheran Churches; one or two Quaker Meeting-houses; two Methodist places; all within *six miles* of the place where I am sitting. And, these, mind, not poor shabby Churches; but each of them larger and better built and far handsomer than Botley Church, with the church-yards kept in the neatest order, with a head-stone to almost every grave. As to the Quaker Meeting-house, it would take Botley Church into its belly, if you were first to knock off the steeple. (Cobbett 1818, 229)

During his travels in the United States during 1830–31, Alexis de Tocqueville had a similar response, noting that "there is not a country in the world where the Christian religion retains a greater influence over the souls of men than in America" ([1835–39] 1956, 314). At mid-century, the Swiss theologian Philip Schaff (1855, 91) observed that attendance at Lutheran Churches was far higher in New York than in Berlin.

If European visitors marveled at American religiousness, Americans who traveled in Europe were equally surprised by the lack of religious participation they observed. Thus, Robert Baird, the first major historian of American religion, reported after an eight-year sojourn on the Continent, that nowhere in Europe did church attendance come close to the level taken for granted by Americans (1844, 188).

Today, no one disputes that religious participation has long been far higher in America than in Europe. What is in dispute, is *why*. The answer to that question seemed obvious to many Europeans who wrote about American religion during the nineteenth century. Almost unanimously, they stressed the powerful competitive forces unleashed by a free market religious economy.

In the 1850s, Karl T. Griesinger, a militantly irreligious German, complained that the separation between church and state fueled religious efforts, observing: "Clergymen in America [are] like other businessmen; they must meet competition and build up a trade, and it is their own fault if their income is not large enough. Now it is clear why heaven and hell are moved to drive the people to the churches, and why attendance is more common here than anywhere else in the world" (1858; translated in Handlin 1949, 261).

Some twenty years earlier, the Austrian journalist Frances Grund had made similar points, noting that establishment makes the clergy "indolent and lazy" because

> a person provided for cannot, by the rules of common sense, be supposed to work as hard as one who has to exert himself for a living.... Not only have Americans a greater number of clergymen than, in proportion to the population, can be found either on the Continent or in England; but they have not one idler amongst them; all of them are obliged to exert themselves for the spiritual welfare of their respective congregations. Americans, therefore, enjoy a threefold advantage: they have more preachers; they have more active preachers, and they have cheaper preachers than can be found in any part of Europe. (1837; quoted in Powell 1967, 77–80)

William Cobbett, quoted earlier, made the same point that because American clergy were "rewarded [only] for their diligence," they unexcelled in terms of their "piety, talent, and zeal" (1818] 1964, 233). Wittingly or not, these visitors echoed Adam Smith's penetrating analysis of the weaknesses of established churches, which, he said, inevitably produce a clergy content to repose "themselves upon their benefices [while neglecting] to keep up the fervour of faith and the devotion in the great body of the people; and having given themselves up to indolence, were become altogether incapable of making any vigorous exertion in defence even of their own establishment" ([1776] 1981:789).

Ernst Troeltsch and Max Weber, two of the most famous early sociologists of religion, were well aware of Smith's work when they also concluded that pluralism produces vigorous religious organizations. But where Smith saw virtue in vigorous religious bodies, Troeltsch and Weber saw danger and therefore condemned pluralism, lest there be vigorous churches in Germany. In 1904, accompanied by their wives, Troeltsch and Weber spent five weeks touring America.

Upon their return, each wrote about the proliferation of competing sects they had observed during their visit. Troeltsch warned his fellow Germans about the dangers of permitting free market religious "disestablishment" because, under these conditions, the more "orthodox" religious bodies always attract the greatest following, and orthodox religion invariably poses a danger to "scientific education." To guard against a vigorous orthodoxy, Troeltsch advised that states grant "corporate privileges grounded in law" to a small number of suitable churches, selected for their "contribution to public life," and provide each with the needed "material base of support" ([1906] 1991, 109–17). That is, competition is to be prevented and religious energy thereby drained away by the imposition of state churches. Weber was a bit less antagonistic to the sects he had observed in America, but he too did not wish them to prosper in Germany, asserting that they were by definition anti-intellectual and hence the enemies of high culture ([1906] 1985, 11–12).

However, by the turn of the twentieth century, awareness of the invigorating consequences of religious competition was fading rapidly. Smith's writings on religion were of so little interest that they were (and are) deleted from most editions of *The Wealth of Nations*. In similar fashion, the passages in Troeltsch and Weber reported above went unnoticed until rescued from oblivion by Irving Hexham and Karla Poewe (1997). For a century, the received wisdom was that pluralism harms religion because competing religious bodies undercut one another's credibility. Here social scientists uncritically accepted the old adage of comparative atheism that "each refutes each," which, ironically, was affirmed by monopoly churches, which have invariably charged that should they be supplanted, religion will be dangerously weakened. Eventually these views were formulated into elegant sociology by Peter Berger (1967; 1979), who repeatedly argued that pluralism inevitably destroys the plausibility of all religions and only where one faith prevails can there exist a "sacred canopy" able to inspire universal confidence and assent. It was not until the 1980s that anyone challenged Berger's claims (Finke 1984; Stark 1985b; Finke and Stark 1988). Nevertheless, this view of the corrosive effects of pluralism was and is utterly inconsistent with the American experience. If competition erodes the plausibility of religions, why is the most pluralistic nation on earth among the most religious?

The many efforts to "explain away" American exceptionalism within the confines of the old paradigm are hardly worth repeating. For example, Bryan Wilson (1966; 1982) was content to assert that American religion is without depth and therefore its apparent popularity is illusory. Roy Wallis (1986b) thought that what appears in America to be religious commitment is merely ethnic loyalty, so that the reality of secularization is concealed. This ignores the fact that it is the nonethnic religious groups that are by far the most vigorous in the United States. And many European scholars have been content to blame the whole thing on the cultural backwardness of America as a land of unsophisticated and credulous masses, where intellectuals have too little cultural impact.

However, the real reason for the vigor of American religion is to be found on the supply side rather than on the demand side, just as Adam Smith and a host of nineteenth century observers recognized. Indeed, having now had more than two centuries to develop under free market conditions, the American religious economy surpasses Adam Smith's wildest dreams about the creative forces of a free market (Moore 1994). There are more than 1,500 separate religious "denominations" (Melton 1989), many of them very sizable—24 have more than 1 million members each. Each of these bodies is entirely dependent on voluntary contributions, and American religious donations currently total more than $60 billion per year or more than $330 per person over age 18. These totals omit many contributions to church construction funds (new church construction amounted to $3 billion in 1993), as well as most donations to religious schools, hospitals, and foreign missions. In 1996, more than $2.3 billion was donated to support missionaries and a significant amount of this was spent on missionaries to Europe (Siewert and Valdez 1997).

Not only do Americans donate huge sums to their churches, many denominations are quite dependent on volunteer labor (see chapter 6). Some, including the Mormons and Jehovah's Witnesses, rely entirely on an unpaid clergy and many more depend on volunteers to perform all of the needed clerical and maintenance services.

Thus, it is obvious to all American denominations that they are as subject to market forces as is any commercial firm, and that they live or die depending on their ability to attract, hold, and motivate members. As a result, Americans are very accustomed to religious marketing (Moore 1994). Direct mail solicitations, newspaper advertising, and billboards with religious messages are common, and most households will be visited at least once a year (and probably more often) by someone wishing to interest them in joining a church.

Government interference in the affairs of religious organizations is relatively rare—even for the most controversial groups, such as self-identified Satanists and Protestant snake-handlers. Of course some religious groups are considered deviant by most Americans. And of course groups constantly attack one another's legitimacy. But the range of conventionality is far, far wider than in nations with regulated religious economies and state churches. And the range of legality is wider still.

COMPETITION AND COMMITMENT IN AMERICA

It is frequent in science for important results to first be reported by investigators who failed to recognize their implications. So it was in the 1920s when a dedicated opponent of pluralism discovered that religious competition greatly increased community levels of participation. In an effort to show that rural America was "lamentably overchurched" and in dire need of consolidated churches, Edmund deS. Brunner conducted a series of exceptionally well executed studies

TABLE 19   Competition and Commitment in American Towns and Villages, 1923–25

| | Churches per 1,000 Population | | | |
	One	Two	Three	Four or More
Percentage who belong to a church	27.4	36.0	34.8	43.4
Percentage enrolled in Sunday schools	15.8	22.3	25.2	37.4

SOURCE: Adapted from Brunner 1927, 74.

of religious life in 138 small towns and villages. As can be seen in table 19, in places where his proposed standard of no more than one church per 1,000 population was met, church membership and Sunday school enrollments were low. And as the number of churches competing for followers per 1,000 increased, so did religious participation.

Brunner was a competent statistician who recognized the relationship he had uncovered, noting that "judged by these superficial tests of their total impact on the community, competitive denominational churches would seem to succeed in proportion to their relative number. An organized church of each small sectarian group enlists more people." However, he was quick to dismiss these apparent fruits of pluralism as contrary to "the spiritual effects of overchurching," noting too that small competitive churches were unable to pay a salary sufficient to sustain "full-time resident ministers with a liberal education" (Brunner 1927, 80).

That Brunner's findings were entirely contrary to the received wisdom that religious competition weakens faith went unremarked for more than sixty years (Finke and Stark 1992). In 1987, Kevin Christiano also reported positive effects of pluralism in an analysis based on American cities at the start of the twentieth century, noting that the "Protestant denominations may have gown in *conjunction with,* and not in spite of, increases in internal differentiation [pluralism]" (1987, 128–29). Christiano recognized that his findings were entirely contrary to the prevailing theory that the proliferation of religious groups would speed secularization, but did not pursue the issue.

So much for hindsight. The first published findings on the positive effects of pluralism and competition presented in conjunction with a new theoretical view appeared the next year (Finke and Stark 1988). Based on an analysis of data for the 150 largest American cities in 1906, the study proposed to test the thesis that the "more pluralism, the greater the religious mobilization ... the more highly specialized and aggressive the churches are, the greater the odds that any given individual will be activated" (ibid., 43). When the percentage of Catholics was controlled for, the results were strong and as hypothesized—the more diverse the local religious economy, the higher the percentage of the population who belonged to a church. Subsequently, these findings were replicated when data for 1890, 1916, and 1926 were substituted for the 1906 data (Finke 1992).

In *The Churching of America* (1992), we used the growth of a competitive, free market religious economy to explain the dramatic rise in American church membership over the past two centuries. It is instructive that European visitors did not begin to remark on the unusual religiousness of America until about forty years after the Revolution, because in the beginning there was nothing remarkable about American religion. In 1776, about 17 percent of Americans belonged to a church, about the same percentage as in England at that time. And it may have been even lower in earlier days, if we can credit the judgment by the Church of England's Society for the Propagation of the Gospel, which, in 1701, decried the lack of "Publick Worshipp of God" and widespread "Infidelity" in America (Pascoe 1901, 1: 87).

However, as free market conditions developed and dozens of vigorous new denominations appeared, church membership and attendance soared. By 1850, about 34 percent of Americans were church members, or twice the percentage in Britain that year. By 1900, half of Americans were churched, and today nearly two-thirds are enrolled in a specific local congregation (Finke and Stark 1992). It is this that requires explanation. And the most plausible and best-tested explanation is the rise of a free-market religious economy wherein eager and efficient firms compete for support, as demonstrated by another study that traces the effect of competition on religious participation in the State of New York (Finke, Guest, and Stark 1996).

In 1776, the Church of England was the subsidized and official church in the Colony of New York, having supplanted the Dutch Reformed Church as the established faith when the English seized the colony from Holland. In addition to these denominations, there were nine other active religious bodies in the colony, most of them very new and very small. As would be expected, religious participation was very low; only about 15 percent of the New York population belonged to a church. Having backed the losing side in the American Revolution, the Church of England lost its established status and free market conditions soon prevailed. Subsequently, the New York State census of 1865 revealed a church membership rate of 34 percent, spread across 53 active denominations, and 26 percent of New York's residents attended church weekly.

Precisely as hypothesized, analysis of data for the 942 towns and cities of New York State found that both the membership rate and the weekly attendance rate rose very substantially with the degree of pluralism. Of perhaps even greater interest is the fact that the increase in average weekly church attendance attenuates as the pluralism index reaches very high levels as can be seen in table 20. This is the *saturation effect* mentioned earlier. The largest increase is between *no* pluralism (the town has only one denomination) and *some* diversity—the percentage who attend weekly more than doubles. The next increase in pluralism results in a significant, but rather smaller, increase in church atten-

TABLE 20   Pluralism and Weekly Church Attendance
in 900 New York State Towns, 1865

Pluralism Index Score	Percentage Who Attended Weekly	Number of Towns
0	10.6	86
.001–.549	22.9	233
.550–.699	29.9	293
.700–.799	33.6	231
.800+	33.9	57

SOURCE: New York, Secretary of State, *Census of the State of New York for 1865* (Albany: C. Van Benthuysen & Sons, 1867).

dance. But above that level, additional pluralism has little or no effect on attendance. That is to be expected, since any market has a saturation point. Given the way it is calculated, the Herfindal Index does not reach maximum value until each person belongs to his or her own unique denomination—an obvious absurdity. Long before that point is reached, there exists an adequate array of choices to maximize the effects of choice and competition. We stress this point because levels of pluralism in contemporary America are, in most places, above the level of saturation and we would not anticipate finding overall pluralism effects on religious participation.

However, this saturation limit only applies to pluralism effects. The conclusion that specific denominations will be more energetic to the degree that they lack market share should be applicable to the contemporary American situation. And it is strongly supported by available studies. Discussion of several of these will be postponed to a later section devoted to Catholic applications of the model, but two important studies not based on Catholic data can be reported here. In a study of Jewish fund-raising appeals, Richard Silberstein and his colleagues (1987) found that per capita contributions were inverse to the percentage of Jews in American metropolitan areas—the smaller the Jewish minority, the more each person gave. In another study, Peter A. Zalenski and Charles E. Zech (1995) found that per capita church contributions varied across Catholic, Episcopalian, Lutheran, and Methodist congregations inversely to each denomination's share of the local market, thus replicating the results for Jewish communities.

There are, of course, a few contrary findings. Kenneth Land, Glenn Dean, and Judith Blau (1991) reported a negative effect of pluralism based on American county data for 1906, 1916, and 1926. What they actually found was a positive effect of pluralism in the urban counties and a negative effect in the rural counties.[2] As noted elsewhere (Finke, Guest, and Stark 1996), large counties distort the results of the pluralism index as a measure of religious choice, and rural counties, in particular, pose measurement problems for the index and the adherence rate. Kevin Breault (1989) and Dan Olson (1998) also reported a negative pluralism effect for contemporary U.S. counties, a finding beset with measurement problems and relying on counties as the unit of analysis. But, as just noted in our comments on the saturation effect, even if we were to ignore these measurement problems, we think it is questionable whether overall effects of pluralism will exist in recent American data. Few areas in contemporary America, even areas where one religion effectively dominates the market, are lacking in religious choices or competition.

This may help account for an additional finding seemingly inconsistent with the market theory: that Mormon commitment is highest in the areas having the largest percentage of Mormons. Rick Phillips (1998) has suggested that this is the result of the greater density of Mormon social networks: that the more Mormon the area, the more that this network pressure overcomes any tendency for the church to become lazy. However, we note that church attendance and church membership rates among non-Mormons also are higher in Utah than elsewhere in the United States. That suggests that local religious competition may be intensified where there are Mormon majorities. In any event, we are unwilling to grant that the Mormon church is immune from competitive forces, but we agree that fascinating special cases may exist and invite closer study—possibly close-up qualitative research. Having mentioned this method of research, we would be remiss not to mention several such studies that add depth to understanding how religious competition is experienced in positive ways.

In her observational study of Catholic charismatics, Mary Jo Neitz found that their full awareness of religious choices "did not undermine their own beliefs. Rather they felt they had 'tested' the belief system and had been convinced of its superiority" (1987, 257–58). Neitz emphasizes that converts use a "rational decision-making process—weighing alternatives, categorizing, and comparing—before coming to a choice."

In her field study of upper-middle-class Jewish women who converted to Orthodoxy, Lynn Davidman stresses the benefits of intra-Jewish pluralism—"specialization of institutions and options for 'being Jewish' brings vitality to Jewish life." Moreover, "pluralization and multiplicity of choices available in the contemporary United States can actually strengthen Jewish communities." (Davidman 1991, 204).

Indeed, R. Stephen Warner has reported that his field studies in Northern California and in Chicago during the late 1970s and early 1980s led him to reject the notion that pluralism corrodes faith several years before he read our similar conclusion: "I was being drawn toward the idea that conservative religion thrives precisely under the mobile, pluralist conditions of the modern United States, and simultaneously I was growing skeptical of theories (e.g. Hunter, 1983) that could grasp such vitality only as an exception to the rule" (Warner 1997, 90).

More recently, when Christian Smith and his colleagues interviewed 178 evangelicals from 23 states, they concluded that making a choice from many religious options can actually enhance religious commitment: "For evangelicals, it is precisely by making a choice for Christ that one's faith becomes valid and secure. There is little reason to believe, therefore, that the modern necessity of having to choose one's own religion makes that religion any less real, powerful, or meaningful to modern believers" (Smith et al. 1998, 104).

More informally, both of us grew up in small midwestern communities where most people were certain that they attended the best church in town *because* they had visited many of the others.

EUROPEAN RELIGIOUS ECONOMIES

If the evidence seems overwhelming that religious competition causes the high levels of religiousness found in the United States, that fails to convince proponents of the old paradigm that such a principle could account for the low levels of religious participation in Europe, past or present. Some have suggested that competitive religious effects are inseparable from an excessively capitalist economy and therefore could not work in Europe. They're about half right! European religion suffers from the weaknesses now well known to plague socialism, because, whatever the character of their commercial economies, most European nations sustain a *socialized* religious economy, while in all the others one (or several) religious group enjoys special status and privileges. Because the situation in eastern Europe and the countries that made up the former Soviet Union is in such flux, we limit our discussion in this section to the principal nations of western Europe and devote a later section to eastern Europe.

WESTERN EUROPE

All of the Protestant nations of Europe maintain official state churches, fully supported by religious taxes or other state revenues, except in Great Britain, where the Anglican Church lives substantially off of property and endowments accrued during its centuries of mandatory tithes (Pickering 1985). In several of the Catholic nations, the Roman Catholic Church is also state-supported, while in others Catholicism enjoys many special advantages and some degree of establishment (a subsequent section is devoted to the Catholic nations).

Socialized religious economies weaken religious organizations in several ways. First, the state often intrudes, even to the point of imposing its views on church teachings and practices—invariably in ways that make the church less strict. Second, as Adam Smith pointed out, kept clergy are lazy. Thirdly, kept laity are lazy too, being trained to regard religion as free. This not only weakens commitment to the state church but indirectly hinders all unsubsidized faiths as well. Finally, despite claims of religious freedom, in all of these nations, the state directly interferes with and otherwise limits potential competitors of the state churches. It will be useful to document each of these points. Before doing so, however, it seems equally useful to point out the amazingly one-sided attention given to European church-state relations. Much is written about the decline in church influence on the state, but the growing influence of the state on the church has been almost entirely ignored.

State Theology

It is an obvious, but nonetheless profound, truth that those who pay the piper call the tune. Politicians who fund state churches usually claim the right to control ecclesiastical appointments and often use this power to select on the basis of doctrinal views. Moreover, governments sometimes impose their doctrinal preferences on the state church directly. Both tendencies are especially pronounced in Scandinavia (Gustafsson 1990).

When the Social Democrats took power in Denmark, Norway, and Sweden during the 1930s, many expected them to dismantle or at least to disestablish the state churches, in keeping with their anti-religious ideologies. Instead, the socialists were content to include the state church as an institution of the welfare state—"religious needs are legitimate welfare needs that the state has a duty to support," according to Norwegian Labour Party doctrine (Førde 1985 quoted in Gustafsson 1990, 111). However, as with all components of the welfare state, politicians have assumed responsibility for what the churches teach and how they conduct their affairs. Consequently, local church governance was shifted from parish assemblies elected by local parishioners to parish councils selected in general elections from candidates nominated by and supported by the national political parties. In Sweden, the government eliminated all religious qualifications for serving on local church boards and councils, and, as a result, control of the state church of Sweden passed into the hands of avowed atheists:

> Members of parish boards and the church council are elected more for their political positions and convictions than for their religious faith. No religious qualifications are required of the candidates—indeed, they need not even be baptized or confirmed. The state church is governed by a majority of nonbelievers—citizens who seldom or never attend church services. (Rydenfelt 1985, A25)

For some years Sweden's minister of ecclesiastical affairs was Alva Myrdal, wife of Gunnar Myrdal and herself a famous leftist economist and nonbeliever. It is both typical and diagnostic of the situation of the Swedish church that Myrdal appointed a government commission to compose a new translation of the New Testament for "general cultural reasons" (Asberg 1990, 16). Published in 1981, even its ardent supporters acknowledged that the translation contained "sweeping transformation[s] of accepted interpretations.... In important ways, it must of necessity run against the grain of Bible traditions" (Asberg 1990, 18). This translation is now the official Church of Sweden version.[3]

Elsewhere in Scandinavia, similar legislative and administrative interference with the state church also is common, even if it is not so extreme as in Sweden (Gustafsson 1990). In Norway and Iceland, the power of church leaders is "rather restricted, and most important decisions concerning the Church still rest with the government," while in Denmark, "decisions about church law, church membership, the hymn book, and so on are taken by the government and the parliament" (Gustafsson 1990, 114). Peter Lodberg, general secretary of the Ecumenical Council in Denmark, noted that the Danish Parliament, having "absolute power in the Administration of the National Church [the Evangelical Lutheran Church]" passed a law authorizing female pastors in the state church over the opposition of all but one of the bishops. "It is characteristic that this question was not seen as a matter of the inner life of the church, but as something concerning the administrative system of the National Church, that is, it was regarded as being an issue for Parliament rather than the bishops," Lodberg commented (1989, 7).

We admonish readers that neither their support of gender equality nor ours is the issue here. The issue is the naked secularity of theological decision-making in socialized churches.

Because it is an international church, Roman Catholicism is much less vulnerable to local pressures. However, recall from chapter 7 that the Portuguese and Spanish churches initially resisted all liberalizing measures adopted by Vatican II because of state control over the appointment of bishops. Conversely, as we see later in this chapter, similar government screening of Catholic bishops resulted in the Netherlands having by far the most liberal Catholic hierarchy in Europe by the time of Vatican II, with rather dire results on Catholic commitment.

Complacent Clergy

One need not have recourse to esoteric economic principles in order to realize that when people have little need or motive to work, they tend not to work, and that subsidized churches will therefore be lazy. Throughout Scandinavia, and in Germany as well, the clergy of the state churches are civil servants as well as union members. As such, they cannot be expected to exhaust themselves in an effort to attract large numbers to worship services, for their incomes and tenure are secure regardless of attendance. Indeed, they are better off with empty churches, which make little demand on their time, than with full ones. Consequently, the clergy of these Protestant state churches are inclined to repose "themselves upon their benefices" even beyond Adam Smith's expectations. A close look at the Swedish religious economy is informative.

Like any massive state concern, the Church of Sweden runs on tax funds. The state imposes a special church tax, and even those who do not belong to the state church must pay 40 percent of this assessment. Tax money pays the salaries of the Lutheran clergy and covers the cost of church construction and maintenance. Direct contributions and payments from worshipers amount to almost nothing. As civil servants, the clergy maintain the country's vital statistics and perform other municipal functions. They are

> integrated into the ordinary bureaucracy. About 85 percent of them are members of trade unions, negotiating with their employer—the government—over salaries, the number of working hours and pensions. Like other Swedish civil servants they have the legal right to strike, though they have not yet exercised that right. But they are dissatisfied with their long working week, and their union steward often threatens to strike. (Rydenfelt 1985, A25)

The Swedish clergy are well paid and have civil service job security. Indeed, the archbishop's salary is nearly as high as that of the prime minister. Not surprisingly, the Church of Sweden suffers from high costs and low productivity. Typically, Sunday services in huge churches able to seat many hundreds, even thousands, of people are attended by a handful of individuals. These tiny congregations are served by large staffs. In the end, "only a very small fraction of capacity is ever utilized" (Rydenfelt 1985). Here an anecdote may be pertinent. An American Lutheran minister had the following experience at the Stockholm Cathedral some years ago. He went there to attend Sunday services and found himself in a huge structure, surrounded by a mere handful of fellow worshipers. At the end of the service, he spoke to the pastor, who bemoaned the paucity of worshipers, and described the large, professional staff attached to the cathedral. The American remarked, "But surely, the staff and their families alone should have made up a much larger audience." The pastor replied, "Yes, but they work so hard all week. They like to take Sunday off."[4]

Free Religion and Commitment

Socialized religion not only breeds a lazy clergy (and parish staff), it breeds a lazy laity. A considerable literature shows that people tend to a value a thing according to its cost, and that principle seems to apply to public attitudes toward state churches. Where religion is perceived to be "free," in that it is provided by the government and is independent of voluntary contributions, it is not accorded much value (see chapter 6). In addition to the fact that people tend not to value what they perceive to be free, the presence of "free" religion greatly impedes the capacity of unsubsidized firms to compete. If I can attend services whenever I wish without encountering a collection plate, why would I want to attend a church that expects me to pay? That was precisely Max Weber's reaction when he became aware of the price of religion in the United States. After his trip to America, he wrote:

> [C]hurch affiliation in the U.S.A. brings with it incomparably higher financial burdens, especially for the poor, than anywhere in Germany.... I have personally known of many burdened cases in a congregation in a city on Lake Erie, which

was composed almost entirely of German immigrant lumberjacks. Their regular contributions amounted to almost $80 annually, being paid out of an average annual income of about $1,000.[5] Everyone knows that even a small fraction of this financial burden in Germany would lead to a mass exodus from the church. (1946, 342)

The recent failure of American-style televangelism in Germany was in part because of the widespread belief that the state churches provide all the religion that is needed (Schmied 1996).[6] The price of free religion is, of course, a low level of commitment. "Another important implication of the religious monopoly is that the [Danish] National Church is marked by the same tendencies as other National Churches in Scandinavia. The participation in Sunday Morning Worship is low," Peter Lodberg remarked (1989, 7).

Religious Regulation

Finally, when religious economies are controlled by subsidized, "official" religious firms, a variety of measures are employed to disable potential competitors—and this goes on even when nations claim to enjoy religious freedom. It is here, on the actual substance of religious freedom, that there is the greatest misunderstanding between European and American scholars. Europeans often claim that their nations, too, offer religious freedom, but to those accustomed to American standards of freedom, what is called freedom in Europe would only be called *toleration* in the United States—and often not that. In the abstract, most nations of western Europe assert freedom of worship, but permit almost unlimited discretion to bureaucrats and parliaments concerning specific policies and decisions to impose sanctions on minority religions, while not providing effective legal recourse as guaranteed in the United States. In America, new religions are able to "struggle on equal terms with their adversaries," James Beckford has noted, but in Europe the lack of constitutional protections "creates conditions in which piecemeal, administrative sanctions can be applied behind a curtain of official detachment" (1985a, 274, 286). In 1984, the European Parliament overwhelmingly passed a resolution allowing member states to curtail the "activity of certain new religious movements," thus giving official approval to repression of minority religions. At present the European Parliament is considering an amendment to the constitution of the European Union permitting member states to discriminate against all religious groups without local "constitutional" status, which means nearly all Protestant groups, as well as all non-Christian faiths (Dixon 1997). It will be helpful to organize this discussion by nation.

Germany

When Germans point to the existence of a variety of "free churches" as proof of religious freedom, Americans note the many ways in which these churches are hindered, harassed, and closely regulated, how they are stigmatized by the media and government, and how this "official" disapproval generates public antagonism. For example, various Protestant sects are singled out by the media and are attacked as deviant and illegitimate—the lead article in the magazine *Stern* (May 4, 1995) warned against the grave dangers posed by Charismatic Christian sects (*Sekten*), characterizing members as fanatics and potential terrorists. Many American evangelical Protestant missionaries in Germany complain that *all* denominations other than the two state churches are considered cults by the German news media, a judgment that often is encouraged by the government (Selthoffer 1997, 18). Thus, recently, the Berlin Senate officially declared a large, charismatic Berlin congregation to be a cult, warning Germans not to become involved. Such government hostility has, in fact, led to police raids on several small Pentecostal churches (Introvigne 1997).

The attempt by the Germans to suppress Scientology has, of course, received immense recent publicity. As yet Scientology has not actually been banned, although the government has placed it under surveillance by the secret service (Introvigne 1997). Moreover, administrative action has excluded Scientologists from the possibility of government employment, as are members of various other *Sekten* (Freedom House 1995). Administrative actions also have caused the refusal of entry visas to various prominent Americans known to be members of or sympathetic to Scientology. It now is proposed by some officials that Jehovah's Witnesses also be placed under secret service watch.

Nevertheless, day-to-day government interference may offer the most serious impact on religious competition in Germany. "Free churches" are routinely hindered by the bureaucracy as they seek necessary licenses, especially building permits. Many Pentecostal groups are denied tax-free status unless they register as secular groups such as sports clubs, rather than as churches (Selthoffer 1995, 18). In 1996, the government revoked the tax-free status as a church of a charismatic congregation in Cologne, and by making the revocation retroactive, now seeks $284,000 in back payments (Selthoffer 1997). And, as mentioned, members of some unpopular religious groups are barred from employment in the civil service (Freedom House 1995). Not surprisingly, public opinion tends to be shaped by these policies, and Protestant Pentecostal churches in Germany report frequent anonymous threats, and high levels of vandalism (Selthoffer 1995, 18). Given this level of intolerance for Christian "free churches," it is not surprising that non-Christian religions are the targets of serious prejudice and discrimination. Thus, Karl-Fritz Daiber (1996, 413) attributes the "persistent social discrimination against Muslims," not primarily to their status as foreigners, but to their religious deviance.

Unfortunately, Germany differs from most other European nations only in having had its actions against religious dissenters given considerable recent attention by the press.

France

On June 22, 1998, the French tax authority placed a $50 million lien for back taxes on all property of the Jehovah's Witnesses. This action was based on a decision that the Witnesses were ineligible for tax-exempt status, and hence owed taxes retroactively, because they are not a legitimate religious group, but rather a dangerous sect. No matter that they are the third largest Christian body in France. In fact, the Witnesses are only one of 173 sects, including Baptists and most other evangelical Protestant groups, determined to have "dangerous characteristics," in an official report on "Cults in France" issued by the French parliament after secret hearings (Witham 1998). Essentially, all religious bodies that are not members of the World Council of Churches are now classified as dangerous. Since that organization is regarded with disdain by many Christian groups, they are regarded as cults, along with all non-Christian bodies.

The report did not advocate new legislation, but proposed a number of administrative actions, including a national Observatory of Cults, which was soon established (Introvigne 1997). Moreover, by giving official standing to claims that these groups aren't valid religions, the report justified the action by tax authorities against the Witnesses and it is expected that similar actions will follow against other groups. In addition, the report is cited as the basis for a good deal of other kinds of administrative discrimination—teachers have been fired from the public schools when it was revealed that they were Jehovah's Witnesses, and a Catholic theatrical group was systematically refused use of public theaters until French bishops rallied to their cause (Introvigne 1997). Indeed, the city of Lyon now denies all public facilities to groups listed in the report, and the Ministry of Youth and Sport in each French department employs a cult expert to educate youth against such groups (Introvigne 1997).

At a different level of interference, all Roman Catholic appointments to bishop must be approved by the French government, and in return Catholicism continues to enjoy many formal and informal special privileges. For example, state television provides ninety minutes free to the Catholic Church every Sunday, thirty minutes every other week to be shared by all other Christian groups, and none for non-Christians, despite there being more Muslims than Protestants in France. Beginning in 1959, the French government agreed to fund some private schools, including those created by certain religious communities. Today, 20 percent of all French schoolchildren attend these schools, most of which are Catholic, with a few serving Protestant and Jewish students. No Muslim schools receive such funding (Liederman 1995). This is entirely consistent with official French forms of anti-Muslim religious discrimination—the most significant being the decision to prohibit Muslim schoolgirls from wearing an Islamic headscarf. Despite vigorous protests, this policy has been repeatedly reaffirmed on the grounds that true separation of church and state extends to prohibiting "ostentatious" religious expression in public settings (Liederman

1995). This rule would also apply to orthodox Jews. But they are secure from such state intrusions because their schools are "private," although funded by the state. At a more mundane level, in 1991, after many appeals, the Jehovah's Witnesses finally received permission from the French government to print religious materials in color, rather than only in black and white (*Yearbook of Jehovah's Witnesses*, 1992, 15). Now, of course, all of their presses are under threat of seizure by the government to satisfy claims for back taxes.

Belgium

On October 30, 1981, the Belgian government finally withdrew its absolute ban on the transportation of Jehovah's Witnesses' publications, including Bibles, by the railroad or postal systems (*Yearbook of Jehovah's Witnesses*, 1984, 110). This did not mark the beginning of an era of greater toleration, however. On April 28, 1997, the Belgian Parliament's Commission on Cults issued its 600-page report, in which the Jehovah's Witnesses are named, along with 188 other religious groups. The Belgian "document is even more extreme than the French report. It included a number of bizarre allegations against many groups ... including the Catholic Charismatic Renewal, Quakers, the YWCA (but, for some reason, not the YMCA), Hasidic Jews, and almost all Buddhists" (Introvigne 1997, 42). Also listed as cults by the Belgian government are the Seventh-day Adventists, the Assemblies of God, the Amish, and the Plymouth Brethren. In addition, the Belgian report proposes making "mind control" a crime.

Switzerland

In Switzerland the Canton of Geneva already has made "mind control" a felony. Indeed, pending legislation also proposes that members of dangerous cults be prohibited from government positions and the establishment of a national cult observatory like the one in France.

Italy

William F. Bainbridge,[7] a prominent American Baptist official, reported that during a visit to Rome in the 1880s, "the police detectives of Pius IX searched all our baggage to keep us from taking a Bible into the Holy City" (1882, 247). That was, of course, long ago. However, as recently as the 1970s, only Catholic priests could perform valid religious marriage services in Italy, and Protestants could not obtain marriage annulments, since these could only be granted by the Catholic Church. Moreover, Italian law still specifies that criminal offenses committed against Catholic clergy are "aggravated," while similar offenses against Protestant ministers are not. The government-owned radio and television services broadcast many hours of Catholic programming weekly. Beginning in 1973, Protestants have been granted twenty minutes a week on radio and fifteen minutes a week on TV (Barrett 1982).

Portugal

Until the Jehovah's Witnesses were given legal recognition in December 1974, the police in Portugal routinely confiscated Bibles and tracts from Witnesses and often beat them severely as well. The Lisbon newspaper *Diario Popular* admitted that until then, "To be one of Jehovah's Witnesses ... was dangerous and even subversive. But times have changed. Now it is possible not only to be a Witness in Portugal but also to assemble in public" (quoted in *Yearbook of Jehovah's Witnesses*, 1983, 235). Moreover, having been allowed to come out from underground, the Witnesses have become the second-largest Christian denomination in Portugal—as they are in many European nations (Brierley 1997). In January 1991, Portugal amended a law that permitted only Catholics to teach religion, extending the right to Protestants as well.

Spain

In 1970, Spain passed a religious toleration act that, for the first time in centuries, gave non-Catholics the right to hold services. In 1992, the Spanish government extended tax-exempt status to a federation of evangelical Protestant groups, gave them the right to organize schools, and recognized "Protestant minister" as a legal profession. However, these new rights were not extended to Protestant groups that were not part of the federation or to non-Christians (Miller 1991). In general, however, Spain has not joined in the "anti-cult" and religious re-regulation campaigns of its northern neighbors.

Scandinavia

Consider three laws governing religion in Norway (Barrett 1982). First, all religious bodies are required to register with the government. Second, it is illegal to belong to more than one religious group at a time. Third, a person must be over age 20 in order to take religious vows. Originally, of course, the latter was aimed at Catholic orders, but today the focus is on "cults."

Moreover, although all of the Scandinavian nations permit other faiths to operate, even evangelical Protestant groups often find it difficult to get the proper permits to qualify a building as suitable for public meetings and to otherwise deal with a state bureaucracy that has no sympathy for "unnecessary" challenges to state Lutheranism. The clergy of the Danish National Church regard all other Christian denominations "as either superfluous or directly harmful," acknowledges Peter Lodberg (1989, 7).

COMPETITION AND RELIGIOUS PRACTICE IN WESTERN EUROPE

The initial attempt to apply a supply-side explanation to account for contrasts in religious participation between the United States and Europe was based on fourteen major European nations plus Australia, New Zealand, Canada, and the United States (Iannaccone 1991). Religious competition was assessed on the basis of pluralism as measured by a standard index of market concentration (the Herfindahl Index), which calculates the odds that any two randomly selected members of a population will belong to the same religious body. Religious participation was measured by rates of weekly church attendance. The results were extremely strong—competition accounted for more than 90 percent of the total variation in church attendance across these nations. Moreover, the United States is not a deviant case, but lies close to the regression line—its unusually high rate of church attendance being entirely consistent with its high level of pluralism. Nations more than 80 percent Catholic were omitted from the analysis, having yielded sufficiently deviant results to require separate consideration.

Next came the first of what are now three impressive studies based on the 284 municipalities in Sweden. Eva M. Hamberg and Thorleif Pettersson (1994; 1997; Pettersson and Hamberg 1997) showed that religious competition within Sweden greatly influences overall rates of church attendance. Competition was measured in two primary ways: as pluralism in terms of religious bodies and as diversity of Sunday sermons. Where Swedes have more options as to religious bodies and in terms of the number, time, and denominational variety of Sunday sermons, church attendance is higher. The findings remained strong when changes in pluralism and attendance were examined over time—increases in pluralism were followed by increases in attendance. Hamberg and Pettersson also found evidence of a ceiling effect on pluralism. As with any market, religious markets have a saturation point beyond which additional options do not raise levels of participation. Thus they found that initial increases in pluralism produced sharp rises in attendance rate, but subsequent additions had far "less impact" (Hamburg and Pettersson 1997; Pettersson and Hamburg 1997).

However, when Steve Bruce (1992) analyzed data from the 1851 religious census of England and Wales, he reported lower rates of church attendance the higher the level of denominational pluralism in 66 cities. Since Bruce is among the most vociferous proponents of the secularization thesis and of the old paradigm generally, his negative findings were regarded as of major importance. However, when efforts were made to replicate his results using exactly the same data, but including all 73 cities reported in the census rather than the 66 reported by Bruce, the results were weak, if still negative. Moreover, using this same 1851 religious census (the only one ever conducted in Britain), robust and positive effects of competition on church attendance were found for the counties of England and Wales and an additional analysis limited to the 48 registration districts of Wales also found strong positive effects.

The heart of our position is that Europeans are poor attenders because of the ineffective efforts of their churches, and that faced with American-style churches, Europeans would respond as Americans do. In a ruthless world ruled by social scientists, it would be possible to conduct a crucial experiment to test that claim. First, a large sample of Europeans would be selected randomly. Then they would be moved to the United States. If religious competition is the basis for European-American differences in participation, then these transplanted Europeans soon ought to increase their levels of religious participation until, after a generation or two, they were behaving like other Americans. Of course, a properly counterbalanced experiment would also reverse the process by moving a random sample of Americans to Europe, where their religious participation would be expected to decline.

As it turns out, it is possible to approximate such an experiment to some degree by contrasting Germans with German-Americans (Stark 1997). Germans make up by far the largest single ethnic identity in America—23 percent give "German" as their ancestry. Moreover, a significant number of German-Americans are of recent origin. Based on the logic of the proposed experiment, we would expect Americans born in Germany to be more like people still in Germany in terms of their religiousness, with subsequent generations becoming progressively more like other Americans. And that's precisely what the data show. First of all, while Lutheran is the main denominational preference of first-generation German-American Protestants, by the third generation most have switched to nonethnic denominations such as the Methodists, Baptists, and a variety of smaller evangelical bodies. In addition, first-generation German-Americans attend church like Germans—not very often. But, within a generation they attend as often as other Americans do.

Thus, when confronted with efficient churches, offering a full spectrum of worship styles and theological orientations, German-Americans have responded in full measure. And, by doing so, they fulfilled the worst fears expressed more than a century ago by Friedrich Conrad Dietrich Wyneken (Gustafson 1994; Wyneken [1843] 1982).

An ordained Lutheran pastor born in Hannover, Wyneken went to America in 1838 in response to a call for clergy to serve immigrant German-Lutheran parishes in Indiana. Upon his arrival, he was shocked by what he described as the "most awful gyrations and gestures" used by Baptist and Methodist revival preachers (Gustafson 1994, 135). He was even more appalled at the large number of German Lutherans who had defected to these upstart sects. He sent many letters back to Germany appealing for help, asking that a large number of trained clergy, along with substantial funding, be sent immediately to enable the Lutherans to withstand the "Methodistic spirit." In 1841, Wyneken took his appeal directly to Germany, remaining until 1843. During his stay, in 1842, he published an essay on "The Distress of German Lutherans in North America," in the distinguished church newspaper *Zeitschrift für Protestantismus und Kirche*. In it he detailed how German-American Lutherans were at the mercy of the sects:

The Lutheran Church has very dangerous enemies in America in the large number of sects ... unless the Lord sends help very soon, [they] will certainly even wipe out the name of the Lutheran church in the West.

... there is hardly a Lutheran or Reformed congregation which does not have to suffer from these swarming pests. Many congregations have been completely scattered by them.... Suddenly a sectarian preacher comes bursting into the congregation and, with noise, screaming and howling, announces the judgement they must face if they do not honestly convert....

With what monstrous swiftness the Methodist spirit has soured and infected almost all of Christendom.... The flood will soon enough flow across the Atlantic toward our German fatherland.... What is to stop them? Just observe the tremendous missionary efforts of the Baptists and Methodists. (Wyneken 1982, 29–33, 49–50)

Why were the Lutherans at the mercy of the sects? According to Wyneken, it was because they lacked clergy, prayer books, hymnals, and Bibles and could not afford to build churches. Notice, however, that the Baptists and Methodists were not dependent on a foreign state church for funding or clergy. They found an abundance of both locally. Yet, faced not only with the Baptist and Methodist challenge, but also with their example, neither Wyneken nor any of his Lutheran clerical colleagues could think of anything better to do than to write home. That is precisely how establishment drains the vigor out of religious organizations.

CONFLICT AS COMPETITION

But what about societies lacking pluralism and competition, but that nevertheless have sustained high levels of religious participation? Several defenders of the old paradigm who have cited these exceptions as fatal to our theory could only have done so disingenuously (see Lechner 1996), for we have made it clear from the start (Finke and Stark 1988) that under certain circumstances conflict as well as competition can create energetic religious bodies. In similar fashion, several critics (Bruce 1995; Lechner 1996) have attempted to defend the old paradigm by misinterpreting our theory as incompatible with any substantial decline in religious participation, leaving secularization as the only possible explanation when declines occur. That is equally wrong. We aim to explain variations in religiousness and therefore must account for declines as well as increases (and for periods of stability as well).

Quebec

Let us begin with Quebec. At first glance it would seem that our theory would predict that very low levels of religious participation would prevail in Quebec, because its religious life is dominated by the Roman Catholic Church. Instead, French Canadians long displayed remarkably high levels of commitment—the overwhelming majority attended mass at least once a week. According to national surveys reported by Barrett (1982), 83 percent of Catholics attended weekly in 1946, as did 65 percent in 1970. Why? Because the church was the only major organization under the control of French Canadians; all other institutions including political parties were dominated by English Canadians. Canada had been seized from France by force of arms, and those French residents not deported to Louisiana remained a subjugated ethnic minority. In this situation, mass attendance was inseparable from political and cultural resistance. However, in recent times, French Canadians have come to power in Quebec and now dominate business and finance as well as politics. The result has been a rapid decline in religious practice as, stripped of its significance as the organizational basis for resisting outside domination, the Catholic Church in Quebec quickly began to display the typical inefficiencies of a monopoly faith. Indeed, based on the 1990 World Values Survey, Catholic mass attendance is now significantly lower in Quebec (29 percent weekly) than elsewhere in Canada (47 percent weekly), fully in accord with the thesis that the Catholic Church generates greater commitment in places where it is a minority faith, discussed in the next section. Given the church's greatly reduced sociopolitical role, both the high level of Catholic practice in the past and its recent rapid decline, are consistent with our theory—indeed, had there been no decline in religious practice in response to the decline in conflict, *that* would have called our theory into question.

Poland

A similar shift has taken place in Poland and for similar reasons. In 1977, when the Catholic Church served as the primary organizational basis for resistance to the Soviet-imposed Communist regime, a survey placed weekly mass attendance at 80 percent (Barrett 1982). In 1990, the World Values Survey found that only 68 percent of Polish Catholics attended mass weekly. More recent polls suggest the decline is continuing, having dropped to perhaps 48 percent by 1995 according to the International Social Survey Program. Why? "For years, the Roman Catholic Church in Poland" was a rallying point for opposition, "the Church versus the State, the Church versus the Communist Party, the Church and the society as a 'we-group' against the communists, and so on. This reality fell to pieces when the communist rule collapsed," explains the Polish sociologist Irena Borowik (1996, 89). This very nicely satisfies our theory—had Catholic commitment in Poland not begun to decline when the church ceased to serve as the vehicle for opposition, that would have called into question our theory, which, although not compatible with just any shift in religiousness, is entirely compatible with what has taken place in Quebec and Poland.

Ireland

The very high level of religious participation in Ireland can be similarly explained, although, since bitter conflicts continue with England concerning the counties of northern Ireland, we would not expect the onset of a very substantial decline. However, dating the onset of the remarkable level of Irish public piety is germane to our theory. It is therefore significant to point out that Irish Catholic piety is recent, and that prior to the middle of the nineteenth century, Ireland displayed precisely the level of religious indifference that we would expect to find in a monopolized religious economy. Consider that in 1800 there were only 120 nuns in the whole of Ireland (Clear 1987), out of a population of 5.2 million (Mitchell 1962). In contrast, in 1820 there were 270 nuns in the United States (Curry 1988), although the Catholic population numbered less than 200,000 (Shaughnessy 1925). The general lack of Irish commitment also showed up in low rates of mass attendance, there being solid evidence that fewer than a third of the Irish attended in 1840 (Larkin 1972) and that attendance was never higher than this as far back as anyone can tell. But then came what historians now generally refer to as the "devotional revolution" (Larkin 1972). The celebrated Irish piety—with mass attendance hovering around 90 percent and with thousands entering religious orders—arose subsequent to the Potato Famine, when the Catholic Church became the primary organizational vehicle for Irish nationalism resisting external domination. Were that function of the church to decline, then we would expect a corresponding decline in religious practice.

The Netherlands

Now let us consider the recent history of the Netherlands, which is alleged to "refute" our theory (Lechner 1996). This is a bit more complex, because Dutch society prior to World War II has been described "pillarized," in that the society enclosed several very distinct subcultures (Dobbelaere 1987; Martin 1978). The image of a pillar was used to clarify the fact that these subcultures did not consist of different class strata but were vertical structures, each including all class strata. As David Martin aptly put it, pillarization consists of "several integrated sub-cultures in which the elites of each negotiate, combine and recombine over the walls of the ghetto" (1978, 189). The pillars were based in religion. Besides the church, the Catholic pillar consisted of an entirely separate Catholic school system, Catholic professional and trade associations, Catholic unions, Catholic newspapers, and even a Catholic political party. Opposed to the Catholic pillar were two Protestant pillars, one based on the Dutch Reformed Church and one based on a much stricter Reformed denomination, sometimes referred to as the Re-reformed Church (Eisinga, Felling, and Lammers 1996). It would not be inaccurate to claim that Dutch society at this time consisted of three Quebecs, each nursing deep grievances and each using religion as the basis of its solidarity.

Our theory would predict an exceptionally high level of religious participation in any religiously pillarized society. While pillarized societies may be wanting in pluralism, they make up for it in the intensity and centrality of religious conflicts, which sustain powerful social norms regarding the need to give public demonstrations of one's commitment and group loyalty. Dutch Catholics flocked to mass to express their solidarity in confronting their Protestant opponents, who responded likewise. This is, in short, another instance of the situation already described in the cases of Quebec, Poland, and Ireland.

Since World War II (and especially since the 1960s), Dutch society has been undergoing depillarization and the historic religious conflicts have lost intensity. Frank Lechner has described the erosion of the Catholic pillar:

> The pillar, a hierarchical structure of secular institutions operating on the basis of a particular world view and under church guidance, was initially erected as a way to defend the cultural and social interests of a threatened minority. Once that minority had achieved substantial equality, and the threats to its subcultural identity had subsided, the defense mechanism lost its function and gradual depillarization set in. (Lechner 1989, 142–43)

As discussed in chapter 7, the Catholic pillar began to crumble rapidly in the wake of the immense changes ushered in by Vatican II, during whose deliberations the Dutch hierarchy revealed themselves to be the most radical national church hierarchy in Europe. The aim of the Dutch bishops was to greatly reduce the tension between their church and secular society. To this end, in 1966, they created a pastoral council that, in addition to members of the clergy, included many Catholic lay members, some Protestant representatives, and even several invited members from the Humanist Union. Almost immediately this council began to issue very controversial statements. "Among its more startling declarations were the affirmation that the papal encyclical *Humanae Vitae* was not convincing in its refusal to sanction contraceptives, and its recommendation that the requirement of celibacy for the priesthood be abolished" (Barrett 1982, 511). And, consistent with Vatican II pronouncements, the council stressed the new doctrine that it was no longer regarded as a sin to not attend mass at least weekly. Told they could backslide on mass attendance, the majority of Dutch Catholics began to sleep in on Sunday. In 1970, the number of those attending mass at least every other week stood at 71 percent, but by 1991 it had dropped to 30 percent. Thus was the Catholic pillar shattered by liberalism: "progressive Catholics challenged the doctrinal core of the faith ... [and] the doctrinal content of the Church disintegrated ..." (Lechner 1989, 143). That is, in the postwar era, the strict Dutch Catholic pillar was replaced with a lax church.

While the Catholic pillar liberalized and dissolved, so did the larger of the Protestant pillars (Eisinga, Felling, and Lammers 1996; Lechner 1996). In contrast, the relatively smaller Protestant pillar has maintained its strictness and, just as would be anticipated on the basis of chapter 6, it has not experienced any decline and continues to enjoy very high levels of church attendance (Becker and Vink 1994).

To sum up: despite a highly regulated religious market controlled by three semi-monopolies, for many years the Netherlands enjoyed a high level of religiousness because these groups stood in vigorous opposition. Depillarization removed the competitive imperative from the Dutch religious economy, with the result that the two largest bodies became lax. And as our theory predicts, these lax firms began to decline as backsliding became the mode. Dutch religiousness thus declined to a level consistent with the new character of its religious economy.

CATHOLICISM AND COMPETITION

Compared with the nations dominated by Protestant state churches, attendance is substantially higher in the Catholic nations of western Europe. This demonstrates that the Roman Catholic Church is more energetic in noncompetitive settings than are established Protestant churches. This contrast was fully anticipated by Adam Smith, who wrote: "In the church of Rome, the industry and zeal of the inferior clergy are kept more alive by the powerful motive of self interest, than perhaps in any established protestant church." This is because, according to Smith, the lower clergy are left to depend for "a very considerable portion of their subsistence from the voluntary oblations of the people." In addition, Smith pointed out, many of the major religious orders are mendicant and "are obliged, therefore, to use every art which can animate the devotion of the common people." Therefore in "Roman catholick countries the spirit of devotion is supported altogether by the monks and the poorer parochial clergy" (Smith [1776] 1981, 789–90).

In addition to being energized by being more dependent on the laity, as an international organization, the Roman Catholic Church has not been subject to direct intervention by secular governments in its doctrinal affairs—albeit that national churches have been shaped to some extent by government influence on appointments of bishops. But nowhere has the Catholic Church been a literal branch of government like the state churches of Scandinavia.

The international character of Catholicism also contributes to its internal diversity. Because the church spans many different countries and cultures, the Vatican has little choice but to condone varying styles of worship and degrees of intensity. This is facilitated by the fact that Catholic religious orders are encapsulated sect movements (Finke and Wittberg in press) and thereby offer substantial variation in doctrinal emphasis and worship styles.

Another important factor is undoubtedly a celibate clergy and religious orders. Priests and nuns do not follow their parents into church "careers," as so often happens among Protestants. Instead, priests and the religious must be recruited anew each generation, and the high levels of sacrifice demanded of them help to ensure that they are recruited from among those with strong preferences for intense religion.

All this having been said, the fact remains that, especially in Latin America, the Catholic Church often displays the symptoms of a lazy monopoly. Moreover, our theory does not exempt the Roman Catholic Church. Rather, it predicts that *Catholic commitment will vary inversely to the proportion nominally Catholic within any appropriate set of units of analysis.* As has been noted, this application of the theory was challenged in the initial study based on the nations of Europe. The marked differences between Protestant and Catholic nations in levels of church attendance necessitated the exclusion of Catholic nations from the analysis. Therefore, let us now pursue competitive effects within Catholic settings.

The first study focused on competition and Catholicism was prompted by an offhand observation while leafing through a copy of the *Catholic Almanac* (Stark 1992a). Nations in which virtually everyone is said to be Catholic seem to be singularly lacking in priests. How is it possible that Honduras can be 96 percent Catholic and have only 64 diocesan priests? Even when the religious priests are added to the total, there is only six-tenths of a priest per 10,000 Catholics in Honduras. It is self-evident that so few priests couldn't possibly serve so many parishioners. The obvious conclusion is that only a fraction of the "Catholics" in Honduras are sufficiently religious to require pastoral services. As we shall see, there is a similar lack of priests throughout Latin America, which also suggests that a rather small fraction of those counted as Catholics in these nations actually practice their faith. This is entirely consistent with a second implication of the lack of priests. The number of priests in a society represents the number of young men sufficiently religious to seek ordination. Ordination rates would seem an accurate barometer of the general level of public religious commitment, and the number of secular priests reflects the history of local ordination. Consequently, a lack of priests undercuts the authenticity of claims about universal Catholicism.

To examine the matter from another perspective, consider that in many Latin American nations where upwards of 90 percent are claimed to be Catholics, there are substantially more full-time Canadian and American evangelical Protestant missionaries than there are diocesan priests (Siewart and Kenyon 1993). In Bolivia, for example, there are 636 missionaries and 221 diocesan priests, or 0.3 priest per missionary. In Honduras, there is 0.2 priest per missionary; in Panama and Guatemala, there is 0.5; in Paraguay, 0.6. For Latin America as a whole, there are only 2.2 diocesan priests per missionary. Keep in mind that the missionary totals do not include more than ten thousand Mormon missionaries. If these are factored in, then for Latin America as a whole, there is only 0.96 diocesan priest per non-Catholic North American missionary. Moreover, if one added in the many thousands of ordained local Protestant clergy, the Catholic clergy would be extremely outnumbered in what has long been depicted as a serenely Catholic world.

Having discovered the somewhat illusory nature of Latin American Catholicism, the study proceeded by analyzing data for 45 nations of the world in which the Roman Catholic Church is active, omitting eastern Europe and the island nations of the Caribbean. The results were as predicted, and powerfully so. The smaller the percentage of Catholics, as claimed by official church statistics, the more priests per 1,000 Catholics. Because the ratio of priests to Catholics has been validated as a measure of local commitment (Stark and McCann 1993; Stark 1998b), these findings sustain the conclusion that Catholic commitment is higher to the extent that the church must confront non-Catholic majorities.

Next came two studies based on American Catholicism (Stark and McCann 1993; Stark 1998b). These proposed an extremely "strong test" of the principle that competition energizes religious organizations. The study reported above (Stark 1992a) contrasted religious participation in nations where the Roman Catholic Church enjoyed centuries as a virtual monopoly with nations where Catholics are an embattled minority. But these new studies compared Catholic dioceses in the United States, all of which are part of a national church that has always been a minority faith forced to compete vigorously to hold its own—which it has proved very adept at doing (Dolan 1978; Finke and Stark 1992). In only 7 of the 171 U.S. Catholic dioceses do Catholics make up the majority of the population. Thus, variations in the percentage of Catholics in local diocesan communities are variations only in the degree to which the church is a minority. One might well suspect that such variations would be insufficient to generate real variations in competition. Nevertheless, even such a weak measure of the independent variable produced very strong results, testifying to the power and scope of the theory.

Four measures of commitment were studied. The ordination rate is the number of secular (or parish) priests ordained in each diocese (such ordinates being of local origins even if they studied elsewhere for the priesthood). The seminarian rate is the number of local men enrolled in seminaries. The priest rate is the number of secular priests per 10,000 Catholics in the diocese. The conversion rate is the number of adult baptisms per 100,000 Catholics. Each of these measures of commitment was very strongly, negatively correlated with the percentage of Catholics. Commitment was highest where the church was numerically weakest—during 1994 and 1995 more than 20 priests per 100,000 Catholics were ordained in the Knoxville, Tennessee, diocese, while Boston ordained 1.25.

These findings were then replicated using the fifty states as the units of analysis (Stark 1998b). In addition to the measures of commitment and of innovation explained above, two additional measures of commitment could be assessed, both very broadly based on lay activities. The *Catholic Digest* rate is the number of copies of this national magazine sold in each state as a percentage of the Catholic population. In South Carolina (which is overwhelmingly Protestant), 3.14 percent of Catholics subscribed to the *Digest,* while in very Catholic Rhode Island, only 0.52 percent subscribed. The Marian apparitions rate is based on the number of shrines and centers devoted to apparitions of the Vir-

gin Mary per 100,000 Catholics. Again South Carolina had the highest rate
(4.0) and Rhode Island the lowest (0.0). Not surprisingly, all of the correlations
are extremely large and negative.

If lack of places where Catholics are an overwhelming majority made the
use of U.S. data a very "strong" test of the theory, a lack of places without an
overwhelming Catholic majority imposed the same burden on efforts to test the
theory in Italy. Nevertheless, an excellent study by Maurizio Pisati (1998) fully
replicated the American and the international findings. Using the regions of
Italy as his cases, Pisati reported a huge, negative correlation (−0.84) between
the percentage of Catholics and the number of priests per 1,000 Catholics. Another recent Italian study by Roberto Marchisio (1998) has identified a set of
niches in the religious market fully consistent with the American results presented in chapter 8.

Ted G. Jelen and Clyde Wilcox (1998) also analyzed European Catholicism
and found:

1. Catholic church attendance is higher in European nations with a smaller
    proportion of Catholics, and, within nations, Catholic attendance is
    higher than that of Protestants, again to the degree that Catholics are in
    the minority.
2. Compared to their non-Catholic countrymen, European Catholics are
    more apt to agree with church social teachings such as opposition to
    abortion and "liberal" female sex roles to the extent that they are in a mi-
    nority situation.

Not only are these results entirely consistent with findings within the United
States, the second set utterly confounds the "sacred canopy" doctrine of the old
paradigm. It *might* be true that religion does gain greater influence over humans
to the degree that it is universal, unquestioned and taken for granted, *if other
things were equal*. That is, universal churches might enjoy unquestioned plausibility if all members of a society had the same religious desires and if religious
monopolies were energetic. But demand always varies and monopoly always
saps the energy of organizations. Consequently, Catholics in Catholic nations
are far more likely to approve of abortion and of liberal gender roles than are
non-Catholics in Catholic nations, while in non-Catholic nations, Catholics are
far more conservative on these issues than is the non-Catholic majority. Jelen
and Wilcox conclude that "minority settings ... are more conducive to effective
religious socialization on the part of the Catholic Church" (1998, 36).

Indeed, effective Catholic socialization translates into religious vocations as
well. In preparation for this volume, we examined the correlation between the
nun rate (see chapter 7) and the percentage of Catholics for the sixteen primary
nations of western Europe. It is strong, negative, and highly significant ($r =
−.53$)—proportionately more Catholic women enter religious orders to the ex-
tent that Catholics are a national minority. For example, there are 105.5 nuns

per 10,000 Catholics in Denmark, 58.5 in Norway, 23.7 in Belgium, and only 18.5 in Spain.

Several additional studies involving Catholics ought to be noted. First, as already commented above, Catholics in Quebec now are less likely to attend mass weekly than are Catholics elsewhere in Canada (Stark and Iannaccone 1996). Second, Catholics in Northern Ireland are more active in their faith than are their counterparts in the Republic of Ireland (Jagodzinski and Greeley forthcoming). Finally, Anthony J. Gill (in press) has found that Catholic seminarian enrollment rates have begun to rise rapidly all across Latin America, probably for the first time, reflective of the more intense Catholicism that is developing in response to the rapid increase in Protestant competition. For Latin America in general, there were 0.19 seminarians per 10,000 Catholics in 1977. In 1997, there were 0.59.

EASTERN EUROPE

In chapter 3 we sketched the revival of religion that has followed the collapse of Soviet communism. Here the pressing issue concerns the future of religiousness in eastern Europe and the former Soviet Union—*after* these revivals, what? This is a matter that deserves and will receive a great deal of study over the next several decades. But, it is not too early to assert flatly that future levels of religiousness in these nations depend upon the degree to which they develop a free market religious economy or (which is more likely) they revert to highly regulated and socialized religious markets.

Monopoly religious traditions die hard. Already the Russian Orthodox Church is demanding restoration of its full establishment and has gained a legal ban on all its religious competitors, even including its own more fundamentalist wing (Schmetzer 1996; Pankhurst 1997). The new Law on Religion attempts to outlaw Western Protestant groups as "ungodly sects" and already has prompted a criminal prosecution of the Jehovah's Witnesses as a "threat to society."[8] The result may be the imposition of a quite lax state church, along the lines of the Scandinavian churches, while millions of Russians—those most actively religious—are forced, once again, into semi-secret worship.

Similar situations are developing in other parts of the former Soviet Union. In Lithuania, it is the old Roman Catholic monopoly that is pressing, quite effectively, for reassertion of the establishment it enjoyed under the communists. Lithuania was always a Roman Catholic nation, and under communist rule, all non-Catholic churches were illegal. During the struggle to free themselves from Soviet rule, Catholics welcomed the aid of non-Catholic religious groups (mainly Pentecostal). But since independence became secure, Catholic leaders have been quite successful in persuading government officials to impede Protestant groups.[9] In similar fashion, although Bulgaria adopted a legal guarantee of religious freedom in 1994, it has subsequently required that all religious groups be registered, and the government has begun deporting evangelical Protestants (Cimino 1996).

Even where the government intends to sustain religious freedom, the tradition of establishment dominates policies. Thus, Hungary now recognizes thirty-six religious groups and provides each with state funding based on its size. This largess does not extend to groups deemed "socially destructive," including the Jehovah's Witnesses, the Hare Krishnas, and several other "obscure Protestant sects" (Esbenshade 1994). Proportional subsidies may be fairer than the Scandinavian and German systems, but they are bound to have an adverse impact on competitive vigor.

In light of such developments, we do not anticipate that the religious revivals in eastern Europe will continue until American-style levels of commitment are achieved. At present the churches generate enthusiasm because, during their period of opposition to the government they were, in effect, strict religious groups and served as the primary vehicles for resistance to oppression (especially that imposed by foreign Soviet power). As these special conditions wane, supply-side weaknesses will reassert themselves unless free market conditions are permitted to apply.

ISLAM

In 1982, Mary Douglas pointed out that social scientists had not "foretold the resurgence of Islam" and asked "why not?" Social scientists (including those employed by the CIA) initially failed to anticipate the enormous religious vitality of Islam because of their faith in secularization. Noting the apparent lack of piety in Islamic nations of those citizens with Western educations, and the relatively rapid pace of modernization, the experts assumed that religion no longer mattered and took it for granted that "the clock would not be turned back." The same biases continue to prevent understanding of the ongoing Islamic "revivals"—that although the Muslim "fundamentalists" may cause political unrest and unpleasantness, they raise no basic questions, because these are merely unfortunate reactions against modernity by the more ignorant and backward segments of the populations of not very modernized nations. This is all nonsense. Granted, the most Westernized elite members of Islamic societies may have been those most prone to secularity, but aside from them, as we saw in chapters 1 and 3, so-called Islamic fundamentalism draws its leadership, and a great deal of support, from among the more educated and privileged and is not a reactionary movement of the "masses."

The vigor of contemporary Islam is based on two important factors, both fully anticipated by our theory. First, Islam currently serves as the institutional basis of nationalism and opposition to colonialism—political, cultural, and economic. As David Martin has explained:

[M]ost Islamic societies approximated the condition of Ireland and Poland in being subject to alien control and influence. Those who spread versions of the enlightenment not only had no native base in the internal history of Islamic societies but were propagating an ideology whose native base was part of the internal history of a Christian and colonialist Europe.

Religion was a bond of the people, and a link with a triumphalist past, whereas secularity came with dependence, weakness and alien infiltration. Thus the intelligentsias in the van of movements against colonialism were susceptible to strong definitions of their native traditions which stressed Islamic purity and severity. They intended to modernize in their own way, and the only way sufficiently rooted in long-term history was Islamic. (Martin 1991, 472)

Secondly, in addition to serving Islamic nations in precisely the way that Catholic piety has served Poland, Quebec, and Ireland, Islam has the added advantage of not being monolithic. Granted, non-Islamic faiths are outlawed in many Islamic societies, and sometimes one branch of Islam persecutes another. In general, however, relatively free market conditions prevail for competing Islamic groups—a level of competition that is quite sufficient to generate high overall levels of commitment. Here the appropriate comparison is with Christian firms within the American religious economy. While there are a large number of non-Christian religious groups active in the United States, in terms of membership, they are insignificant, and their omission would make no appreciable difference in the high levels of religiousness in America. The same applies to Islam in the sense that we ought not to seek diversity primarily in terms of non-Muslim faiths, but within the boundaries of Islam. And within Islam, too, the normal state of affairs is pluralism. Given the unusually close ties between church and state that have typified Islamic societies, for most of its history, Islamic pluralism was "a sociological reality long hidden by an authoritarian power that could not deal with it without threatening its own survival" (Niandou-Souley and Alzouma 1996, 255). Over the past century or so, Islamic pluralism has burst forth in many societies and has generated the same increases in mass mobilization produced by pluralism in the United States.

Finally, research shows that within industrialized nations, Muslims are more apt to undertake the hajj (pilgrimage) to Mecca, the more competitive and unregulated the religious environment (Chaves, Schraeder, and Sprindys 1994).

WEAK COMPETITION AND NEW RELIGIONS

In chapter 8 we proposed that the capacity of new religious firms to successfully enter relatively unregulated markets is inverse to the efficiency and variety of existing religious firms. This is a refinement of the very first proposition ever formulated about "religious economies": "Cults will abound where conventional churches are weakest" (Stark and Bainbridge 1980b, 96). Although originally limited to cult movements (those religious firms offering religious culture beyond the boundaries of culture offered by the conventional religious of a society), eventually we recognized that the proposition applies to all new religious firms, whether within the conventional religious culture or not—we must acknowledge David Nock's (1987) valuable suggestions. In any event, many studies have tested one form or another of this proposition.

The United States

The initial study was based on the fifty U.S. states (Stark and Bainbridge 1980b, 96). The competitive forces in the religious economy of each state were assessed from the strength of conventional churches, measured as the proportion of the population who actually belonged to a local church congregation, as opposed to merely expressing a religious preference. The success of new religious movements was measured in a variety of ways, including the location of more than 500 cult movements, initiation rates into Transcendental Meditation, and a rate based on the number of professional astrologers with ads in the Yellow Pages. All of the correlations were very strong, significant, and negative—religious novelty was thriving where the membership in the conventional churches was low.

A second study was based on data from the U.S. Census of Religion Bodies conducted in 1926, and separate analyses were based on the states and on the 79 cities with populations of 100,000 or more (Stark and Bainbridge 1981b). Again, competition was estimated from rates of membership in the conventional churches. In this study, it was possible to measure the degree of success of new religious movements based on actual membership statistics for five such movements: Christian Science, Theosophy, Liberal Catholic (an Anglican variant of Theosophy), Divine Science, and Baha'i. The results were very strong and consistent. For both the states and the cities, the correlations were very high, negative, and significant. New religions did best where the old churches did worst.

Two very recent studies tested the hypothesis with data on the two most rapidly growing religious movements. Mormon membership rates are highest in states having the lowest overall church membership rates (Stark 1998a). The same is true for Jehovah's Witness membership rates (Stark and Iannaccone 1997).

All of these studies confirm the belief that the West Coast is the land of religious novelty—that's where all unusual religious groups do best. And the reason for this is as theorized, for the West Coast states constitute a relatively "unchurched belt." From California in the south to Alaska in the north, to Hawaii in the west and eastward across Nevada and Colorado, church membership rates are below 40 percent, usually well below. In the rest of the nation, church membership rates never fall below 50 percent and the national average is above 60 percent. A major reason for the lack of church membership in the West is high rates of mobility, which decrease the ability of all voluntary organizations, not just churches, to maintain membership. That is, people move so often that they lack the social ties needed to affiliate with churches, Elk's Clubs, veterans' organizations, civic groups, or political organizations (Welch 1981; 1983; Finke 1989; Stark and Bainbridge 1997). By weakening conventional religious organizations, mobility increases the susceptibility of the population to recruitment by aggressive religious movements willing to go out and seek members.

Canada

This same high level of West Coast mobility exists in Canada too, and, not surprisingly, the percentage of persons reporting that they have "no religion" on their census forms also is highest in the western provinces and cities. And, as hypothesized, that also is where new religious movements thrive in Canada. The initial study was based on the 1976 census and analyzed data for the ten provinces and twenty-two cities, taking advantage of the very detailed information on religious membership collected every five years by the Canadian census (Bainbridge and Stark 1982). Although based on so few cases, the results were so robust (r values ranging from .63 to .83) that they achieved a high level of statistical significance.

David Nock (1987) has replicated the findings using a more recent census. In addition to confirming the strong positive correlations between the percentage reporting "no religion" and membership in groups such as Spiritualists and Baha'i, Nock found similar results for the Adventists and the Jehovah's Witnesses.

As can be seen in table 21, data based on the twenty-five metropolitan areas of Canada from the 1991 census, once again confirm these results. Where more people say they have no religion, new movements attract more members.

TABLE 21   Weak Conventional Competition and Religious Movements
in Canada's 25 Metropolitan Areas, 1991

	Correlation (r) *of Membership Rates with Percentage of Population Reporting "No religion"*
Jehovah's Witnesses	.61
Mormons	.60
Baha'i	.54
Para-religons*	.82

SOURCE: Data based on twenty-five metropolitan areas of Canada from the Canadian Census, 1991.
*Statistics Canada created this category by combining all persons who claimed membership in a variety of unconventional groups including Scientology, New Age, New Thought, Pagan, Theosophical, and Satanic, among others.

PROTESTANT GROWTH IN LATIN AMERICA

Several years ago David Martin told one of his English colleagues that he was planning to write a book about Protestantism in Latin American. The response he received from this stalwart of the old paradigm was, "A very small book, surely" (Martin 1989, 31). Yet, when Martin's *Tongues of Fire: The Explosion of Protestantism in Latin America* appeared in 1990 it was in fact the *second* book on the topic that year, having been preceded by David Stoll's *Is Latin America Turning Protestant? The Politics of Evangelical Growth.*

Until these books were published, the progressive relaxation of legal barriers against non-Catholic religious organizations and the successful entry of aggressive Protestant firms had gone largely unnoticed in scholarly circles. Indeed, according to the old paradigm, such changes were impossible. Some hard-line secularizationists agreed that Catholic Liberation Theology had at least a short-term future in Latin nations, but a successful outbreak of evangelical Protestantism was dismissed as absurd—hence the haughty reactions Martin experienced when he began his study. Eventually, of course, even social scientists became aware that Protestant groups—most of them of the Pentecostal variety—are sweeping over the continent. In Chile an estimated 22 percent are now *active* in evangelical Protestant congregations (even official Catholic statistics for 1995 concede that Chile now is "only" 80.4 percent Catholic), as are at least 20 percent in Guatemala and 16 percent in Brazil. If current rates of Protestant growth hold for another twenty years, Protestants will be the majority in many Latin nations—they already make up by far the majority of those actually in church each Sunday. Keep in mind that as this is taking place, Latin America is undergoing sustained modernization.

While these trends confound the old paradigm, they are entirely in keeping with our theory: when energetic new firms confront lazy erstwhile monopolies on a reasonably level playing field, the newcomers win. It follows that initial Protestant success in Latin America will have been greatest where Catholicism offers the least effective competition, where levels of Catholic commitment are low. Earlier in this chapter we noted that vocations are a valid measure of levels of commitment to the Catholic Church. Therefore, Protestant groups should have grown least where the ratio of priests and of nuns to the Catholic laity is highest. Table 22 supports this prediction from the theory. The proportion of the population who have become Protestants is strongly negatively correlated with the ratios of priests and nuns to nominal Catholics.

Mexico

An even more direct test of the hypothesis can be made in Mexico. The Mexican census asks for religious affiliation, and, as in Canada, the percentage of those who respond "no religion" is reported. The theory predicts that Protestants will be gaining where more people claim to be without a faith, and that is

TABLE 22   Protestant Success in Latin America

	Correlation (r) with Percentage Protestants
Priests per 10,000 Catholics	−.503*
Nuns per 10,000 Catholics	−.541*

NOTE: Chile omitted as an outlying case.
* $p < .05$.

very much the case. Based on the thirty-two states of Mexico, the correlation between percentage responding "no religion" and the percentage responding "Protestant" is 0.81 (significant beyond .001).[10]

EUROPE

The very first article testing this proposition that new movements will succeed to the extent that the conventional churches are weak (Stark and Bainbridge 1980b) acknowledged that many would cite Europe as a contrary case. Given the apparent weaknesses of their churches, European nations ought to abound in new religious movements, especially cults. Indeed, other things being equal, our theory would predict that such movements would be more prevalent in western Europe and Great Britain than they are in the United States. To meet this potential challenge, we noted that "a closer look at Europe supports rather than weakens our analysis. Although it receives little attention from intellectuals and less coverage in the press, cult activity seems to be *quite widespread in Europe*" (Stark and Bainbridge 1980b, 114). To justify this claim, we presented fragmentary data to show that England probably had a substantially higher rate of cult movements per million population than did the United States, and that involvement in astrology was higher in France than in America.

Needless to say, such data failed to satisfy many social scientists—indeed, we were not satisfied with them either. And they certainly could not have been expected to give pause to European social scientists, most of whom were certain that new religious movements, which are so abundant in the United States and Canada, fail to attract followers among the more secularized (and less gullible) populations on the other side of the Atlantic. Describing the European literature on new religious movements, Thomas Robbins and James Beckford noted "a widespread but questionable assumption that [new religious movements] are relatively rare and unusual" (1988, 19).

This prompted a search for a more adequate picture of the real situation in Europe. Eventually, data from a great variety of sources, on many different groups, demonstrated that many parts of Europe abounded in new religious movements, often having rates far above those found in the United States and Canada (Stark 1985a). For example, Indian and Eastern Cult Centers are far more common in Europe (1.8 per million population) than the United States (1.3 per million). Moreover, many European nations, especially those thought to be the more secularized, had rates far higher than the America's. Switzerland's rate was 3.8, Scotland's 3.2, Denmark's 3.1 and England and Wales's 3.0. Indeed, only Belgium (1.0), Italy (0.7), and Spain (0.6) had rates lower than that for the United States.

Unfortunately, the responses of our European colleagues to these findings were primarily methodological rather than substantive. Thus, the late Roy Wallis repeatedly noted that many of these rates were based on very small numbers of cases (Wallis and Bruce 1984; Wallis 1986a; 1986b) and suffered from other grave defects. This prompted Karel Dobbelaere (1987, 120) to use the occasion of the Paul Hanly Furfey Lecture to dismiss these conclusions about the greater prevalence of new religious movements in Europe as "empirically refuted." We were not unsympathetic to these objections, because we knew just how woefully crude and incomplete were the available data on religious groups in Europe, and especially on unusual groups. In fact, the European rates had been patched together out of data from such diverse sources as the back cover of an ISKCON[11] magazine, a New Age travel guide, a Mormon almanac, a book published by Scientology, and from yearbooks published by the Jehovah's Witnesses and the Seventh-day Adventists. Whatever one believes about the prevalence of religious movements in Europe, it is certain that such groups have received scant scholarly attention compared with their American counterparts. As noted: "One cannot simply go to the library and find material on cults and sects in Europe even slightly comparable with such works as J. Gordon Melton's *Encyclopedia of American Religions*, with its more than 1,200 entries"[12] (Stark 1985a, 306).

This is no longer true. J. Gordon Melton and his associates at the Institute for the Study of American Religion have nearly completed a three-volume *Religions Directory International* that attempts to list all the religious groups currently active in each European nation—adding up to thousands. In addition, for each nation, its religious groups are sorted out by "families" following the same scheme Melton developed for his American listings. Thus, it will soon be possible to consult a standard source to count various kinds of religious groups active in European nations—just as earlier computations were made for American religious groups (Stark, Bainbridge and Doyle 1979; Stark and Bainbridge 1981). We have been privileged to have access to drafts of the directories.

Table 23 shows that overall, these European nations have *twice* as high a rate of cult movements as does the United States. Moreover, many European nations have rates many times that of the United States—in fact, Switzerland has a rate about ten times that of the United States. Keep in mind too, that despite the best efforts of Melton and his associates, compared with the United States, European cult movements are undercounted, and the nations with the lowest rates are mainly those where Melton believes the undercounting was greatest. As an example of the magnitudes that might be involved in some of these un-

TABLE 23   New Religious Movements in Europe and America

	Movements per Million	Number of Movements
Switzerland	16.7	108
Iceland	12.0	3
Great Britain	10.7	604
Austria	7.9	60
Sweden	6.8	57
Denmark	4.5	23
Netherlands	4.4	64
Ireland	3.9	14
West Germany	2.5	155
Belgium	2.4	24
Norway	1.9	8
Greece	1.5	15
Italy	1.2	66
Portugal	1.0	10
France	0.9	52
Finland	0.8	4
Spain	0.7	29
Poland	0.5	17
Total Europe*	3.4	1,317
United States	1.7	425

SOURCE: Stark 1993.
*Total based only on the nations listed in the table.

derestimates, consider that in the draft initially available to us, Melton and his associates reported thirty-two cult movements in Italy, for a rate of 0.6. Subsequently, it became possible to dispatch an Italian-speaking researcher to look again. She found an additional thirty-four groups during a four-week stay, thus doubling Italy's rate.[13]

So much, then, for data that are "empirically refuted" and for European immunity to cults. Whatever Europe's true rate of new religious movements, it is far higher than that of the United States. Comparatively speaking, Europe is awash in cult movements, despite the widespread and vigorous government efforts to keep them out. However, the rate of new religious movements is lower ($r = .62$) in nations with less diversity (as measured by the Herfindahl Index), despite the fact that these new movements have such small memberships as to have no effect on the diversity score. There are several plausible interpretations of this correlation. It may be because of undercounting—novel religious groups may simply make themselves less visible the more monolithic the society in order to avoid government interference and public hostility. In addition, such groups may be less common where the tolerance for religious deviance is lacking (apathy not being defined as deviance). In any event, this finding is consistent with the curvilinearity of start-up costs for new religions. As societies become less regulated, it will be easier for new religions to get started. But no European society has yet developed the high level of competition that eventually arises in an unregulated religious economy, and that then impedes new religious firms. In contrast, the United States has developed such a high overall level of competition that new religions do face tougher going than they do in the most pluralistic parts of Europe.

Given the recent decline in religious repression in eastern Europe, we must expect new religious movements to blossom there too. And they are! At Moscow State University, the journalism department's library is designated as the L. Ron Hubbard Reading Room, after the founder of Scientology (Borenstein 1997). According to data gathered by the Institute of Geography of the Russian Academy of Sciences, the Hare Krishnas had established 9 communities in Russia by 1990, their numbers had grown to 120 communities by 1995, and "today they are to be found virtually everywhere, gravitating to the larger cities and urban areas, where they concentrate on proselytism among the younger generation" (Krindatch 1995, 5). Mormons made their first (post-Revolution) appearance in Russia in 1991, and by 1995, they had established 59 branches there. Meanwhile, the Jehovah's Witnesses have emerged from underground and drew 231,176 Russians to their 1997 annual Memorial Service, which is as close to a religious holiday celebration as the Witnesses observe. The Witnesses also reported their average number of Russian "publishers" (members who put in a number of hours of missionary activity each month) for 1997 as 78,868—an increase of 28 percent from the previous year. However, much of the outbreak of new religious movements in Russia does not involve imported faiths, but is based on home-grown movements. Among these are the Great White Brotherhood, whose members wear white robes and worship "a woman who calls herself 'the Mother of the World, Lord Jesus-Maria, Maria Devi Khristos,'{hrs}" and the Mother of God Center, whose clergy "wear purple robes and look to Mary for the salvation of the world" (Borenstein 1997, 2). In fact, throughout the entire period of communist rule, occult groups flourished, having special appeal for party functionaries (Rosenthal 1997).

Growth of new religious movements also is reported for Poland. Melton's data included seventeen different movements, ranging from the Ukrainian White Brotherhood to the Unification Church. Hare Krishna membership in Poland was estimated at 10,000 in 1996 (Zagorska 1998), although that seems rather high compared with 700 members claimed by the Mormons. Moreover, Hare Krishna membership has often been greatly overestimated by outsiders, partly because members are so visible and because the group often draws large crowds to its various public celebrations. Thus, it was widely believed and reported in the press that thousands of young Hungarians had become devotees. But when Freda Ross (1995) visited local Krishna centers in Hungary, the "thousands" melted away, as she determined that the center in Békéscaba had 15 members and the one in Budapest had about 50. In similar fashion, a Toronto magazine once estimated that there were 10,000 Krishna members in that Canadian city, but there actually were only 80 (Hexham, Currie, and Townsend 1985). On the other hand, there is no reason to doubt that there were 123,704 Jehovah's Witness publishers in Poland in 1997.

Similar portraits could be sketched for most other nations in this region. Let us emphasize, however, that we do not think these new movements are the wave of the future. They are merely indicative of weaknesses in the traditional religious institutions in eastern Europe. A potential wave of the future is far more likely to be found in energetic Christian and Islamic movements as these gain access to what historically were Christian and Islamic populations. Indeed, it is fear of these movements that has motivated reactionary laws and policies in eastern Europe and the nations of the former Soviet Union.

CONCLUSION

We have seen that societies with "universal" religions aren't very religious when it comes to organized participation, and we have argued that only in unregulated religious economies with a multitude of competing religious firms will there be high levels of commitment. But how high is high? Put another way, if full-blown pluralism develops in a society, how religious could we expect it to become?

Given the fact that religion is risky goods and that people often can increase their flow of immediate benefits through religious inactivity, it seems unlikely that any amount of pluralism and vigorous marketing can ever achieve anything close to total market penetration. The proportion of Americans who actually belong to a specific church congregation (as opposed to naming a religious preference when asked) has hovered around 65 percent for many decades—showing no tendency to respond even to major economic cycles. Perhaps that is about the ceiling under conditions of modern living. In any event, it is vital to keep in mind how long it took for the free play of pluralism in America to produce these results. It was not until the twentieth century that as many as half of all Americans were churched. There is no reason to suppose that it will take a much shorter time in other societies.

Finally, in this entire discussion of competition, all we really are saying is that, other things being equal, *effort pays*—that to the extent that organizations work harder, they are more successful. What could be more obvious? Moreover, at least in principle, the results of hard work are independent of theology. Thus, we are convinced that many of the declining American liberal denominations, for example, could grow if they could somehow get their current members to work at bringing in new members the way strict denominations do. Keep in mind that, although demand is smaller at the more liberal end of the spectrum than in the more moderate niches, liberal demand also is very underactivated. Hence, if liberal groups such as the Unitarians or Episcopalians could count on most members devoting four hours a month to door-to-door canvassing, they would grow a lot! The trouble is that these denominations are unable to motivate such efforts because in practice religious effort and theology *are* connected. Contrary to the complaints of disingenuous critics that our approach reduces religion to nothing but marketing,[14] we have consistently argued that the inability of the liberal denominations to market themselves effectively is rooted in their doctrines—only vivid conceptions of an active and concerned supernatural can generate vigorous religious action.

CHAPTER 10

Church-to-Sect Movements

It is the received wisdom that, once begun, the sect-to-church process is irreversible, and that "secularization" is an absorbing state from which faith never returns. H. Richard Niebuhr (1929), the originator of sect-to-church theory, took it for granted that transformation was possible only in the churchlike direction—that churches could not reverse the process and become more sectlike. He theorized that only the lower classes want high-tension faith, and that sects are turned into churches when they are taken over by the upper classes. Because, in Niebuhr's view, the lower classes are incapable of reclaiming a church from elite control, no church ever could be transformed back in the sectlike direction. This remains the unanimous opinion of scholars faithful to the notion that religiousness has declined greatly during the past century—as Frank Lechner remarked, "it is hard to see how the process can be reversed" (1991, 1111).

Although there have been several very insightful case studies of individual congregations that switched away from liberalism (especially Warner 1988), we have been unable to find even a hint in the theoretical literature that denominations can become more conservative, except for Benton Johnson's suggestion in a footnote that a shift in that direction "is at least conceivable" (1963, 543). One would suppose that social scientists had never heard of the Counter-Reformation.

In any event, in chapter 8, we developed a more comprehensive theoretical analysis of religious economies, which leads to the conclusion that, under certain conditions, and where religious groups are market-dependent, religious organizations will shift in the direction of higher tension with their environment.

Whether increases in tension should be called shifts toward a less liberal outlook, toward greater strictness, or revivals, may be a matter of taste. But, whatever they are called, should such changes occur, and be accompanied by organizational rejuvenation—a resurgence of membership, attendance, contributions, and other aspects of commitment—this will be a bitter pill indeed for those who continue to deny that "strict" churches are strong (see Marwell 1995).

In this chapter we show that in fact the changes anticipated by the theory are under way and are producing the predicted revival of congregational commitment. That is, within the bosom of some of the lowest-tension American denominations there are sufficient cases of clergy and congregations opting for greater strictness to let us demonstrate that low tension and its inherent lack of commitment are entirely reversible. In particular, we examine pertinent data on Roman Catholics, Methodists, Presbyterians, Unitarian-Universalists, and Reform Jews. But first, it will be helpful to review, clarify, and extend the pertinent portions of the theory.

THE CHURCH-TO-SECT PROCESS

At the end of chapter 8, having given extensive consideration to how and why the clergy (ecclesiastics) play the primary role in moving religious bodies from higher to lower tension, we noted emerging conditions under which we would expect this process to be reversed. Recall that among the motives that tempt clergy to lead their denominations toward lower tension are increased membership and enhanced social status. The very same goals can serve to reverse the trend.

It will be obvious that, other things being equal, the weaker a religious organization becomes, the less rewarding it is for the clergy of that organization: their congregations become smaller, their members tend to be older and less active, and their budgets decline proportionately. Meanwhile, as their denominations are seen to be in decline, clergy of these denominations also experience reduced status in secular society. Were these commercial firms, one would expect managers to switch to the effective tactics displayed by their thriving competitors. But since they have failed to do so for so long, that is not to be expected and we do not propose that, faced with these prospects, many clergy will have a change of outlook. Consequently, what we expect is that any substantial decline in the worldly rewards of the clergy will result in a marked shift only in the motivations and outlook of those who enter the clergy. Recall this proposition:

PROPOSITION 94.   If the secular rewards of religious vocations decline, then religious rewards must play an increasing part in the motivation of those who pursue such vocations.

What we predict is that declining religious organizations will increasingly be unable to recruit clergy except those motivated by personal religious convictions and who are not deterred by reduced benefits and prestige.

However, a religion so tepid that it fails to gather or maintain a flock will not suffice to provide religious motivations sufficient to sustain religious vocations. It follows:

PROPOSITION 95.   To the extent that religious rewards motivate ecclesiastics, they will prefer a relatively higher level of tension for the group.

There is by now a substantial and compelling literature on the organizational decay of low-tension religious groups, which has been summarized in chapters 6 and 7. As noted, these shifts have been seen as irreversible. And why not? Hard times have not prompted second thoughts among prominent liberal clergy; they continue to stress theological and moral positions known to be offensive to the vast majority of their remaining members. Thus, Episcopalian Bishop John Shelby Spong, whose denomination has experienced a severe loss of market share during his clerical career (see table 6) tirelessly proclaims that the Judeo-Christian conception of a conscious and concerned "theistic" God "is doomed to die, no matter how frantically or hysterically people seek to defend it. It will not survive" (1998, 227). And a good thing too, according to the bishop, because this God is an "ogre" whom "I would choose to loathe rather than to worship" (ibid., 95). Doomed too are all notions of the divinity of Jesus, according to Spong. And good riddance says the bishop since, redefined as merely a holy man, "Christ [can never] be used again to denigrate or judge the adequacy of any of the worlds' other great religious traditions" (ibid., 189). As for the Crucifixion, it is a "barbaric" story (ibid., 94) and those who believe the Bible are "idolaters." Little wonder that Spong's own diocese is a disaster area. Rather than serving as a refuge for the millions of "exiles" from traditional beliefs, as Spong proposes, the diocese of Newark has suffered devastating membership losses throughout the bishop's more than twenty years in office. From 1978 to 1996, Spong's diocese declined by more than 40 percent, compared with a decline of 16 percent for the denomination as a whole. Fortunately for the future of the denomination, a return from liberalism does not require liberal clergy to recant, merely that they not be replaced by like-minded heirs. Which is what Propositions 94 and 95 anticipate.

But, if substantially more conservative young clergy do begin to turn up in a liberal denomination, how will they be able to succeed in shifting the organization toward increased tension? The more general theoretical model of religious economies developed in chapter 8 postulates the existence of relatively stable demand niches in the market—that in any society people will tend to be distributed in a rough approximation of a normal curve around a mean representing a modest level of religious tension. That is, most people seem to want religion that has some moral reservations vis-à-vis secularity and that presents a relatively active conception of the supernatural—a religion that is somewhat otherworldly and strict, although most do not want it to be too strict. Other market niches, made up of those who want quite low or quite high tension religion, are smaller than the medium-tension niches in the center of the curve.

From this, several dynamic implications follow. First, as high-tension sects begin to decrease their tension, they shift from smaller to larger market niches, which brings with it the opportunity for increased growth. Second, and conversely, as moderate religious bodies shift toward even lower tension (move to the liberal end of the spectrum), they move away from larger market niches toward smaller ones, with a consequent reduction in their potential membership base. Of course, should a liberal body then reverse the process and move in the direction of higher tension, the potential for growth increases again. Formally:

PROPOSITION 96.   As a religious body in a very low state of tension moves to a higher state of tension, it moves from smaller to larger market niches and has an increased opportunity for growth.

It also must be recognized that at the most liberal end of the church-sect spectrum, the clergy usually are substantially more liberal than the majority of their remaining members (Glock, Ringer, and Babbie 1967; Hadden 1969; Wuthnow 1989) and a return from liberalism ought therefore to generate immediate favorable, face-to-face responses from the rank and file. In denominations notable for weak congregations, the emergence of successful, growing congregations will not go unnoticed. Moreover, the growth of these congregations will be based on recruitment of a more conservative rank and file, which will further solidify the shift in orientation.

Let us now introduce two important qualifiers.

PROPOSITION 98.   Initial shifts toward higher tension will primarily occur at the congregational level and will be reflected at the denominational level as a cumulative result of congregational shifts.

Here we recognize that changes introduced by a new generation of clergy whose motivations are primarily religious, will be bottom-up, since that is where these clergy will enter the system. We thus postulate a reversal of the time-honored conflict between a "progressive" young clergy and their "reactionary" superiors. The "Young Turks" will now seek to free themselves from superiors committed to "progressive" theology. Moreover, as implied in proposition 99:

PROPOSITION 99.   The church-to-sect process is far more likely to occur in relatively unregulated religious economies where the survival of all religious groups rests on market processes than in regulated economies featuring subsidized denominations.

Highly regulated economies are distorted toward inefficiency in a number of critical ways, including the ability to preserve a well-paid, secure clergy, regardless of how empty their churches are on Sunday. The result, however, is not entirely to prevent the process described in the propositions above, but to slow it down very considerably. There have been signs recently that younger clergy in parts of Europe are far more conservative and energetic than their older colleagues, as will be discussed. However, where religious bodies are exposed to unforgiving market forces, where they can *and do* go broke, the church-to-sect process is likely to kick-in far sooner and more powerfully.

Let us now turn to testing the theory. The data are from a great many sources and will be assessed as they are utilized. Moreover, there is variation across denominations in terms of aspects of the theory to which the data apply.

ROMAN CATHOLICS

As outlined in chapter 7, the shifts in doctrine and practice adopted by the Roman Catholic Church during the Vatican II Council (1962–65) caused an extremely rapid period of tension reduction as, almost overnight, core doctrines and liturgical practices that had stood for centuries were abandoned. And almost as quickly, the worst fears of the conservatives who opposed these changes were confirmed by a staggering collapse in religious vocations, as well as a substantial drop in mass attendance.

Many things were involved in the extraordinary decline in vocations. As we noted in chapter 7, both secular and religious rewards fell substantially. However, during the papacy of John Paul II, there have been vigorous efforts to reemphasize the spiritual rewards of vocations (for which the pope has been attacked relentlessly in the liberal Catholic press as a reactionary). Thus far, the pope's efforts have not stimulated an increase in American seminary enrollments, but they seem to have helped stem the decline, inasmuch as the number of seminarians has hovered at about 5,000 for the past six years. However, precisely as predicted by our theory, new research indicates a shift back to spiritual motivation and to traditional Catholicism by those who are entering the priesthood. Dean Hoge, Joseph Shields, and Douglas Griffin report finding:

> a strong pattern of conservative attitudes on institutional church issues among the youngest priests today. Young priests turned conservative on church-related issues beginning sometime in the 1980s, and the trend has intensified. In 1993 the youngest and oldest priests are the most conservative on such issues as optional celibacy, re-admission of resigned priests, allowing parishes to choose their priests and allowing priests to choose their bishops. The priests in their forties and fifties are decidedly more liberal, causing age patterns to be U-shaped. This is an important development in the priesthood that no one foresaw in the 1960s or 1970s; its explanation even today remains unclear. (Hoge, Shields, and Griffin 1995, 212)

The U-shaped age pattern discovered by Hoge, Shields, and Griffin reflects that priests recruited and socialized prior to Vatican II were entering a far more conservative (strict) faith and consequently religious motivations played a substantially greater role among them than among those who entered during the period of enthusiastic liberalization immediately following the council, when it was quite easy for priests and the religious to be released from their vows, and an end to celibacy was widely anticipated. Whereas earlier studies of becoming a priest found that religious motives predominated (Fichter 1961; Schoenherr and Greeley 1974), studies of young priests conducted during the 1970s and 1980s found widespread levels of discontent and unhappiness rooted in worldly concerns. During this period, young Catholic priests blamed their low morale on being overworked, on their opinions and needs being ignored by their superiors, on the slow pace of doctrinal liberalization, and especially on the unwillingness of the hierarchy to accept contraception and to abandon rules of celibacy. It also is significant that the more liberal their views, the more likely priests (and probably the religious as well) were to resign (Greeley 1972a; Hall and Schneider 1973).

Whatever those who entered the clergy during the late 1960s and 1970s may have anticipated, by now it is clear to all that the Roman Catholic Church will not soon become a "democratic" body; nor, in the foreseeable future, will it follow the Anglican example and ordain people without regard for gender, marital status, or sexual orientation and place them in well-paid pulpits. Hence, the decline in seminarians and novices for whom worldly rewards are determinative of cost/benefit ratios and, as we have seen, a decided shift toward religious motivations.

Nor is this shift limited to the United States. A similar study conducted by the Brazilian Bishop's Conference found the same trend. Seminarians in Brazil now reject liberation theology as "something of the past" and have been characterized as far more "evangelical" than their predecessors (Cimino 1996a).

Nor is the return to orthodoxy limited to priests. As demonstrated in chapter 7, it is the higher-tension religious orders that are growing, indicative of the priority of religious motivations. Thus, even if none of the orders that adopted low-tension lifestyles in response to Vatican II ever returns to higher tension, history is being highly selective in favor the higher-tension orders. In summary, we quote a young American sister serving in Africa: "You don't accept a life of sacrifice merely to bring sanitation or even medicine to the less fortunate. You only do it for Christ."

METHODISTS

The Methodists are well known as one of the classic cases of sect-to-church transformation. Although begun in reaction against the worldliness of the Church of England, it was the American branch of Methodism that truly prospered. Unleashed from the threat of state intervention, Bishop Asbury's band of uneducated, poorly dressed, and plain-spoken itinerants sparked revival fires throughout the new nation. At the prodding of Asbury, camp meeting revivals became the "battle ax and weapon of war" for converting sinners, and local class meetings promoted and monitored the renewal efforts throughout the year (Asbury [1852] 1958, 453). The young Methodist movement skyrocketed from 2.5 percent of all church adherents in 1776 to 34.2 percent in 1850, then constituting the largest religious body in the nation, with 117 members per 1,000 Americans.

But changes were on the horizon. In 1855, the famous itinerant Peter Cartwright complained that his Methodists had "almost let camp meetings die out," class meetings were being neglected, and the itinerants were dismounting and replacing the local lay preachers (Cartwright 1856, 523). Changes were also evident in the education and affluence of Methodists. Methodists did not open a seminary until 1847, but by 1880 there were, under official control of the Methodist Episcopal Church, 11 theological seminaries, 44 colleges and universities, and 130 women's seminaries and schools (Sweet 1933, 333). Rapidly rising Methodist affluence was soon evident in attractive clergy salaries and the rapidly increasing value of church properties. Soon Methodist divines received the social prestige and respect once reserved for Congregationalists, Episcopalians, and Presbyterians, the colonial mainline denominations.

Indeed, the Methodists long ago became full members of the mainline, not only in terms of prestige, but also as a source of dissenting sects. This reached crisis proportions with the advent of the Holiness Movement toward the end of the nineteenth century. Fully in accord with the theoretical propositions developed in chapter 8, the Methodist bishops refused to tolerate grass-roots revivalism within the ranks and ejected the most active proponents of Holiness, just as the Wesley brothers had been ejected by the Anglican establishment a century before. In response, the rebels "called for all true holiness Christians to come out of Methodism's church of mammon" (Melton 1989, 37). And come out they did, founding many new religious denominations, including the Church of the Nazarene. By the early twentieth century, the most sectlike congregations and leaders had left, and the Methodist Episcopal Church continued its climb to greater cultural prestige and acceptance.

Throughout most of the twentieth century, the Methodist clergy have pressed for increasing liberalism (Finke and Stark 1992). Their success in doing so has been mirrored by a corresponding decline in membership—what once was by far the largest Protestant body in the nation has experienced a century of decline. In 1890, 84 of every 1,000 Americans were Methodists. In 1990, there were only 36. This was not due to the growth of the Catholic Church or to any general decline in church membership. As the Methodists slumped, the Southern Baptists increased their "market share" from 33 per 1,000 in 1890 to 61 in 1990, while the Assemblies of God and the Church of God in Christ went from 0 to 9 and 22 per 1,000 respectively. Meanwhile, the church membership rate increased from 45 percent of the total population in 1890 to about 65 percent in 1990.

As the century passed and the bad news continued for the Methodists, there has been growing discontent among the rank and file who have remained within the church, and repeated efforts have been made to return to the higher-tension stance on which the church's original success was based. And, in keeping with our theory, these efforts have taken hold in a new generation of young clergy.

CLERGY AND THE NEW HOLY CLUBS

The origins of Methodism can be traced to the Holy Club at Oxford, an organization outside the church for young men determined to revive the spirituality of the Church of England, led by the Wesley brothers.. Today, somewhat similar "Holy Clubs" are attempting to revive the United Methodist Church.

One of the first new "Holy Clubs" was the Good News movement founded by Charles W. Keysor. In 1965, Keysor was asked to write an article for the Methodist ministers' journal, *New Christian Advocate,* outlining the central tenants of evangelical Methodists. After Keysor's essay "Methodism's Silent Minority" appeared, he received over 200 letters and phones calls from other Methodists, mostly pastors, lamenting their lack of contact with other evangelical Methodists and their feelings of being "cut off from the leadership of [their] church."[1] So, less than a year later, Keysor launched *Good News* magazine. Incorporated as "A Forum for Scriptural Christianity" and seeking the revival of the United Methodist Church, *Good News* quickly became more than a magazine. By 1970, the *Good News* board sponsored their first national gathering, attracting 1,600 Methodists; and by 1976, they sponsored a newsletter for seminarians (*Catalyst*), published their own church school literature, launched efforts to promote evangelical delegates and statements at the General Conferences, established the Evangelical Missions Council, and promoted the founding of renewal groups at local conferences (Heidinger 1992, 14–19). As the circulation of the *Good News* magazine swelled to 20,000 and the growing list of services increased, many expected the young movement to split from the church like the holiness groups of the past. But the leaders of the movement have consistently denied any desire to split from the denomination, insisting that they are "dedicated to the spiritual renewal and theological reform of our United Methodist Church."[2] In this they resemble earlier reformers such as Benjamin Titus Roberts (who founded the Free Methodists in 1860 after being expelled by the Methodist Episcopal Church for protesting the move to lower tension) and the many leaders of the Holiness Movement. The ability of contemporary conservatives to avoid expulsion seems due to the unwillingness of the Methodist bishops to impose any corresponding punishment on the constant challenges to their authority from the lower-tension direction.

A second national movement dedicated to the renewal and reform of the Methodists is the Confessing Movement, so called because its members subscribe to a confessional statement issued in the spring of 1994 reaffirming the traditional teachings of the United Methodist Church and pledged to "vigorously challenge and hold accountable those that undermine this confession." *Christianity Today* described the Confessing Movement as seeking to "put boundaries on what is acceptable practice and belief within United Methodism" (Zipperer 1995, 105). By the fall of 1996, the movement had gathered the written support of 960 churches and over 18,000 individuals for this confessional statement.[3] Both the Good News and Confessing Movement are attempting to increase tension with the dominant culture by reestablishing clear boundaries.

Yet, despite all of the attention given to these national movements, some of the most effective efforts to unite evangelical Methodists has occurred in the local conferences. Leaders of the Good News movement estimate that renewal groups are present in 60 percent of the Methodist conferences. One example is the Evangelical Fellowship of the Northern Indiana Conference. Following conversations with the *Good News* founder, Charles Keysor, the Fellowship was started in 1970 to provide ministers fellowship with other evangelical Methodist ministers. The Fellowship now represents a sizable portion of the total conference. Of the 568 ministers assigned to churches in the Northern Indiana Conference in 1994, 21 percent (121) were on the mailing list of the Evangelical Fellowship in 1995;[4] and the percentage of pastors rises to 31 percent when we include only the 322 pastors in "full connection" with the conference.[5]

One of the most striking characteristics of the pastors on the Fellowship's mailing list is how recently they have entered the ministry. The typical pattern for Methodist ministers is to graduate from seminary, serve two years as a probationary member, and then enter full connection with the conference. Of those pastors who have entered into full connection, and are on the Evangelical Fellowship list, 62 percent entered *after* 1980, whereas, of the pastors not listed by the Fellowship, 57 percent entered into full connection *prior* to 1980. Judging from the Evangelical Fellowship list, a new generation of evangelical Methodist leadership is emerging.[6]

So what is the effect of the growing new cohort of evangelical Methodist ministers? Using the 1994, 1995, and 1996 *General Minutes of the Annual Conferences of the United Methodist Church*, we traced the pastors on the Evangelical Fellowship list to the churches they were serving during this period. The first two columns of table 24 show the substantial differences between churches that have at least one pastor on the Evangelical Fellowship list and those churches that have none. The differences are impressive. Where there is an evangelical pastor, attendance and expenditures have risen sharply. And while even the congregations led by evangelicals lost members, the rate of decline had been cut by almost half. However, the most significant contrasts to be seen in table 24 involve the congregations served by *young* evangelical ministers. In this two-year period, these pastors generated truly remarkable increases in attendance and expenditures and nearly halted the decline in membership. No wonder these young evangelical Methodists believe the future of the church belongs to them.

It has become increasingly common for Methodist evangelicals to unite with other non-Methodist evangelicals. When over 39,000 clergy attended the Promise Keepers' 1996 Clergy Conference to rally around the themes of awak-

TABLE 24   The Impact of Evangelical Pastors in the Northern Indiana
Conference of the United Methodist Church

	Without an Evangelical Pastor (n=451)	*With an Evangelical Pastor** (n=75)	*With a Young Evangelical Pastor*** (n=46)
% change in average attendance, 1993–95	−1.3	4.5	7.9
% change in expenditures, 1993–95	6.2	21.6	41.4
% change in membership, 1993–95	−3.9	−2.3	−0.7
Average attendance per 1,000 members, 1995	586	699	803
Expenditures per member, 1995	$596	$789	$931

SOURCE: *General Minutes of the Annual Conferences of the United Methodist Church,* 1994 and 1996.
* One or more of church's clergy included on the Evangelical Fellowship mailing list.
** Accepted into full connection in 1980 or later.

ening, renewal, and cooperation, mainline clergy (including Methodists) were in attendance.[7] Although Promise Keepers did not record the denominational affiliation of each pastor attending, two pastors from Indiana identified over 35 Methodist clergy in attendance from the Northern Indiana Conference alone, and *Good News* (1996) magazine reported that the Aldersgate Renewal Ministries used the conference to host a meeting of 80 United Methodist youth workers. Mainline clergy have found many of the para-church organizations, such as Promise Keepers, Fuller Institute of Church Growth, Focus on the Family, and others, to be a source of support and revival for their own churches.

Among these para-church organizations is the Willow Creek Association. When the Willow Creek Community Church was reporting a weekend attendance of approximately 5,000, only ten years after it was founded, other ministers wanted to know how it was done. The senior pastor Bill Hybels (then 33 years old), reported that after being "barraged" by phone calls he decided to organize a conference for church leaders. The first Church Leadership Conference held on November 8, 1985, included 30 pastors from 17 churches; exactly ten years later (November 8, 1995) the Conference hosted 2,700 pastors. The conferences are now one of many services provided by the Willow Creek Association, including workshops, conferences, a newsletter, classified ads for church staff positions, and resources that include videos, books, and dramas. The stated mission of the association is "to help churches turn irreligious people into fully devoted followers of Christ."[8] On March 20, 1996, the Willow Creek Association reported 1,135 churches (associates) in the United States from over 35 denominations. Most of these were either non-denominational or Baptist, but there were 63 Methodist and 30 Presbyterian congregations on the list.

TABLE 25   Performance of United Methodist Churches Affiliated with the
Willow Creek Association (WCA), 1993–95

	All Unaffiliated Congregations (n=25,881)	Affiliated with WCA (n=53)	Affiliates with Young Pastor* (n=29)
% change in average attendance, 1993–95	1.0	13.8	22.2
% change in expenditures, 1993–95	4.3	14.4	16.6
% change in membership, 1993–95	−1.7	4.1	5.1
Average attendance per 1,000 members, 1995	401	458	581
Expenditures per member, 1995	$416	$547	$669

SOURCE: *General Minutes of the Annual Conferences of the United Methodist Church,* 1994 and 1996. The
Willow Creek Association's "Church and Ministry Associates Directory" was used to identify
churches affiliated with the association.
*Accepted into full connection in 1980 or later.

In table 25, we can see that the trends in member commitment are in favor
of the United Methodist churches affiliated with the Willow Creek Association.
Of greatest significance is that the WCA affiliated churches are growing rapidly
in a declining denomination. And here too the trends are even more favorable
in WCA churches with a young pastor—the average congregation grew by 5.1
percent. Keep in mind the very short time that these young evangelicals have
had to produce these results.

It also follows from the implied obverse of Proposition 96, that if clergy in
the lower-tension religious bodies press toward even lower tension, they ought
to accelerate their loss of market share. We already have noted the example of
Bishop Spong, whose efforts to transform Episcopalianism into a "Godless" religion have been matched by the loss of nearly half the members of his diocese.
But a recent event provides adequate statistical evidence.

At the moment, few topics polarize the liberal churches more than the question of same-sex marriage. Thus, the highly publicized marriage of a lesbian
couple at St. Mark's United Methodist Church in Sacramento, California, in
early 1999 allows clear identification of 92 Methodist clergy from the Califor-
nia-Nevada Conference who are pressing for an even lower-tension Methodism—clergy who served as co-officiants at the wedding. Of these, 72 were present and another 20 served in absentia.

Table 26 reveals the sharp differences between *congregations* in the California-
Nevada Conference having a pastor who served as an officiant for the same-sex
marriage at St. Mark's and those who didn't (since three congregations had two
pastors who were co-officants, there are only 38 congregations in column 2).
The first column shows that churches being served by pastors who did not serve

TABLE 26   Impact of Pastors Officiating at Same-Sex Marriage
in the California–Nevada Conference of the United Methodist Church

	Without *an Officiant Pastor* *in 1996* *(n=351)*	*With* *an Officiant Pastor* *in 1996* *(n=38)*	*With Same* *Officiant Pastor,* *1994–96* *(n=21)*
% change in average attendance, 1994–96	2.8	−4.9	−3.57
% change in expenditures, 1994–96	6.7	−2.2	−6.0
% change in membership, 1994–96	0.0	−4.0	−2.3
Average attendance per 1,000 members, 1996	501	454	443

SOURCE: The list of clergy serving as co-officiants for the same-sex marriage was taken from the Affirmation web site (http://www.UMAFFIRM.ORG) two days after the wedding ceremony (January 18, 1999). Data on congregations were taken from the *General Minutes of the Annual Conferences of the United Methodist Church,* 1995 and 1997.

as officiants (the vast majority of the conference) showed no decline in membership and actually increased their average attendance and total contributions. In contrast, the congregations served by pastors who served as officiants experienced substantial declines in attendance, giving, and membership. These same declines can be observed in column 3, where we have included only congregations where the same co-officiant pastor served for the entire three-year period.

Clearly, then, it isn't merely that an *activist* clergy can revive a congregation that accounts for the gains we have observed by more traditional Methodist clergy; an activist liberal clergy produces congregational decline.

PRESBYTERIANS

Like the Methodists, the Presbyterians have felt the full force of the limited market appeal of low tension. Between 1960 and 1990, while Methodist market share fell by 39 percent, the United Presbyterian Church (USA) declined by 34 percent (table 6 above). But, unlike in the case of the Methodists, for whom this has been mainly a twentieth-century affliction, the Presbyterian market share has been slipping for nearly 200 years (Finke and Stark 1992). Is it too late? Or is a more "religious" young clergy coming to the rescue here as well?

Table 27 demonstrates that Presbyterian (USA) churches belonging to the Willow Creek Association also exhibit very favorable trends in member commitment. Moreover, in a denomination with a long history of declining membership, the pastors affiliated with WCA have almost reversed the tide.

TABLE 27   Performance of Presbyterian Churches Affiliated
with the Willow Creek Association (WCA), 1994–96

	All Unaffiliated Congregations (n=11,361)	Affiliated with WCA (n=30)
% change in average attendance, 1994–96	−0.3	5.0
% change in contributions, 1994–96	8.1	15.7
% change in membership, 1994–96	−2.5	−0.8
Average attendance per 1,000 members, 1996	463	581
Contributions per member, 1996	$611	$925

SOURCE: *Presbyterian Church (USA) Minutes,* 1994 and 1996. The Willow Creek Association's "Church and Ministry Associates Directory" was used to identify churches affiliated with the association.

UNITARIAN-UNIVERSALISTS

The Unitarians began as a church movement within New England Congregationalism during the eighteenth century and emerged as a distinct denomination in 1825. Meanwhile, the Universalists originated in England, but failed to achieve organizational life until the Independent Christian Society was founded in Philadelphia in 1790.

From the start, both groups have provided a realistic test of Bishop John Spong's notions concerning the future salvation of Christianity as a "religion" of unbelief. Both the Unitarians and the Universalists opted for a very minimal form of deism (at best an impersonal higher power), dismissed the divinity of Christ and rejected most of the Bible as myth and legend. In doing so the Unitarians and Universalists ought to have maximized their appeal to rationalists and others too enlightened to embrace "superstition." If so, such people are exceedingly rare, because neither denomination ever attracted more than a tiny following. Indeed, when the two merged in 1961, they claimed only a combined total of 151,000 members. Subsequent to the merger, membership continued to decline, and by 1982 it had fallen to 135,000, the same as their combined membership in 1906.[9] However, we do not think these membership figures reflect the proportion of true unbelievers in America. What we think they reflect is the rather obvious fact that unbelievers have no earthly (and surely no heavenly) reason to join a church. For an irreligious person to join a church—even a church of irreligion—would be like going shopping in an empty store for things you don't want.

Recently there have been some remarkable changes in the Unitarian-Universalist "store," and the shelves are no longer so empty. Instead, those attending this denomination now encounter religious ritual, ceremony, and various modes of spirituality. The pastor of New York City's Church of All Souls admits that a few years ago he was sometimes booed in other Unitarian-Universalist churches when he concluded services with a benediction that invoked God. But, he says, "I get away with God language with impunity now."[10] A Boston Unitarian pastor recently explained: "The last generation of Unitarian-Universalists were fleeing Methodism, Roman Catholicism, Judaism. What this generation is fleeing is the emptiness of the culture" (Niebuhr 1996, 14). Rev. Thomas J. S. Mikelson, the Unitarian-Universalist pastor in Cambridge, Mass., recalled that in the early 1970s, "I called myself a religious humanist ... I didn't talk about God." Now he does, and he says that his new-found faith in the existence of God "opens the door for me to feel a relationship with a personal God, to pray, to express my gratitude for my life and the world, and to have a deeper sense of vocation" (ibid., 14).

These shifts parallel those among the rank and file. In a survey of members conducted in 1967, Unitarian-Universalists tended to dismiss "worship" as a motive for attending church. Only 24 percent rated it as "very important," while 33 percent said it was "not important." Twenty years later, this had changed dramatically: 44 percent said worship was "very important," and only 12 percent thought it "not important." In similar fashion, the proportion of Unitarian-Universalists who dismissed God as an "irrelevant concept" dropped from 28 percent to 18 percent (Unitarian-Universalist Association 1967; 1989).

Does it matter? Well, 1982 was the low point in Unitarian-Universalist membership, there being only 135,487. Each year since then has shown a modest increase, and by 1997 the Unitarian-Universalists had 151,213 members—an increase of 11.6 percent. That may not seem like a lot. But for a denomination that had been shrinking for decades until a shift toward higher tension set in, this growth is rather more than suggestive.

REFORM JEWS

Reform Judaism also originated as a church movement, being a response to the emancipation of Jews in Europe early in the nineteenth century (Steinberg 1965). At long last given the opportunity to participate fully in civic and social life, many Jews found themselves prevented from doing so by the demands of orthodox observance. Kosher dietary restrictions, for example, prevented Jews from freely associating with gentiles, just as their distinctive dress and appearance made them unacceptably unfashionable. Some Jews dealt with this problem by converting to Christianity. But for many others who wished to retain some ties to their roots, the solution lay in a new form of Judaism that abandoned the "Law"—a Judaism freed from ethnicity (Steinberg 1965; Stark 1996). The extent to which the Reform Jews rejected traditional observance was quite remarkable. During the early years, they even refused to use the title of rabbi, instead referring to their clergy as "reverend." Indeed, as proclaimed by the Pittsburgh Platform, Reform Judaism rejected all aspects of orthodoxy that were not adapted to the views and habits of modern civilization.

We hold that all such Mosaic and Rabbinical laws as regulated diet, priestly purity and dress originated in ages and under the influence of ideas altogether foreign to our present mental and spiritual state.

We recognize Judaism as a progressive religion, ever striving to be in accord with the postulates of reason. (quoted in Sternberg 1965, 125)

From these radical beginnings, Reform Judaism became progressively more liberal, until it came to be regarded as a religion virtually devoid of conceptions of the sacred or of the supernatural—more philosophy than faith. And, as we have come to expect of the lowest-tension faiths, Reform Jews came to display a pronounced lack of commitment: declining membership, poor attendance, waning contributions (Wertheimer 1993).

Then in the aftermath of World War II, there was growing pressure from the Reform rank and file to reinstate certain traditional rituals in order to more fully identify with historic Judaism. In part this was a response to the horrors of the Holocaust and in part it stemmed from a growing membership of descendants of Jews from eastern Europe who were accustomed to a more traditional Judaism (the original Reform Movement began in Germany, and in America it had depended largely on German-American Jews). However, the Reform clergy would have no part of renewed observance. Anticipating Bishop Spong, a leading rabbi explained in 1959 that "many [Reform Jews] seek comfort in the nostalgia of a romanticized Jewish past which never existed. We cannot lead our people forward by stumbling backward" (quoted in Wertheimer 1993, 11). In this same spirit, in 1955, the central policy committee ruled that traditional customs could not be observed at bar mitzvah and wedding ceremonies. But then something changed. We suspect that a new generation of rabbis had rather more spiritual interests than did their predecessors. In any event, in 1979, the central policy committee reversed its 1955 ruling and acknowledged that such customs could now be observed "if a new generation finds them meaningful and useful in the practice of Judaism" (Wertheimer 1993, 96).

And the new generation, clergy as well as laity, have found meaning in many of the orthodox religious observances and practices so vehemently discarded when the Reform Movement broke with Orthodoxy during the nineteenth century. There has been a marked increase in the use of Hebrew in services, and "in many temples men don yarmulkes and prayer shawls, [and] kosher meals are prepared" (Wertheimer 1993, 96). Meanwhile, a movement to reinstate the mikveh ritual bath following menstruation has been spreading among Reform women. And so it has gone.

Table 28 offers insights into the extent of the church-to-sect transformation of Reform Judaism. The data display very strong reverse relationships between age and Jewish observance—those under 30 being by far the group most apt to be observant, while those over 50 are the least observant group. When religious bodies are in transit from sect to church, the opposite pattern holds: younger

TABLE 28   Age and Observance among American Reform Jews

	Age				
	18–29 (n=136)	30–39 (n=244)	40–49 (n=187)	Over 50 (n=229)	Gamma
% who always or usually light Hanukkah candles	74	71	68	53	.228**
% who very often attend Seder	78	72	65	65	.157**
% who had a bar or bath mitzvah	67	51	55	45	.179**
% who fast on Yom Kippur	61	50	51	44	.124*
% who buy kosher meat	39	37	29	24	.188**

SOURCE: 1990 National Jewish Population Survey cited in Kosmin and Lachman 1993.
*$p < 0.05$. **$p < 0.01$.

people always show up as more liberal. But among members of Reform Temples, those under 30 are far more likely than those over 50 to light Hanukkah candles, to attend Seder, to have had a bar or bath mitzvah, to fast on Yom Kippur, or to buy kosher meat.

Like the Unitarian-Universalists, the move toward higher tension by Reform Jews also has reversed many years of declining membership. Between 1980 and 1998, the number of households enrolled in a Reform Temple had risen by 24 percent and the number of congregations has increased by 15 percent.

CONCLUSION

For decades, liberal religious spokespersons have been hailing a new day, when a newly restored and invigorated church will rise from the wreckage of "antique" faiths utterly unsuited for our sophisticated times. Ironically, every sign of life in the religious marketplace is associated with the antique faiths. Most of those liberals willing to acknowledge this fact find it incomprehensible, since their Holy Writ holds that traditional religion is incompatible with modern times. In frustration and impatience, each new outburst of religious vigor is quickly dismissed as a last spasm of anti-modernity, as the last gasp of irrationality, soon to be routed in the final battle of the culture wars. What is overlooked in this literature is that liberal religious doctrines fail to mobilize support, not because of what they offer, but because of what they lack. If the basis of the most effective religions resides in an image of God as active, dependable, responsive, and all-powerful, then the phrase "modern religion" borders on being an oxymoron. That is, modern theologies fail for want of religious content.

Consider the new, invigorated, modernized religion recommended by Episcopalian Bishop John Shelby Spong. In his book *Why Christianity Must Change or Die*, Spong explains that the Apostle's Creed "is quite alien to the world in which I live." He continues:

> If the God I worship must be identified with these ancient creedal words in any literal sense, God would become for me not just unbelievable, but in fact no longer worthy of being the subject of my devotion. I am not alone in this conclusion. Indeed, I am one of a countless host of modern men and women for whom traditional religious understandings have lost much of their ancient power. We are that silent majority of believers. (Spong 1998, 4)

But believers in what? In God, according to Spong. But what does he mean? Well, his "God is not a person ... is not a being ... is not an external, personal force." God is, instead, the "infinite center of life ... the mystical presence in which all personhood could flourish ... [only] an internal reality ... the Ground of Being" (ibid., 64). Notice that Spong uses clear language in saying what God is not, but his words become elusive and allusive when he writes of what God is. In this respect, Bishop Spong is not even slightly unusual. What no proponent of religious modernism ever has explained is what they *believe* as opposed to what they reject. To follow Paul Tillich in limiting God to an impersonal "ground of our being," sounds good, but neither Tillich nor any of his interpreters ever defined the positive aspect of this phrase in any meaningful way, as opposed to what so obviously is excluded by it. In our judgment, modernism, whether in the form expressed by Tillich or by his students such as Bishop Spong, is a faith of irreligion couched in metaphor and embroidered with poetry.

At the start of his career, the senior author collaborated on the first major surveys of American religiousness (Glock and Stark 1965; 1966; Stark and Glock 1965; 1968). Having written a lengthy battery of belief items, he submitted these in late 1962 to a number of prominent religious figures for evaluation, among them Paul Tillich, James A. Pike, Langdon Gilkey, and Martin E. Marty. Almost unanimously they complained that the items only measured traditional beliefs, and thereby relegated liberal Christianity to being measured only in terms of what it did not believe. Each of these critics was then invited to submit draft questions, or even suggestions for questions, that could serve as positive measures of liberal belief. Some submitted a few entirely secular political belief items (including one on behalf of a more steeply "progressive" income tax and several favoring unilateral American nuclear disarmament), but no detectably religious items were ever forthcoming. Our attempts to create such measures by interviewing liberals as to their positive beliefs produced only metaphors or references to clever, but unfathomable, wordplays, such as Dietrich Bonhoeffer's proposal of a Christianity without religion.

In a subsequent study of Protestant clergy in California, respondents were given a chance to identify themselves in terms of generic theological labels in common use: liberal, neo-orthodox, conservative, and fundamentalist (Stark and Foster 1970). Clergy found no difficulty in identifying themselves; indeed, only 2 out of 1,580 failed to do so. It turned out that which of these theological labels clergy selected could be predicted almost perfectly by an Orthodoxy Index made up of firm belief in four core Christian doctrines: the existence of God, the divinity of Christ, the reality of life after death, and the existence of the Devil. Liberals were easily distinguished, in that only 4 percent of them accepted all four beliefs, despite the fact that they were free to reinterpret each in purely symbolic fashion; 26 percent of self-identified liberals rejected all four beliefs, and another 29 percent only accepted the existence of God, while rejecting the other three beliefs. In contrast, 97 percent of clergy self-identified as a "fundamentalist" subscribed to all four of these beliefs, while 3 percent expressed doubt about the Devil. Thus, at least for measurement purposes, it suffices to define liberalism as the lack of belief rather than as a different set of religious beliefs.

In any event, whatever the intellectual merits of very low tension, modernized religion, it is clearly a failure on sociological grounds—in its inability to motivate and sustain religious organizations or activity. Spong's notions that Christianity can be renewed by dispensing with all supernaturalism and inviting the "silent majority" to rejoin is nonsense. The majority of Americans are not silent at all, but are busy participating in churches where God is still a "being."

Surely those who have refused to be persuaded by Dean Kelley's (1972) assessment of why the conservative churches are growing (while the liberals decline), must now accept his point, given the many, dramatic, repeated, and successful recent reversals of the process:

Sermons about sin and salvation preached from Presbyterian and Methodist pulpits, to full churches.

Unitarian-Universalist pastors in clerical robes ending their services with the benediction.

Yarmulkes and mikveh baths in Reform temples.

New, growing, Catholic orders, with their members wearing habits.

Miracles, indeed!

Propositions and Definitions

CHAPTER 4. THE MICRO FOUNDATIONS OF RELIGION

PROPOSITION 1.   Within the limits of their information and understanding, restricted by available options, guided by their preferences and tastes, humans attempt to make rational choices.

PROPOSITION 2.   Humans are conscious beings having memory and intelligence who are able to formulate **explanations** about how rewards can be gained and costs avoided.

Definition 1.   **Explanations** are conceptual simplifications or models of reality that often provide plans designed to guide action.

PROPOSITION 3.   Humans will attempt to evaluate explanations on the basis of results, retaining those that seem to work most efficiently.

PROPOSITION 4.   Rewards are always limited in supply, including some that simply do not exist in the observable world.

PROPOSITION 5.   To the degree that rewards are scarce, or are not directly available at all, humans will tend to formulate and accept explanations for obtaining the reward in the distant future or in some other nonverifiable context.

Definition 2.   **Otherworldly rewards** are those that will be obtained only in a nonempirical (usually posthumous) context.

Definition 3.   **Supernatural** refers to forces or entities beyond or outside nature that can suspend, alter, or ignore physical forces.

PROPOSITION 6.   In pursuit of rewards, humans will seek to utilize and manipulate the supernatural.

PROPOSITION 7.   Humans will not have recourse to the supernatural when a cheaper or more efficient alternative is known and available.

Definition 4.   **Gods** are supernatural "beings" having consciousness and desire.

PROPOSITION 8.   In pursuit of rewards, humans will seek to exchange with a god or gods.

Definition 5.   **Religion** consists of very general explanations of existence, including the terms of exchange with a god or gods.

PROPOSITION 9.   The greater the number of gods worshipped by a group, the lower the price of exchanging with each.

PROPOSITION 10.   In exchanging with the gods, humans will pay higher prices to the extent that the gods are believed to be more **dependable.**

Definition 6.   **Dependable** means the gods can be relied upon to keep their word and to be consistent in their orientations towards humans.

> *Definition 6a.*   **Good gods** are those who intend to allow humans to profit from their exchanges.

> *Definition 6b.*   **Evil gods** are those who intend to inflict coercive exchanges or deceptions on humans, resulting in losses for human exchange partners.

> *Definition 6c.*   **Inconsistent gods** are those who alternate unpredictably between benign and evil orientations toward humans.

PROPOSITION 11.   In exchanging with the gods, humans will pay higher prices to the extent that the gods are believed to be more **responsive.**

Definition 7.   **Responsive** means the gods are concerned about, are informed about, and act on behalf of humans.

PROPOSITION 12.   In exchanging with the gods, humans will pay higher prices to the extent that the gods are believed to be of greater **scope.**

Definition 8.   The **scope** of the gods refers to the diversity of their powers and the range of their influence.

PROPOSITION 13.   The greater their scope (and the more responsive they are), the more plausible it will be that gods can provide otherworldly rewards. Conversely, exchanges with gods of smaller scope will tend to be limited to worldly rewards.

PROPOSITION 14.   In pursuit of otherworldly rewards, humans will accept an **extended exchange relationship.**

Definition 9.   An **extended exchange relationship** is one in which the human makes periodic payments over a substantial length of time, often until death.

PROPOSITION 15.   In pursuit of otherworldly rewards, humans will accept an **exclusive exchange relationship.**

Definition 10.   An **exclusive exchange relationship** is one in which the human may exchange only with one specific god (and approved subordinate gods, such as angels).

PROPOSITION 16.   People will seek to delay their payment of religious costs.

PROPOSITION 17.   People will seek to minimize their religious costs.

Definition 11.   An **ecclesiastic** is anyone who specializes in religion—in explaining, supervising, and/or conducting exchanges with a god or gods.

Definition 12.   **Religious organizations** are social enterprises whose primary purpose is to create, maintain, and supply religion to some set of individuals and to support and supervise their exchanges with a god or gods.

PROPOSITION 18.   A religious organization will be able to require extended and exclusive commitments to the extent that it offers otherworldly rewards.

Definition 13.   **Religious commitment** is the degree to which humans promptly meet the terms of exchange with a god or gods as specified by the explanations of a given religious organization.

Definition 14.   **Objective religious commitment** refers to all behavior in accord with the explanations sustained by a religious organization.

Definition 15.   **Subjective religious commitment** involves belief in, and knowledge of, the explanations sustained by a religious organization and having the appropriate emotions.

Definition 16.   **Magic** refers to all efforts to manipulate supernatural forces to gain rewards (or avoid costs) without reference to a god or gods or to general explanations of existence.

PROPOSITION 19.   Magic cannot generate extended or exclusive patterns of exchange.

PROPOSITION 20.   Magicians will serve individual clients, not lead an organization.

PROPOSITION 21.   All religious explanations, and especially those concerning otherworldly rewards, entail risk.

PROPOSITION 22.   An individual's confidence in religious explanations is strengthened to the extent that others express their confidence in them.

PROPOSITION 23.   Confidence in religious explanations increases to the extent that people participate in **religious rituals.**

Definition 17. **Religious rituals** are collective ceremonies having a common focus and mood in which the common focus is on a god or gods, while the common mood may vary.

PROPOSITION 24. **Prayer** builds bonds of affection and confidence between humans and a god or gods.

Definition 18. **Prayer** is a communication addressed to a god or gods.

PROPOSITION 25. Confidence in religious explanations will increase to the degree that **miracles** are credited to the religion.

Definition 19. **Miracles** are desirable effects believed to be caused by the intervention of a god or gods in worldly matters.

PROPOSITION 26. Confidence in religious explanations will increase to the degree that people have **mystical experiences.**

Definition 20. **Mystical experiences** are some sense of contact, however fleeting, with a god or gods.

PROPOSITION 27. Confidence in the explanations offered by a religion will be greater to the extent that its ecclesiastics display levels of commitment greater than that expected of followers.

PROPOSITION 28. Vigorous efforts by religious organizations are required to motivate and sustain high levels of individual religious commitment.

CHAPTER 5. RELIGIOUS CHOICES: CONVERSION AND REAFFILIATION

Definition 21. **Conversion** refers to shifts across religious traditions.

Definition 22. **Reaffiliation** refers to shifts within religious traditions.

Definition 23. **Social capital** consists of interpersonal attachments.

PROPOSITION 29. In making religious choices, people will attempt to conserve their **social capital.**

PROPOSITION 30. Under normal circumstances, most people will neither convert nor reaffiliate.

PROPOSITION 31. To the extent that people have or develop stronger attachments to those committed to a different version of their traditional religion, they will reaffiliate.

PROPOSITION 32. To the extent that people have or develop stronger attachments to those committed to a religion in a different tradition, they will convert.

Definition 24.   **Religious capital** consists of the degree of mastery of and attachment to a particular religious culture.

PROPOSITION 33.   In making religious choices, people will attempt to conserve their religious capital.

PROPOSITION 34.   The greater their religious capital, the less likely people are either to reaffiliate or to convert.

PROPOSITION 35.   Reaffiliation will be far more prevalent than conversion (under normal conditions).

PROPOSITION 36.   When people reaffiliate, they will tend to select an option that maximizes their conservation of religious capital.

PROPOSITION 37.   When people convert, they will tend to select an option that maximizes their conservation of religious capital.

PROPOSITION 38.   Most people will marry within their religious group.

PROPOSITION 39.   In mixed religious marriages, spouses usually will be of very similar religious backgrounds, belonging to groups within the same religious tradition.

PROPOSITION 40.   Mixed religious marriages are more likely to the degree that one or both spouses lack religious capital.

PROPOSITION 41.   When mixed religious marriages occur, the couple maximize their religious capital when the partner with the lower level of commitment reaffiliates or converts to the religion of the more committed partner.

CHAPTER 6. RELIGIOUS GROUP DYNAMICS

PROPOSITION 42.   Among religious organizations, there is a reciprocal relationship between the degree of lay commitment and the degree of exclusivity.

PROPOSITION 43.   All religious groups can be located along an axis of **tension** between the group and its sociocultural environment.

Definition 25.   **Tension** refers to the degree of distinctiveness, separation, and antagonism in the relationship between a religious group and the "outside" world.

Definition 26.   **Churches** are religious bodies in relatively lower tension with their surroundings.

Definition 27.   **Sects** are religious bodies in relatively higher tension with their surroundings.

PROPOSITION 44. The higher its level of tension with its surroundings, the more **extensive** the commitment to a religious organization.

Definition 28. As applied to religious commitment, **extensive** refers to the range and depth of religious effects on the individual.

PROPOSITION 45. The higher its level of tension with its surroundings, the more **expensive** it is belong to a religious group.

Definition 29. As applied to religious commitment, **expensive** refers to the material, social, and psychic costs of belonging to a religious group.

PROPOSITION 46. The higher its level of tension with its surroundings, the more exclusive, extensive, and expensive is the level of commitment required by a religious group.

PROPOSITION 47. The higher a group's level of tension with its surroundings, the higher its average level of member commitment.

PROPOSITION 48. Among religious organizations, there is a reciprocal relationship between expense and the value of the rewards of membership.

PROPOSITION 49. There is a reciprocal relationship between commitment and growth.

PROPOSITION 50. As religious organizations grow, their **congregations** will tend to become larger.

Definition 30. **Congregation** refers to the smallest, relatively autonomous membership unit within a religious organization.

PROPOSITION 51. Congregational size is inversely related to the average level of member commitment.

PROPOSITION 52. The larger the congregation, the less dense the social networks within the group.

PROPOSITION 53. The less dense the networks within a congregation are, the lower the average level of reinforcement provided for commitment.

PROPOSITION 54. The less dense networks within a congregation are, the less efficient the monitoring of member behavior.

PROPOSITION 55. The larger the congregation, the higher the proportion of free-riders.

PROPOSITION 56. The less dense the networks within a congregation, the stronger the ties maintained to external networks.

PROPOSITION 57. The more prevalent member ties to external networks, the greater the pressure on the group to reduce tension.

PROPOSITION 58.   As religious organizations grow, their administrative sector grows more rapidly.

PROPOSITION 59.   As the administrative sector expands, authority will become more centralized and policies will be standardized.

PROPOSITION 60.   As authority becomes more centralized it will tend to be more exclusively in the hands of **professional** ecclesiastics.

Definition 31.   A **profession** is an occupational group claiming sole possession of the training, talent, or other qualifications needed to perform a specific occupational role.

PROPOSITION 61.   Professional ecclesiastics will seek to define the necessary qualifications for the performance of their role.

PROPOSITION 62.   Professional ecclesiastics will attempt to control entry into the profession.

PROPOSITION 63.   Professional ecclesiastics will seek to improve their ratio of rewards to costs.

PROPOSITION 64.   Professional ecclesiastics will favor growth.

PROPOSITION 65.   To the extent that ecclesiastics enjoy a favorable reward ratio, religious motives will be less important among those entering the position.

PROPOSITION 66.   Growth (especially at the congregational level) and the professionalization of their ecclesiastics will tend to shift religious organizations from higher to lower tension—from sects to churches.

PROPOSITION 67.   Professional ecclesiastics will seek to minimize diversity, especially with respect to organizational practices.

PROPOSITION 68.   To the extent that tendencies toward greater tension are suppressed, the average level of commitment of a religious group will be reduced by the departure or expulsion of the most highly committed members.

CHAPTER 8. A THEORETICAL MODEL OF RELIGIOUS ECONOMIES

Definition 32.   A **religious economy** consists of all the religious activity going on in any society: a "market" of current and potential adherents, a set of one or more organizations seeking to attract or maintain adherents, and the religious culture offered by the organization(s).

PROPOSITION 69.   Because exclusive religious organizations offer more valuable and apparently less risky religious rewards, when exclusive firms appear in religious economies previously dominated by nonexclusive groups, the exclusive firm(s) become dominant.

PROPOSITION 70.   All religious economies include a set of relatively stable market **niches.**

Definition 33.   **Niches** are market segments of potential adherents sharing particular religious preferences (needs, tastes, and expectations).

PROPOSITION 71.   To the degree that a religious economy is unregulated, it will tend to be very **pluralistic.**

Definition 34.   **Pluralistic** refers to the number of firms active in the economy; the more firms there are with significant market shares, the greater the degree of pluralism.

PROPOSITION 72.   The capacity of a single religious firm to monopolize a religious economy depends upon the degree to which the state uses coercive force to regulate the religious economy.

PROPOSITION 73.   To the degree that a religious firm achieves a monopoly, it will seek to exert its influence over other institutions, and the society will thus be **sacralized.**

Definition 35.   **Sacralized** means that there is little differentiation between religious and secular institutions and that the primary aspects of life, from family to politics, are suffused with religious symbols, rhetoric, and ritual.

PROPOSITION 74.   To the degree that deregulation of the religious economy occurs in a previously highly regulated economy, the society will be desacralized.

PROPOSITION 75.   To the degree that religious economies are unregulated and competitive, overall levels of religious commitment will be high. (Conversely, lacking competition, the dominant firm[s] will be too inefficient to sustain vigorous marketing efforts, and the result will be a low overall level of religious commitment, with the average person minimizing and delaying payment of religious costs.)

PROPOSITION 76.   Even where competition is limited, religious firms can generate high levels of commitment to the extent that the firms serve as the primary organizational vehicles for social conflict. (Conversely, if religious firms become significantly less important as vehicles for social conflict, they will be correspondingly less able to generate commitment.)

PROPOSITION 77.   Societies with low levels of religious participation will be lacking in effective religious socialization.

PROPOSITION 78.   Where large numbers of people receive ineffective religious socialization, subjective religiousness will tend to be idiosyncratic and heterodox but far more widespread than organized religious participation.

PROPOSITION 79.   The capacity of new religious firms to enter relatively unregulated markets successfully is inverse to the efficiency and variety of existing religious firms.

PROPOSITION 80.   Religious organizations mainly originate through sect formation.

PROPOSITION 81.   Sect movements that endure and grow will tend to reduce their tension with the sociocultural environment, thereby moving away from the market niche(s) in which they originally were based (a process referred to as the sect-to-church transformation).

PROPOSITION 82.   As sects initially lower their tension they become more appealing to larger niches and will therefore grow.

PROPOSITION 83.   As religious groups move into range of the largest niches and abandon their original market niche(s), they tend to suffer schisms as sect movements break away to serve members with higher tension preferences.

PROPOSITION 84.   Where free market conditions prevail, given the relative size of niches, at any given moment, religious bodies based on medium tension niches will enroll the larger portion of the population.

PROPOSITION 85.   As moderate religious bodies continue to reduce their tension, they move away from the larger niches and cease to grow.

PROPOSITION 86.   At any given moment, religious growth will therefore be limited primarily to somewhat higher tension bodies.

PROPOSITION 87.   Because of the transformation of sects into churches, there will tend to be an oversupply of lower-tension religious bodies.

PROPOSITION 88.   Low-tension bodies will typically have declining memberships and will tend to disappear via mergers.

PROPOSITION 89.   Because of the transformation of sects into churches, there will tend to be an undersupply of religious bodies serving the medium-tension niches, creating an opportunity for new bodies, most of which will migrate from stricter niches.

PROPOSITION 90.   Religious organizations are easier to form to the extent that they can be sustained by a small number of members.

PROPOSITION 91.   Most religious groups will begin in a relatively high state of tension.

PROPOSITION 92.   Most sects do not reduce their initial level of tension and do not grow, and the high-tension end of the church-sect spectrum will therefore abound in small, unsuccessful religious organizations.

PROPOSITION 93. **Church movements** are formed by dissidents wishing to shift to a lower-tension niche who lack the power to shift the organization.

Definition 36. **Church movements** are schismatic movements that break away to enter a lower level of tension.

PROPOSITION 94. If the secular rewards of religious vocations decline, then religious rewards must play an increasing part in the motivation of those who pursue such vocations.

PROPOSITION 95. To the extent that religious rewards motivate religious leaders, they will prefer a relatively higher level of tension for the group.

PROPOSITION 96. As a religious body in a low state of tension moves to a higher state of tension, it moves from smaller to larger niches and has an increased opportunity for growth.

PROPOSITION 97. In an unregulated religious economy, where the survival of all religious groups rests on market processes, growth will facilitate the efforts of clergy to move a group into lower or higher tension.

CHAPTER 10. CHURCH-TO-SECT MOVEMENTS

PROPOSITION 98. Initial shifts toward higher tension will occur primarily at the congregational level and will be reflected at the denominational level as a cumulative result of congregational shifts.

PROPOSITION 99. The church-to-sect process is far more likely to occur in relatively unregulated religious economies where the survival of all religious groups rests on market processes than in regulated economies featuring subsidized denominations.

NOTES

INTRODUCTION: ATHEISM, FAITH, AND THE SOCIAL SCIENTIFIC STUDY OF RELIGION

1. Jean Bodin's *Colloquium of the Seven about Secrets of the Sublime* finally was published in 1857.

2. In keeping with this psychological tradition, the 1860 U.S. census classified inmates of mental hospitals according to the *cause* of their psychopathology, finding that one of the most common was "religious excitement" (Stark and Bainbridge 1997).

3. William Swatos (1989) carefully refutes the "received wisdom" that American sociology was founded by pious Protestants whose religiousness governed the early agenda of the field.

4. Note the appropriate acronym

5. Joseph P. Fitzpatrick, S.J. (1989, 391) writes:

> In 1934, the General of the Society of Jesus, Vladimir Ledechowski, S.J., sent a letter to the American Jesuit Provincials, insisting that they send large numbers of their men to get their doctorates in the most prestigious universities of the United States and abroad. It was important, he said, that we prepare Jesuits to maintain the prestige and competence of Jesuit colleges and universities in the United States. As a result, many of us, such as myself and Father Joseph Fichter, S.J., found ourselves at Harvard University and elsewhere; and large numbers returned to our Jesuit colleges and universities with a high level of training in a wide variety of disciplines in secular universities.

6. Graduate students at Berkeley during the 1960s who have published at least one significant article or book within the social scientific study of religion include Robert Alford, Randall H. Alfred, Earl R. Babbie, Laile E. Bartlett, H. Taylor Buckner, Fred Byrd, Randall Collins, Ian Currie, N.J. Demerath III, Henry C. Finney, Bruce D. Foster, Toyomasa Fuse, Stephen Hart, Donald Heinz, Max Heirich, Travis Hirschi, Barclay Johnson, Jonathan Kelley, Arthur Leibman, John Lofland, Gary T. Marx, Armand L. Mauss, Jean Messer, Donald Metz, Michael Otten, Thomas Piazza, Melvin Pollner, Whitney

Pope, Linda Pritchard, Harold E. Quinley, Philip Roos, Guenther Roth, Metta Spencer, Rodney Stark, Donald Stone, Stephen Steinberg, Ann Swidler, Alan Toby, Jean-Guy Vaillancourt, Ruth Wallace, R. Stephen Warner, and Robert Wuthnow.

7. We find this perverse, despite the fact that these same people cite our work as representative of what this new religious studies curriculum would stress.

CHAPTER 1. A NEW LOOK AT OLD ISSUES

1. We thank Mansoor Moadell for a copy of Charles C. Torrey's *The Commercial-Theological Terms in the Koran* (Leyden: E.J. Brill, 1892).

CHAPTER 2. RATIONALITY AND THE "RELIGIOUS MIND"

1. The conversations were informal in style, and the question was not always worded precisely this way.

2. They also are as likely to have read part of a book other than the Bible during the past seven days (65% versus 68%) and even as apt to have watched MTV during the past week (30% versus 29%).

CHAPTER 3. SECULARIZATION, R.I.P.

1. Rodney Stark's translation from Middle English.

2. "All our ancestors were literal Christian believers, all of the time" (Laslett 1965, 7).

3. Century of supposed Christianization: Austria (9th), Belgium (7th), Denmark (11th), Finland (13th), France (6th), Germany (9th), Great Britain (9th), Iceland (11th), Ireland (5th), Italy (4th), Netherlands (8th), Norway (11th), Portugal (4th), Spain (4th), Sweden (12th), and Switzerland (8th).

4. In a 1968 sample of Protestant clergy in California, only 45 percent of pastors of the United Church of Christ could agree "I know God really exists and I have no doubts about it" (Stark, Foster, Glock and Quinley 1971). Of Methodist clergy, 52 percent agreed. Notice that this item is much less stringent than the one used by Leuba since clergy were free to define God as they wished. Given that the majority of these same clergy doubted the divinity of Jesus, one must suppose that many of them asserted their beliefs in a rather remote and vague conception of God, not one who hears and answers prayers.

CHAPTER 4. THE MICRO FOUNDATIONS OF RELIGION

1. "Religious systems may change in accordance with changes in the social structure; but they may also change for demographic or ecological reasons, because of personal decisions by leaders, or from the logic of the internal character of the system," Raymond Firth observed in a classic essay. "Such changes occur even in what are apparently static societies," he added, illustrating this with a detailed description of doctrinal and ritual changes among the Tikopia and the Hopi (Firth 1959, 140).

2. In what may be the most widely cited essay ever written on religion by an anthropologist, Clifford Geertz noted "the surely untrue proposition" that individual religious-

ness is universal in traditional socities. "But if the anthropological study of religious commitment is underdeveloped, the anthropological study of religious non-commitment is non-existent. The anthropology of religion will have come of age when some more subtle Malinowski writes a book called 'Belief and Unbelief (or even 'Faith and Hypocrisy') in a Savage Society'{hrs}" (Geertz 1966, 43).

3. In previous work, explanations for obtaining rewards in nonverifiable contexts were identified as "compensators." We always disliked using that term as it implies unmeant negative connotations about the validity of religious promises. As we reworked the theory, it became evident that there is no need to distinguish these kinds of explanations by use of a special term. It suffices to analyze aspects of the religious means of fulfillment of such explanations and the issues of risk and plausibility entailed therein.

4. Since the Middle (or Near) East is in Asia, Tyler here refers to Judaism, Christianity, and Islam, as well as religions of the Far East.

5. "It was Durkheim, not the savage, who made society into a god," Evans-Pritchard remarked (1956, 313).

6. Clyde Kluckhohn frankly acknowledged that all functionalist "analyses [are] from an observer's point of view and with a minimum of content" (1952, 420–21).

7. It is likely that a proper statistical study of rain dances and rain would produce a relatively strong positive correlation. Just as "primitives" do not attempt to make it snow in summer, rain dances are not held in the dry season. Moreover, rain dances are not prompted primarily by *lack* of rain. Rather, they are done in *anticipation* of rain.

8. In an overlooked but methodologically quite remarkable discussion, Herbert Spencer quotes reports by several teachers of adult deaf mutes that their students had grown up without wondering about religious questions, citing "an American lady who was deaf and dumb, but at a mature age was instructed, and who said the idea that the world must have had a Creator never occurred to her" (1893, 2: 671–72). Spencer regarded this as proof that there is no religious instinct.

9. Stark 1981, 159, comments that "the differences between supernatural and non-supernatural or naturalistic systems are so profound that it makes no more sense to equate them than to equate totem poles and telephone poles."

CHAPTER 5. RELIGIOUS CHOICES:
CONVERSION AND REAFFILIATION

1. Large public religious meetings such as those conducted by Billy Graham or by the Promise Keepers do not produce mass conversions (or any kind of conversion) and rarely even reaffiliation. They are no more spontaneous than the Super Bowl and are attended by people with relatively high levels of commitment who are seeking merely to "revive" or "renew" it.

2. Eventually Rigdon was excommunicated by the Mormons and went on to other affiliations.

3. Note the similarity with Muhammad's public revelations during which he dictated the Qur'ān.

4. Morley went on to play an important role in Mormon history, serving as a member of the Council of Fifty (Quinn 1997, 248).

5. In fact, many of those who did "give in" had been taken captive following their desertion from their American units.

CHAPTER 6. RELIGIOUS GROUP DYNAMICS

1. There are "godless" religions, but their followings are limited to small elites—as in the case of the elite forms of Buddhism, Taoism, and Confucianism.

2. Despite their favorable assessment of sects' ability to generate commitment and conformity, Smith and Troeltsch did not admire the sects. Smith noted that their morals "have frequently been rather disagreeably rigorous and unsocial" (1776, 748). When offering his final assessment on the various "forms" of religious organizations, Troeltsch concluded that the "Church-type is obviously superior to the sect-type and to mysticism" ([1911] 1991b, 1007).

3. We thank the Public Affairs Office of the Latter-Day Saints, Salt Lake City, Utah, for providing this information.

4. As with the Nazarenes (see Table 5), attendance is far higher than membership at Willow Creek. Attendance at the weekend "seeker" services was 13,000 in 1990, and the midweek believer services attracted approximately 4,000, while the total membership was only 1,865 (Mellado 1991).

5. The Yoido Full Gospel Church uses small groups as a powerful tool for evangelism, encouraging "each cell group to win at least one person to the Lord every six months" (Hurston 1994, 99).

6. If it seems unreasonable to compare a denomination to a single church, realize that whereas in 1785, Francis Asbury's Methodists reported 18,000 members, in 1990, the Yoido Full Gospel Church reported worship attendance of 600,000 per week (Vaughan 1992, 367).

7. To better understand the procedures used for starting new churches, we conducted phone interviews with the denominational representatives responsible for starting new churches in each of the fifteen largest denominations. We asked them to "describe the procedures used to start a new church" and followed their description with a series of questions about the financial support and leadership provided for new churches.

8. This varies from one denomination to the next, but the most typical plan is 100 percent support for the first year, 80 percent for second, and so on, until they are receiving no support at the end of five years.

9. The representative from the Progressive National Baptists was emphatic that most of the splits resulted from "fights" and not from carefully planned divisions.

CHAPTER 7. CATHOLIC RELIGIOUS VOCATIONS: DECLINE AND REVIVAL

1. Ebaugh and her co-authors were entirely misinformed when they justified use of 1960 data on the status of women on grounds that "[i]nsufficient educational and occupational data [are available for] 1990" (Ebaugh et al. 1996, 177). Much better data for a far larger selection of nations are available now than for 1960. For example, the GDI measure is available for 129 nations, and the GEM is available for 116. A comprehensive electronic source of contemporary cross-national data is MicroCase Corporation's *Nations of the Globe*, which provides data on all 174 nations with populations of 200,000 or more.

2. We encountered several obvious typographical errors in the *Catholic Almanac* data, as when a number increased or decreased by an order of magnitude for one year because a digit had been dropped or added and sometimes data for one nation were simply

repeated from the previous year. We corrected these data as indicated. Missing years were assigned the average value of the preceding and the following years.

3. Constitutional documents hold more status than other Vatican documents, such as apostolic letters or decrees.

4. These three items were included in a single index with a Cronbach's alpha of .77.

CHAPTER 8. A THEORETICAL MODEL OF RELIGIOUS ECONOMIES

1. The other two basic assumptions of rational choice are maximizing behavior and market equilibrium (Becker 1976).

2. Religious groups have a membership of persons "in similar social circumstances, of similar status. ... Those who voluntarily associate with each other in a sectarian movement generally show considerable similarity of social characteristics," Bryan Wilson asserted (1966, 184), for example.

3. This may well be the reason why sociologists regard religious monopolies as the basis for strong faith and pluralism as inevitably eroding faith. If Peter Berger's notion of the "sacred canopy" is equated with the sacralization of societies, then it is true that a single canopy is necessary, and that multiple canopies do not suffice. But when the sacred canopy line of thought is construed to mean that personal piety is more abundant under monopoly faith that is clearly wrong.

4. Non-Christians were omitted because of the Christian content of many of the items.

5. We discarded all cases of people who could name only a generic preference as opposed to naming a specific body. That is, people who couldn't identify a specific Lutheran, Methodist, Baptist, or Presbyterian body were not coded. Coding was as follows: *Ultraliberal:* Unitarian Universalist, Unity Church, Unity, Spiritualist; *Liberal:* United Methodist, United Presbyterian, Episcopal, Congregationalist, United Church of Christ, Disciples of Christ; *Moderate:* American Lutheran, Lutheran Church in America, American Baptist, less than "strong" Catholics; *Conservative:* Southern Baptist, Missouri Lutheran, Wisconsin Lutheran, "strong" Catholics, United Brethren, Christian, Christian Reform, Church of Christ; *Strict:* Christian and Missionary Alliance, Assemblies of God, Holiness (Nazarene), Brethren, Open Bible, Churches of God, Full Gospel, Four-Square Gospel, Church of Holiness, Jehovah's Witnesses, Mormons (LDS), Nazarene, Pentecostal Assembly of God, Seventh-Day Adventist, Wesleyan, Missionary Baptist, Grace Brethren, Charismatic; *Ultrastrict:* Bible Fellowship, Apostolic Faith, Free Will Baptist, Church of God in Christ Holiness, Pentecostal Church of God, Pentecostal Holiness, Zion Union Apostolic, Holiness Church of God, Pentecostal Apostolic, Bible Missionary, Mennonite Brethren, Church of the First Born.

6. A staff member of the United Church of Christ has claimed that it is so well endowed that it need not be responsive to the laity. Perhaps.

CHAPTER 9. RELIGIOUS COMPETITION AND COMMITMENT: AN INTERNATIONAL ASSESSMENT

1. A cautionary example is Michael P. Carroll's (1987) offensive interpretation of the Roman Catholic practice of praying the Rosary as anal-erotic behavior (literally as turd

squeezing), while demonstrating his complete ignorance of the use of prayer beads in many other religions, including Buddhism.

2. A subsequent study, Blau, Land, and Redding 1992, concluded that "religious monopoly—not diversity—fuels religious expansion," but it fails to control for the Catholic percentage.

3. Our Swedish colleague Eva M. Hamberg has informed us that members of the theological faculties at Swedish Universities regard this translation as theologically superior to the one it replaced.

4. We thank Laurence Iannaccone for this anecdote.

5. Notice that these lumberjacks weren't tithing.

6. The failure was also owing in part to the very low quality of the programs, many of which were tapes of American programs with German subtitles.

7. Great-grandfather of our colleague William Sims Bainbridge.

8. "Jehovah's Witnesses Are on Trial in Russia," *Seattle Times,* Feb. 10, 1999, A12.

9. "Roman Catholics Pressure Pentecostals in Lithuania," *Charisma,* November 1996, 29–30.

10. Data from the *Anuario Estadisticio di los Estado Unidos Mexicanos,* 1990.

11. ISKCON = International Society for Krishna Consciousness, popularly referred to as the Hare Krishnas.

12. There were 1,730 in the fourth edition of J. Gordon Melton's *Encyclopedia of American Religions,* published in 1993.

13. The researcher also learned of the probable existence of several dozen more cult groups in Italy, but was unable to obtain current addresses in the time available.

14. On the first and last pages of *The Churching of America* (and on many pages in between), we specifically said that doctrine holds the key to the success or failure of groups over the course of American history: "[T]o the degree that denominations rejected traditional doctrines and ceased to make serious demands on their followers, they ceased to prosper. The churching of America was accomplied by aggressive churches committed to vivid otherworldliness" (p. 1). Nevertheless, Martin E. Marty was sufficiently dishonest to write of our thesis: "No God or religion or spirituality, no issue of truth of beauty or goodness, no faith or hope or love, no justice or mercy; only winning or losing in the churching game matters." He must have confused our book with one of his own. His cookbook perhaps?

CHAPTER 10. CHURCH-TO-SECT MOVEMENTS

1. "The Good News Movement: Is It Good for United Methodists," *Circuit Rider,* April 1989, 6.

2. Ibid.

3. The confessional statement is available from Dr. John Ed Mathison, Frazer Memorial United Methodist Church, 6000 Atlanta Highway, Montgomery, AL 36117, or the Confessing Movement's website: www.confessingumc.org. We would like to thank Cy Mathison for providing information on the number of churches and individuals signing the confessing statement.

4. We thank Reverend Michael Brown, Reverend Riley Case, and Reverend Dwight Monical for information about the Evangelical Fellowship.

5. The majority of the pastors *not* in "full connection" are "local pastors." Local pastors are not members of the annual conference, have not completed three years of seminary, do not have the voting privileges given to conference pastors, and are frequently bivocational. For these reasons they are less involved in clergy organizations and their work schedules seldom allow them to attend the day-time meetings of the Evangelical Fellowship.

6. This supports the claim of Thomas Oden, Confessing Movement co-founder and professor of theology at Drew University, that the "emerging leadership" of young evangelical United Methodist students will soon be hard to ignore (Zipperer 1995).

7. For a mainline pastor's reflections on his attendance at the Clergy Conference, see *Christian Century*, 1996: 695–97. He reports that the "most poignant reaction to the experience came from a United Methodist district superintendent" when he said: 'This is what we used to be like. John Wesley would love this.'{hrs}"

8. This information was taken from Mellado 1991, several Willow Creek brochures, and the Willow Creek Association Web site, http://www.willowcreek.org/wca.

9. Data for 1906 are from the U.S. religious census for that year; more recent data were provided by the Unitarian-Universalist Association.

10. Terry Mattingly, "When a Unitarian Minister Goes Too Far," Scripps Howard News Service, *East Side Journal*, April 26, 1997, E6.

REFERENCES

Abbott, Andrew. 1988. *The System of Professions: An Essay on the Division of Expert Labor.* Chicago: University of Chicago Press.

Aberele, David F., Albert K. Cohen, Arthur K. Davis, Marion J. Levy, Jr., and Francis X. Sutton. 1950. "The Functional Prerequisites of a Society." *Ethics* 60: 100–111.

Adorno, Theodore W., Else Frankle-Brunswik, Daniel J. Levinson, and R. Nevitt Sanford. 1950. *The Authoritarian Personality.* New York: Harper & Sons.

Ahmad, Mumtaz. 1991. "Islamic Fundamentalism in South Asia: The Jamaat-i-Islami and the Tablighi Jamaat of South Asia." In *Fundamentalisms Observed,* edited by Martin E. Marty and R. Scott Appleby, 457–528. Chicago: University of Chicago Press.

Allen, Charlotte. 1996. "Is Nothing Sacred?: Casting Out the Gods from Religious Studies." *Lingua Franca* (November) 31–40.

Allen, James B., and Glen M. Leonard. 1992. *The Story of the Latter-Day Saints.* 2d ed. Salt Lake City: Deseret.

Allen, James B., Ronald K. Esplin, and David J. Whittaker. 1992. *Men With a Mission, 1837–1841: The Quorum of the Twelve Apostles in the British Isles.* Salt Lake City: Deseret.

Allport, Gordon W. 1960. *The Individual and His Religion.* New York: Macmillan.

———. 1963. "Behavioral Science, Religion, and Mental Health." *Journal of Religion and Health* 2: 187–97.

Alston, Jon P., and B. E. Aguirre. 1970. "Congregational Size and the Decline of Sectarian Commitment: The Case of the Jehovah's Witnesses in South and North America." *Sociological Analysis* 40: 63–70.

Ammerman, Nancy Tatom. 1990. *Baptist Battles: Social Change and Religious Conflict in the Southern Baptist Convention.* New Brunswick, N.J.: Rutgers University Press.

Anderson, Karl Ricks. 1996. *Joseph Smith's Kirtland: Eyewitness Accounts.* Salt Lake City: Deseret.

Anderson, Richard Lloyd. 1971. "The Impact of the First Preaching in Ohio." *Brigham Young University Studies* 11: 474–96.

Anthony, Dick. 1990. "Religious Movements and Brainwashing Litigation: Evaluating Key Testimony." In *In Gods We Trust,* edited by Thomas Robbins and Dick Anthony, 295–343. 2d ed. New Brunswick, N.J.: Transaction Publishers.

Argyle, Michael, 1959. *Religious Behavior.* Glencoe, Ill.: Free Press.

Argyle, Michael, and Benjamin Beit-Hallahmi. 1975. *The Social Psychology of Religion.* London: Routledge & Kegan Paul.

Arrington, Leonard J. 1985. *Brigham Young: American Moses.* New York: Knopf.

Arrington, Leonard J., and Davis Bitton. 1979. *The Mormon Experience: A History of the Latter-Day Saints.* New York: Knopf.

Asberg, Christer. 1990. "The Swedish Bible Commission and Project NT 81." In *Bible Reading in Sweden,* edited by Gunnar Hansson, 15–22. Uppsala: University of Uppsala.

Asbury, Francis. [1852] 1958. *The Letters of Francis Asbury.* Nashville: Abingdon Press.

Babbit, Beth, ed. 1998. *1997 General Minutes of the Annual Conferences of the United Methodist Church.* Evanston, Ill.: General Council on Finance and Administration.

Backman, Milton V., Jr. 1983. *The Heavens Resound: A History of the Latter-Day Saints in Ohio, 1830–1838.* Salt Lake City: Deseret.

———. 1988. "Lo, Here! Lo, There! Early in the Spring of 1820." In *The Prophet Joseph: Essays on the Life and Mission of Joseph Smith,* edited by Larry C. Porter and Susan Easton Black, 19–35. Salt Lake City: Deseret.

Bainbridge, William F. 1882. *Along the Lines at the Front: A General Survey of Baptist Home and Foreign Missions.* Philadelphia: American Baptist Publication Society.

Bainbridge, William Sims. 1978. *Satan's Power: A Deviant Psychotherapy Cult.* Berkeley and Los Angeles: University of California Press.

———. 1985. "Cultural Genetics." In *Religious Movements: Genesis, Exodus, and Numbers,* edited by Rodney Stark, 157–98. New York: Paragon House.

Bainbridge, William Sims, and Rodney Stark. 1982. "Church and Cult in Canada." *Canadian Journal of Sociology,* 7: 351–66.

Baird, Robert. 1844. *Religion in America; or, An Account of the Origin, Progress, Relation to the State, and Present Condition of the Evangelical Churches in the United States.* New York: Harper & Bros.

Baldwin, Stephen L. 1900. *Foreign Missions of the Protestant Churches.* Chicago: Missionary Campaign Library.

Barbour, Ian. 1990. *Religion in an Age of Science.* San Francisco: HarperSanFrancisco.

Barker, Eileen. 1984. *The Making of a Moonie: Brainwashing or Choice.* Oxford: Basil Blackwell.

———. 1986. "Religious Movements: Cult and Anti-Cult since Jonestown." *Annual Review of Sociology* 12: 329–46.

Barkun, Michael. 1986. *Crucible of the Millennium.* Syracuse, N.Y.: Syracuse University Press.

Barna, George. 1992. *The Barna Reports, 1992–93.* Ventura, Calif.: Regal Books.

Barrett, Clive. 1996. *The Egyptian Gods and Goddesses: The Mythology and Beliefs of Ancient Egypt.* London: Hammersmith.

Barrett, David B. 1982. *World Christian Encyclopedia.* Oxford: Oxford University Press

Barron, F. 1953. "An Ego Strength Scale Which Predicts Response to Psychotherapy." *Journal of Consulting Psychology* 17: 327–33.

Bateson, C. Daniel, Patricia Schoenrade, and W. Larry Ventis. 1993. *Religion and the Individual.* New York: Oxford University Press.

Baumer, Franklin L. 1960. *Religion and the Rise of Scepticism.* New York: Harcourt, Brace.

Beattie, John. 1966. "Ritual and Social Change." *Man* 1: 60–74.

Becker, Gary S. 1964. *Human Capital: A Theoretical and Empirical Analysis.* New York: Columbia University Press.

———. 1975. *Human Capital: A Theoretical and Empirical Analysis, with Special Reference to Education.* New York: Columbia University Press.

———. 1976. *The Economic Approach to Human Behavior.* Chicago: University of Chicago Press.

———. 1996. *Accounting for Tastes.* Cambridge, Mass.: Harvard University Press.

Becker, Gary S., Elizabeth M. Landis, and Robert T. Michael. 1977. "An Economic Analysis of Marital Instability." *Journal of Political Economy* 85: 1141–87.

Becker, J. W., and R. Vink. 1994. *Secularisatie in Nederland, 1966–1991.* Rijswijk: Sociaal en Cultureel Planbureau.

Beckford, James A. 1978. "Accounting for Conversion." *British Journal of Sociology* 29: 249–62.

———. 1985a. *Cult Controversies: The Societal Response to New Religious Movements.* London: Tavistock Publications.

———. 1985b. "The Insulation and Isolation of the Sociology of Religion." *Sociological Analysis* 46: 347–54.

———. 1990. "The Sociology of Religion, 1945–1989." *Social Compass* 37: 45–64.

Bede. [730] 1955. *Ecclesiastical History of the English People.* London: Penguin Classics.

Bedell, Kenneth B., ed. 1995. *The Yearbook of American and Canadian Churches.* Nashville: Abingdon Press.

———. 1996. *The Yearbook of American and Canadian Churches.* Nashville: Abingdon Press.

Bedell, Kenneth B., and Alice M. Jones, eds. 1992. *The Yearbook of American and Canadian Churches.* Nashville: Abingdon Press.

Beit-Hallahmi, Benjamin, and Michael Argyle. 1997. *The Psychology of Religious Behaviour, Belief and Experience.* London: Routledge.

Bellah, Robert N. 1964. "Religious Evolution." *American Sociological Review* 29: 358–74.

———. 1967. "Civil Religion in America." *Daedalus* 96: 1–21.

———. 1970. *Beyond Belief.* New York: Harper & Row.

Benedict, Ruth. 1938. "Religion." In *General Anthropology,* edited by Franz Boas, 627–65. New York: C. D. Heath.

Berger, Peter. 1968. "A Bleak Outlook Is Seen for Religion." *New York Times,* April 25, 3.

———. 1969. *The Sacred Canopy.* New York: Doubleday.

———. 1979. *The Heretical Imperative: Contemporary Possibilities of Religious Affiliation.* New York: Doubleday.

———. 1997. "Epistemological Modesty: An Interview with Peter Berger." *Christian Century* 114 (October 29): 972–75, 978.

Bergin, Allen E. 1983. "Religiosity and Mental Health: A Critical Reevaluation and Meta-Analysis." *Professional Psychology: Research and Practice* 14: 170–84.

Berrett, LaMar C. 1988. "Joseph, a Family Man." In *The Prophet Joseph: Essays on the Life and Mission of Joseph Smith,* edited by Larry C. Porter and Susan Easton Black, 36–48. Salt Lake City: Deseret.

Berriot, François. 1984. *Athèismes et athéistes au XVI siècle en France.* Lille: Cerf.

Beyer, Peter. 1994. *Religion and Globalization.* London: Sage.

Bibby, Reginald W., and Merlin B. Brinkerhoff. 1973. "The Circulation of the Saints: A Study of People Who Join Conservative Churches." *Journal for the Scientific Study of Religion* 12: 273–83.

Blau, Judith R., Kenneth C. Land, and Kent Redding. 1992. "The Expansion of Religious Affiliation." *Social Science Research* 21: 329–52.

Blau, Peter M. 1970. "A Formal Theory of Differentiation in Organizations." *American Journal of Sociology* 35: 201–18.

———. 1972. "Size and the Structure of Organizations: A Causal Analysis." *American Sociological Review* 37: 434–40.

———. 1977. *Inequality and Heterogeneity: A Primitive Theory of Social Structure.* New York: Free Press.

———. 1994. *Structural Contexts of Opportunities.* Chicago: University of Chicago Press.

Blumer, Herbert. 1969. *Symbolic Interactionism: Perspective and Method.* Englewood Cliffs, N.J.: Prentice-Hall.

Bonhoeffer, Dietrich. 1959. *Ethics.* New York: Macmillan, 1959.

Borenstien, Eliot. 1997. "Indigenous and Eclectic Religious Faiths Find Following in Russia." *Religion Watch* 12 (September): 1–2.

Borg, Marcus. 1995. *Meeting Jesus Again for the First Time: The Historical Jesus and the Heart of Contemporary Faith.* San Francisco: HarperSanFranciso.

Borowik, Irena. 1996. "Religion and Sexual Values in Poland." *Journal of Contemporary Religion* 11: 89–94.

Bossy, John. 1985. *Christianity in the West, 1400–1700.* New York: Oxford University Press.

Boudon, Raymond. 1993. "Toward a Synthetic Theory of Rationality." *International Studies in the Philosophy of Science* 7: 5–19.

Bourdieu, Pierre. 1984. *Distinction: A Social Critique of the Judgement of Taste.* Cambridge, Mass.: Harvard University Press.

Breault, Kevin D. 1989. "New Evidence on Religious Pluralism, Urbanism, and Religious Participation." *American Sociological Review* 54: 1048–53.

Brierley, Peter. 1993. "Europe: Where Christianity Matters—and Is in Decline." *MARC Newletter* 93 (September): 2.

Brøndsted, Johannes. 1965. *The Vikings.* Baltimore: Penguin Books.

Brooke, Rosalind, and Christopher Brooke. 1984. *Popular Religion in the Middle Ages.* London: Thames & Hudson.

Bruce, Steve. 1986. *God Save Ulster!: The Religion and Politics of Paisleyism.* New York: Oxford University Press.

———. 1992. *Religion and Modernization.* Oxford: Clarendon Press.

———. 1993. "Religion and Rational Choice: A Critique of Economic Explanations of Religious Behavior." *Sociology of Religion* 54: 193–205.

———. 1995. "The Truth about Religion in Britain." *Journal for the Scientific Study of Religion* 34: 417–30.

———. 1997. "The Prevasive World-View: Religion in Pre-Modern Britain." *British Journal of Sociology* 48: 667–80.

Brunner, Edmund deS. 1927. *Village Communities.* New York: George H. Doran.

Bultina, Louis. 1949. "Church Membership and Church Attendance in Madison, Wisconsin." *American Sociological Review* 14: 385–88.

Burchinal, Lee G. 1959. "Some Social Status Criteria and Church Membership and Church Attendance." *Journal of Social Psychology* 49: 53–64.

Burns, Gene. 1992. *The Frontiers of Catholicism.* Berkeley and Los Angeles: University of California Press.

Bush, Lester E. 1976. "Birth Control among the Mormons: Introduction to an Insistent Question." *Dialogue* 10: 12–44.

Bushman, Richard L. 1984. *Joseph Smith and the Beginnings of Mormonism*. Urbana: University of Illinois Press.

———. 1988. "Joseph Smith's Family Background." In *The Prophet Joseph:Essays on the Life and Mission of Joseph Smith*, edited by Larry C. Porter and Susan Easton Black, 1–18. Salt Lake City: Deseret.

Butler, Jon. 1982. "Enthusiasm Described and Decried: The Great Awakenings as Interpretative Fiction." *Journal of American History* 69: 305–25.

———. 1990. *Awash in a Sea of Faith: Christianizing the American People*. Cambridge, Mass.: Harvard University Press.

Byock, Jesse L. 1988. *Medieval Iceland: Society, Sagas, and Power*. Berkeley and Los Angeles: University of California Press.

Cantril, Hadley S. 1943. "Educational and Economic Composition of Religious Groups." *American Journal of Sociology* 48: 574–79.

Caplovitz, David and Fred Sherrow. 1977. *The Religious Drop-Outs*. Beverly Hills, Calif.: Sage.

Carroll, Michael P. 1987. "Praying the Rosary: The Anal-Erotic Origins of a Popular Catholic Devotion." *Journal for the Scientific Study of Religion* 26: 486–98.

———. 1996. "Stark Realities and Androcentric/Eurocentric Bias in the Sociology of Religion." *Sociology of Religion* 57: 225–39.

Casanova, Jose. 1994. *Public Religions in the Modern World*. Chicago: University of Chicago Press.

Chao, Hsing-Kuang. In press. "The Converts in Taiwanese Immigrant Church." *Soochow Journal of Sociology* 9 (March 2000)

Cartwright, Peter. 1856. *Autobiography of Peter Cartwright, the Backwoods Preacher*. Edited by W. P. Strickland. New York: Carlton & Porter.

Chaves, Mark. 1995. "On the Rational Choice Approach to Religion." *Journal for the Scientific Study of Religion* 34: 98–104.

Chaves, Mark, and David E. Cann. 1992. "Regulation, Pluralism, and Religious Market Structure: Explaining Religion's Vitality." *Rationality and Society* 4 (3): 272–90.

Chaves, Mark, Peter J. Schraeder, and Mario Sprindys. 1994. "State Regulation of Religion and Muslim Religious Vitality in the Industrialized West." *Journal of Politics* 56: 1087–97.

Chee-Beng, Tan. 1994. "Chinese Religion: Continuity, Transformation, and Identity, with Special Reference to Malaysia." In *Religions sans frontières?* edited by Roberto Cipriani, 257–89. Rome: Dipartimento per l'informazione e editoria.

Chen, Hsinchih. 1995. "The Development of Taiwanese Folk Religion, 1683–1945." Ph.D. diss., Department of Sociology, University of Washington.

Christian, William A., Jr. 1981. *Apparitions in Late Medieval and Renaissance Spain*. Princeton: Princeton University Press.

Christiano, Kevin. 1987. *Religious Diversity and Social Change: American Cities, 1890–1906*. New York: Cambridge University Press.

Cimino, Richard P. 1996a. "Brazilian Seminarians Indifferent to Liberationist Concerns." *Religion Watch* 11 (April): 5.

———. 1996b. "Charismatics Facing Restrictions in Bulgaria ..." *Religion Watch* 12 (November): 6.

————. 1996c. "Church of England Sees Increased Giving Rates, New Parishes." *Religion Watch* 11 (April): 5.

Clear, Caitriona. 1987. *Nuns in Nineteenth Century Ireland.* Dublin: Gill & Macmillan.

Cobbett, William. 1818. *Journal of a Year's Residence in the United States of America.*Reprint. London: Centaur, 1964.

Codrington, R. H. 1891. *The Melanesians.* Oxford: Oxford University Press.

Cohen, Gershon D. 1967. "Messianic Postures of Ashkenazim and Sephardim (Pior to Sabbatai Zevi)." In *Studies of the Leo Baeck Institute,* edited by Max Kreutzberger, 117–56. New York: Frederick Ungar.

Cohn, Norman. 1961. *The Pursuit of the Millennium.* New York: Harper & Row.

Coleman, James S. 1990. *Foundations of Social Theory.* Cambridge: Belknap Press, Harvard University Press.

Collins, Randall. 1997. "Stark and Bainbridge, Durkheim and Weber: Theoretical Comparisons." In *Rational Choice Theory and Religion: Summary and Assessment,* edited by Lawrence A. Young, 163–80. New York: Routledge.

————. 1998. *The Sociology of Philosophies: A Global Theory of Intellectual Change.* Cambridge, Mass.: Harvard University Press.

Collins, Ross William. 1968. *Calvin and the Libertines of Geneva.* Toronto: Clarke, Irwin & Co.

Comte, Auguste. 1896. *The Positive Philosophy.* 2 vols. Translated and edited by Harriet Martineau. London: George Bell & Sons.

Cornwall, Marie. 1988. "The Influence of Three Agents of Socialization." In *The Religion and Family Connection,* edited by Darwin Thomas, 207–31. Provo, Utah: Religious Studies Center, Brigham Young University.

Coulton, G. G. 1930. *Life in the Middle Ages.* 4 vols. Cambridge: Cambridge University Press.

—. 1938. *Medieval Panorama.* Cambridge: Cambridge University Press.

Cox, Harvey. 1983. "Interview." In *Hare Krishna, Hare Krishna,* edited by Steven J. Gelberg. New York: Grove Press.

Crawley, A. E. 1905. *The Tree of Life: A Study of Religion.* London: Hutchinson.

Crossan, John Dominic. 1991. *The Historical Jesus: The Life of a Mediterranean Jewish Peasant.* San Francisco: HarperSanFrancisco.

Cupitt, Don. 1997. *After God: The Future of Religion.* New York: Basic Books.

Currie, Robert, Alan Gilbert, and Lee Horsley. 1977. *Churches and Churchgoers: Patterns of Church Growth in the British Isles since 1700.* Oxford: Clarendon Press.

Curry, Catherine Ann. 1988. "Statistical Study of Religious Women in the United States." Available from George C. Stewart, Jr., P.O. Box 7, Fayetteville, NC 29302.

Daiber, Karl-Fritz. 1996. "Religion and Modernity in Germany." *Social Compass* 43: 411–23.

Darwin, Charles. [1839] 1906. *Voyage of the Beagle, 1931–36.* New York: P. F. Collier & Son.

Davidman, Lynn. 1991. *Tradition in a Rootless World: Women Turn to Orthodox Judaism.* Berkeley and Los Angeles: University of California Press.

Davie, Grace. 1990a. "Believing Without Belonging: Is this the Future of Religion in Britain?" *Social Compass* 37: 455–69.

————. 1990b. "'An Ordinary God': The Paradox of Religions in Contemporary Britain." *British Journal of Sociology* 41: 395–420.

————. 1994. *Religion in Britain since 1945: Believing Without Belonging.* Oxford: Blackwell.

Davies, Norman. 1996. *Europe: A History.* Oxford: Oxford University Press.

Davis, Deborah. 1984. *The Children of God: The Inside Story.* Grand Rapids, Mich.: Zondervan.

Davis, Kingsley. 1949. *Human Society.* New York: Macmillan.

Delumeau, Jean. 1977. *Catholicism between Luther and Voltaire.* Philadelphia: Westminster Press.

Demerath, Nicholas J., III. 1965. *Social Class in American Protestantism.* Chicago: Rand McNally.

————. 1995. "Rational Paradigms, A-Rational Religion and the Debate over Secularization." *Journal for the Scientific Study of Religion* 34: 105–12.

Demerath, Nicholas J., III, and Phillip E. Hammond. 1969. *Religion in Social Context: Tradition and Transition.* New York: Random House.

Dennis, James S. 1902. *Centennial Survey of Foreign Missions.* New York: Fleming H. Revell.

DiIanni, Albert. 1987. "Vocations and the Laicization of Religious Life." *America* (March 14): 207–11.

————. 1993. "Religious Vocations: A New Sign of the Times." *Review for Religious* 52: 745–63.

DiMaggio, Paul J., and Walter W. Powell. 1991. "The Iron Cage Revisited: Institutional Isomorphism and Collective Rationality in Organizational Fields." *American Sociological Review.* 48: 147–60.

Dittes, James E. 1971. "Typing the Typologies: Some Parallels in the Career of Church-Sect and Extrinsic-Intrinsic." *Journal for the Scientific Study of Religion* 10: 375–83.

Dives and Pauper. [Ca. 1410] 1976. London: Oxford University Press.

Dixon, Tomas. 1997. "Are Minority Churches Targets for Discrimination?" *Christianity Today* 41 (8): 74.

Dobbelaere, Karel. 1987. "Some Trends in European Sociology of Religion: The Secularization Debate." *Sociological Analysis* 48: 107–37.

————. 1989. "CISR, An Alternative Approach to Sociology of Religion in Europe: ACSS and CISR Compared." *Sociological Analysis.* 50: 377–87.

————. 1997. "Towards an Integrated Perspective of the Processes Related to the Descriptive Concept of Secularization: A Position Paper," Paper read at the annual meeeting of the Society for the Scientific Study of Religion.

Dolan, Jay P. 1978. *Catholic Revivalism: The American Experience, 1830–1900.* Notre Dame: University of Notre Dame Press.

Doughty, C.M. 1926. *Travels in Arabia Deserta.* 3d ed. New York: Boni & Liveright.

Douglas, Mary. 1975. *Implicit Meanings: Essays in Anthropology.* London: Routledge & Kegan Paul.

————. 1982. "The Effects of Modernization on Religious Change." In *Religion and America: Spirituality in a Secular Age,* edited by Mary Douglas and Steven M. Tipton, 25–43. Boston: Beacon Press.

————. 1986. *How Institutions Think.* Syracuse, N.Y.: Syracuse University Press.

Douglass, H. Paul, and Edmund deS. Brunner. 1935. *The Protestant Church as a Social Institution.* New York: Russell & Russell.

Duffy, Eamon. 1987. "The Late Middle Ages: Vitality or Decline." In *Atlas of the Christian Church,* edited by Henry Chadwick and G.R. Evans, 86–95. New York: Facts on File.

————. 1992. *Stripping of the Altars.* New Haven: Yale University Press.

Duke, James T. 1997. "Church Callings as an Organizational Device in the LDS Church." Paper read at the annual meeting of the Association for the Sociology of Religion.

Duke, James T., Barry L. Johnson, and James B. Duke. 1993. "Rate of Religious Conversion: A Macrosociological Study." *Research in the Sociology of Religion* (JAI Press) 5: 89–121.

Durant, Will, and Ariel Durant. 1963. *The Age of Louis XIV.* New York: Simon and Schuster.

————. 1965. *The Age of Voltaire.* New York: Simon & Schuster.

Durkheim, Emile. 1913. Review of *Les fonctions mentales dans les sociétés inférieures,* by Lucien Lévy-Bruhl (Paris: F. Alcan, 1910). *L'Année sociologique* 12: 33–37.

————. 1915. *The Elementary Forms of the Religious Life.* London: George Allen & Unwin. Originally published as *Les formes élémentaires de la vie religieuse, le système totémique en Australie* (Paris: F. Alcan, 1912).

————. [1897] 1951. *Suicide.* Glencoe, Il.: Free Press.

Durkin, John, Jr., and Andrew M. Greeley. 1991. "A Model of Religious Choice Under Uncertainty: On Responding Rationally to the Nonrational." *Rationality and Society* 3: 178–96.

Dynes, Russell R. 1955. "Church-Sect Typology and Socio-Economic Status." *American Sociological Review* 20: 555–60.

Ebaugh, Helen Rose. 1977. *Out of the Cloister: A Study of Organizational Dilemmas.* Austin: University of Texas Press.

————. 1993. *Women in the Vanishing Cloister: Organizational Decline in Catholic Religious Orders in the United States.* New Brunswick, N.J.: Rutgers University Press.

Ebaugh, Helen Rose, Jon Lorence, and Janet Saltzman Chafetz. 1996. "The Growth and Decline of the Population of Catholic Nuns Cross-Nationally, 1960–1990: A Case of Secularization as Social Structural Change." *Journal for the Scientific Study of Religion* 35: 171–83.

Echikson, William. 1990. *Lighting the Night: Revolution in Eastern Europe.* New York: William Morrow.

Eichhorn, Werner. 1959. "Taoism." In *The Concise Encyclopaedia of Living Faiths,* edited by R. C. Zaehner, 385–401. Boston: Beacon Press.

Eisenman, Robert. 1997. *James the Brother of Jesus.* New York: Viking.

Eisinga, Rob, Albert Felling, and Jan Lammers. 1996. "Deconfessionalisation in the Netherlands, 1964–1992." *Journal of Contemporary Religion* 11: 77–88.

Ellison, Christopher G. 1991. "Religious Involvement and Subjective Well-Being." *Journal of Health and Social Behavior* 32: 80–99.

————. 1994. "Religion, The Life Stress Paradigm, and the Study of Depression." In *Religion in Aging and Health: Theoretical Foundations and Methodological Frontiers,* edited by Jeffrey S. Levin, 78–121. Newbury Park, Calif.: Sage.

————. 1995. "Rational Choice Explanations of Individual Religious Behavior: Notes on the Problem of Social Embeddedness." *Journal for the Scientific Study of Religion* 34: 89–97.

Ellison, Christopher G., and Darren E. Sherkat. 1990. "Patterns of Religious Mobility Among Black Americans." *Sociological Quarterly* 31: 551–68.

————. 1995. "The 'Semi-Involuntary Institution' Revisited: Regional Differences in Church Participation Among Black Americans." *Social Forces* 73: 1415–37.

Ellwood, Robert S. 1993. "A Japanese Mythic Trickster Figure: Susa-no-o." In *Mythical Trickster Figures: Contours, Contexts, and Criticisms,* edited by William J. Hynes and William G. Doty, 141–58. Tuscaloosa: University of Alabama Press.

Esbanshade, Richard S. 1994. *Hungary.* New York: Marshall Cavendish.

Eusebius. [Ca. 325] 1965. *The History of the Church.* Translated by G. A. Williamson. Harmondsworth, Middlesex: Penguin Books.

Evans-Pritchard, E. E. 1956. *Nuer Religion.* Oxford: Oxford University Press.

———. 1960. "Introduction" to Robert Hertz. *Death and the Right Hand.* New York: Free Press.

———. 1965. *Theories of Primitive Religion.* Oxford: Clarendon Press.

———. 1967. *The Zande Trickster.* Oxford: Clarendon Press.

———. 1981. *A History of Anthropological Thought.* New York: Basic Books.

Falk, M. Marcelline. 1980. "Vocations: Identity and Commitment." *Review for Religious* 39: 357–65.

Fauset, Arthur H. 1944. *Black Gods of the Metropolis.* Philadelphia: University of Pennsylvania Press.

Feldman, Kenneth A., and Theodore M. Newcomb. 1970. *The Impact of College on Students.* San Francisco: Jossey-Bass.

Ferejohn, John A. 1991. "Rationality and Interpretation: Parliamentary Elections in Early Stuart England." In *The Economic Approach to Politics: A Critical Reassessment of the Theory of Rational Action,* edited by Kristen Renwick Monroe, 279–305. New York: HarperCollins,

Ferraro, Kenneth F., and Cynthia M. Albrecht-Jenson. 1991. "Does Religion Influence Adult Health?" *Journal for the Scientific Study of Religion* 30: 193–202.

Festinger, Leon. 1957. *A Theory of Cognitive Dissonance.* Stanford: Stanford University Press.

Feuerbach, Ludwig von. [1841] 1957. *The Essence of Christianity.* New York: Harper Torchbooks.

Fichter, Joseph H. 1961. *Religion as an Occupation: A Study in the Sociology of Professions.* Notre Dame: University of Notre Dame Press.

Fields, Karen E. 1995. "Translator's Introduction." In Emile Durkheim, *The Elelmentary Forms of the Religious Life.* New translation. New York: Free Press.

Finke, Roger. 1984. "The Churching of America, 1850–1980." Ph.D. diss., University of Washington, Seattle.

———. 1989. "The Demographics of Religious Participation: An Ecological Approach, 1850–1980." *Journal for the Scientific Study of Religion* 28: 45–58.

———. 1990. "Religious Deregulation: Origins and Consequences." *Journal of Church and State* 32: 609–26.

———. 1992 "An Unsecular America." In *Religion and Modernization: Sociologists and Historians Debate the Secularization Thesis,* edited by Steve Bruce. Oxford: Clarendon Press.

———. 1994. "The Quiet Transformation: Changes in Size and Leadership of Southern Baptist Churches." *Review of Religious Research* 36: 3–22.

———. 1997a. "The Consequences of Religious Competition: Supply-Side Explanations for Religious Change." In *Assessing Rational Choice Theories of Religion,* edited by Lawrence A. Young, 46–65. New York: Routledge.

———. 1997b. "The Illusion of Shifting Demand: Supply-Side Interpretations of American Religious History." In *Retelling U.S. Religious History,* edited by Thomas Tweed, 108–24. Berkeley and Los Angeles: University of California Press.

————. 1997c. "An Orderly Return to Tradition: Explaining Membership Recruitment to Catholic Religious Orders." *Journal for the Scientific Study of Religion* 36: 218–30.

Finke, Roger, Avery M. Guest, and Rodney Stark. 1996. "Pluralism and Religious Participation: New York, 1855–1865." *American Sociological Review* 61: 203–18.

Finke, Roger, and Laurence R. Iannaccone. 1993. "Supply-Side Explanations for Religious Change in America." *The Annals* 527: 27–39.

Finke, Roger, and Rodney Stark. 1988. "Religious Economies and Sacred Canopies: Religious Mobilization in American Cities, 1906." *American Sociological Review* 53: 41–49.

————. 1992. *The Churching of America, 1776–1990: Winners and Losers in Our Religious Economy.* New Brunswick, N.J.: Rutgers University Press.

Finke, Roger, and Patricia Wittberg. In press. "Organizational Revival from Within: Explaining Revivalism and Reform in the Roman Catholic Church." *Journal for the Scientific Study of Religion.*

Firth, Raymond. 1959. "Problem and Assumption in an Anthropological Study of Religion." *Journal of the Royal Anthropological Institute* 89: 129–48.

————. 1963. "Offering and Sacrifice: Problems of Organization." *Journal of the Royal Anthropological Institute* 93: 12–24.

————. 1996. *Religion: A Humanist Interpretation.* London: Routledge.

Fitzpatrick, Joseph P., S.J. 1989. "Introducing Religion to Social Science." *Sociological Analysis* 50: 391–92.

Flannery, Austin, ed. 1975 [1992]. *Vatican Council II: The Conciliar and Post Conciliar Documents.* Grand Rapids, Mich.: Eerdmans.

Fletcher, Richard. 1997. *The Barbarian Conversion: From Paganism to Christianity.* New York: Holt.

Forde, Daryll. "Spirits, Witches, and Sorcerers in the Supernatural Economy of the Yakö." *Journal of the Royal Anthropological Institute* 88: 165–78.

Frazer, Sir James G. [1890–1915] 1922. *The Golden Bough.* New York: Macmillan.

Freedom House. 1995. *Freedom in the World.* New York: Freedom House.

Freidson, Eliot. 1986. *Professional Powers: A Study of the Institutionalization of Formal Knowledge.* Chicago: University of Chicago Press.

Freud, Sigmund. [1912–13] 1950. *Totem and Taboo: Some Points of Agreement Between the Mental Lives of Savages and Neurotics.* New York: Norton.

————. 1922. *Group Psychology and the Analysis of the Ego.* London: Hogarth Press.

————. [1927] 1961. *The Future of an Illusion.* Garden City, N.Y.: Doubleday.

Gager, John G. 1975. *Kingdom and Community: The Social World of Early Christianity.* Englewood Cliffs, N.J.: Prentice-Hall.

Gallup International. 1984. *Human Values and Beliefs.* London.

Galton, Francis. 1890. *Narrative of an Explorer in Tropical South Africa.* New York: Ward, Lock.

Gaskin, J. C. A. 1989. *Varieties of Unbelief: From Epicurius to Sartre.* New York: Macmillan.

Gauna, Max. 1992. *Upwellings: First Expresssions of Unbelief in the Printed Literature of the French Renaissance.* Rutherford, N.J.: Fairleigh Dickinson University Press.

Gay, Peter. 1969. *The Enlightenment: An Interpretation.* Vol. 2: *The Science of Freedom.* New York: Knopf. Norton reprint, 1977.

Geertz, Clifford. 1966. "Religion as a Cultural System." In *Athropological Approaches to the Study of Religion,* edited by Michael Banton, 1–46. London: Tavistock Publications.

Gentilcore, David. 1992. *Bishop to Witch.* Manchester: Manchester University Press.

George, Carl F. 1992. *Prepare Your Church for the Future.* Grand Rapids, Mich.: Baker Book House.

Gill, Anthony J. 1998. *Rendering unto Caesar: The Roman Catholic Church and the State in Latin America.* Chicago: University of Chicago Press.

Gill, Anthony J. 1994. "Rendering unto Caesar? Religious Competition and Catholic Political Strategy in Latin America, 1962–1979." *American Journal of Political Science* 38: 403–25.

Glock, Charles Y. 1964. "The Role of Deprivation in the Origin and Evolution of Religious Groups." In *Religion and Social Conflict,* edited by Robert Lee and Martin E. Marty, 24–36. New York: Oxford University Press.

Glock, Charles Y., and Phillip E. Hammond, eds. 1973. *Beyond the Classics?* New York: Harper & Row.

Glock, Charles Y., Benjamin B. Ringer, and Earl R. Babbie. 1967. *To Comfort and to Challenge: A Dilemma of the Contemporary Church.* Berkeley and Los Angeles: University of California Press.

Glock, Charles Y., and Rodney Stark. 1965. *Religion and Society in Tension.* Chicago: Rand McNally.

———. *Christian Beliefs and Anti-Semitism.* New York: Harper & Row.

Goldenweiser, Alexander A. 1915. Review of *Les formes élémentaires de la vie religieuse, le système totémique en Australie,* by Emile Durkheim (Paris: F. Alcan, 1912). *American Anthropologist* 17: 719–35.

Goldman, Marion. 2000. *Passionate Journeys: Why Successful Women Joined a Cult.* Ann Arbor: University of Michigan Press.

Goode, William J. 1951. *Religion Among the Primitives.* New York: Free Press.

"The Good News Movement: Is It Good for United Methodists." 1989. *Circuit Rider,* April: 6–8.

Goody, Jack. 1961. "Religion and Ritual: The Definitional Problem." *British Journal of Sociology* 12: 142–64.

Gordon-McCutchan, R. C. 1983. "Great Awakenings." *Sociological Analysis* 44: 83–95.

Gottfredson, Michael, and Travis Hirschi. 1990. *A General Theory of Crime.* Stanford, Calif.: Stanford University Press.

Grandstaff, Mark R., and Milton V. Backman, Jr. 1990. "The Social Origins of Kirtland Mormons." *Brigham Young University Studies.* 30: 47–66

Greeley, Andrew M. 1972a. *The Catholic Priest in the United States: Sociological Investigations.* Washington, D.C: United States Catholic Conference.

———. 1972b. *Unsecular Man: The Persistence of Religion.* New York: Schocken Books.

———. 1975. *Sociology of the Paranormal: A Reconnaissance.* Beverly Hills: Sage.

———. 1982. "The Failures of Vatican II after Twenty Years." *America,* February 6: 86–89.

———. 1988. "American Exceptionalism: The Religious Phenomenon." Paper presented at a conference at Nuffield College, Oxford.

———. 1989a. *Myths of Religion.* New York: Warner Books.

———. 1989b. *Religious Change in America.* Cambridge, Mass.: Harvard University Press.

———. 1994. "A Religious Revival in Russia?" *Journal for the Scientific Study of Religion.* 33: 253–72.

———. 1995. *Religion as Poetry.* New Brunswick, N.J.: Transaction Publishers.

————. 1996. "The New American Paradigm: A Modest Critique." Paper read at the German Sociological Association annual meeting, Cologne.

Griffith, Mearle L. 1995. *A Profile of United Methodists Based on the Survey of United Methodist Opinion.* A research report printed by the General Council on Ministries.

Grubb, Kenneth G., ed. 1949. *World Christian Handbook.* London: World Dominion Press.

Grund, Francis. 1837. *The Americans in Their Moral, Social, and Political Relations.* Excerpted in Powell 1967 (New York: Macmillan).

Gustafson, David A. 1994. "A Confessional Lutheran Encounters American Religion." In *Missionary to America: The History of Lutheran Outreach to Americans,* edited by Marvin A. Huggins. Minneapolis: Augsburg Fortress Publishers.

Gustafsson, Göran. 1990. "Politicization of State Churches—A Welfare State Model." *Social Compass* 37: 107–16.

Hadden, Jeffrey K. 1969. *The Gathering Storm in the Churches.* Garden City, N.Y.: Doubleday.

————. 1974. "A Brief Social History of the Religious Research Association." *Review of Religious Research* 15: 128–36.

————. 1987. "Toward Desacralizing Secularization Theory." *Social Forces* 65: 587–611.

Hamberg, Eva M., and Thorleif Pettersson. 1994. "The Religious Market: Denominational Competition and Religious Participation in Contemporary Sweden." *Journal for the Scientific Study of Religion* 33: 205–16.

————. 1997. "Short-Term Changes in Religious Supply and Church Attendance in Contemporary Sweden." *Research in the Social Scientific Study of Religion* 8: 35–51.

Hamilton, Richard F. 1996. *The Social Misconstruction of Reality.* New Haven: Yale University Press.

Hammond, Phillip E., ed. 1985. *The Sacred in a Secular Age* Berkeley and Los Angeles: University of California Press.

Handlin, Oscar. ed. 1949. *This Was America.* Cambridge, Mass.: Harvard University Press.

Hanson, Sharon. 1997. "The Secularization Thesis: Talking at Cross Purposes." *Journal of Contemporary Religion* 12:159–79.

Hansson, Gunnar, ed. 1990. *Bible Reading in Sweden.* Uppsala: University of Uppsala.

Harnack, Adolph von. 1908. *The Mission and Expansion of Christianity in the First Three Centuries.* 2 vols. Translated by James Moffatt. New York: G. P. Putnam's Sons. Originally published as *Die Mission und Ausbreitung des Christentums in den ersten drei Jahrhunderten* (Leipzig: J. C. Hinrichs, 1902).

Healy, Robert M. 1984. "Jefferson on Judaism and the Jews: 'Divided We Stand, United, We Fall!'{hrs}" *American Jewish History* 78: 359–74.

Heath, Anthony. 1976. *Rational Choice and Social Exchange.* Cambridge: Cambridge University Press.

Heaton, Tim B. 1986a. "How Does Religion Influence Fertility? The Case of Mormons." *Journal for the Scientific Study of Religion* 25: 248–58.

————. 1986b. "Socio-Demographic Characteristics of Religious Groups in Canada." *Sociological Analysis* 47: 54–65.

Hechter, Michael, ed. 1983. *Microfoundations of Macrosociology.* Philadelphia: Temple University Press.

————. 1987. *Principles of Group Solidarity.* Berkeley and Los Angeles: University of California Press.

————. 1994. "The Role of Values in Rational Choice Theory." *Rationality and Society* 6: 318–33.

————. 1997. "Religion and Rational Choice Theory." In *Rational Choice Theory and Religion: Summary and Assessment,* edited by Lawrence A. Young, 147–59. New York: Routledge.

Hechter, Michael, and Satoshi Kanazawa. 1997. "Sociological Rational Choice Theory." *Annual Review of Sociology* 23: 191–214.

Heidinger, James V., II. 1992. "25 Years of Vision." *Good News,* March–April: 14–19.

Herodotus. [Ca. 450 B.C.] 1987. *The History.* Translated by David Grene. Chicago: University of Chicago Press.

Hexham, Irving, Raymond F. Currie, and Joan B. Townsend. 1985. "New Religious Movements." In *The Canadian Encyclopedia.* Edmonton: Hurtig.

Hexham, Irving, and Karla Poewe. 1997. *New Religions as Global Cultures: Making the Human Sacred.* Boulder, Colo.: Westview Press.

Hirschi, Travis. 1969. *Causes of Delinquency.* Berkeley and Los Angeles: University of California Press.

Hobbes, Thomas. [1651] 1956. *Leviathan, I.* Chicago: Regnery.

Hodgson, Marshall G. S. 1974. *The Venture of Islam,* vol 1: *The Classical Age of Islam.* Chicago: University of Chicago Press.

Hoge, Dean R. 1994. "Introduction: The Problem of Church Giving." *Review of Religious Research* 36: 101–10.

Hoge, Dean R., Joseph J. Shields, and Douglas L. Griffin. "Changes in Satisfaction and Institutional Attitudes of Catholic Priests, 1970–1993." *Sociology of Religion* 56: 195–213.

Hoge, Dean, Joseph J. Shields, and Mary Jeanne Verdieck. 1988. "Changing Age Distribution and Theological Attitudes of Catholic Priests, 1970–1985." *Sociological Analysis* 49: 264–80.

Hoge, Dean R., and Fenggang Yang. 1994. "Determinants of Religious Giving in American Denominations: Data from Two Nationwide Surveys." *Review of Religious Research* 36: 123–48.

Holmberg, A. R. 1950. *Nomads of the Long Bow.* Washington: Smithsonian Institution.

Homans, George. 1941. "Anxiety and Ritual: The Theories of Malinowski and Radcliffe-Brown." *American Anthropologist* 43:164–72.

————. 1974. *Social Behavior: Its Elementary Forms.* Rev. ed. New York: Harcourt Brace Jovanovich.

Hood, Ralph W., Jr. 1985. "Mysticism," In *The Sacred in a Secular Age,* edited by Phillip E. Hammond, 285–97. Berkeley and Los Angeles: University of California Press.

Horton, Robin. 1960. "A Definition of Religion and Its Uses." *The Journal of the Royal Anthropological Institute* 90: 201–26.

Hougland, James G., and James R. Wood. 1980. "Control in Organizations and the Commitment of Members." *Social Forces* 59: 85–105.

Howell, Julia Day. 1997. "ASC Induction Techniques, Spiritual Experiences, and Commitment to New Religious Movements." *Sociology of Religion* 58: 141–64.

Hume, David. [1741] 1882. *Essays: Moral, Political, and Literary.* London: Longmans Green.

————. [1748] 1962. *Inquiry Concerning Human Understanding.* New York: Macmillan.

————. [1739–40] 1969. *A Treatise of Human Nature.* London: Penguin Books.

Hunter, James Davison. 1983. *American Evangelicalism: Conservative Religion and the Quandary of Modernity.* New Brunswick, N.J.: Rutgers University Press.

———. 1987. *Evangelicalism: The Coming Generation.* Chicago: University of Chicago Press.

Hurston, Karen. 1994. *Growing the World's Largest Church.* Springfield, Mo.: Gospel Publishing House.

Hynes, William J., and William G. Doty, eds. 1993. *Mythical Trickster Figures: Contours, Contexts, and Criticisms.* Tuscaloosa: University of Alabama Press.

Iannaccone, Laurence R. 1988. "A Formal Model of Church and Sect." *American Journal of Sociology* 94 (Supplement) S241-S268.

———. 1990. "Religious Practice: A Human Capital Approach." *Journal for the Scientific Study of Religion* 29: 297–314.

———. 1991. "The Consequences of Religious Market Regulation: Adam Smith and the Economics of Religion." *Rationality and Society* 3: 156–77.

———. 1992. "Sacrifice and Stigma: Reducing Free-Riding in Cults, Communes, and Other Collectives." *Journal of Political Economy.* 100 (2):271–92.

———. 1994."Why Strict Churches Are Strong." *American Journal of Sociology* 99: 1180–1211.

———. 1995a. "Risk, Rationality, and Religious Portfolios." *Economic Inquiry* 33: 285–95.

———. 1995b. "Voodoo Economics? Reviewing the Rational Choice Approach to Religion." *Journal for the Scientific Study of Religion* 34: 76–89.

———. 1996. "Looking Backward: Estimating Long-Run Church Attendance Trends Across Eighteen Countries." Paper read at annual meetings of the Society for the Scientific Study of Religion.

———. 1997. "Skewness Explained: A Rational Choice Model of Religious Giving." *Journal for the Scientific Study of Religion* 36: 141–57.

Iannaccone, Laurence R., Roger Finke, and Rodney Stark. 1996. "Deregulating Religion: The Economics of Church and State." *Economic Inquiry* 35: 350–64.

Iannaccone, Laurence R., Daniel Olson, and Rodney Stark. 1995. "Religious Resources and Church Growth." *Social Forces* 74: 705–31.

Idler, Ellen L., and Stanislav V. Kasl. 1997a. "Religion among Disabled and Nondisabled Persons, I: Cross-Sectional Patterns in Health Practices, Social Activities, and Well-being." *Journal of Gerontology* 52B (6): S294–305.

———. 1997b. "Religion among Disabled and Nondisabled Persons, II: Attendance at Religious Services as a Predictor of the Course of Disability. *Journal of Gerontology* 52B (6): S306–16.

Introvigne, Massimo. 1997. "Religious Liberty in Western Europe," *Iskcon Communications Journal* 5: 2:37–48.

Jagodzinski, Wolfgang, and Andrew Greeley. Forthcoming."The Demand for Religion: Hard Core Atheism and 'Supply Side' Theory."

James, William. [1902] 1958. *The Varieties of Religious Experience.* New York: Mentor Books.

Jarvie, I. C. 1970. "Explaining Cargo Cults." In *Rationality,* edited by Bryan Wilson, 50–61. Oxford: Basil Blackwell.

Jarvis, G. K., and H. C. Northcutt. 1987. "Religion Differences in Morbidity and Mortality." *Social Sciences and Medicine* 25: 813–24.

Jelen, Ted G., and Clyde Wilcox. 1998. "Context and Conscience: The Catholic Church as an Agent of Political Socialization in Western Europe." *Journal for the Social Scientific Study of Religion* 37: 28–40.

Johnson, Benton. 1961. "Do Holiness Sects Socialize into Dominant Values." *Social Forces* 39: 309–16.

———. 1963. "On Church and Sect." *American Sociological Review* 28: 539–49.

———. 1996. "Response: Amplified Verson." Paper read at the Colloquium on Rational Choice Theory and Religion, Loyola University, Chicago, April 17.

Johnson, Paul. 1976. *A History of Christianity.* New York: Harper & Row.

Johnson, Stephen D., and Joseph B. Tamney. 1988. "Factors Related to Inconsistent Life-Views." *Review of Religious Research* 30: 40–46.

Jones, Ernest. 1953. *Life and Works of Sigmund Freud.* Vol. 1. New York: Hogarth Press.

Jones, Gwyn. 1968. *A History of the Vikings.* London: Oxford University Press.

Judge, E. A. 1960. *The Social Patterns of Christian Groups in the First Century.* London: Tyndale.

Kelley, Dean M. 1972. *Why Conservative Churches are Growing.* New York: Harper & Row.

King, Eleace. 1990. "Introduction and Statistical Overview." In *CARA Formation Directory for Men and Women Religious, 1991.* Washington, D.C.: Georgetown University.

———. 1992. "Introduction and Statistical Overview." In *CARA Formation Directory for Men and Women Religious, 1993.* Washington, D.C.: Georgetown University.

———. 1993. "Introduction and Statistical Overview." In *CARA Formation Directory for Men and Women Religious, 1994–1995.* Washington, D.C.: Georgetown University.

Kirkpatrick, Lee A., and Ralph W. Hood, Jr. 1990. "Intrinsic-Extrinsic Religious Orientation: The Boon or Bane of Contemporary Psychology of Religion?" *Journal for the Scientific Study of Religion* 29: 442–62.

Kluckhohn, Clyde. 1952. "Values and Value Orientations in the Theory of Action: An Exploration in Definition and Classification." In *Toward a General Theory of Action,* edited by Talcott Parsons and Edward A. Shils, 127–39. Cambridge, Mass.: Harvard University Press.

Kluegel, James R. 1980. "Denominational Mobility." *Journal for the Scientific Study of Religion* 19: 26–39.

Kosko, Bart. 1992. *Neural Networks and Fuzzy Systems.* Englewood Cliffs, N.J.: Prentice-Hall.

Kosmin, Barry Alexander, and Seymour P. Lachman, 1993. *One Nation under God: Religion in Contemporary American Society.* New York: Harmony Books.

Kox, Willem, Wim Meeus, and Harm t'Hart. 1991. "Religious Conversion of Adolescents: Testing the Lofland and Stark Model of Religious Conversion." *Sociological Analysis* 52: 227–40.

Krause, Neal. 1997. "Religion, Aging, and Health: Current Status and Future Prospects." *Journal of Gerontology* 52B (6): S291–93.

Krindatch, A. D. 1995. "Geography of Religions in Russia." Paper presented at the meetings of the Society for the Scientific Study of Religion.

La Barre, Weston. 1969. *They Shall Take Up Serpents.* New York: Schocken Books.

———. 1972. *The Ghost Dance.* New York: Dell.

La Bras', Gabriel. 1963. "Dechristianisation: Mot fallacieux." *Social Compass* 10: 448–51.

Lambert, Frank. 1990. "{hrs}'Peddlar in Divinity': George Whitefield and the Great Awakening, 1737–1745." *Journal of American History* 77: 812–837.

Lambert, Malcolm. 1992. *Medieval Heresy: Popular Movements from the Gregorian Reform to the Reformation.* 2d ed. Oxford: Basil Blackwell.

Land, Kenneth C., Glenn Deane, and Judith Blau. 1991. "Religious Pluralism and Church Membership: A Spatial Diffusion Model." *American Sociological Review* 56: 237–49.

Lang, Graeme, and Lars Ragvold. 1993. *The Rise of a Refugee God: Hong Kong's Wong Tai Sin.* Oxford: Oxford University Press.

Langer, Suzanne. 1942. *Philosophy in a New Key.* Cambridge, Mass.: Harvard University Press.

Larkin, Emmet. 1972. "The Devotional Revolution in Ireland, 1850–1875." *American Historical Review* 77: 625–52.

Larson, Edward J., and Larry Withan. 1997. "Scientists Are Still Keeping the Faith." *Nature* 386 (3 April): 435.

Laslett, Peter. 1965. *The World We Have Lost.* London: Methuen.

Lawson, Ronald. 1995. "Sect-State Relations: Accounting for the Differing Trajectories of the Seventh-Day Adventists and Jehovah's Witnesses." *Sociology of Religion* 56: 351–77.

Leatham, Miguel C. 1997. "Rethinking Religious Decision-Making in Peasant Millenarianism: The Case of Nueva Jeruslén." *Journal of Contemporary Religion* 12: 295–309.

Le Bon, Gustave. 1896. *The Crowd: A Study of the Popular Mind.* London: Ernest Benn.

Lechner, Frank J. 1989. "Catholicism and Social Change in the Netherlands: A Case of Radical Secularization?" *Journal for the Scientific Study of Religion* 28: 136–47.

———. 1991. "The Case Against Secularization: A Rebuttal. *Social Forces* 69: 1103–19.

———. 1996. "Secularization in the Netherlands?" *Journal for the Scientific Study of Religion* 35: 252–64.

Lenski, Gerhard E. 1953. "Social Correlates of Religious Interest." *American Sociological Review* 18: 533–44.

———. 1966. *Power and Privilege: A Theory of Social Stratification.* New York: McGraw-Hill.

Lessa, William A., and Evon Z. Vogt. 1972. *Reader in Comparative Religion: An Anthropological Approach.* 3d ed. New York: Harper & Row.

Leuba, James H. [1916] 1921. *The Belief in God and Immortality.* Chicago: Open Court.

———. 1934. "Religious Beliefs of American Scientists," *Harper's Magazine* 169: 291–300.

Levin, Jeffrey S. 1996. "How Religion Influences Morbidity and Health." *Social Science and Medicine* 43 (5): 849–64.

Levin, Jeffrey S., and P. L. Schiller. 1987. "Is There a Religious Factor in Health?" *Journal of Religion and Health* 26: 9–36.

Lévy-Bruhl, Lucien. 1899. *History of Modern Philosophy in France.* Chicago: Open Court.

———. 1923. *Primitive Mentality.* Translated by Lilian A. Clare. New York: Macmillan. Originally published as *La mentalité primitive* (Paris: F. Alcan, 1922).

———. [1926] 1979. *How Natives Think.* Translated by Lilian A. Clare. Salem, N.H.: Ayer. Originally published as *Les fonctions mentales dans les sociétés inférieures* (Paris: F. Alcan, 1910).

Lewis, C. S. [1949] 1996. *The Weight of Glory.* New York: Simon & Schuster.

Liebman, Robert C., John R. Sutton, and Robert Wuthnow. 1988. "Exploring the Social Sources of Denominationalism: Schisms in American Protestant Denominations, 1890–1980." *American Sociological Review* 53: 343–52.

Liederman, Lina Molokotos. 1995. "The Headscarf Affair: A Case Study of Religion, Society and Mass Media in Contemporary France." Unpublished thesis, Ecole Pratique des Hautes Etudes, Sorbonne.

Lienhardt, Godfrey. 1961. *Divinity and Experience: The Religion of the Dinka*. Oxford: Oxford University Press.

Lodberg, Peter. 1989. "The Churches in Denmark." In *Danish Christian Handbook* edited by Peter Brierly, 6–8. London: MARC Europe.

Lofland, John. 1966. *Doomsday Cult: A Study of Conversion, Proselytization, and Maintenance of Faith*. Englewood Cliffs, N.J.: Prentice-Hall.

———, ed. 1976. *Doing Social Life: The Qualitative Study of Human Interaction in Natural Settings*. New York: John Wiley.

———. 1977. "{hrs}'Becoming a World-Saver' Revisited" *American Behavioral Scientist* 20: 805–18.

Lofland, John, and Rodney Stark. 1965. "Becoming a World-Saver: A Theory of Conversion to a Deviant Perspective." *American Sociological Review* 30: 862–75.

Lowry, James A. 1989. "Selected SBC Trends." *Quarterly Review* 49: 51–56.

Luckmann, Thomas. 1967. *The Invisible Religion*. New York: Macmillan.

Machalek, Richard, and David A. Snow. 1993. "Conversion to New Religious Movements." *Religion and the Social Order* 3B: 53–74.

Mack, Burton L. 1996. *Who Wrote the New Testament? The Making of the Christian Myth*. San Francisco: Harper San Francisco.

MacMullen, Ramsey. 1981. *Paganism in the Roman Empire*. New Haven: Yale University Press.

Malinowski, Bronislaw. [1925] 1992. *Magic, Science and Religion*. Prospect Heights, Ill.: Waveland Press.

Mandelbaum, David G. 1966. "Transcendental and Pragmatic Aspects of Religion." *American Anthropologist* 68: 1174–91.

Manuel, Frank E. 1959. *The Eighteenth Century Confronts the Gods*. Cambridge, Mass.: Harvard University Press.

March, James G. 1978. "Bounded Rationality, Ambiguity, and the Engineering of Choice." *Bell Journal of Economics* 9: 587–607

———. 1988. "Variable Risk Preferences and Adaptive Aspirations." *Journal of Economic Behavior and Organization* 9: 5–24.

Marchisio, Roberto. 1998. "Il tempo delle scelte: La religiosità individual nell'economia religiosa italiana." *Polis* 12: 33–52.

Martin, David. 1965. "Towards Eliminating the Concept of Secularization." In *Penguin Survey of the Social Sciences*, edited by Julius Gould. Harmondsworth, Eng.: Pengiun Books.

———. 1978. *A General Theory of Secularization*. New York: Harper & Row.

———. 1989. "Speaking in Latin Tongues." *National Review*, September 29, 30–35.

———. 1990. *Tongues of Fire: The Explosion of Protestantism in Latin America*. Oxford: Basil Blackwell.

———. 1991. "The Secularization Issue: Prospect and Retrospect." *British Journal of Sociuology* 42: 465–74.

Martin, Everett D. 1920. *The Behavior of Crowds*. New York: Harper.

Marty, Martin.1984. *Pilgrims in Their Own Land*. Boston: Little Brown.

Marx, Karl, and Friedrich Engels. 1964. *On Religion*. New York: Schocken Books. Undated Scholars Press reprint.

Marwell, Gerald. 1995. "We Still Don't Know If Strict Churches Are Strong, Much Less Why: Comment on Iannaccone." *American Journal of Sociology* 101: 1097–1104.

Mathews, Shailer. 1921. *A History of New Testament Times in Palestine*. New York: Macmillan.

McFarland, H. Neill. 1967. *Rush Hour of the Gods: A Study of New Religious Movements in Japan*. New York: Macmillan.

McLoughlin, William G. 1971. *New England Dissent, 1630—1833: The Baptists and the Separation of Church and State*. 2 vols. Cambridge, Mass.: Harvard University Press.

———. 1978. *Revivals, Awakenings, and Reform*. Chicago: University of Chicago Press.

McNeill, William H. 1976. *Plagues and Peoples*. Garden City, N.Y.: Doubleday.

McPherson, J. Miller. 1981. "A Dynamic Model of Voluntary Affiliation." *Social Forces* 59: 705–28.

McPherson, J. Miller, Pamela A. Popielarz, and Sonja Drobnic. 1992. "Social Networks and Organizational Dynamics." *American Sociological Review* 57: 153–70.

McPherson, J. Miller, and Lynn Smith-Lovin. 1987. "Homophily in Voluntary Organization: Status Distance and the Composition of Face to Face Groups." *American Sociological Review* 52: 370–79.

Mead, George Herbert. 1934. *Mind, Self, and Society: From the Standpoint of a Social Behaviorist*. Chicago: University of Chicago Press.

Meeks, Wayne A. 1983. *The First Urban Christians*. New Haven: Yale University Press.

Mellado, James. 1991. *Willow Creek Community Church*. Case study. Cambridge, Mass.: Harvard Business School.

Melton, J. Gordon. 1988. "Testing Truisms about the 'Cults': Toward a New Perspective on Nonconventional Religion." Paper presented at the annual meetings of the American Academy of Religion, Chicago.

———. 1989. *The Encyclopedia of American Religions*. 3d ed. Detroit: Gale Research.

Merton, Robert K. 1995. "The Thomas Theorem and the Matthew Effect." *Social Forces* 74: 379–424.

Middleton, John, ed. 1967a. *Gods and Rituals*. Austin: University of Texas Press.

———, ed. 1967b. *Magic, Witchcraft, and Curing*. Austin: University of Texas Press.

Miller, Alan. 1995. "A Rational Choice Model of Religious Behavior in Japan." *Journal for the Scientific Study of Religion* 34: 234–44.

Miller, Alan S., and John P. Hoffmann. 1995. "Risk and Religion: An Explanation of Gender Differences in Religiosity." *Journal for the Scientific Study of Religion* 34:63–75.

Miller, Dave. 1991. "Law Promises New Freedom for Protestants." *Christianity Today* (November 25): 60–62.

Miller, Donald E. 1997. *Reinventing American Protestantism*. Berkeley, Calif.: University of California Press.

Mitchell, B. R. 1962. *Abstract of British Historical Statistics*. Cambridge: Cambridge University Press.

Money-Kyrle, R[oger]. 1929. *The Meaning of Sacrifice*. London: Hogarth Press.

Moore, R. Lawrence. 1994. *Selling God: American Religion in the Marketplace of Culture*. New York: Oxford University Press.

Moroto, Aiko. 1976. "Conditions for Accepting a New Religious Belief: A Case Study of Myochikai Members in Japan." M.A. thesis, Dept. of Sociology, University of Washington.

Morris, Colin. 1993. "Christian Civilization (1050–1400)." In *The Oxford History of Christianity,* edited by John McManners, 205–42. Oxford: Oxford University Press.

Müller, F. Max. 1880. *Lectures on the Origin and Growth of Religion as Illustrated by the Religions of India. Delivered in the Chapter House, Westminster Abbey, in April, May, and June, 1878.* London: Longmans Green.

Murphy, Tim. 1994. *"Wesen und Erscheinung* in the History of the Study of Religion: A Post-Structuralist Perspective." *Method and Theory in the Study of Religion* 6: 119–46.

Murray, Alexander. 1972. "Piety and Impiety in Thirteenth-Century Italy." *Studies in Church History* 8: 83–106.

Mutlu, Kayhan. 1996. "Examining Religious Beliefs among University Students in Ankara." *British Journal of Sociology* 47: 353–59.

Nauta, André. 1994. "{hrs}'That They All May Be One': Can Denominationalism Die?" *Research in the Social Scientific Study of Religion* (JAI Press) 6: 35–51.

Needham, Rodney. 1972. *Belief, Language and Experience.* Chicago: University of Chicago Press.

Neitz, Mary Jo. 1987. *Charisma and Community: A Study of Religious Commitment within the Charismatic Renewal.* New Brunswick: Transaction Publishers.

Neitz, Mary Jo, and Peter R. Mueser. 1997. "A Critique of the Rational Choice Approach." In *Assessing Rational Choice Theories of Religion,* edited by Lawrence A. Young, 105–18. New York: Routledge.

Neitz, Mary Jo, and James V. Spickard. 1990. "Steps Toward a Sociology of Religious Experience: The Theories of Mihal Csikszentmihayi and Alfred Schutz." *Sociological Analysis* 51:15–33.

Nelson, John. 1992. "Shinto Ritual: Managing Chaos in Contemporary Japan." *Ethnos* 57: 77–104.

Newman, William M. 1974. "The Society for the Scientific Study of Religion: The Development of an Academic Society." *Review of Religious Research* 15: 137–51.

Niandou-Souley, Abdoulaye, and Gado Alzouma. 1996. "Islamic Renewal in Niger: From Monolith to Plurality." *Social Compass* 43: 249–65.

Niebuhr, Gustav. 1996. "Unitarians Striking Chord of Spirituality." *New York Times,* December 8 (National Report), 14.

Niebuhr, H. Richard. 1929. *The Social Sources of Denominationalism.* New York: Holt.

Nielsen, Daniel A., ed. 1995. *1994 General Minutes of the Annual Conferences of the United Methodist Church.* Evanston, Ill.: General Council on Finance and Administration.

———, ed. 1996. *1995 General Minutes of the Annual Conferences of the United Methodist Church.* Evanston, Ill.: General Council on Finance and Administration.

Nineham, Dennis. 1997. "In Praise of Solar Living." *Times Literary Supplement,* December 26, 5.

Nock, David A. 1987. "Cult, Sect, and Church in Canada: A Reexamination of Stark and Bainbridge." *Canadian Review of Sociology and Anthropology* 24: 514–25.

Norbeck, Edward. 1961. *Religion in Primitive Society.* New York: Harper.

Obelkevich. James. 1979. *Religion and the People, 800–1700.* Chapel Hill: University of North Carolina Press.

Olson, Daniel V. A. 1998. "Comment: Religious Pluralism in Contemporary U.S. Counties." *American Sociological Review* 63: 759–61.

Olson, Mancur. 1965. *The Logic of Collective Action.* Cambridge, Mass.: Harvard University Press.

Ostow, Mortimer. 1990. "The Fundamentalist Phenomenon: A Psychological Perspective." In *The Fundamentalist Phenomenon: A View from Within, a Response from Without,* edited by Noman J. Cohen, 99–125. Grand Rapids, Mich.: Eerdmans, 1990.

O'Toole, Roger. 1977. *The Precipitous Path: Studies in Political Sects.* Toronto: PMA Associates.

———. 1984. *Religion: Classic Sociological Approaches.* Toronto: McGraw-Hill Ryerson.

Otto, Rudolf. 1923. *The Idea of the Holy: An Inquiry into the Non-Rational Factor in the Idea of the Divine and Its Relation to the Rational.* Translated by John W. Harvey. Rev. ed. Oxford: Oxford University Press. Originally published as *Das Heilige. Über das Irrationale in der Idee des göttlichen und sein Verhältnis zum Rationalen* (Breslau, 1917).

Pagels, Elaine. 1979. *The Gnostic Gospels.* New York: Random House.

Pals, Daniel L. 1996. *Seven Theories of Religion.* New York: Oxford University Press.

Pargament, K. I., and C. L. Park. 1995. "Merely a Defense? The Variety of Religious Ends and Means." *Journal of Social Issues* 51 (2): 13–32.

Parrinder, Geoffrey, ed. 1983. *World Religions: From Ancient History to the Present.* New York: Facts on File.

Parsons, Talcott. 1939. *The Structure of Social Action.* New York: McGraw-Hill.

———. 1951. *The Social System.* Glencoe, Ill.: Free Press.

Pascal, Blaise. [1670] 1966. *Pensées.* London: Penguin Classics.

Pascoe, C. F. 1901. *Two Hundred Years of the SPG.* 2 vols. London: SPG.

Payne, Robert. 1959. *The History of Islam.* New York: Barnes & Noble.

Pettersson, Thorleif, and Eva Hamberg. 1997. "Denominational Pluralism and Church Membership in Contemporary Sweden: A Longitudinal Study of the Period, 1974–1995." *Journal of Empirical Theology* 10: 61–78.

Phillips, Rick. 1998. "Religious Market Share and Mormon Church Activity." *Sociology of Religion* 59: 117–30.

Pickering, J. F. 1985. "Giving in the Church of England: An Econometric Analysis." *Applied Economics* 17: 619–32.

Pinto, Leonard J., and Kenneth E. Crow. 1982. "The Effects of Size on Other Structural Attributes of Congregations within the Same Denomination." *Journal for the Scientific Study of Religion* 21: 304–16.

Pisati, Maurizio. 1998. "Non di solo Cattolicesimo: Elementi per un'analaisi dell'offerta religiosa in Italia." *Polis* 12: 53–73.

Plantinga, Alvin. 1993. *Warrant: The Current Debate.* New York: Oxford University Press.

Pollner, Melvin L. 1989. "Divine Relations, Social Relations, and Well-being." *Journal of Health and Social Behavior* 30: 92–104.

Poloma, Margaret. 1987. *The Charismatic Movement: Is There a New Pentecost?* Boston: Twayne Publishers.

———. 1989. *The Assemblies of God at the Crossroads.* Knoxville: University of Tennessee Press.

Poloma, Margaret, and George H. Gallup, Jr. 1991. *Varieties of Prayer: A Survey Report.* Philadelphia: Trinity Press International.

Popielarz, Pamela A., and J. Miller McPherson. 1995. "On the Edge or in Between: Niche Position, Niche Overlap, and the Duration of Voluntary Association Memberships." *American Journal of Sociology* 101: 698–720.

Popper, Karl. 1959. *The Logic of Scientific Discovery.* New York: Basic Books.

———. 1962. *Conjectures and Refutations.* New York: Basic Books.

Porter, Larry C. 1988. "{hrs}'The Field Is White Already to Harvest': Earliest Missionary Labors and the Book of Mormon." In *The Prophet Joseph: Essays on the Life and Mission of Joseph Smith,* edited by Larry C. Porter and Susan Easton Black, 73–89. Salt
Lake City: Deseret Book Company.

Powell, Milton B., ed., 1967. *The Voluntary Church: Religious Life, 1740–1860, Seen through the
Eyes of European Visitors.* New York: Macmillan.

Pratt, Parley P. [1873] 1985. *The Autobiography of Parley P. Pratt.* Salt Lake City: Deseret.

Presbyterian Church (USA). Office of the General Assembly. 1995. *Presbyterian (USA)
1994 Minutes: 206th General Assembly.* Louisville, Ky.: Office of the General Assembly.

———. 1996. *Presbyterian (USA) 1995 Minutes: 207th General Assembly.* Louisville, Ky.: Office
of the General Assembly.

———. 1997. *Presbyterian (USA) 1996 Minutes: 208th General Assembly.* Louisville, Ky.: Office
of the General Assembly.

Preus, J. Samuel. 1987. *Explaining Religion: Criticism and Theory from Bodin to Freud.* New
Haven: Yale University Press.

Price, S. R. F. 1984. *Rituals and Power: The Roman Imperial Cult in Asia Minor.* Cambridge:
Cambridge University Press.

Quinn, D. Michael. 1994. *The Mormon Hierarchy: Origins of Power.* Salt Lake City: Signature Books.

———. 1997. *The Mormon Hierarchy: Extensions of Power.* Salt Lake City: Signature Books.

Radcliffe-Brown, A. R. 1939. *Taboo.* Cambridge: Cambridge University Press.

———. 1952. *Structure and Function in Primitive Society.* Glencoe: Free Press.

Radin, Paul. 1956. *The Trickster.* London: Routledge and Kegan Paul.

———. [1937] 1957. *Primitive Religion.* New York: Dover Books.

Redman, Ben Ray. 1949. *The Portable Voltaire.* New York: Penguin Books.

Reichard, Gladys A. 1950. *Navaho Religion.* 2 vols. New York: Pantheon Books.

Reichenbach, Hans. 1959. *The Rise of Scientific Philosophy.* Berkeley and Los Angeles: University of California Press.

Richardson, James T. 1985. "The Active vs. Passive Convert: Paradigm Conflict in Con-
version/Recruitment Research." *Journal for the Scientific Study of Religion* 24: 163–79.

Robbins, Thomas. 1988. *Cults, Converts & Charisma.* Beverly Hills, Calif.: Sage.

Robbins, Thomas, and James Beckford. 1988. "Introduction." In Thomas Robbins,
Cults, Converts and Charisma, 1–23. Beverley Hills, Calif.: Sage.

Robinson, John A. T. 1963. *Honest to God.* Philadelphia: Westminster.

Roesdahl, Else. 1980. "The Scandinavians at Home." In *The Northern World,* edited by
David M. Wilson, 145–58. New York: Harry N. Abrams.

Rosenthal, Bernice Glatzer, ed. 1997 *The Occult in Russian and Soviet Culture.* Ithaca, N.Y.:
Cornell University Press.

Ross, Freda. 1995. "The Krishna Movement in Hungary." *Religion, State, and Society* 23:
207–12.

Ross, Thomas W. 1985. "The Implicit Theology of Carl Sagan." *Pacific Theological Review*
18: 24–32.

Runcimen, W. G. 1969. "The Sociological Explanation of 'Religious' Beliefs." *Archives
Européennes de Sociologie* 10: 149–91.

Rydenfelt, Sven. 1985. "Sweden and Its Bishops." *Wall Street Journal,* August 21, A25.

Sawyer, P. H. 1982. *Kings and Vikings: Scandinavia and Europe, a.d. 700–1100.* London:
Methuen.

Sawyer, Peter, and Birgit Sawyer. 1993. *Medieval Scandinavia: From Conversion to Reformation, circa 800–1500.* Minneapolis: University of Minnesota Press.

Schaff, Philip. 1961 [1855]. *America: A Sketch of Its Political, Social, and Religious Character.* Cambridge, Mass.: Harvard University Press, Belknap Press.

Schaller, Lyle E. 1991. *Forty-four Questions for Church Planters.* Nashville: Abingdon Press.

Scheflin, Alan, and Edward M. Opton. 1978. *The Mind Manipulators.* New York: Paddington Press.

Schmied, Gerhard. 1996. "US-Televangelism on German TV." *Journal of Contemporary Religion* 11: 95–99.

Schmetzer, Uli. 1996. "Religion Thrives in Russia, but Church Comes in for Criticism." *Chicago Tribune* Service. *Seattle Times,* November 28, F17.

Schneider, Jane. 1990. "Spirits and the Spirit of Capitalism." In *Religious Orthodoxy and Popular Faith in European Society,* edited by Ellen Badone, 24–54. Princeton: Princeton University Press.

Schoenherr, Richard A., and Andrew M. Greeley. 1974. "Role Commitment Processes and the American Catholic Priesthood." *American Sociological Review* 39: 407–25.

Scroggs, Robin. 1980. "The Sociological Interpretation of the New Testament: The Present State of Research." *New Testament Studies* 26: 164–79.

Selthoffer, Steve. 1997. "German Government Harasses Charismatic Christians." *Charisma,* June, 22–24.

Seidler, John, and Katherine Meyer. 1989. *Conflict and Change in the Catholic Church.* New Brunswick, N.J.: Rutgers University Press.

Shaftesbury, Anthony Ashley Cooper, third earl of. [1711] 1978. *Characteristics of Men, Manners, Opinions, Times.* 3 vol. Facsimile edition. Hildesheim, Germany: Georg Olms Verlag.

Shahar, Meir, and Robert P. Weller, eds. 1996. *Unruly Gods: Divinity and Society in China.* Honolulu: University of Hawaii Press.

Sharot, Stephen. 1982. *Messianism, Mysticism, and Magic: A Sociological Analysis of Jewish Religious Movements.* Chapel Hill: University of North Carolina Press.

Shaughnessy, Gerald. 1925. *Has the Immigrant Kept the Faith?* New York: Macmillan.

Shepherd, William R. 1980. *Shepherd's Historical Atlas.* Rev. 9th ed. Totowa, N.J.: Barnes & Noble.

Sherkat, Darren E. 1991. "Leaving the Faith: Testing Theories of Religious Switching Using Survival Models." *Social Science Research* 20: 171–87.

———. 1993. "Theory and Method in Religious Mobility Research." *Social Science Research* 22: 208–27.

———. 1997. "Embedding Religious Choices: Preferences and Social Constraints into Rational Choice Theories of Religious Behavior." In *Rational Choice Theory and Religion: Summary and Assessment,* edited by Lawrence A. Young, 65–85. New York: Routledge.

———. 1998a. "Tracking the Restructuring of American Religion: Changes in Patterns of Religious Mobility between 1973 and 1996." Paper presented at the annual meetings of the Southern Sociological Society. Atlanta, Ga.

———. 1998b. "Counterculture or Continuity? Competing Influences on Baby Boomers' Religious Orientations and Participation." *Social Forces* 76: 1087–1115.

Sherkat, Darren E., and John Wilson. 1995. "Preferences, Constraints, and Choices in Religious Markets: An Examination of Religious Switching and Apostasy." *Social Forces* 73: 993–1026.

Shiner, Larry. 1967. "The Concept of Secularization in Empirical Research." *Journal for the Scientific Study of Religion* 6: 207–20.

Siewert, John A., and John A. Kenyon, eds. 1993. *Mission Handbook.* 15th ed. Monrovia, Calif.: MARC.

Siewert, John A., and Edna G. Valdez, eds. 1997. *Mission Handbook.* 17th ed. Monrovia, Calif.: MARC.

Silberstein, Richard, Jonathan Rabinowitz, Paul Ritterband, and Barry Kosmin. 1987. "Giving to Jewish Philanthropic Causes: A Preliminary Reconnaissance." In *Spring Research Forum Working Papers,* 1–8. New York: United Way Institute.

Simmel, Georg. [Ca. 1905] 1959. *Sociology of Religion.* New York: Wisdom.

Simon, Herbert A. 1957. *Models of Man: Social and Rational.* New York: John Wiley & Sons.

————. 1982. *Models of Bounded Rationality.* Cambridge: Cambridge University Press.

Simpson, George Eaton. 1978. *Black Religions in the New World.* New York: Columbia University Press.

Singelenberg, Richard. 1989. "{hrs}'It Separated the Wheat from the Chaff': The '1975' Prophesy and Its Impact on Dutch Jehovah's Witnesses." *Sociological Analysis* 50: 23–40.

Singer, Margaret. 1979. "Coming Out of the Cults." *Psychology Today,* January, 72–83.

Smart, Ninian. 1984. *The Religious Experience of Mankind.* 3d ed. New York: Charles Scribner's Sons.

Smith, Adam. [1776] 1981. *An Inquiry into the Nature and Causes of the Wealth of Nations.* 2 vols. Indianapolis: Liberty Fund.

Smith, Adam. [1759] 1982. *The Theory of Moral Sentiments.* Indianapolis: Liberty Fund.

Smith, Christian. 2000. *Christian America? What Evangelicals Really Want.* Berkeley and Los Angeles: University of California Press.

Smith, Christian, with Michael Emerson, Sally Gallagher, Paul Kennedy, and David Sikkink. 1998. *American Evangelism: Embattled and Thriving.* Chicago: University of Chicago Press.

Smith, Greg. 1996. "The Unsecular City: The Revival of Religion in East London." In *Rising in the East: The Regeneration of East London,* edited by Tim Butler and Michael Rustin, 108–57. London: Lawrence & Wishart.

Smith, Lucy Mack. [1853] 1996. *History of Joseph Smith by His Mother.* Edited by Scot Facer Procter and Maurine Jensen Procter. Salt Lake City: Bookcraft.

Smith, Mark. 1996. *Religion in Industrial Society: Oldham and Saddleworth, 1740–1865.* Oxford: Oxford University Press.

Smith, Timothy L. 1983. "My Rejection of the Cyclical View 'Great Awakenings' in American Religious History." *Sociological Analysis* 44: 97–101.

Smith, W. Robertson. [1889] 1907. *Lectures on the Religion of the Semites.* New ed. London: Adam and Charles Black.

Snow, David A., and Richard Machalek. 1983. "The Convert as a Social Type." In *Sociological Theory, 1983,* edited by Randall Collins, 259–88. San Francisco: Jossey-Bass.

Snow, David A., and Cynthia L. Phillips. 1980. "The Lofland-Stark Conversion Model: A Critical Reassessment." *Social Problems* 27: 430–47.

Soden, Wolfram von. 1994. *The Ancient Orient.* Grand Rapids, Mich.: Eerdman's.

Sommerville, C. John. 1992. *The Secularization of Early Modern England.* New York: Oxford University Press.

Spencer, Herbert. [1876–96] 1893, 1896. *Principles of Sociology.* London. 3 vols. Revised edition. New York: D. Appleton. Vol. 2 of the U.S. edition appeared in 1893, followed by vol. 1 in 1896.

Sperber, Dan. 1975. *Rethinking Symbolism.* Cambridge: Cambridge University Press.

Spickard, James V. 1997. Review of *Rational Choice Theory and Religion: Summary and Assessment,* edited by Lawrence A. Young. *Contemporary Sociology* 26: 768–69.

Spiro, Melford E. 1964. "Religion and the Irrational." In *Symposium on New Approaches to the Study of Religion,* edited by June Helm, 102–15. Seattle: University of Washington Press.

———. 1966a. "Buddhism and Economic Action in Burma." *American Anthropologist* 68: 1163–73.

———. 1966b. "Religion: Problems of Definition and Explanation." In *Anthropological Aporoaches to the Study of Religion,* edited by Michael Banton, 85–126. London: Tavistock Publications.

Spong, John Shelby. 1998. *Why Christianity Must Change or Die.* San Francisco: HarperSanFrancisco.

Staples, Clifford L., and Armand L. Mauss. 1987. "Conversion or Commitment? A Reassessment of the Snow and Machalek Approach to the Study of Conversion." *Journal for the Scientific Study of Religion* 26: 133–47.

Stark, Rodney. 1963. "On the Incompatibility of Religion and Science: A Survey of American Graduate Students." *Journal for the Scientific Study of Religion* 3: 3–20.

———. 1964. "Class, Radicalism, and Religious Involvement." *American Sociological Review* 29: 698–706.

———. 1965. "A Taxonomy of Religious Experience." *Journal for the Scientific Study of Religion* 5: 97–100.

———. 1971a. "The Economics of Piety: Religion and Social Class." In *Issues in Social Inequality,* edited by Gerald W. Theilbar and Saul D. Feldman, 483–503. Boston: Little, Brown.

———. 1971b. "Psychopathology and Religious Commitment." *Review of Religious Research* 12: 165–76.

———. 1981. "Must All Religions Be Supernatural?" In *The Social Impact of New Religious Movements,* edited by Bryan Wilson, 159–77. New York: Rose of Sharon Press,

———. 1983. "Religious Economies: A New Perspective." Paper delivered at Conference on New Directions in Religious Research, University of Lethbridge.

———. 1984a. "Religion and Conformity: Reaffirming a *Sociology* of Religion." *Sociological Analysis* 43: 53–68.

———. 1984b. "The Rise of New World Faith." *Review of Religious Research* 26: 18–27.

———. 1985a. "Europe's Receptivity to Religious Movements." In *Religious Movements: Genesis, Exodus, and Numbers,* edited by Rodney Stark, 301–43. New York: Paragon.

———. 1985b. "From Church-Sect to Religious Economies." In *The Sacred in a Post-Secular Age,* edited by Phillip E. Hammond, 139–49. Berkeley and Los Angeles: University of California Press.

———. 1987. "How New Religions Succeed: A Theoretical Model." In *The Future of New Religious Movements,* edited by David G. Bromley and Phillip E. Hammond, 11–29. Macon, Ga.: Mercer University Press.

———. 1992a. "Do Catholic Societies Really Exist?" *Rationality and Society* 4: 261–71.

———. 1992b. "How Sane People Talk to the Gods: A Rational Theory of Revelations." In *Innovation in Religious Traditions: Essays in the Interpretation of Religious Change*, edited by Michael A. Williams, Collet Cox, and Martin S. Jaffe, 19–34. Berlin: Mouton de Gruyter.

———. 1993. "Europe's Receptivity to New Religious Movements: Round Two." *Journal for the Scientific Study of Religion* 32: 389–97.

———. 1996a. *The Rise of Christianity: A Sociologist Reconsiders History.* Princeton: Princeton University Press.

———. 1996b. "Why Religious Movements Succeed or Fail: A Revised General Model." *Journal of Contemporary Religion* 11:133–46.

———. 1997. "German and German-American Religion: Approximating a Crucial Experiment." *Journal for the Scientific Study of Religion* 36: 182–93.

———. 1998a. "The Basis of Mormon Success: A Theoretical Application." In *Latter-Day Saint Social Life: Social Research on the LDS Church and Its Members*, edited by James T. Duke, 29–70. Provo, Utah: Religious Studies Center, Brigham Young University.

———. 1998b. "Catholic Contexts: Competition, Commitment, and Innovation." *Review of Religious Research* 39: 197–208.

———. 1998c. "Spiegare le variazioni della religiosita: Il modello del mercato" ["Explaining International Variations in Religiousness: The Market Model"]. Translated by Maurizio Pisati. *Polis: Ricerche e studi su società e politica in Italia* 12: 11–31.

———. 1998d. "The Rise and Fall of Christian Science." *Journal of Contemporary Religion* 13: 189–214.

Stark, Rodney, and William Sims Bainbridge. 1979. "Of Churches, Sects, and Cults: Preliminary Concepts for a Theory of Religious Movements." *Journal for the Scientific Study of Religion* 18: 117–131.

———. 1980a. "Networks of Faith: Interpersonal Bonds and Recruitment to Cults and Sects." *American Journal of Sociology* 85: 1376–95.

———. 1980b. "Secularization, Revival, and Cult Formation. *Annual Review of the Social Sciences of Religion* 4: 85–119.

———. 1980c. "Towards a Theory of Religion: Religious Commitment." *Journal for the Scientific Study of Religion* 19: 114–28.

———. 1981a. "American-Born Sects: Initial Findings." *Journal for the Scientific Study of Religion* 20: 130–49.

———. 1981b. "Secularization and Cult Formation in the Jazz Age." *Journal for the Scientific Study of Religion* 20: 360–73.

———. 1985. *The Future of Religion: Secularization, Revival, and Cult Formation.* Berkeley and Los Angeles: University of California Press.

———. [1987] 1996. *A Theory of Religion.* Republished edition. New Brunswick, N.J.: Rutgers University Press.

———. 1997. *Religion, Deviance, and Social Control.* New York: Routledge.

Stark, Rodney, W. S. Bainbridge, and Daniel P. Doyle. 1979. "Cults of America: A Reconnaissance in Space and Time." *Sociological Analysis* 40: 347–59.

Stark, Rodney, Roger Finke, and Laurence R. Iannaccone. 1995. "Pluralism and Piety: England and Wales, 1851." *Journal for the Scientific Study of Religion* 34: 431–44.

Stark, Rodney, and Bruce D. Foster. 1970. "In Defense of Orthodoxy: Notes on the Validity of an Index." *Social Forces* 48: 383–93.

Stark, Rodney, Bruce D. Foster, Charles Y. Glock and Harold E. Quinley. 1971. *Wayward Shepherds: Prejudice and the Protestant Clergy.* New York: Harper & Row.

Stark, Rodney, and Charles Y. Glock. 1965. "The New Denominationalism." *Review of Religious Research* 7: 17–28.

———. 1968. *American Piety.* Berkeley and Los Angeles: University of California Press.

Stark, Rodney, and Laurence R. Iannaccone, 1993. "Rational Choice Propositions about Religious Movements." In *Religion and the Social Order,* vol. 3A: *Handbook on Cults and Sects in America,* edited by David G. Bromley and Jeffrey K. Hadden, 241–61. Greenwich, Conn.: JAI Press.

———. 1994. "A Supply-Side Reinterpretation of the "Secularization" of Europe." *Journal for the Scientific Study of Religion* 33: 230–52.

———. 1995. "Truth? A Reply to Bruce." *Journal for the Scientific Study of Religion* 34: 516–19.

———. 1996. "Recent Religious Declines in Quebec, Poland, and the Netherlands: A Theory Vindicated." *Journal for the Scientific Study of Religion* 35: 265–71.

———. 1997. "Why the Jehovah's Witnesses Grow So Rapidly: A Thoretical Application." *Journal of Contemporary Religion* 12: 133–57.

Stark, Rodney, Laurence R. Iannaccone, and Roger Finke. 1996. "Religion, Science and Rationality." *American Economic Review Papers and Proceedings:* 433–37.

———. 1998. "Rationality and the Religious Mind." *Economic Inquiry* 36: 373–89.

Stark, Rodney, and James C. McCann. 1993. "Market Forces and Catholic Commitment: Exploring the New Paradigm." *Journal for the Scientific Study of Religion* 32: 111–23.

Stark, Rodney, and Lynne Roberts. 1982. "The Arithmetic of Social Movements: Theoretical Implications." *Sociological Analysis* 43: 53–68.

Steinberg, Stephen. 1965. "Reform Judaism: The Origin and Evolution of a Church Movement." *Review of Religious Research* 7: 1–8.

Stoll, David. 1990. *Is Latin America Turning Protestant?* Berkeley and Los Angeles: University of California Press.

Stolzenberg, Ross M., Mary Blair-Loy, and Linda J. Waite. 1994. "Religious Participation in Early Adulthood: Age and Family Life Cycle Effects on Church Membership." *American Sociological Review* 60: 84–103.

Sundén, Hjalmar. [1959] 1966. *Die Religion und die Rollen.* Berlin: Topelmann. Originally published in Swedish as *Religionen och Rollerna.*

———. 1987. "Saint Augustine and the Psalter in the Light of Role-Psychology." *Journal for the Scientific Study of Religion* 26: 375–82.

Swatos, William H., Jr. 1984. "The Relevance of Religion: Iceland and Secularization Theory." *Journal for the Scientific Study of Religion* 23: 32–43.

———. 1989. "Religious Sociology and the Sociology of Religion in America at the Turn of the Twentieth Century: Divergences from a Common Theme." *Sociological Analysis* 50: 363–75.

Swatos, William H., Jr., and Loftur Reimar Gissurarson. 1997. *Icelandic Spiritualism: Mediumship and Modernity in Iceland.* New Brunswick, N.J.: Transaction Publishers.

Sweet, William Warren. 1933. *Methodism in American History.* New York: Methodist Book Concern.

———. 1964. *Religion on the American Frontier, 1783–1840: The Baptists.* New York: Cooper Square Publishers.

Tamney, Joseph B. 1979. "Established Religiosity in Modern Society: Islam in Indonesia." *Sociological Analysis* 40: 125–35.

———. 1980. "Fasting and Modernization." *Journal for the Scientific Study of Religion* 19: 129–37.

———. 1992. *The Resilience of Christianity in the Modern World.* Albany: State University of New York Press.

Tamney, Joseph B., and John G. Condran. 1980. "The Decline of Religious Homogeneity: The Indonesian Situation." *Journal for the Scientific Study of Religion* 19: 267–80.

Tamney, Joseph B., and Riaz Hassan. 1987. *Religious Switching in Singapore.* Flinders, Australia: Select Books.

Thalheimer, Fred. 1973. "Religiosity and Secularization in the Academic Professions." *Sociology of Education* 46: 183–202.

Thomas, George M. 1989. *Revivalism and Cultural Change.* Chicago: University of Chicago Press.

Thomas, Keith. 1971. *Religion and the Decline of Magic.* New York: Scribner's.

Thompson, Edward H. 1991. "Beneath the Status Characteristic: Gender Variations in Religiousness." *Journal for the Scientific Study of Religion* 30: 381–94.

Thompson, Kenneth. 1990. "Religion: The British Contribution." *British Journal of Sociology* 41: 531–35.

Thompson, Margaret. 1986. "Discovering Foremothers: Sisters, Society, and the American Catholic Experience." *U.S. Catholic Historian* 5: 273–90.

Thomsen, Harry. 1963. *The New Religions of Japan.* Rutland, Vt.: Charles E. Tuttle.

Thornton, Arland. 1979. "Religion and Fertility: The Case of Mormonism." *Journal of Marriage and the Family* 41:131–42.

Tillich, Paul. 1962. *The Courage to Be.* London: Collins.

Tiryakian, Edward A. 1993. "American Religious Exceptionalism: A Reconsideration." *The Annals* 527: 40–54.

Toby, Jackson. 1957. "Social Disorganization and Stake in Conformity: Complementary Factors in the Predatory Behavior of Hoodlums." *Journal of Criminal Law, Criminology, and Police Science* 48: 12–17.

Tocqueville, Alexis de. [1835–39] 1956. *Democracy in America.* 2 vols. New York: Vintage Books.

Tomasson, Richard F. 1980. *Iceland.* Minneapolis: University of Minnesota Press.

Tooker, Deborah E. 1992. "Identity Systems in Highland Burma." *Man* 27: 799–819.

Torrey, Charles C. 1892. *The Commercial-Theological Terms in the Koran.* Leyden: E.J. Brill.

Trenchard, John, and Thomas Gordon. [1720–24] 1995. *Cato's Letters: Or, Essays on Liberty, Civil and Religious, and Other Important Subjects.* Indianapolis: Liberty Fund.

Troeltsch, Ernst. [1912] 1931. *The Social Teaching of the Christian Churches.* 2 vols. New York: Macmillan.

———. [1906] 1991a. "The Separation of Church and State and the Teaching of Religion." Translated by James Luther Adams and Walter F. Bense. In *Religion in History.* Minneapolis: Fortress Press. Originally published in *Heidelberger Akademische Rede.*

———. [1911] 1991b. "Stoic-Christian Natural Law and Modern Secular Natural Law." Translated by James Luther Adams and Walter F. Bense. In *Religion in History.* Minneapolis: Fortress Press. Originally published in *Gesammelte Schriften.*

Trotter, Wilfred. 1919. *Instincts of the Herd in Peace and War: 1916–1919.* 2d ed. London: Oxford University Press.

Trueheart, Charles. 1996. "The Next Church." *Atlantic Monthly*, August, 37–58.

Tschannen, Oliver. 1991. "The Secularization Paradigm: A Systematization." *Journal for the Scientific Study of Religion* 30: 395–415.

Turner, Ralph H., and Lewis M. Killian. 1987. *Collective Behavior.* 3d ed. Englewood Cliffs, N.J.: Prentice-Hall.

Turner, Mark. 1996. *The Literary Mind.* New York: Oxford University Press.

Tylor, Sir Edward Burnett . [1871] 1958. *Primitive Culture.* 2 vols. New York: Harper & Brothers.

Unitarian Universalist Association. 1967. *Report of the Committee on Goals.* Boston: Unitarian Universalist Association.

———. 1989. *The Quality of Religious Life in Unitarian Universalist Congregations.* Boston: Unitarian Universalist Association.

Van Wagoner, Richard S. 1994. *Sidney Rigdon: A Portrait of Religious Excess.* Salt Lake City: Signature Books.

Vauchez, Andre. 1997. *Sainthood in the Later Middle Ages.* New York: Cambridge University Press.

Vaughan, John. 1992. As reported in *The Almanac of the Christian World*, edited by E. Draper. Wheaton, Ill.: Tyndale House Publishers.

Verdieck, Mary Jeanne, Joseph J. Shields, and Dean R. Hoge. 1988. "Role Commitment Processes Revisited: American Catholic Priests 1970 and 1985." *Journal for the Scientific Study of Religion* 27: 524–35.

Voyé, Liliane, and Karel Dobbelaere. 1994. "Roman Catholicism: Universalism at Stake." In *Religions sans frontières?* edited by Roberto Cipriani, 83–113. Rome: Dipartimento per l'informazione e editoria.

Wagner, Melinda Bollar. 1983. "Spiritual Frontiers Fellowship." In *Alternatives to American Mainline Churches*, edited by Joseph H. Fichter. New York: Rose of Sharon Press.

———. 1990. *God's Schools: Choice and Compromise in American Society.* New Brunswick, N.J.: Rutgers University Press.

Wallace, Anthony F. C. 1966. *Religion: An Anthropological View.* New York: Random House.

Wallace, Ruth A. 1975. "A Model of Change of Religious Affiliation." *Journal for the Scientific Study of Religion* 14: 345–55.

Wallis, Roy. 1986a. "The Caplow–De Tocqueville Account of Contrasts in European and American Religion: Confounding Considerations." *Sociological Analysis* 47: 50–52.

———. 1986b. "Figuring Out Cult Receptivity." *Journal for the Scientific Study of Religion* 25: 494–503.

Wallis, Roy, and Steve Bruce. 1984. "The Stark-Bainbridge Theory of Religion: A Critical Analysis and Counter Proposals." *Sociological Analysis* 45:11–27.

Warner, R. Stephen. 1979. "Theoretical Barriers to the Understanding of Evangelical Christianity." *Sociological Analysis.* 40: 1–9.

———. 1988. *New Wine in Old Wineskins: Evangelicals and Liberals in a Small-Town Church.* Berkeley and Los Angeles: University of California Press.

———. 1993. "Work in Progress towards a New Paradigm for the Sociological Study of Religion in the United States." *American Journal of Sociology* 98: 1044–93.

———. 1997. "Convergence Toward the New Paradigm: A Case of Induction." In *Assessing Rational Choice Theories of Religion*, edited by Lawrence A. Young, 87–101. New York: Routledge.

Weber, Max. [1913] 1946. *From Max Weber: Essays in Sociology*. Edited by H. H. Gerth and C. Wright Mills. New York: Oxford University Press.

——. 1947. *The Theory of Social and Economic Organization*. Glencoe: Free Press.

——. [1906] 1985. "{hrs}'Churches' and 'Sects'" in North America: An Ecclesiastical Socio-Political Sketch." Translated by Colin Loader. *Sociological Theory* 3: 7–13.

——. [1922] 1993. *The Sociology of Religion*. Boston: Beacon Press.

Welch, Kevin. 1981. "An Interpersonal Influence Model of Traditional Religious Commitment." *Sociological Quarterly* 22: 81–92.

——. 1983. "Community Development and Metropolitan Religious Commitment: A Test of Two Competing Models." *Journal for the Scientific Study of Religion* 22: 167–81.

Wertheimer, Jack. 1993. *A People Divided: Judaism in Contemporary America*. New York: Basic Books.

Whitefield, George. [1747] 1969. *George Whitefield's Journals*. Gainsville, Fla.: Scholars' Facsimiles and Reprints.

Whittaker, Thomas. 1911. *Priests, Philosophers and Prophets: A Dissertation on Revealed Religion*. London: Adam and Charles Black.

Wilken, Paul H. 1971. "Size of Organizations and Member Participation in Church Congregations." *Administrative Science Quarterly* 16: 173–79.

Williams, Michael Allen. 1996. *Rethinking "Gnosticism": An Argument for Dismantling a Dubious Category*. Princeton: Princeton University Press.

Wilson, Bryan. 1959. "An Analysis of Sect Development." *American Sociological Review* 24: 2–15.

——. 1966. *Religion in Secular Society*. London: C. A. Watts.

——. 1967. *Patterns of Sectarianism*. London: Heinemann.

——. 1968. "Religion and the Churches in Contemporary America." In *Religion in America*, edited by William G. McLoughlin and Robert N. Bellah, 77–84. Boston: Houghton Mifflin.

——. 1975a. "The Debate over Secularization; Religion, Society and Faith." *Encounter* 45: 77–84.

——. 1975b. *Magic and the Millennium*. Frogmore, Eng.: Paladin.

——. 1982. *Religion in Sociological Perspective*. Oxford: Oxford University Press.

Wilson, John, and Darren E. Sherkat. 1994. "Returning to the Fold." *Journal for the Scientific Study of Religion* 33: 148–61.

Wilson, Monica Hunter. 1957. *Rituals of Kinship among the Nyakyusa*. New York: Oxford University Press.

Wilson, Warren H. 1925. *The Farmer's Church*. New York: Century Co.

Winter, Michael, and Christopher Short. 1993. "Believing and Belonging: Religion and Rural England." *British Journal of Sociology* 44: 635–51.

Witham, Larry. 1998. "France Determines Jehovah's Witnesses Are Not a Religion." *Washington Times*, National Weekly Edition, July 6–12, 21.

Wittberg, Patricia. 1994. *The Rise and Fall of Catholic Religious Orders*. Albany: State University of New York Press.

——. 1996. "{hrs}'Real' Religious Communities: A Study of Authentication in New Roman Catholic Religious Orders." *Religion and the Social Order* 6: 149–74.

Wood, Gordon S. 1993. "Founding a Nation, 986–1787." In *The Almanac of American History*, edited by Arthur M. Schlesinger, Jr. New York: Barnes & Noble.

Woolston, Thomas. 1735. *Works of Thomas Woolston*. London: J. Roberts.

Wuthnow, Robert. 1978. *Experimentation in American Religion.* Berkeley and Los Angeles: University of California Press.

———, ed. 1979. *The Religious Dimension: New Directions in Quantitative Research.* New York: Academic Press.

———. 1985. "Science and the Sacred." In *The Sacred in a Secular Age,* edited by Phillip E. Hammond, 187–203. Berkeley and Los Angeles: University of California Press.

———. 1989. *The Struggle for America's Soul.* Grand Rapids, Mich.: Eerdmans.

Wyneken, Friedrich Conrad Dietrich. [1843] 1982. *The Distress of the German Lutherans in North America.* Translated by S. Edgar Schmidt and edited by R. F. Rehmer. Fort Wayne, Ind.: Concordia Theological Seminary Press.

Yamane, David. 1997. "Secularization on Trial: In Defense of a Neosecularization Paradigm." *Journal for the Scientific Study of Religion* 36: 109–22.

Yamane, David, and Megan Polzer. 1994. "Ways of Seeing Ecstasy in Modern Society: Experiential-Expressive and Cultural-Linguistic Views." *Sociology of Religion* 55: 1–25.

Yang, Fenggang. 1998. "Chinese Conversion to Evangelical Christianity." *Sociology of Religion* 59: 237–58.

Yearbook of Jehovah's Witnesses. Published annually. Brooklyn: Watchtower Bible and Tract Society of New York.

Yerkes, Royden Keith. 1952. *Sacrifice in Greek and Roman Religions and Early Judaism.* New York: Scribner's.

Yinger, J. Milton. 1957. *Religion, Society and the Individual.* New York: Macmillan.

———. 1970. *The Scientific Study of Religion.* New York: Macmillan.

Young, Lawrence A. 1997. "Phenomenological Images of Religion and Rational Choice Theory." In *Rational Choice Theory and Religion: Summary and Assessment,* edited by Lawrence A. Young, 133–45. New York: Routledge.

Zalenski, Peter A., and Charles E. Zech. 1995. "The Effect of Religious Market Competition on Church Giving." *Review of Social Economy* 3: 350–67.

Zagorska, Anna. 1998. "Sharing the Power: The Growth of Non-Traditional Religions in Poland." *Religion in Eastern Europe* 18 (2): 1–16.

Zekoff, Steven E., ed. 1997. *1996 General Minutes of the Annual Conferences of the United Methodist Church.* Evanston, Ill.: General Council on Finance and Administration.

Zimdars-Swartz, Sandra L. 1991. *Encountering Mary.* Princeton: Princeton University Press.

Zipperer, John. 1995. "Confessing Movement Grows Amid Doctrinal Disputes." *Christianity Today,* October, 105.

INDEX

abortion, 20

actions: religious, 96, 103, 108, 120–21, 273–74. *See also* church attendance; commitment; ecclesiastics; miracles; morality; mysticism; participation; prayer; rituals; volunteers

Adams, James Luther, 16

administration: organizational, 162–67. *See also* ecclesiastics; state

Adorno, T. W., 12, 18

Adrian Dominican community, 186

affiliation. *See* commitment; denominations; organizations; reaffiliation; religious groups; unaffiliated persons

Africa, 4, 7, 97, 108

After God: The Future of Religion (Cupitt), 146

afterlife, 99, 100, 276

age: and conversion, 119; and Jewish observance, 273–74, 274*table*; and religion's effect on health, 32; of religious vows, 236

"Age of Faith," 63–67, 71, 78–79, 199–200

aggiornamento, 177

Albigensians, 67

Aldergate Renewal Ministries, 268

Allport, Gordon W., 11, 13, 16, 44

altruism, 39. *See also* sacrifices

American Anthropologist, 89–90

American Catholic Sociological Review, 15–16

American Catholic Sociological Society (ACSS), 15–16

American Man of Science, 73

Americans. *See* United States

American Sociological Association, 18

American Sociological Society, 15

Amish, 213, 235

Anglicans, 228, 250; church attendance, 68; "democratic" ordinations, 264; Methodists vs., 167, 264, 265; New York, 225; ridiculing belief, 2; secularization thesis and, 60; Society for the Propagation of the Gospel, 225. *See also* Episcopalians

animism, 71

anthropologists: on magic, 105–6; on religion, 6–8, 84, 89–90, 92–96, 101, 107, 113, 288–89n2; religiousness of faculty, 54; on rituals, 107–8

Antonino, St., 64, 66

Apa Tanus, 93–94

Apostle's Creed, 65, 275

Archives de Sciences sociales des Religions, 16

Arrington, Leonard J., 130

Asbury, Francis, 157, 159*fig*, 264, 290n6

asceticism, 112

Asia, 4, 6, 93; Chenchu nomads of India, 102; communist "brainwashing," 135–36; folk religions, 75–76, 97, 99, 194; philosophy rejecting gods, 1; polytheistic, 142; Sōka Gakkai, 194; Yoido Full Gospel Church, 157, 290nn5,6. *See also* Chinese

Assemblies of God, 212, 235, 265

Association for the Sociology of Religion, 16

astrology, 250, 253

atheism, 1, 2–3, 13–14, 73, 113; "all refute all," 31; "each refutes each," 222; scientific, 3–13, 19, 62–63, 73; village, 14

Text:	10/12 Baskerville
Display:	Baskerville
Composition:	Impressions Book and Journal Services, Inc.
Printing and binding:	Maple-Vail Book Manufacturing Group
Index:	Barbara Roos